A CHURCH DIVIDED

Matthew D. Hockenos

A CHURCH DIVIDED

German Protestants Confront the Nazi Past

INDIANA UNIVERSITY PRESS
BLOOMINGTON AND INDIANAPOLIS

This book is a publication of

Indiana University Press
601 North Morton Street
Bloomington, IN 47404-3797 USA

http://iupress.indiana.edu

Telephone orders   800-842-6796
Fax orders   812-855-7931
Orders by e-mail   iuporder@indiana.edu

The paper used in this publication meets the minimum requirements
of American National Standard for Information Sciences—Permanence
of Paper for Printed Library Materials, ANSI Z39.48-1984.

Manufactured in the United States of America

Library of Congress Cataloging-in-Publication Data

Hockenos, Matthew D., date
    A church divided : German Protestants confront the Nazi past /
Matthew D. Hockenos.
      p.   cm.
    Includes bibliographical references and index.
    ISBN 0-253-34448-4 (cloth : alk. paper)
    1. Germany—Church history—1945–   2. Protestant churches—
Germany—History—20th century.   3. Guilt—Religious aspects—
Christianity—History of doctrines—20th century.   4. National
socialism and religion.   5. Germany—Church history—1933–1945.
6. Church and state—Germany—History—1933–1945.   I. Title.
BR856.H685 2004
280'.4'094309044—dc22

                                                        2004003740

1   2   3   4   5   09   08   07   06   05   04

To my
Parents

One simply does not want to suffer any more. One wants to escape the misery [and] to live, but does not wish to ponder. The mood is as if one expects to be compensated after the terrible suffering or at least to be comforted; but one does not want to be burdened with guilt.

—Karl Jaspers, *The Question of German Guilt*

The guilt exists, there is no doubt about it. Even if there were no other guilt than that of the six million clay urns, containing the ashes of burnt Jews from all over Europe.

—Martin Niemöller, *Of Guilt and Hope*

CONTENTS

ACKNOWLEDGMENTS

The completion of this book would not have been possible without the wisdom and generous support of many individuals and organizations. Of the many colleagues and mentors who influenced this project at every stage, Molly Nolan and Stewart Stehlin of New York University, and John S. Conway, professor emeritus at the University of British Columbia, in particular deserve my warm appreciation. From the beginning, their persistent criticisms and gentle persuasion improved the quality of the manuscript. I'm grateful for their unflagging support and enthusiasm for this project—even when I didn't heed all of their advice.

Early drafts of various chapters presented as conference papers also profited from the insightful comments of several scholars and professors, including Doris Bergen, Donald Dietrich, Helga Doblin, Robert Ericksen, Robert Herzstein, Dianne Kirby, Hartmut Lehmann, and Richard Rubenstein. The chapter on Bishop Wurm benefited immensely from David Diephouse's extensive knowledge of Württemberg's Lutheran bishop. Tony Judt of New York University offered thoughtful advice during the early stages of this project and assisted me as a junior visiting fellow at the Institut für die Wissenschaften vom Menschen in Vienna in 1995, where he was writing a book while on sabbatical. Of my supportive colleagues at Skidmore College, I wish to especially thank Barry Goldensohn for encouragement and advice on the reorganization of the chapters; Undine Giguere for editing the notes and bibliography; reference librarians Amy Syrell and Marilyn Sheffer for their cheerful willingness to track down obscure German theology texts; and Sarah Rubin for reading and offering perceptive comments on the final draft.

Professor Gerhard Besier of the University of Heidelberg and Jörg Conzelmann of the Karlshöhe Lutheran charity and deacon's seminary helped me to secure housing in Heidelberg and Karlshöhe Ludwigsburg during an archival research trip in 2001. Lively discussions with the former director of Karlshöhe, Dr. Winfried Fischer, clarified some of the more opaque aspects of the structure and organization of the Protestant Church in Germany. The friendly assistance and recommendations from Professor Michael Brenner of the University of Munich were critical for attaining financial support from a number of institutions, including the Institut für Europäische Geschichte in Mainz, where Professor Heinz Duchhardt and his colleagues provided insightful guidance in fall 2001. The Deutscher Akademischer Austauschdienst (DAAD) generously supported two research trips to Germany, the first in 1994–95 and the second in conjunction with the Leo Baeck Institute in 2001.

I was also fortunate to participate in the scholar-in-residence program through the Faculty Resource Network at New York University in 2002. The NYU history department, whose chair at the time was Molly Nolan, provided a friendly and familiar setting in which to complete the manuscript. Lectures and roundtable discussions at the Remarque Institute for European Studies and the Leo Baeck Institute provided further stimulation during my time as scholar-in-residence at NYU. The opportunity to finish my research in Germany and write the final chapters of the manuscript would not have been possible without the support of Skidmore College, in particular a year-long sabbatical (2001–2002) and financial support from the Office of the Dean of Faculty.

The assistance and patience of all the archivists I encountered in Germany was a pleasant surprise. During my first research trip to Germany I spent much of my time at the Evangelisches Zentralarchiv in Berlin, where Friedrich Künzel introduced me to the art of archival research. Peter Honigmann and his staff in Heidelberg at the Zentralarchiv zur Erforschung der Geschichte der Juden in Deutschland were particularly accommodating while the reading room was under construction. Hermann Ehmer and his colleagues at the Landeskirchliches Archiv Stuttgart deserve particular thanks for copying hundreds of pages of documents. I will also remember their warmth and sensitivity in the wake of the September 11, 2001, terrorist attacks on the World Trade Center. Both Holger Bogs at the Evangelische Kirche Hauptarchiv Hessen-Nassau and the late Christoph Freiherr von Brandenstein at the Landeskirchliches Archiv Nürnberg and their staffs were always obliging. Michael Häusler and his assistants at the Archiv des Diakonischen Werkes der EKD in Dahlem provided expert assistance and welcome advice. I also received archival assistance in the United States from Sara Mummert, the reference librarian at the Gettysburg Lutheran Theological Seminary's A. R. Wentz Library in Gettysburg, Pennsylvania, where Stewart Herman's papers are housed and from which many of the photographs in this book come. Cliff Anderson, curator of the Reformed Research Collections at the Princeton Theological Seminary, assisted me in obtaining photos from the Karl Barth Archiv in Basel, Switzerland.

I wish to thank my editor at Indiana University Press, Robert Sloan, who has been patient with my delays and quick to respond to my questions, and my copyeditor, Elizabeth Yoder, for her meticulous reading of the manuscript. The anonymous criticisms and suggestions by two readers for the press enabled me to significantly improve certain chapters.

Finally, I would like to thank my family and friends who have listened to my ideas and shared their opinions, and in doing so have greatly enriched the experience of writing this book.

A CHURCH DIVIDED

Introduction

When Allied bombs stopped falling on Germany in May 1945, German men, women, and children emerged, dazed and scared, from their makeshift basement bunkers in Berlin, Dresden, Frankfurt, and other German cities. Colossal destruction confronted them everywhere. The English journalist Isaac Deutscher described Berlin as evoking "the impression of a miraculously well-preserved ruin of classical antiquity—like Pompeii or Ostia—on a gigantic scale."[1] While the Allies celebrated their victory over the most murderous regime in the Western world, Germans, many of whom had supported Hitler's Third Reich, began the arduous tasks of clearing the rubble, searching for loved ones, securing medical assistance, finding places to live, obtaining food, and rebuilding their cities. They also sought answers. How could this have happened? Who's to blame? What will happen to us now? Although the Allies offered answers to many of these questions, they were not the answers most Germans wanted to hear. In their misery, few Germans wanted to be reminded about the extermination camps or the tens of thousands of Jews and Slavs murdered by the German Army and the Nazi mobile killing units on the eastern front. Instead, most Germans focused on their own suffering and perceived their immediate plight as the fault of the Allies: *they* bombed our apartments, post offices, tram cars, gas mains, schools, and churches into rubble; *they* rape and exploit our women and girls; *they* imprison our men and accuse us all of supporting the Nazi regime.

Rather than seek assistance from the occupying forces that they mistakenly perceived as their enemy, even after Germany's unconditional surrender in May 1945, many Germans turned to the Protestant and Catholic churches for material relief, emotional comfort, and answers to their urgent questions. The clergy, especially the Protestant clergy, had a reputation among Germans for service loyal to the nation. In contrast to the Allies, they, at least, could be trusted to put German interests first. From the heady days in 1933 when Hitler first came to power to the bleak months in the spring of 1945 when bombs rained down on German cities, the

Protestant clergy had demonstrated their devotion to the Fatherland as well as their distrust of the Jews and their antipathy to communism. Most important for the hungry and desperate German population, the churches had proven track records for providing social services and spiritual comfort. Who better for Germans to turn to in this time of dire need?

After decades in the background, the churches were suddenly thrust into the limelight, playing the role they believed was rightly theirs. Germans called on their pastors and priests for assistance that ran the gamut from finding housing to writing character references for discredited spouses, brothers, and sons who had joined the Nazi Party. Most of all, these anguished survivors craved assurance that life would get better. Churchmen could do little to solve the acute problems of severe shortages, but they could offer a message of comfort. And they could try to provide Christian answers to their unsettling questions: Why did this happen? And what are we to do now?

This book is an analysis of how Protestant pastors, church leaders, theologians, and laypeople sought to shape the historical record and alleviate German distress through their responses to these questions in the years immediately following Germany's defeat. That these community leaders, whose professional lives had been devoted to the provision of moral guidance, should think it their duty to provide answers to their parishioners was natural. Most, however, had little insight into the difficulties such a task would involve.

These difficulties are conspicuously evident in a typical declaration that clergymen from the northeastern regional church of Berlin-Brandenburg issued in November 1945. The occasion for drafting this statement was the Day of Repentance and Prayer (*Buss- und Bettag*), an annual Protestant holy day in late November when clergymen encouraged parishioners to examine their conscience, repent for their sins, and pray for forgiveness. Clergymen across Germany used this day in 1945 to deliberate on the twelve years of Nazi rule and the desperate plight of Germans in the wake of the war. The new church leadership in Berlin-Brandenburg took the opportunity to reflect on why Nazism flourished in Germany and who was to blame for both the destruction of Germany's cities and the atrocities committed against the Jews and other "enemies" of the Reich:

> We did not fear God above all the powers of men and governments, we did not trust and obey God unconditionally—that is what brought us under the sway of the tempter, that is what cast us into the abyss! That is what gave the demon of inhumanity free rein among us.
>
> And now the righteous judgment of our holy God has fallen upon us. Before His judgment seat we are not subject to the verdicts and standards of other human beings who also stand in fear of His judgment and are thrown upon His grace. Before God we are being questioned concerning our own guilt, our great, immeasurable guilt. Before God we cannot excuse ourselves.
>
> Before Him there cries out against us all the innocently shed blood, all the blaspheming of His Holy Name and all the inhumanities which occurred in our midst es-

pecially against the Jews. If we know ourselves to be innocent—humanly speaking—of participating in the atrocities . . . we yet cannot, before God, escape the great burden of need and guilt which rests upon us.[2]

It was not at all unusual for clergymen to pepper their sermons and declarations with the biblical language of tempters, demons, the abyss, and God's righteous judgment and compassionate forgiveness. But what did it mean? On the one hand, the statement is frustratingly vague and obscure. Is Hitler the "tempter" under whose sway the German people were "cast into the abyss"? Is God's righteous judgment a reference to the Allied destruction of Germany and the raping of German women by Soviet soldiers? Did the Berlin clerics really mean to say that German Protestants are "innocent humanly speaking" and "not subject to the verdicts and standards of other human beings"? On the other hand, the statement is at times surprisingly concrete and critical. The authors acknowledge that inhumanities occurred against Jews in their midst and that there was no escaping or excusing the great burden of guilt weighing on the collective shoulders of Germans. The clear emphasis on sinfulness, suffering, and salvation are underlying themes in many of the statements issued by churchmen.

Although the November 1945 declaration issued by the clerics from Berlin-Brandenburg was representative of most of the statements issued by Protestant clergy and laity, there were other Protestant church leaders and parishioners who put forth explanations for Nazism and understood Protestant responsibility for the crimes of the Third Reich quite differently. Despite disagreements among churchmen about who was responsible for Nazism and why, they carried out their debates using a uniquely Protestant discourse, focusing on sin, suffering, and salvation. To be sure, this discourse both influenced and at times overlapped with the wider discourse about guilt and responsibility taking place in postwar Germany, but the emphasis on divine judgment, repentance, and God's compassionate forgiveness was Protestant to the core. The crux of this study is an analysis of this discourse and the intense debates that took place in Germany within the hierarchy of the Protestant Church over how to understand the Nazi past and the church's role in that past.

Ideally, this study would investigate both Catholic and Protestant churches and extend beyond 1950. But all historical studies are necessarily incomplete, and this one is no exception. By limiting my investigation to Protestant clergy and laity from the first postwar conference of church leaders in August 1945 to their first official declaration on the "Jewish question" in April 1950, I can analyze in detail the motivations at work in the strategies these churchmen used to confront the Nazi past.

The Individuals, Groups, and Institutional Bodies

All of the pastors and church leaders investigated in this study were ardent Protestants who adhered to one of the three Protestant denominations or traditions in Germany: Lutheran, United, or Reformed (Calvinist). Prior to the seizure of power by the Nazis in 1933, many of these churchmen had already achieved positions of leadership within the twenty-seven regional churches that comprised the German Evangelical Church (*Deutsche Evangelische Kirche*, DEK). In 1933 and 1934 the Nazis and their supporters among the Protestant clergy, the German Christians (*Deutsche Christen*), hounded many of the established church leaders out of power, leading the outcasts and their like-minded colleagues to create the Confessing Church (*Bekennende Kirche*) as an alternative to the official German Evangelical Church. The Confessing Church operated parallel to the official Nazified church from 1934 to 1945. When the war ended in 1945, the discredited German Christians stepped aside, most often without a struggle, from positions of power. Pastors and church leaders who had to varying degrees supported the Confessing Church assumed the leadership of the postwar Evangelical Church in Germany (*Evangelische Kirche in Deutschland*, EKD).[3] By placing the designation "Evangelical" first, postwar church leaders sought to emphasize the church's denominational basis, a change that deemphasized the national character of the church.

In contrast to the Roman Catholic Church, where the pope played the central role, the EKD had no single leader and was by no means monolithic. It was not a unified church in the doctrinal sense but rather a federation of independent regional churches (*Landeskirchen*). During the period this study covers, the EKD consisted of twenty-seven autonomous regional churches, which included Lutheran, Reformed, and United denominations or traditions. (See map of the boundaries of the regional churches.)

In 1933 approximately 41 million Germans were officially registered as Evangelical (Protestant) and 21 million as Catholic from a total population of 65 million. The Lutheran regional churches embraced nearly half of the Protestants, and the United regional churches the other half. The United churches, the largest of which was the Church of the Old Prussian Union prior to the break-up of Prussia after the Second World War, were shaped predominately by Lutheran practices and traditions even though they had been administered since 1817 as a union of Lutheran and Reformed.[4] The two small Reformed regional churches in northwestern Germany consisted of 400,000 and 500,000 parishioners. Of the 65 million Germans, fewer than 1 percent were Jewish.[5]

The National Socialist revolution in 1933 further exacerbated these divisions. Unlike the Catholic Church, which signed a concordat with the Nazis in 1933, the Protestants split into essentially three groups—the ultranationalist, antisemitic, and pro-Nazi German Christian movement; the somewhat oppositional Confessing Church; and the uncommitted neutrals. Each of these groups enjoyed support from clergy and laity from all three Protestant traditions (Lutheran, United, and Reformed). To complicate matters further, the intensely antisemitic German Christians as well as the pastors in the Confessing Church were divided amongst themselves. Recent studies estimate the total number of German Christians to have

The Provincial Churches of the Evangelical Church in Germany

Of the Evangelical Church's twenty-seven regional churches—each with its own administration and leadership—nearly half were Lutheran and the other half United. Two of the smallest regional churches identified themselves as Reformed (Calvinist). *Frederic Spotts,* The Churches and Politics in Germany *(Middletown, Conn.: Wesleyan University Press), 14.*

hovered around 600,000.[6] Of the 18,000 Protestant pastors in Germany, fewer than one-third were adherents of the German Christian movement.[7] Although the number of pastors who joined the Confessing Church reached just over 7,000 in January 1934, for most of the period of the church struggle from 1933 to 1945 the number was fewer than 5,000.[8] Unfortunately, there are no reliable figures on how many laypersons belonged to the Confessing Church. Approximately 80 percent of the laity was in the middle, subscribing to neither the beliefs of the German Christians nor the Confessing Church.

Although there was a political dimension to the divisions in the Confessing Church, differences in politics were not paramount. Politically, virtually all clergymen were conservative supporters of either the Nazi party or a conservative-nationalist party. The first split that became evident in the Confessing Church in 1934 was not political but theological or doctrinal, occurring between Lutherans who emphasized different tenets of Lutheranism. With the exception of Swiss Calvinist theologian Karl Barth and a few German Reformed Church leaders, the vast majority of Confessing Church leaders were Lutherans who accepted and subscribed in varying degrees to the Christian doctrines originating from Martin Luther and taught by the Lutheran Church. To be designated a Lutheran meant accepting and adhering to the Lutheran confessions—in particular, the Augsburg Confession (1530), the Articles of Smalcald (1537), and the Formula of Concord (1577). Over the centuries, however, Lutherans interpreted these confessions differently, resulting in factionalism among Lutherans.

Most of the leaders of the EKD and its constituent churches were born in the last three decades of the nineteenth century, and many were the sons of pastors or were raised in traditional Protestant households. Otto Dibelius (1880–1967), a leading Lutheran churchman in Berlin and bishop of the Berlin-Brandenburg church after the war, described the pious atmosphere in his parents' house in his autobiography:

> I came of a family where a firm Christian faith was the accepted basis in life. The picture of our grandfather, who taught religion at the Prenzlau high school, had looked down upon us all through our childhood, filling us with awe. His straightforward, profoundly Christian personality had earned him extraordinary respect. . . . It was taken for granted that one attended church regularly, that one prayed, and that the day began with family prayers. It was a Christianity without problems, a conservative Christianity resting simply upon its own evidence.[9]

Like Dibelius, all postwar church leaders had studied theology as young men and taken positions as prelates, pastors, vicars, deans, seminary directors, and as theology or church history professors. In the postwar period many of them were elected or appointed to the two primary leadership bodies of the EKD: the twelve-member EKD council, the church's executive; and the 120-member EKD legislative body or synod, which passes resolutions and establishes church policy. (See chart, diagramming the structure, organizations, and offices of the EKD.) In addition to the EKD council and synod, which were the national leadership bodies of the church, there were also regional councils and synods. An additional noteworthy postwar leadership body was the reform-oriented council of brethren (*Bruderrat*), which had been the leadership council of the Confessing Church from 1934 to 1945. Although the Confessing Church officially disbanded after the war, the council of brethren continued to exist as an alternative voice within the EKD.

Not only did several of the churchmen discussed in this book serve on these councils and in synods, but they also rose to the rank of bishop, president, or superintendent—the highest positions in the regional churches. By the end of the war they were middle-aged and well established as theologians or church leaders. Theophil Wurm (1868–1953), the conservative Lutheran bishop of Württemberg in southwest Germany and a central figure in the postwar church, was older; he was seventy-six when the war ended in May 1945. Hans Meiser (1881–1956), the archconservative bishop of Bavaria, and Otto Dibelius, the postwar bishop of Berlin-Brandenburg, were both in their mid-sixties. Martin Niemöller (1892–1984), the fiery Berlin pastor who spent 1937–45 in concentration camps for his opposition to Nazi church policy and later led the reform-minded faction in the postwar church, was fifty-three. The Lutheran theologians Hans Asmussen (1898–1968), Hermann Diem (1900–75), Hans Iwand (1899–1960), and Walter Künneth (1901–97), all of whom engaged vociferously in the postwar debates, were in their thirties when the Nazis came to power and between forty-six and forty-nine when the war ended. Karl Barth (1886–1968), the controversial Swiss Reformed (Calvinist) theologian who clashed frequently with Asmussen after 1945 and who was the theological mentor for many in the reform wing[10] of the church, was fifty-nine. One of the youngest men discussed in this book is Helmut Thielicke (1908–86), who had been a theology professor at the University of Heidelberg until the Nazis dismissed him in 1939. When he took a teaching position at the University of Tübingen after the war he was thirty-seven.

All of these men and many of their colleagues experienced the Third Reich as mature adults. Several, including Niemöller, lost sons who fought for Germany on the eastern front. Many had close friends or relatives who had been Nazi Party members; Bishop Wurm's son Hans, for instance, joined the Nazi Party in 1922 and was jailed for a year after the war for lying about it. As these churchmen struggled to comprehend their personal fates, the fate of the church, and the fate of Germany in the immediate postwar years, they frequently fell back on the answers they found in their interpretations of Scripture. Although they were all Protestants and had supported the Confessing Church in varying degrees, they did not see eye-to-eye either theologically or politically.

Appreciation for the widely divergent theological perspectives within the Protestant churches is crucial for understanding the conflicting and overlapping ways representatives of the Lutheran, Reformed, and United Protestant traditions in

Structure, Organisations and Offices of the Evangelical Church in Germany

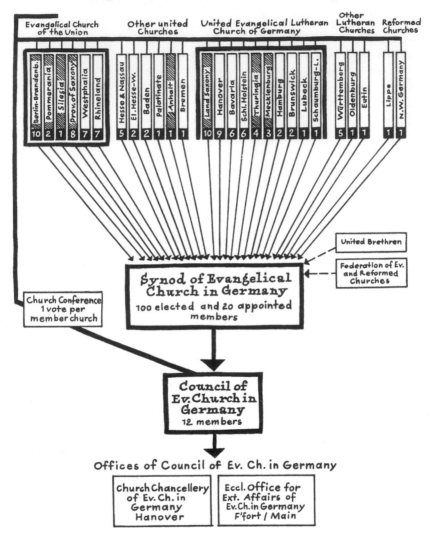

Twenty-seven regional churches comprised the Evangelical Church in Germany. Each church was represented in the synod, the church's legislative body, from which elected members formed the executive body, the Council of the EKD. *Otto Dibelius,* The Evangelical Church in Berlin and the Soviet-Zone of Germany *(Berlin: Eckart, 1959), 51.*

Germany grappled with the church's ambivalent relationship to Nazi policies. To be sure, the full range of motivational factors of the participants in the dialogue must be analyzed, including their experiences during the Nazi period, their political convictions, and the historical context of war-torn Germany under Allied occupation. But at the core of the debate over the past conduct of churchmen in the Third Reich were theological issues, some of which had divided Protestants in Germany since the Reformation in the sixteenth century and others that arose in the extremely volatile atmosphere of Hitler's brutal regime. Frequently implicit and occasionally explicit in the debates over the Nazi past were disagreements over key orthodox Lutheran doctrines: the doctrine of two kingdoms, the law-gospel dualism, the doctrine of divine orders, and the theory of supersessionism. Churchmen were deliberating in the immediate postwar years on more than just their action or inaction in Hitler's Germany; they were coming to grips with the whole Lutheran theological and political tradition in Germany. In fact, one of the major obstacles to confronting Nazism when it first appeared in the late 1920s and early 1930s was that the prior issues of Protestant nationalism, deference to the state, and a hierarchical church polity had been ignored. The failure to confront or acknowledge these issues not only caused the church to splinter under pressure from the Nazis into German Christian, Confessing Church, and neutral factions but also helps to explain the failure of many churchmen after the war to acknowledge the church's mistakes.

Strategies for Confronting the Nazi Past

For the conservative Lutheran majority in the church, coming to terms with the Nazi past meant minimizing or excusing the church's vacillation between complacency and complicity during Nazi rule while it simultaneously sought international recognition for the suffering that the German people endured during the war and Allied occupation. These politically conservative and theologically orthodox Lutherans, many of whom had sought modus vivendi with the Nazis, tended in the postwar years to favor a spiritual rebirth based on Lutheran tradition and nationalism rather than to undertake a detailed examination of their motivations for their actions and inaction under Nazism. The majority of Lutherans had accepted without protest the elimination of democratic rights, civil liberties, and the rule of law in the 1930s; they remained silent while the Nazis rounded up political opponents, even such prominent churchmen as Martin Niemöller, as well as their Jewish neighbors, and deported them to concentration and extermination camps. Following the war these clergymen defended their conservative nationalist politics and in some cases their Christian-based antisemitism as well.

The silence of church conservatives about their role in the Nazi past was, in fact, a noisy affair. In their efforts to influence the historical record, they propagated what

German historian Harold Marcuse refers to in his book *Legacies of Dachau* (2001) as the myths of victimization, ignorance, and resistance.[11] The dissemination of these myths required that church leaders mount frequent and vocal attacks on those persons in the churches, on the political Left, and among the Allies, who accused the church of being instrumental in fostering a mentality conducive to Nazism. Conservatives such as Bishops Otto Dibelius, Hans Mesier, and Theophil Wurm falsely identified the German population as victims of both the Nazis and the Allies, claimed ignorance of the extermination camps, and maintained that they had been active in the resistance against the Nazis. They emphasized at one and the same time the Protestant Church's struggle against the Nazis *and* the guilt that burdened all Christian peoples for their failure to live by the Word of God.

Honest, open postwar discussions of the church's complacency and complicity in the face of the Nazis' illegal, inhumane, and unchristian policies were extremely rare. When conservative church leaders did discuss the atrocities committed by Germans, they blamed either the Nazi leaders or the destructive impact of secularization on modern society. They expressed more concern about the German loss of dignity and the subsequent onset of despair and depression within the German population than about the crimes committed by Germans against defenseless men, women, and children.

On the other hand, a minority of Protestant Church leaders and clergymen harshly criticized these apologist attitudes as inconsistent with Christian values and sought to redress past wrongs by acknowledging the church's share of responsibility for the Third Reich. These Lutheran and Reformed churchmen, foremost among them Hermann Diem, Hans Iwand, and Martin Niemöller, had distanced themselves politically from the Nazis after their initial enthusiasm and subscribed to a modified version of Reformed (Calvinist) theology associated with Swiss Calvinist theologian Karl Barth, who had taught at German universities from 1921 to 1935. After the war they demanded structural as well as theological reforms in the church in order to ensure a more active Christian resistance to totalitarianism in the future. Although some individuals from the reform wing of the postwar church addressed the roots of their antisemitism and anti-Judaism, these reformers were, for the most part, as negligent as the conservatives about confronting the church's wholly inadequate response to the systematic extermination of millions of Jews. This study covers the church debates up to 1950 when the EKD finally broke its silence and, in its highly controversial "Statement on the Jewish Question," acknowledged its guilt toward the Jewish people.[12]

Not all churchmen in the postwar era are easily categorized as either reformers or conservatives. Nor are these black-and-white categories with precise definitions. On the Day of Repentance and Prayer in November 1945, the Berlin-Brandenburg clerics, for instance, used images and explanations in their statement that were typical of both reformers and conservatives. The authors of the statement acknowledged that "inhumanities" had been perpetrated against Jews—a bold admission even for reformers in 1945—but simultaneously maintained that churchmen and their flocks were innocent "humanly speaking." The guilt of the church, conservatives were fond of saying, was guilt before God for not trusting and obeying God unconditionally. Even leaders of the reform movement like Niemöller were on occasion willing to join forces with conservatives to protest the harshness of Allied denazification policies and to advocate for the clemency of convicted Nazis on death row.[13] But whether their declarations and sermons resounded with language typical of reformers or conservatives, all churchmen relied on theological concepts and doctrine to make their points and explain their conduct from 1933 to 1945.

Historiography and Methodology

Scholars as diverse as Frankfurt School philosopher Theodor Adorno, psychoanalysts Alexander and Margaret Mitscherlich, and neoconservative critic Hermann Lübbe have maintained that Germans living through the postwar "rubble years" had neither the desire nor the energy to discuss, confront, or reflect on their role in the twelve years of National Socialist rule.[14] Working from this assumption, many historians and social scientists argue that the first genuine confrontation with the Nazi past took place in the late 1960s when presumptuous students demanded an accounting of their parents' generation. While the "sixty-eighters" did initiate an important new stage in the German process of critically understanding the Nazi past, it was in the relatively unexplored decade following the Holocaust that Germans first established a discourse that would shape the discussion about German guilt and responsibility for the remainder of the twentieth century and beyond. As historian of postwar Germany Robert Moeller has convincingly argued, the debates that continue to rage over responsibility for Nazi crimes nearly sixty years after the ruination and exposure of the Nazi regime echo similar debates that took place throughout West Germany in the late 1940s and early 1950s.[15] Churchmen were powerful and influential voices in the disputes over what the German philosopher Karl Jaspers called *die Schuldfrage* (the guilt question).[16]

Scholars of German Protestant Church history and theology have developed a sophisticated and nuanced understanding of German Protestantism during the Third Reich. Hundreds of scholarly articles and monographs—featuring a wide variety of methodologies and historiographical perspectives—explore various facets of the Protestant churches under Nazi rule.[17] In addition to conventional studies focusing on leading churchmen and ecclesiastical politics, recent studies now explore the role of gender and social class in the church, Christian-Jewish relations, university theological faculties, specific regional churches, and even individual parishes. The historiography of this topic was not always so rich. As late as the 1970s, Wolfgang Gerlach, a pastor and church historian in West Germany, had difficulty finding a German publisher for his controversial manuscript on antisemitism in the Protestant churches from 1933 to 1945. Today there are several studies on Christian antisemitism and anti-Judaism during the Nazi era, and Gerlach's superb study is available in both German and English.[18]

The literature on various aspects of *Vergangenheitsbewältigung* (coming to terms with the past) by historians also continues to expand.[19] The history of how the churches sought to come to terms with antisemitism and their role in the Nazi past has received much less attention, but this too is changing as the most recent contribution, *Die evangelische Christenheit und die deutsche Geschichte nach 1945: Weichenstellungen in der Nachkriegszeit* (2002) by German church historian Martin Greschat suggests.[20] The number of books in English that specifically address the manner in which Protestant churchmen handled the question of guilt after the war can be counted on one hand.[21] Histories of the Catholic encounter with the Nazi past in the immediate postwar years are also few in number.[22]

Any explanation for the paucity of studies on *Vergangenheitsbewältigung* in the churches must begin with the obvious: a precondition for such studies is an accurate and critical account of the churches from 1933 to 1945. Such a record simply did not exist until the mid-1960s. In the immediate postwar decades the erroneous assumption underlying the majority of studies on the churches in the Third Reich was that churchmen either enthusiastically supported or valiantly opposed the Nazi regime. Since the early postwar studies of the Protestant Church in the Nazi era tended to be written by laity and clergy who opposed the Nazis or sought to foster a myth of church resistance, their focus was on the real and perceived resistance of the Confessing Church.[23] Memoirs by churchmen who had participated in the church struggle from 1933 to 1945 contributed to this historiography by juxtaposing the Confessing Church, fighting for the freedom to preach the gospel and its message "love thy neighbor," to the German Christians, venerating Hitler alongside an Aryan Jesus.[24] Scholars said little about the collaborationist German Christians or the vast majority of pastors and laypersons, most of whom sought to avoid trouble by refusing to join either the Confessing Church or the German Christian movement. The immediacy of the horrific events, the inaccessibility of substantial documentation, and the tendency to inflate the resistance side of the church struggle meant that few scholars in the 1950s and early 1960s scrutinized the church in light of its legacy of antisemitism and accommodation with Nazism.[25]

The late 1960s and 1970s saw a more critical revisionist approach with the publication of two groundbreaking studies on the churches in Nazi Germany, one by British-born church historian John S. Conway and the other by German church historian Klaus Scholder.[26] The myth of a resistance church locked in battle with a small group of brown-shirted clerics and their Nazi cohorts began to dissolve. In the 1970s and 1980s the number of sympathetic studies on the churches decreased as scholars focused greater attention on the Confessing Church's complacency toward, and at times complicity in, National Socialism. The recognition that opposition to Nazism within the churches was an exception to the rule has led some scholars to shift the focus of their research from the Nazi period to the postwar strategies employed by churchmen to explain the church's complicity with Nazism. In the past two decades several scholars, in particular Gerhard Besier and Martin Greschat, have published rigorous studies on various aspects of the church's uneven attempts to address its complex legacy.[27]

The central purpose of this book is to analyze the postwar actions and pronouncements of Protestant clergymen and laypersons through a critical reading of their correspondence, sermons, speeches, newspaper articles, and, when relevant, their theological treatises. The present literature on *Vergangenheitsbewältigung* in the Protestant churches places more emphasis on *how* churchmen addressed the past than on *why* they addressed it as they did. This book tries to answer both the "how" and the "why." It stresses the importance of theology, especially certain Lutheran tenets such as the doctrine of two kingdoms, that reinforced the nationalist sentiments of many churchmen and provided them with ready-made rationales for their accommodation with Nazi policies in the Third Reich.

The chapters that follow begin with a brief analysis of the divisions within the Confessing Church during the period of the church struggle (1933–45). Based on the extensive secondary source literature, this chapter provides necessary background for understanding the seven chapters on the immediate postwar years. The common thread that runs through these chapters is the theological and political underpinnings of conflicts that erupted between conservatives and reformers as they attempted to steer the church through the chaotic half-decade from 1945 to 1950. The second and third chapters examine the decisions and declarations made at the first postwar conference of church leaders in the town of Treysa in August 1945. Although church leaders agreed upon a twelve-man provisional leadership council at this meeting, tempers flared over Niemöller's demand for far-reaching reforms in the structure and doctrine of the church. The fourth and fifth chapters analyze the origin and content of two highly controversial statements issued by church leaders in the fall of 1945: the October 1945 Stuttgart Declaration of Guilt, and an open letter by Bishop Wurm to Christians in England one month later. Both of these chapters pay special attention to the volatile response by the Protestant grass roots to these public interpretations of guilt. The sixth chapter explores the reformers' critique of the church's politically conservative past and their redefinition of the church's social and political mission to include progressive political causes. Finally, the last two chapters provide a detailed investigation of the changing relationship between Protestants and Jews from 1945 to 1950.

This study analyzes the Protestant Church's halting and often contradictory process of confronting the Nazi past. Some historians consider the five years it took the official church to condemn antisemitism and anti-Judaism a blink of the eye when compared to the centuries-old practice within the church of teaching contempt for Jews. To others the five years between the liberation of the extermination camps and an official sign of *metanoia* by the church was shamefully long. Although half a decade was an excruciatingly long wait for the church to address its anti-semitism and anti-Judaism, no doubt it was better for the church to wait and issue a statement that embraced real and lasting changes in the church's relation to Jews than to issue a hastily written statement that did not recognize the necessity of fundamental changes in church doctrine.

The inclination to avoid an aggressive confrontation with the Nazi past was stronger among Protestant Church leaders than the drive to reform the church's ecclesiastical structure, theology, and political practice. The refusal by the conservative majority to draw any practical lessons from the church's complicity with National Socialism only further placated an already unapologetic German population. Nevertheless, an outspoken reform-minded minority in the church (often with international support) did succeed in forcing the EKD to grapple with the issues of political and ethical responsibility for the atrocities committed during the Third Reich. These reformers preempted a restoration of the pre-1933 church and had some success in encouraging pastors and laypeople to take independent positions on social and political issues regardless of the official conservative church policy.

This book challenges the common assumption, prevalent in most works on post-1945 Germany, that Germans were either too exhausted or simply unwilling to confront the question of German guilt. Exhausted and demoralized they certainly were, but not to such a degree that they could not or would not discuss the course of events that had brought them to their present circumstances. While many Protestants passionately debated the past, it is true, only a minority acknowledged the widespread enthusiasm for Nazism within the church and saw the necessity of taking the steps necessary to prevent such a possibility in the future.

1

The Church Struggle
Ecclesiastical, Political, and Theological
Disunity in the Third Reich

Origins of the Church Struggle and the Formation of the
Confessing Church, 1933–34

In the period 1933–45 Protestant responses to National Socialism in Germany ranged from enthusiastic endorsement to active opposition. These reflected the variety of theological and political perspectives of Protestant clergy and laity to the crises that had beset Germany since the First World War. Twelve years of Nazi dictatorship only made these divisions more entrenched and obvious. The divisions among pastors, church leaders, and theologians after the Second World War reflected many of the conflicts that had emerged during the period of Nazi rule, commonly referred to as "the church struggle."

The church struggle involved three interwoven dimensions: the struggle between the Confessing Church and the German Christian movement for control of the Protestant Church; the struggle between the Confessing Church and the Nazi state over spheres of influence; and the conflict within the Confessing Church between the conservative and radical wings over the nature of the church's opposition to the German Christians and the Nazi state.[1] The postwar debates about the Nazi past are an indisputable legacy of this final dimension of the church struggle.

The church struggle began as a defensive struggle waged by established church authorities who grouped together loosely in the Confessing Church against the ultranationalist pro-Nazi faction within the church, the German Christians.[2] The German Christians sought to incorporate the twenty-seven Protestant regional churches into a united German Evangelical Reich church headed by a Reich bishop with close ties to Hitler. Their goal to integrate Christianity and National Socialism in a racially pure "people's church" was a direct challenge not only to the autonomy of the regional churches but to Lutheran and Reformed doctrinal principles as well. Thus, in addition to the ecclesiastical dimension of this conflict over who would control the churches administratively, the German Christian and Confessing Church clergy were often tenacious theological antagonists as well. Although there were clear and definite distinctions between the theology of the German Christians and that of the Confessing Church, these distinctions should not overshadow the continuities between the mainstream Protestant theology adhered to by many Confessing clergy and German Christian theology. In fact, the nationalism, antisemitism, and anticommunism at the heart of the German Christian movement were widely accepted and defended by reputable theologians in university faculties across Germany.[3]

The second dimension to the church struggle—conflict between the Confessing Church and the Nazi state—is often erroneously conceived as the primary (even the only) struggle.[4] It is imperative to understand the church's opposition to the state for what it really was: occasional critiques by a small group of churchmen against particular state policies, such as the Nazi euthanasia program and, most importantly, Nazi church policy.

The final dimension of the church struggle, and the one most relevant to the postwar period, was the intense feuding within the Confessing Church itself between its radical and conservative wings. The divisions between these two wings of the Confessing Church became visible in 1934. Whereas the radicals, led by Pastor Martin Niemöller of Berlin-Dahlem, took a firm stand against the German Christians, conservatives, especially in the south German churches, showed a willingness to work alongside the more reputable churchmen in the German Christian movement. The radicals in the Confessing Church, it is important to note, were *not* socially or politically radical; in social and political matters they differed very little from the conservatives, most of whom had supported one of the right-wing political parties—the German People's Party, the German National People's Party, or the National Socialist German Workers' Party (NSDAP)—in Weimar elections. In the context of the persecution of the churches by the Nazi state, however, their opposition to Hitler's church policy was decidedly radical. After the war the Niemöller wing of the Confessing Church continued to differentiate themselves from the conservatives by advocating reform of the church's strict ecclesiastical hierarchy, dogmatic Lutheran doctrine, and conservative-nationalist political orientation. Although the Communist authorities in the Soviet occupation zone did not make life easy for churchmen after the war, there was little cause in the immediate postwar years for a continuation of radical opposition by Niemöller and his colleagues to the church policies of the new authorities in the eastern or western zones of occupation. Thus, while the designation "radical" is appropriate for describing their opposition to the church policy of the Third Reich, "reformist" or "reform-minded" is more suitable when defining their goals in the immediate postwar years.

The central issue underlying the struggle between radicals and conservatives during the Nazi era was whether the Confessing Church's opposition to attempts to incorporate the church into the Third Reich by force necessarily involved wider opposition to the Nazi state. Some pastors and church leaders in the Niemöller wing of the Confessing Church believed that it *was* necessary to publicly protest state laws and decrees that interfered with the church's control over its administrative, financial, legal, and pastoral offices. State policies that undermined civil liberties but were not directly harmful to the church elicited few condemnations from the pulpit. The same was true of state-orchestrated violence against those perceived to be enemies of the regime, particularly Communists and Jews. Nevertheless, this limited step toward political disobedience by the radicals led to bitter quarrels within the ranks of the Confessing Church. The rift became so great that no concerted or unified stance was ever possible against the Nazi state. In the postwar era, churchmen continued to differ in their assessment of the church's legacy of these years.[5]

When Adolf Hitler came to power in January 1933, Protestant churchmen across the country shared in the general enthusiasm for his nationalist, anticommunist, and antisemitic rhetoric. The experience of the Weimar Republic (1918–33) for most Protestant churchmen convinced them of the need for strong national leadership and moral renewal—two prominent platforms in Hitler's campaign. Protestant bishops, pastors, theologians, and church officials made up a particularly important segment of the group of conservative elites who willingly compromised with Hitler when he first came to power.[6] Influential and prominent church leaders such as Otto Dibelius and Martin Niemöller in Berlin and Bishops Theophil Wurm, Hans Meiser, and August Marahrens of Württemberg, Bavaria, and Hannover respectively wholeheartedly welcomed Hitler's rise to power while at the same time staking out their claim to the church's sphere of influence. In this they shared many of the same concerns for their established role in society as did elites in the armed forces, civil service, and economy. Bishop Wurm, for instance, welcomed "the struggle against undermining influences in our cultural life" but warned that "we must be careful not to lose . . . the freedom of movement with respect to the Reich and the State" that had been gained during the Weimar period.[7] In Bavaria, Bishop Meiser had pastors read a statement from the pulpit on Easter Sunday 1933 lauding the new state:

> A state which brings into being again government according to God's Laws should, in doing so, be assured not only of the applause but also of the glad and active cooperation of the Church. With gratitude and joy the Church takes note that the new state bans blasphemy, assails immorality, establishes discipline and order, with a strong hand, while at the same time calling upon man to fear God, espousing the sanctity of marriage and Christian training for the young, bringing into honor again the deeds of our fathers and kindling in thousands of hearts, in place of disparagement, an ardent love of *Volk* and Fatherland.[8]

The executive council of the Church of the Old Prussian Union, by far the largest of the twenty-seven regional churches, issued an Easter message declaring it was "joyfully prepared to play its part in the national and moral renewal of our people."[9]

In addition to the political support of church leaders, the prestigious Lutheran theologians Paul Althaus (1886–1966), Werner Elert (1885–1954), Friedrich Gogarten (1887–1967), and Emanuel Hirsch (1888–1972) lent theological justification to the National Socialist revolution.[10] Thus, alongside far less reputable churchmen in the ultranationalist and fanatically antisemitic German Christian movement—for example, pastor Joachim Hossenfelder (1899–1976), a thirty-three-year-old firebrand and ardent Nazi, and Ludwig Müller (1883–1945), a former naval chaplain who would become Reich bishop in fall 1933—respectable and influential authorities in the church also applauded the National Socialist government.

Most Protestants, then, found nothing incompatible with practicing their faith and supporting Hitler. If some were disturbed by the violence in word and deed of this new movement, they hoped that such excessive rhetoric and brutality would subside once order had been established. Protestant leaders admired Hitler's courage in attacking atheistic leftists and liberals and believed his goals were similar to theirs. Even when Hitler backed the German Christians in the July 1933 church elections and championed their leader, Ludwig Müller, as the new Reich bishop, only a small segment of regional church leaders drew the obvious conclusion that Hitler would not let them decide the church's future, especially when they envisioned a future of strong, independent, and confessionally defined regional churches.[11] Even after a year of state interference in church affairs, the majority of churchmen continued to harbor the illusion that Hitler was simply misinformed and misled by Müller, his church liaison.[12] Consequently, in 1933 and 1934 there was little evidence of a church-state struggle. Church elites directed the bulk of their wrath at the German Christians who sought to modify church doctrine in accordance with National Socialism and its racial policies.

During this period, the German Christians, with essential support from Hitler and the Nazi state, won control of all but three regional churches (Bavaria, Hannover, and Württemberg) and were partially successful in reorganizing the regional churches into a united Reich church with Reich Bishop Müller at its apex. According to the German Christians' June 1932 "Guiding Principles," they sought to reorganize the Protestant churches into one "dynamic national church (*Volkskirche*), which expresses the living faith of our people."[13] Their guiding principles go on to condemn the German Evangelical Federation of Churches (*Kirchenbund*) for being too weak in its struggle against parliamentarianism, Marxist-bolshevism, and Judaism. Prioritizing their service to the German race, or *Volk*, and nation, the German Christians saw the church as an integral part of Hitler's program of national renewal.[14]

A year after Hitler came to power, the German Christians had achieved many of their goals. Through a combination of elections and strong-arm tactics, they had successfully gained control of the largest of the regional churches, the Prussian, as well as those in Saxony, Thuringia, Schleswig-Holstein, Mecklenburg, Brunswick, Hesse, and several smaller regional churches.[15] Established church leaders who were removed from leadership positions in these regional churches referred to the German Christian–controlled churches as "destroyed churches."[16] The Lutheran churches in the south and Hannover remained in the hands of the old leadership and were thus designated "intact churches." Immediately after gaining control of the destroyed churches, the German Christians passed racial legislation, the infamous Aryan paragraph, which sought to exclude Christians of Jewish descent from holding positions in the church.[17] German Christians as well as many Confessing churchmen considered Christians of Jewish descent—"non-Aryans," according to Nazi racial legislation—a "grave danger" to the church and to German culture.[18]

The birth of the church opposition movement came from those traditional leaders who were appalled by the German Christians' energetic overthrow of the familiar landmarks of church life. Established church leaders who suddenly found themselves removed from their positions in the regional churches were naturally upset by the German Christians' actions. Hence, opposition to the German Christians arose, by and large, in the realm of ecclesiastical or church politics, as opposed to theology, during the turbulent spring, summer, and fall of 1933. The opposition sought to preserve traditional patterns in such matters as voting rights in church elections, the leadership principle within the church, the degree of autonomy allotted to the regional churches, the appointment of church officials, and the use of church funds. They sought to preserve their former theological and church political positions unchanged and to block any further extension of the German Christians' takeover of church life.

When these defensive measures failed, the opponents of the German Christians gathered in the Confessing Church, which began to take shape under the leadership of Martin Niemöller in the winter of 1933–34. In the spring of 1933 some opposition clergy, especially younger pastors and theologians, articulated the need for change beyond simply ridding the pulpits and ecclesiastical offices of German Christians. Calling themselves the Young Reformation movement, they sought to introduce a new vision of the church based on clearly drawn theological premises. The Young Reformers' program was hardly a radical new alternative; rather, it called for the formal political independence of the church from the state (a condition many churchmen had come to enjoy during the Weimar period), a unified Reich church, and younger men in the church administration.[19] On purely political questions, they were ready to support Hitler and the National Socialist revolution. But their principal aim was to refute the accusation that the church was no longer relevant to German society or national life. Led by the Lutherans Walter Künneth, a theologian and lecturer at Berlin University, and Hanns Lilje, general secretary of the German Student Christian movement, and including among their members Martin Niemöller and Dietrich Bonhoeffer (1906–45), they sought to distinguish themselves from both the German Christians and established church leaders.

It was, however, symptomatic of their ambivalence toward Nazism that, on the vital question of the place of Jews in German society, they compromised.[20] In early April 1933 the Nazi state passed a law that purged most Jews—"non-Aryans," according to the legislation—from the civil service. Since there were Christians of Jewish descent in the Protestant churches, a tiny fraction of whom (twenty-nine to be exact) were ordained pastors or held ecclesiastical offices, the question arose how the church would treat these Christians of Jewish descent.[21] Not surprisingly, the German Christians favored adopting the state's racial legislation and officially excluding "non-Aryans" from the pulpits and unofficially from the pews. The Young Reformers rejected legislation that would exclude Christians of Jewish descent from the church but were silent when the Nazis took exclusionary measures against Jews and Christians of Jewish descent in the wider society.[22]

First appearances notwithstanding, the Young Reformers' rejection of racial legislation in the church was not a sign of their resolve to oppose antisemitism but rather of their pique at the German Christians' arrogance for thinking they could willy-nilly disregard the sacrament of baptism and modify the church's established policy toward baptized Jews in order to accommodate their vision of a racially pure church.[23] The Young Reformers charged that "organized exclusion [of Jewish Christians] means an interference with the power of the sacraments. The Jewish Christian has been accepted into our church through the will of God in the sacrament of baptism. Through this baptism he is bound indissoluble to this church, and this church to him."[24] It is clear that this stance was motivated by concern for the integrity of the church's autonomy rather than by any humanitarian sympathy for the victims of Nazi racial discrimination. Confessing churchmen said virtually nothing about the Nazi mistreatment of Jewish Germans who had not converted to Christianity. Nor did the discrimination against the approximately 50,000 Jewish Christians in the secular sphere receive strong condemnation.[25] It was, in fact, an embarrassment to many Confessing Church members when the issue of the Christian Jews was raised, since it exposed only too clearly the divergence between their racial attitudes and their Christian witness. Even when it came to protecting Jewish Christians from the state, only a handful of Confessing churchmen were willing to take a risk for a "non-Aryan."

How deeply influenced even these Confessing Church clergy were by anti-Judaic Christian doctrine and the existing currents of anti-Jewish prejudice in German society can be seen from the attitudes of two of their most prominent theologians, Walter Künneth and Dietrich Bonhoeffer.[26] Künneth referred to Jews as "the people of the curse" and "germ carriers," and supported "the elimination of Jewish influence" from Germany.[27] He defended the right of baptized Jews to hold the positions of pastor and church administrator but believed that "the post of Bishop and other positions of leadership in the Church should be reserved for those of the German race."[28] The Young Reformers' distinction between Jews and Jewish Christians, their acceptance of the Aryan paragraph in the secular sphere, and their lukewarm defense of Jewish Christians within the church were early signs that Jews, whether baptized or not, could not count on the church to protect them.

Another revealing response to this issue was the stance taken by Dietrich Bonhoeffer, one of the brightest of Germany's younger generation of theologians. His highly acclaimed April 1933 "The Church and the Jewish Question" employed traditional anti-Judaic language typical of the Lutheran churches.[29] Bonhoeffer was not antisemitic. He did, however, advocate the conversion of Jews to Christianity, since he believed that only through faith in Jesus as the Messiah was salvation possible. It is worth quoting from Bonhoeffer's text at some length to demonstrate just how deeply ingrained anti-Judaic thinking was.

> The Church of Christ has never lost sight of the thought that the "chosen people" who nailed the redeemer of the world to the cross must bear the curse for its action through a long history of suffering. . . . But the history of the suffering of this people, loved and punished by God, stands under the sign of the final homecoming of Israel [the Jews] to its God. And this homecoming happens in the conversion of Israel to Christ. . . . The conversion of Israel, that is to be the end of the people's period of suffering. From here the Christian Church sees the history of the people of Israel with trembling as God's own, free, fearful way with his people, because God is not yet finished with it. Each new attempt to solve "the Jewish question" comes to naught . . . nevertheless such attempts must be made.[30]

Despite his anti-Judaism, Bonhoeffer distinguished himself from the Young Reformers by *actively* opposing implementation of racial legislation in the church and arguing that Christians had a responsibility to show Christian kindness and charity to all Jews by assisting those who suffered as a result of the state's racial legislation.[31]

Although Swiss theologian Karl Barth did not think it was necessary in early 1933 to speak out passionately on the behalf of Jews or Jewish Christians, he did express his disappointment in the Young Reformers' conservative and half-hearted opposition. He minced no words in his 1933 pamphlet *Theological Existence Today!* when he asserted that in principle the Young Reformers were no different than "those heretics [the German Christians]."[32] "These 'New Reformers' are only in disagreement with the 'German Christians' as regards the formal independence or dependence of the Church, but do not disagree concerning the nature of the Church."[33] As far as Barth was concerned, both were guilty of the theological "error" of acknowledging secondary revelations alongside the revelation of Jesus Christ. What the opposition needed to build first and foremost, he insisted, was a spiritual or theological center of resistance based on the Word of God. In contrast to the ecclesiastical opposition of the Young Reformers, Barth proposed a theological opposition that would be directed against any theology, whether German Christian or orthodox Lutheran, that did not acknowledge the infinite qualitative distinction between God and man.[34]

Barth's criticism of the theological "flabbiness" of the church's opposition in the spring of 1933 provided some pastors and theologians with the resolve to hold firm theologically against the German Christians. In September 1933, Martin

Niemöller and Gerhard Jacobi (1891–1971), a pastor of the Kaiser Wilhelm Memorial Church in Berlin, founded the Pastors' Emergency League (PEL). In a matter of weeks some 2,300 pastors, many of whom played a part in the Young Reformation movement, signed the PEL pledge to defend church doctrine against any encroachments by the German Christians on the Reformation confessions, to extend solidarity to those persecuted on account of their confessional stand, and to block any application of the Aryan paragraph within the church.[35] By January 1934 approximately 6,000, slightly over one-third, of the Protestant clergymen in Germany had committed themselves to PEL's confessional stand.[36] PEL, more so than the Young Reformation movement, was the precursor to the Confessing Church and remained the heart and soul of church opposition right up to 1945. Based on their understanding of the gospel and their inherited view of the church-state relationship, neither Niemöller nor the majority of pastors who joined PEL in 1933–34 thought to stand against the Nazi state or in defense of Jews. Their priorities were first and foremost the reclamation of the church from the pernicious secular forces attacking it.

The conservative Lutherans in the intact churches believed that Hitler's support for the German Christian takeover of the churches was the result of a misunderstanding. Hitler, they convinced themselves, did not fully understand that the struggle within the church was an internal church conflict between the legitimate leadership of the regional churches and the illegitimate attempts by the German Christians to usurp authority. Even after Hitler rebuffed established church leaders in a January 1934 meeting, they continued to delude themselves that they could work out a modus vivendi with the Nazi state. This attitude exacerbated the division between the opposition in the destroyed Prussian churches organized around PEL and the more cautious opposition of the conservative Lutherans in the intact churches.

In the midst of this dismal situation that threatened the church's very existence, it was Barth who called for a united theological stance. He forcefully addressed the theological situation in a manner that sought to speak for Reformed, United, and Lutheran churchmen from destroyed churches in the north to intact churches in the south. Barth urged the churches to recognize the unity of their faith through their confession of the exclusivity of Jesus Christ and the gospel as sources of God's revelation. Motivated by a sense of urgency in the midst of the forced coordination (*Gleichschaltung*) of the churches by the Nazis, churchmen from across Germany gathered for the First General Confessional synod in Barmen in late May 1934. In addition to issuing the famous Barmen theological declaration, the delegates elected a leadership body, the Reich council of brethren (*Reichsbruderrat*), to direct the national affairs of what would become known as the Confessing Church.[37] Although the confessional unity achieved at Barmen would turn out to be ephemeral, the synod marked a high point for the Confessing Church. For German church historian Klaus Scholder, the Barmen synod marked an extraordinary and unprecedented event in the four centuries of Protestant history: "The fact that this Church could articulate a common confession for the first time since the sixteenth century gave this synod a significance which extended far beyond the immediate occasion."[38] Although most of the churchmen present, especially many Lutherans, would not have agreed with Scholder's designation of the Barmen declaration as an official confession, Scholder's statement nevertheless captures the historical magnitude of the Barmen synod for many of the Confessing churchmen.

The Barmen Declaration and the Confessional Dispute

The Theological Declaration of Barmen, as it was officially called, was an attempt to achieve consensus among the three Evangelical (Protestant) traditions and to reassert or reclaim church independence, particularly theological independence, from the Nazi-influenced German Christian movement (see appendix 1). Although there were a significant number of pastors and church leaders from all three traditions—Lutheran, Reformed, United—who were willing to make doctrinal concessions in order to achieve a consensus in the face of the German Christian threat, there was also a powerful group of Lutherans, including some of the most respected and world-renowned Lutheran theologians in Germany, who believed strongly that the theological consensus reached at Barmen was an unacceptable dilution of Lutheran theology. To be sure, all Lutherans present at Barmen voted in favor of the declaration. But the number of critics of the Barmen declaration increased when the German Christian threat diminished after 1934, and especially after 1945 when confessional unity was no longer an urgent necessity. Some Lutherans, like Erlangen theologian and church historian Hermann Sasse (1895–1976), opposed Barmen because its theological content clashed with the traditional Lutheran Confessions.[39] Others, such as Paul Althaus, a Lutheran professor of systematic theology at Erlangen University, seemed more agitated by what they believed were Barmen's political implications, particularly a curtailment of the state's authority. Bishop Hans Meiser of Bavaria exemplifies those who voted for Barmen primarily to register their protest against the German Christians' storm-trooper tactics and theological excesses—not because they held the declaration itself in high esteem.

Many conservative Lutherans shared Meiser's strategy and beliefs. After 1945, and in some cases as early as 1934, these Lutherans distanced themselves from the declaration; they felt Barmen's revision of core Lutheran doctrine was too drastic. They quite rightly perceived that the Barmen declaration challenged four of the conservative Lutherans' most sacred tenets: the law-gospel dialectic, the orders of creation or divine orders, natural revelation, and the orthodox Lutheran understanding of Martin Luther's doctrine of the two kingdoms.

The Barmen declaration consists of a preamble, six theses, and a conclusion.[40]

Each of the six theses begins by quoting Scripture, followed by an explanation of the passage and a condemnation of error or *damnatio*. The theological committee designated to draft the declaration for the Barmen synod consisted of Karl Barth, the Swiss dialectical theologian; the relatively unknown Bavarian Lutheran churchman Thomas Breit (1880–1966); and Hans Asmussen, a Lutheran pastor and theologian from Altona near Hamburg. Although Asmussen was a Lutheran, and after the war a rather conservative one, he was influential in the radical wing of the Confessing Church and sympathetic to Barth's theology during the church struggle. At the request of Meiser, Hermann Sasse was to have participated in the deliberations of the committee but could not due to illness.[41] Sasse was, however, given opportunities to read and contribute suggestions to drafts of the document. Ultimately, Sasse chose not to support the final draft and left the synod before the final vote was taken. Despite the presence of Lutherans on the theological committee, scholars agree that Barth was the principal author of the declaration.

The first thesis grounded the church in a theology centered on Christ and committed the church's proclamation to the principle of *sola scriptura,* based on Scripture alone. The second article asserted that Christ's message, which unites God's grace and God's law, had authority in all areas and aspects of life. Thesis III declared that the church's ecclesiastical structure derived from Christ's message and that neither the church's structure nor its message could be changed to satisfy current political or ideological trends. The fourth thesis stated that the purpose of the church's ecclesiastical offices was to fulfill the church's special commission to preach the gospel and administer pastoral care—not for personal advancement or aggrandizement. Thesis V acknowledged the state's divine origins and its right to use force to maintain order; at the same time, it asserted that the church's message and worldly engagement should remind the state of its ultimate origins in God. Finally, Barmen VI explained the mission of the church as spreading the message of God's free grace through its office of preaching. The Barmen declaration did not address the increasingly prevalent attacks on Jews and Judaism articulated by clergymen from both the German Christian movement and sections of the Confessing Church. Although theses III, IV, and VI contributed to the confessional dispute between conservatives and radicals, it was theses I, II, and V that caused the greatest alarm among Lutheran conservatives and had the greatest impact on the post-1945 differences between conservatives and reformers over guilt, repentance, political engagement, and Christian-Jewish relations.

The first thesis was meant to reinforce *to whom* and *to what* the church must listen, *from where* the church's knowledge of God must come, and *from what source* the church's proclamation must be derived. According to this fundamental thesis, "Jesus Christ, as he is attested to us in Holy Scripture, is the one Word of God that we have to hear, and which we have to trust and obey in life and death." Barmen I rejected all claims that the church could proclaim that the message of God's saving grace could be found in a source other than Jesus Christ as attested to in the Scriptures.

Barth explained in the late 1930s that the primary aim of Barmen I (and the declaration as a whole, for that matter) was to tackle the problem of natural theology in general and its crude manipulation by the German Christians in particular.[42] The vulgar natural theology espoused by the German Christians placed the events of 1933, German history, German blood, and even Adolf Hitler alongside the gospel as revelations of God's will. Walter Grundmann, a leader of the German Christians in Saxony, provided one of the more brazen distortions of natural theology in his explanation of the significance of the Nazi insignia for Christianity: "The Swastika is a sign of sacrifice which lets the cross of Christ shine out for us in a new light."[43] Directed primarily but not exclusively against this type of theological error, Barmen's first thesis rejected the placing of the swastika next to the cross, the Third Reich next to God's Reich, or Hitler next to Christ in church proclamation. Thus, the rejection of natural theology in the first thesis was for Barth and many of his supporters the foundation over which the entire church struggle was to be fought.

Conservatives, however, detected correctly a challenge not only to the German Christians' blatant heresy of placing Hitler next to Christ but also a challenge to the long doctrinal tradition of natural theology and natural revelation in Christianity, particularly Luther's theory of the divine orders. Several highly respected Lutheran theologians, including Paul Althaus, Werner Elert, Friedrich Gogarten, Emanuel Hirsch, and Hermann Sasse, to name a few, maintained a twofold revelation of God: in Jesus Christ, and in the divine orders (family, state, and *Volk*). They did not, of course, maintain that the two revelations were of equal importance to Christians. The revelation of God in Jesus Christ was always given priority. But the very fact that they took a second revelation in the divine orders with resolute seriousness meant that it was highly unlikely that they could support the Barmen declaration unconditionally. Sasse believed that Barth's attack on natural theology and the divine orders was a grave mistake because such a critique alienated not only the German Christians but the conservative Lutherans as well.

Barth did not mind alienating both German Christians and conservative Lutherans. He wanted to stress that German Christian theology was merely the logical outcome of orthodox Lutheranism. Since Barth saw no adequate way to check or limit the prioritizing of a natural revelation over the revelation of God in Christ as attested in the Scriptures, he maintained that all natural theologies must be eliminated from church proclamation. Barth wrote the declaration, to be sure, with an eye to pleasing Lutherans as well as Reformed churchmen. The Lutherans Barth wanted most to meet halfway, however, were Asmussen, Niemöller, and their colleagues who sought confessional unity—not conservative Lutheran confessionalists like Althaus, Elert, and Sasse.

The import of the Lutheran critique of the first thesis was equally relevant to the second thesis. Barmen II challenged another of the most guarded tenets of Lutheran doctrine: the distinction between law and gospel. By maintaining that Jesus Christ was both our assurance of forgiveness (gospel) and claim upon our whole life (law), Barmen emphasized, according to the Lutheran critics, the *unity* of gospel and law in Jesus Christ. In the theological context of the first half of the twentieth century, this particular thesis more than the others rightfully deserved to be labeled "Reformed" or "Barthian" as Werner Elert has argued.[44]

The Lutherans took exception to the identification of law with gospel because they understood that divine law and gospel offered two very different messages. According to the Lutheran Reformation confessions, God's law accused and convicted man, whereas the gospel comforted and consoled him. They also insisted that the chronological order *law-gospel* was essential and that any change in that order belittled the miracle of the gospel and its message of forgiveness. The joyful and consoling message of the gospel—that God will forgive sinners for the sake of Christ—lost its significance, its miraculousness, if the law—God's judgment—had not previously condemned man as a contemptible sinner. Lutheranism maintained such a separation in order to preserve the purity of God's love as expressed in the gospel from any mention of God's wrath at the same time.

The flurry of criticism in 1934, especially from theologians at Erlangen University, led Barth to respond with the essay "Gospel and Law," reversing in his title the traditional Lutheran order. Barth maintained that true knowledge of God's law must come *after* God's revelation in the gospel.[45] Moreover, Barth disapproved of the Lutheran separation of law and gospel. Convinced that the Lutheran separation of gospel and law had its corollary in the separation of church and state in the Lutheran doctrine of two kingdoms, Barth believed that the independence of the law from the gospel, and the state from the church, opened the way for the German Christians' correlation of the divine law with the laws of the National Socialist state. One need only skim Elert and Althaus's response to the Barmen declaration, the "Ansbach Memorandum," to see that they accepted the correlation of divine law with the law of the National Socialist state.[46] By arguing that the gospel was the source of the law, Barth hoped to block the linking of God's law to the laws of man. As one commentator acknowledges, "The dialectic between law and gospel therefore had to be subordinated to Barth's concern that the Word of God not be confused with the words of men."[47] The unity of gospel and law according to Barth was a theme that ran through the entire Barmen declaration. Thus, the premise of the second thesis is much the same as the first—to reinforce the infinite qualitative distinction between God and man.

For conservative Lutherans, however, Barth's reformulation was unacceptable. All attempts to elevate the Barmen declaration to the status of a binding doctrinal confession for Lutherans, Elert argued in 1948, ought to be dropped.[48] As regrettable as the German Christian perversion of the law-gospel doctrine was, it did not justify a major change in the established doctrine. Barth's undermining of the traditional distinction between law and gospel had equally troubling repercussions, as far as the conservative Lutherans were concerned, for understanding the relationship between church and state, which the highly controversial fifth thesis addressed.

Of the six theses, the fifth is most important for an appreciation of the political and theological debates within the church in the aftermath of the war. At issue was the degree of authority Christians ought to allot the state. Conservatives granted it more, radicals less. The authors of Barmen V modified the orthodox Lutheran interpretation of Luther's doctrine of two kingdoms in order to map out an alternative view of the relation of church and state that would address the totalitarian claims of the Nazi state.

Lutherans, both radical and conservative, agreed that the state existed by reason of man's sin. Since Christians and non-Christians failed to conduct themselves in accordance with the dictates of the gospel, it was necessary for God to rule the earth by means other than the consoling promise of the gospel. Accordingly, God created a second government, the worldly government or regiment (*das weltliche Regiment*), alongside the spiritual government or regiment (*das geistliche Regiment*), in order to preserve life and property in the not-yet-redeemed world. Whereas the Holy Spirit ruled the church or spiritual kingdom by means of the gospel, the state ruled civil society or the earthly kingdom by means of coercion and force. The two kingdoms within which every Christian lived simultaneously were both kingdoms of God. However, God commissioned them with different tasks, ruled them with different governments, and placed different means at the disposal of the two governments. The task of a church minister was to proclaim the gospel of Christ; the task of a state minister was to keep the peace. Barmen V did not explicitly challenge this accepted interpretation of Luther's doctrine, but it did modify it.

The fifth thesis emphasized the ties between the two kingdoms as much as their separateness when the authors declared that the church "calls to mind the Kingdom of God, God's commandment and righteousness, and thereby the responsibility both of rulers and ruled." In doing so, the church reminded the state that it was divinely sanctioned not only in its role to maintain order but also in its responsibility to the kingdom of God and the Word of God. This strongly suggested, although it was never explicitly stated in the Barmen declaration, that the honor due the secular authority was contingent on the state's fulfillment of, or at least the genuine attempt to fulfill, its God-given task in accordance with commonly recognized Christian principles. Conservative Lutherans denounced this link between the two kingdoms as a departure from orthodoxy. For them, Barth's interpretation undermined the orthodox Lutheran distinction between God's alien work and God's proper work, between law and gospel, between *das geistliche Regiment* and *das weltliche Regiment*. Thus, Barmen V implicitly limited the autonomy and authority of the state and in doing so lost the support of many conservative Lutherans.

The different ways in which the two wings of the Confessing Church understood the confessional basis of the church was obviously not a matter of mere semantics.

The confessional dispute involved the significant question: What constitutes the church's confession, that is, what are the defining doctrines of the Evangelical Church? For the supporters of Barmen, the traditional interpretation of the Lutheran confessions provided inadequate doctrinal resources to withstand attempts by the German Christians to fuse Christianity and National Socialism. In view of the German Christian heresies, Barth and his followers sought not simply to restore the traditional Lutheran vision but to revise that vision by restricting the church's proclamation to God's word alone. They defined the church as the brethren gathered together to profess Jesus Christ as the sole mediator between God and man. Conservative Lutherans, relying on other mediating links between God and man such as the state, accused the radicals of acting like a sect determined to exclude anyone who did not accept and adhere to their unorthodox declaration.[49] Although Asmussen tried in his exegesis to guard against the accusation that the radical wing of the Confessing Church was unfaithful to the Lutheran confessions, it became the rallying call of the conservative Lutherans into the postwar period.

Conservative Lutherans who opposed the Barmen declaration in 1934 continued to maintain throughout the Nazi period and afterwards that Barmen held no weight in the Lutheran Church since it conflicted in several places with Lutheran doctrine and was neither written nor accepted by a Lutheran synod. Those conservative Lutherans who put aside their reservations in light of the ecclesiastical situation in the spring of 1934 and voted for Barmen interpreted it after the war as a significant theological statement but certainly not a legitimate confession in the sense of the Reformation confessions.[50] The radicals, in contrast, viewed the Barmen declaration as more than a theological declaration; many accorded it the stature of a confession equal to, if not superseding, the sixteenth-century confessions. When the Allies finally defeated the Nazis, Martin Niemöller and his colleagues completely rejected both a restoration of either the pre-1933 church or the Reich church, and they declared their intention to redefine the church along the theological lines set down at Barmen.[51]

The Fragmentation of the Confessing Church (1934–39)

Five months after Barmen, a follow-up synod of the same opposition forces in the Confessing Church was held in Pastor Niemöller's church in the Berlin suburb of Dahlem. It was a call for battle against the errors of the German Christians. The radical wing of the Confessing Church declared in effect that the leaders of the official Reich church had cut themselves off from the Christian church as a result of their unconstitutional and unchristian behavior. Moreover, the misuse of the legal machinery of the Reich church by the German Christian leaders necessitated the implementation of emergency rights (*Notrecht*) by the Confessing Church and the replacement of the administrative and governing bodies of the Reich church with Confessing synods and councils of brethren.[52] One resolution called on all parishes

> to accept no instructions from the former Reich Church government or its adminis-
> trative offices, and to withdraw from further cooperation with those who continue to
> obey this church regime. We summon them [the congregations] to follow the in-
> structions of the Confessional Synod of the German Evangelical Church and those
> bodies it recognizes.[53]

And finally, the Dahlem resolution requested the official recognition of the Confessing Church and its synods and councils as the legitimate leadership of the German Evangelical Church by the Nazi state.[54] In effect, the drafters of the Dahlem resolutions declared an outright schism in the church between the Confessing Church and the German Christians. In so doing, they also caused a rupture between radicals and conservatives in the Confessing Church.

These controversies were to have long-lasting effects. The first postwar church conference held in Treysa in August 1945 nearly collapsed under the tension between those who wanted to establish a new church on the basis of the declarations made at Barmen *and* Dahlem and those who wanted the foundation to be orthodox Lutheranism as it was defined in the nineteenth and early twentieth centuries.

The assertions made at Dahlem were highly controversial within the Confessing Church for practical as well as theological reasons. In practice, Dahlem meant that two church governments—the official Reich church government under Bishop Müller's leadership, with its thousands of administrative, judicial, and spiritual offices, and the government of the Confessing Church—would exist side by side. Of the two, there was no doubt that the Confessing Church was the least well-equipped to take up the tasks of governing. Not only did the Confessing churches profess goals in contradiction with those of the state and therefore lack its support, they also lacked majorities in most of the regional churches. Even more problematic was the theological claim that the Confessing clergymen had the right, the power, or the ability to distinguish between true and false Christians and excommunicate those they deemed false.

The Dahlem synod brought into the open the divisions that had simmered below the surface at Barmen. The Dahlemites, on the one hand, argued that the Dahlem resolutions were the logical outcome of the theological declaration made at Barmen. Barmen, they argued, laid out the Confessing Church's theology, and Dahlem its praxis. The authors of the Barmen declaration asserted that the gospel of Jesus Christ was the one word that the church must hear and obey. The Dahlemites put this into practice by contending that the basis of the Reich church was something other than the gospel and that therefore it was their duty as true Christians to sever ties with the leadership of the Reich church and to erect new laws and bodies that corresponded with the gospel. Conservative Lutherans, on the other hand, interpreted Barmen as a necessary and timely reminder that the gospel and not National Socialist politics took priority in the church. The practical implementation of this conservative interpretation of Barmen was the removal of the radical German Christians and a restoration of the old leadership of the regional churches.

Conservatives' eagerness to avoid any unnecessary tension with the state guided their actions in the months following the Dahlem synod. Consequently, the Confessing Church's leadership council, the Reich council of brethren, split into two distinct leadership bodies; each aimed to implement their interpretation of the mandate given to them at Barmen, or in the case of the Dahlemites, at Barmen and Dahlem. On one side, there was the Council of the German Evangelical Church (*Rat der DEK*), consisting primarily of Dahlemites who saw no room for compromise with the German Christians or Nazi church policies. On the other side, there was the Provisional Church Directory (*Vorläufige Leitung*), led by Bishop Marahrens and conservative church leaders primarily from the intact churches.

Fiery exchanges took place between the two groups, with Barth calling the Provisional Church Directory "a demolition firm as far as the decisions made at Dahlem are concerned," and the ultraconservative Bishop Marahrens declaring that "the greatest danger to the Evangelical Church comes from Karl Barth."[55] An exasperated Niemöller pointed out the obvious: the Confessing Church could not have two competing church administrations. Nevertheless, from November 1934 onwards it did.

The intensification of state pressure in early 1935 led to new attempts to achieve unity within the Confessing Church. In March 1935 Wilhelm Frick (1877–1946), Hitler's minister of the interior, had more than 700 pastors arrested, the majority from Prussia, to prevent them from reading a declaration from their pulpits denouncing the blasphemous pronouncements of a particularly *völkisch* faction of German Christians.[56] The recognition that division within the Confessing Church precluded a unified response to the arrests led the two wings to patch up their differences temporarily at the third general confessional synod in Augsburg in May 1935.[57] Typically, however, the professed unity in the ranks of the Confessing Church was more ephemeral than real. Marga Meusel (1897–1953), a parish worker in Berlin, and Martin Albertz (1883–1956), a Berlin pastor with close ties to the Dahlem wing, tried without success to get the Confessing Church to discuss the plight of Jews and Jewish Christians.[58] Bishop Meiser, who agreed to host the synod on the condition that Barth not come, had his way, and Barth did not attend.[59] Barth, in turn, had only caustic words for the compromising positions taken by both wings of the Confessing Church at Augsburg, declaring: "It [the Confessing Church] still has no heart for the millions who suffer unjustly. It still has nothing to say on the simplest questions of public honesty. When it speaks, it speaks only about its own affairs."[60] He sarcastically branded the synod "a new Peace of Augsburg" and ominously predicted that this peace would not last.[61]

It was one of Hitler's tried and true strategies to change tactics and alliances when a desired goal was not achieved or when a particular alliance proved politically problematic. Hitler had thrown his support and the support of the Nazi state behind the German Christians in the spring of 1933 because they had demonstrated the desire and capacity to "coordinate" the Reich's twenty-seven regional churches with the Nazi state. When the German Christians proved incapable of carrying out this task, Hitler decided on a more direct form of pressure. This involved the creation of a new ministry of church affairs, which was then entrusted to one of the Führer's old cronies, Hanns Kerrl, who had first been appointed as Prussian minister of justice. Kerrl's church committees, established on the Reich and regional level, were meant to create an administrative umbrella under which the German Christians and both wings of the Confessing Church could co-exist.[62] The Dahlemites refused to work with the committees, describing the state's interference in church affairs through the committees as "worse than it was in the time of Ludwig Müller."[63] Otto Dibelius, who was removed from his post as superintendent-general of Kurmark in the Berlin-Brandenburg Church in 1933, responded to the establishment of the church committees with a hard-hitting memorandum, "The State Church Is Here," which lambasted Kerrl and the attempt by the state to undermine the independence of the church.[64]

The fourth and last general confessional synod took place in Bad Oeynhausen in mid-February 1936. The relationship between the two wings of the Confessing Church had soured to the point where reconciliation was impossible. Conservatives established the Lutheran council (*Lutherrat*), whose membership included Bishops Marahrens, Meiser, and Wurm among others.[65] It quickly became the leading voice of conservative Lutheranism in Germany and remained so into the postwar period. The Dahlemites elected their own to a Second Provisional Directory, which had the support of Lutherans in the destroyed churches but not the intact churches.[66] The palpable acrimony at Bad Oeynhausen brought to its logical conclusion the long-simmering debate between the two wings of the Confessing Church. From this point on, two groups with two different leadership bodies existed side by side in the Confessing Church.[67] Each side adopted a different ecclesiastical course: conservatives in the intact churches concerned themselves with safeguarding their church functions and continually demonstrated a willingness to compromise with the German Christians and the state in order to achieve this; Dahlemites in the destroyed churches, many of whom already had lost their positions, demonstrated a greater degree of independence from the state's ministry of church affairs and an occasional willingness to make critical public statements about the Nazi state and its church policy. Even after the war these two groups continued to clash head-on again and again over everything from the administration of the sacraments to relations with the occupying powers and the founding of two German states.

With political power increasingly centralized in the hands of Hitler and his closest subordinates in the mid-1930s, the churches were starkly confronted with the question: What was the proper relationship between church and state? Since his expulsion to Switzerland in June 1935, Barth had taken a more radical position on the church's political role. He reproached the Confessing Church for not recognizing that the decision to place emphasis on the First Commandment in the six theses of the Barmen declaration was not only a religious decision but also a political one in the context of Nazi Germany and the Nazi deification of Hitler.[68] By failing to discern the political nature of its religious commitments, Barth believed, the Confessing Church was incapable of supplying a penetrating critique of National Socialism. The Dahlemites, no longer constrained by the conservative Lutherans after the Bad Oeynhausen split, expressed a similarly critical position in a strongly worded confidential letter to Hitler in early June 1936 that openly criticized the state-initiated dechristianization of the Reich.[69] Two key paragraphs read:

> When blood, race, nationality, and honor are thus raised to the rank of qualities that guarantee eternity, the Evangelical Christian is bound, by the First Commandment, to reject the assumption. When the "Aryan" human being is glorified, God's Word bears witness to the sinfulness of all men. When, within the compass of the National Socialist view of life, an anti-Semitism is forced on the Christian that binds him to hatred of the Jew, the Christian injunction to love one's neighbor still stands . . . .
>
> The Evangelical conscience, which shares the responsibility for the people and the government, is most heavily burdened by the fact that there are still concentration camps in Germany—which describes itself as a country in which justice is administered—and that the measures and actions of the secret State police are exempt from any judicial control.[70]

The letter to Hitler, drafted by Hans Asmussen, signaled a new clarity in the approach taken by the Dahlem wing of the Confessing Church in internal church relations as well as external relations with the Nazi state. This less compromising stance by the Dahlemites can be attributed to three factors: the harsher police measures implemented in the second half of the 1930s, the attempts to dilute the Dahlem line by Bishop Marahrens and the conservatives, and the realization that a commitment to certain theological principles had political ramifications. No longer was it possible to hold firm to the declarations passed at Barmen and Dahlem without coming into conflict with state law. It was one thing to lampoon the hapless Reich Bishop Müller, something conservatives and Dahlemites alike participated in, and quite another to openly criticize state policy as the confidential letter to Hitler did. Theologically, ecclesiastically, and psychologically, Lutherans were sorely unprepared to oppose the state. For many Lutherans, opposition to state interference in church affairs was a major step, but questioning the legality of the state and its motives, as the letter to Hitler did, was virtually unthinkable. Conservatives went so far as to charge the small minority that persisted in open opposition with risking the lives and livelihoods of everyone else in the church.[71] Although the church struggle took on a new dimension that included a struggle between church and state in

the mid-1930s, the internal church struggle between the various factions continued to dominate the activities of most churchmen.

Leadership of the churches was still solidly divided when the Second World War
began in September 1939. As the nation geared up for war and the state clamped
down on any sign of disloyalty, churchmen were increasingly confronted with
conflicts of interest between their political and ideological loyalty to the Nazi state
and their religious and spiritual loyalty to the church and their ordination vows.
Whereas the German Christians' readiness to adapt their religious convictions to
the National Socialist *Weltanschauung* meant they rarely experienced a conflict of
interest, pastors in the Confessing Church continually struggled with how to meet
the contradictory demands required of a patriotic citizen and a pious cleric. Pre-
dictably, responses by the Dahlem and conservative wings of the Confessing
Church to the dual demands of the gospel and National Socialism diverged considerably in certain instances but only slightly in others. For the most part the
Lutheran traditionalists, such as Marahrens and Meiser, strove to reconcile their
political loyalty to Hitler and their religious loyalty to the Lutheran confessions by
maintaining that the state leadership was divinely ordained. They hypocritically
charged the Dahlem wing of the Confessing Church as well as extremists in the
German Christian movement with mixing politics and religion and thus failing to
recognize Luther's admonishment to keep the worldly and spiritual kingdoms separate. To be sure, Marahrens and Meiser's support for the Nazi regime was certainly more restrained than that of the German Christians, but their quietism was
no less political.

Pastors in the Dahlem wing of the Confessing Church distinguished between
love for the fatherland and unmitigated support for Hitler, making it possible to
express their patriotism, even chauvinism, while maintaining that, as the fifth thesis of the Barmen declaration stated, Christians should not allow the state to become
"the single and totalitarian order of human life." Typical of most opposition in Nazi
Germany, the Dahlemites in the Confessing Church enthusiastically supported certain facets of Nazi rule, opposed others, and were indifferent or complacent toward
others. But in contrast to the first few years of Nazi rule, after 1937 the regime sought
total control over individuals and groups in the public sphere and hence also sought
to quash even the smallest signs of public dissent. Thus, despite their professed allegiance to the fatherland, pastors from the Dahlem wing who strove to preach according to the dictates set down in the Barmen declaration—which clearly limited
the role of the state—were considered enemies of the Reich.

Niemöller was the quintessential example of a churchman who struggled simultaneously to remain true to his nationalist and to his religious convictions, and
as a consequence, he spent eight years in concentration camps. Niemöller's nationalist sympathies were well known throughout Germany from his 1933 autobiography *From U-Boat to Pulpit* (1934), which enthusiastically recounted his days
as a U-boat commander in the First World War and the shame he felt at Germany's

defeat in 1918.[72] His combined feelings of detachment from the Weimar Republic and enthusiasm for Hitler's vision of a strong moral order led Niemöller to vote for the Nazis in the 1924 election.[73] He built his reputation as a dynamic preacher in perhaps the most influential parish in Germany—the posh and powerful Berlin suburb of Dahlem.

Yet after Hitler came to power, he quickly became disillusioned by the Nazis' support for the German Christian movement, paganist attacks on Christian doctrine, and deification of Hitler. He became a staunch defender of the Barmen-Dahlem line. In his last sermon before his arrest Niemöller preached, "We are no more ready to keep silent at man's behest, when God commands us to speak. For it is, and must remain the case, that we must obey God rather than man."[74] Arrested on 1 July 1937 for his outspoken criticism of the state's church policy and charged with causing unrest, Niemöller was acquitted the following March after a highly publicized show trial. Hitler was furious at Niemöller's acquittal and the international support he received as a result of the trial. He ordered Niemöller locked up and held indefinitely. After eight months in Berlin's Moabit prison, Niemöller spent the rest of the Third Reich in Sachsenhausen concentration camp outside Berlin and after 1941 in Dachau near Munich.

At the outbreak of the hostilities, to the surprise and disapproval of some of his friends in the Dahlemite wing of the Confessing Church and supporters abroad, Niemöller requested from his cell at Sachsenhausen that he be allowed to rejoin the German navy to fight for his country.[75] Hitler denied his request. Although Niemöller and some of his colleagues in the Dahlem wing distinguished themselves from their conservative colleagues by openly protesting the state's church policy, the two wings were for the most part in agreement in their support for the war once it started. In fact, when the German Christians challenged Confessing churchmen to sign a loyalty oath to Hitler in 1938, most were willing to take the oath as long as it was understood that their ultimate allegiance as Christians was to God.[76]

Just as the controversy over the loyalty oath was dying down, a new confrontation over the relationship between politics and religion broke out in the ranks of the Confessing Church. In late September 1938, when war seemed imminent, the Dahlemites proposed that a day of prayer be held on 30 September to ask for God's forgiveness for the sins of the nation. The text contained among other things the following confession:

> We have tolerated altogether too much false gospel. . . . We confess before Thee the sins of our people. Your name is derided among them, your word is attacked, your truth has been oppressed. Openly and in secret much injustice has taken place.[77]

Understandably, the Nazis interpreted the prayer liturgy as a veiled attack on the state and a justification for acts of rebellion at a moment when they regarded foreign affairs as particularly sensitive. Although only a handful of pastors read the prayer liturgy from their pulpits, the Nazi Party accused the Confessing Church of treason. The bishops of the intact churches took the opportunity to condemn the prayer liturgy and to disassociate themselves further from the Dahlemites and the councils of brethren.[78]

To add fuel to the fire, a letter by Karl Barth to a colleague in Prague, urging the Czechs to offer the greatest possible resistance to a German invasion, was made public. The letter declared that Czechs who defended their border against the Germans would be acting not only on behalf of "freedom . . . but also for the Christian Church."[79] Later, Barth explained that he was not encouraging the Czechs to go to war against Germany in the name of the church but rather to resist the expansion of National Socialism in order to spare the Czech churches the ordeal that had befallen the German churches. Although the Czech crisis passed for the moment without armed conflict, the prayer liturgy and Barth's letter made clear where the different factions of the church stood concerning the church's role in politics.

The Second World War and the Holocaust

Many Protestant pastors greeted the invasion of Poland in September 1939 enthusiastically, convinced by Nazi propaganda that Germans, including Protestant clergy in the Polish corridor and upper Silesia, were being abused by the Poles.[80] John S. Conway, author of *The Nazi Persecution of the Churches, 1933–1945*, rightly suggests that the churches' reaction to the beginning of the Second World War was entirely predictable:

> The whole sorry process of accommodation and compromise that had gone on since 1933 now reached its logical conclusion when, in face of Hitler's attack on Poland in September 1939, the Churches stood dumb and confused, unable to raise a voice of protest, spiritless and without initiative.[81]

The same lack of resolve was evident in their response to Nazi racial policy in the late 1930s. On the night of 9 November 1938, the infamous *Kristallnacht*, the SS (*Schutzstaffel*) organized and carried out a massive pogrom on Germany's Jewish population that resulted in more than 200 synagogues burned or destroyed, more than 7,500 Jewish businesses wrecked, 91 Jews killed, and scores more wounded and raped. The Nazis arrested some 26,000 Jews and placed them in concentration camps.[82] The official response from the Confessing Church was silence. Some individual Confessing Church pastors, including Niemöller's replacement, Helmut Gollwitzer (1908–93), and a Württembergian pastor, Julius von Jan, took advantage of Germany's Prayer and Repentance Day (*Buss- und Bettag*) the following week to protest the Nazi orchestrated pogrom, but the leaders whose voices carried the most weight—Bishops Marahrens, Meiser, and Wurm—made no formal protest.[83]

Although a unified response from the Confessing Church was virtually impossible, the real stumbling block to an official Confessing Church protest was not the confessional, organizational, or even political divisions but the traditional antipathy toward Judaism derived from centuries of Lutheran teaching that the Jew was a godless outcast who would always be a danger to a Christian nation unless he converted to Christianity. Racial antisemitism was certainly prevalent in the Confessing Church, but anti-Judaism was the church's official doctrine on the Jews. According to this doctrine the Jewish threat to Christian society came, not from the Jews' race or biology, but because they rejected Jesus Christ as the Messiah.[84]

Most churchmen from the Confessing Church put Jews and Jewish Christians in very different categories. It was only the latter group—the converts—that the Confessing Church felt obliged to defend against Nazi racial laws. But these attempts to defend Jewish Christians were the exception and not the rule, and they had the effect of legitimizing much of the Nazis' murderous racial policy. By 1939 not only had the state's persecution of the churches reached new heights but the Nazis were clamping down on anyone aiding or abetting any person defined as a Jew by the Nazis. Even if the larger body of the Confessing Church had had a change of heart—which they did not—assistance to Jews would have been extremely difficult and risky.

Although too late to have a major impact on Nazi racial policy, the violence of *Kristallnacht* did spur some individuals to take a more active role in trying to assist their Jewish countrymen. With institutional support from the leadership body of the Dahlem wing of the Confessing Church, Martin Albertz, Dietrich Bonhoeffer, Heinrich Grüber (1891–1975), Hermann Maas (1877–1970), and others provided relief and help with emigration for Jews and Christians of Jewish descent.[85] Barth and Bonhoeffer also toned down their earlier anti-Judaic explanations for Jewish suffering and became proactive defenders of European Jews.[86]

Bonhoeffer's opposition was more political and consequently more perilous than Barth's. From a large, wealthy, and influential Lutheran family of scholars, scientists, and military officers, Dietrich Bonhoeffer had begun lecturing at Berlin University at the age of twenty-two. Active in resistance work for a number of years, he eventually joined the conspiracy against Hitler led by Admiral Wilhelm Canaris and Major General Hans Oster in the counterintelligence office of the High Military Command. During trips abroad he smuggled out information on behalf of the resistance, and on a trip to Italy he even made contact with the Italian Resistance. When the Gestapo uncovered a plan of the conspirators to smuggle Jews out of Germany in April 1943, they arrested Bonhoeffer and held him in Tegel prison in Berlin. On 9 April 1945 the Nazis executed the thirty-nine-year-old theologian with his fellow conspirators Canaris and Oster at Flossenburg concentration camp.[87] Within a month the Nazis executed Bonhoeffer's brother and two brothers-in-law for "antiwar activity." Bonhoeffer's attitude toward the Jews had changed significantly. Gone from his theology was the traditional Lutheran separation between the people of the Old Testament and those of the New Testament. Aiding the Jews was no longer an act of Christian charity, as he had advocated in 1933, but it was a theological necessity based on the unity of Jews and Christians in the person of Jesus Christ.[88]

When the slaughter of innocent Jews and Slavs began in earnest in 1941 across eastern Europe, the Confessing Church was paralyzed by fear and prejudice. Soon after the German army began its drive eastward, stories of atrocities against Jews filtered back to civilians and churchmen in Germany. Stewart Herman, pastor of the American Church in Berlin until December 1941, reported in 1943 that "it became definitely known through the soldiers returning from the front that in occupied Russia . . . Jewish civilians—men, women, and babies—were being lined up and machine-gunned by the thousands."[89] Bishop Wurm also alluded to the rumors of mass killings in a letter to the Reich minister of church affairs dated December 1941.[90]

Despite the prevalence from late 1941 onward of rumors and eyewitness accounts that mass killings were taking place, the Protestant Church issued only one public condemnation during the Holocaust—and this was a partially veiled criticism in October 1943 by the twelfth confessional synod of the Church of the Old Prussian Union held in Breslau. In its statement to the congregations the Prussian Confessional synod declared, "The murdering of men solely because they are members of a foreign race, or because they are old, or mentally ill, or the relatives of a criminal, cannot be considered as carrying out the authority entrusted to the State by God."[91] The synod also called on the congregations to show spiritual fellowship and brotherly love to "our non-Aryan fellow Christians," that is, baptized Jews. Unfortunately, this plea went unrecognized by Protestants in all but a few exceptional instances.

Even Bishop Wurm, who openly asserted that Jews were dangerous and destructive and needed to be combated, sent a letter to Hitler protesting "in God's name" the "persecution and annihilation to which many men and women under German domination are being subjected."[92] Tellingly, he could not convince his conservative colleagues Bishops Marahrens and Meiser to sign the letter with him. As the letter to Hitler makes clear, Wurm minced no words in expressing his belief that the inhuman treatment of men and women was contrary to God's commands. Be that as it may, it would be a misinterpretation of the private protests of Wurm and other church leaders to present them as championing the cause of the Jews. The notion that antisemitism was justified as long as it stayed within "biblical limits," as one pastor put it, was widely accepted within the church.[93] Although never explicitly defined, "biblical limits" seemed to exclude extermination and brutal mistreatment but not the denial of civil liberties or expulsion from Germany.

By the end of 1941, at the age of seventy-three, Wurm had acquired great respect from both wings of the Confessing Church for his outspoken statements against unnecessary cruelty in the war as well as against the euthanasia program. In the early 1940s when he used this prestige to attempt to unify the two wings of the Confessing Church (*Einigungswerk*), he found his efforts greeted with cautious enthusiasm from both sides.[94] Over the next few years Wurm often addressed letters to all the pastors in Germany stressing the areas of unity among them and encouraging a more united stand. On Easter Sunday in 1943 a statement, "Task and Service of the Church" (*Auftrag und Dienst der Kirche*), signed by eighty-six prominent churchmen, outlined in thirteen theses the church's tasks and obligations.[95] This document was a "classic compromise statement."[96] It declared the Bible as the source of church proclamation, rejected outside interference in church matters, and reiterated the church's obligation and right to preach the Word of God publicly before the people and the state. Despite the broad support this statement elicited, Wurm's efforts had only limited success during the war, and attempts to rehabilitate it at the first postwar conference of church leaders in Treysa in August 1945 were met with skepticism by hard-liners in the Lutheran council and the Reich council of brethren. Nevertheless, it laid the foundation for at least the possibility of a reconciliation between the two wings of the Confessing Church in the postwar period.

The Relevance of the Church Struggle for the Postwar Period

Despite the many public statements professing church unity, the divisions that racked the Confessing Church during the church struggle essentially carried over into the postwar period. The defeat of the Nazi regime brought about the rapid and complete eclipse of those churchmen in the ranks of the German Christians who had held office for all these years. It remained for the surviving leaders of the Confessing Church to tackle the horrific burdens now facing both church and nation. In fact, their policy toward their former enemies in the German Christian movement was very moderate. The overwhelming majority in the Confessing Church wanted to rid the church of its worst German Christian elements, welcome the rest back into the fold, forget the past, and end recrimination.

Three groups emerged from the wreckage in 1945 to lead the church's reconstruction: ultraconservative Lutherans aligned with Hans Meiser and the Lutheran council; conservatives from Lutheran and United churches aligned with Bishop Wurm; and a reform-minded group of churchmen from all three Protestant traditions associated with Niemöller, Barth, and the councils of brethren. The issues of how to organize the church and what role to give to the Barmen declaration became major bones of contention because the outcome would determine which interpretation of the church struggle would become official church history.[97] Even more to the point, these issues were issues of power and control in one of the most powerful and influential institutions in modern German history. Although a tiny minority of German Christians continued to maintain regional and national leadership positions in the postwar period, the bulk of the church's postwar leaders came from the ranks of the Confessing Church's Dahlem or conservative wings. Even before Germany's surrender, Confessing Church leaders in the destroyed churches began to reclaim high-ranking positions vacated by German Christians. At the same time, bishops and officers from the intact churches sought positions of national leadership within the church.

Meiser and his colleagues wanted to take advantage of the unsettled conditions within the church to found a loosely united Lutheran Church consisting of the Lutheran-dominated regional churches. Their goal was to give conservative Lutheranism a more powerful voice in church affairs after it was so successfully challenged by leaders of the reform wing of the Confessing Church at Barmen and later. For Meiser and the Lutheran council, the Barmen declaration was an important declaration in the context of the German Christian threat but not a binding confession that would play a major role in the future United Evangelical Lutheran Church of Germany (*Vereinigte Evangelisch-Lutherische Kirche Deutschlands*, VELKD).[98]

At the other extreme, Niemöller and his colleagues wanted to end the centuries-old system of regional churches and rebuild a more unified (less confessionally divided) church from the congregations up.[99] Niemöller fiercely opposed the "enthronement of new bishops" and "the episcopal absolutism" of conservatives like Dibelius, which he considered a continuation of the very problems that led to the church's easy accommodation with Nazism.[100] Moreover, the former Dahlemites wanted to ensure that the church would not be refounded as an Erastian Church, that is, a church characterized by state supremacy in ecclesiastical affairs.[101] They advocated a church run by councils of brethren with strong representation of laymen.[102]

And Bishop Wurm, backed by the venerable director of the Bethel Institute for Epileptics and one-time Reich bishop, Pastor Friedrich von Bodelschwingh, wanted a loosely united Evangelical Church, led but not entirely dominated by the Lutheran churches, that would be based on the traditional system of regional churches.[103] Despite the rift that developed between Meiser and Wurm over Meiser's insistence on an exclusively Lutheran Church, the ultraconservatives who aligned with Meiser and the conservatives who aligned with Wurm had two things in common: they both wanted to rebuild the church from the top down and to retain the regional churches and the hierarchical decision-making procedures associated with the regional churches.[104] The difference between them was that Meiser wanted to exclude the voice of Reformed and United churches (which in practice often meant excluding the voice of the Dahlemites), while Wurm intended to include them—albeit not as equal partners. In the end, it was Wurm's vision that appealed to most churchmen.

To be sure, not all prominent church leaders adhered strictly to one of these three agendas. For instance, many notable churchmen from the former councils of brethren, like Asmussen, sought a compromise position closer to Wurm than to

Niemöller. There were also conservative Lutherans from United churches, such as Bishop Dibelius of Berlin, who were not prepared to follow Meiser all the way to a United Evangelical Lutheran Church if it meant eliminating the chances for a loosely united Evangelical Church.

Prior to the Treysa conference in late August 1945, there were months of intense activity in the churches. Churchmen jockeyed for favorable positions in the emerging denazified church, sought influential contacts with the Allies, began the sensitive task of re-establishing ecumenical ties with foreign churches, sought replacements for church officials and pastors who had died in the war or had been discredited by their complicity with the German Christians, and sought means to repair the material damage inflicted on church property during the war. They also reflected on the church's distant and immediate past, discussed the organizational and theological basis of the postwar church, chose national and regional leadership bodies, and provided direction to local pastors. And not least of all, they began the arduous job of offering physical and spiritual assistance to the defeated and war-weary population.[105] Each of these activities sparked contention because they referred back to the church's role during the past twelve years, over which the three groups were in sharp disagreement.

Those who took part in the church struggle, whether as conservatives or Dahlemites in the Confessing Church, tended to carry with them into the postwar period one of two lasting impressions of the churches in the Third Reich. The church struggle convinced them either of the theological and ecclesiastical irreconcilability of the regional churches, or, conversely, of the unlimited potential for greater unity between the churches precisely because of their mutual experiences. For the great majority for whom the church struggle provided further evidence of the incompatibility of the Lutheran, Reformed, and United traditions, the end of the war offered the opportunity to restore the traditional system and leadership of autonomous regional churches. They regarded the common confession made at Barmen in May 1934 to be of great significance for the church struggle but not necessarily for the postwar period. Conservatives favored a church-organized denazification of the churches, which for them meant accepting all but the most extreme German Christians back into the fold.[106] Conservative Lutherans like Hans Meiser never forgot the criticisms they had to endure from the Lutheran supporters of Karl Barth, Niemöller, and Diem among them, who accused them of abandoning the Barmen declaration and thereby weakening the oppositional front.[107] The legacy of the church struggle for conservative Lutherans was the unbridgeable gap that had developed between themselves and those they deemed radical sectarians.

The Dahlemites who conferred such importance on the Barmen declaration and its practical application in the Dahlem resolutions wanted to carry over the confessional unity into the post-1945 church. The legacy of the church struggle for the Dahlemites was twofold. First, in the sphere of ecclesiastical politics, the church struggle proved that the structure of confessionally divided regional churches impaired the churches' ability to organize a united front against the encroachments of the German Christians and the Nazi state. And second, the church struggle demonstrated the inadequacy of orthodox Lutheran theology to provide the theoretical foundation to resist or oppose measures taken by the state, in particular the state's racial policy. This reasoning led many from the Dahlem wing to advocate fundamental reforms in the postwar church.

2

Representations of the Nazi Past
in Early 1945

In spring 1945 Germany prostrate, destroyed by Allied bombs and disgraced by twelve years of Nazi rule. Its dreams of victory had been abandoned. Its government had been overthrown. Its territory had been invaded and occupied. Its enemies were now expected to take their revenge, and indeed tales of raping and pillaging by Soviet troops in the eastern provinces sent panic waves through every household. Its cities were filled with skeletons of bombed-out buildings. Communications were entirely severed. Hunger and disease, homelessness and death were apparent on all sides. The institutions of the past seemed irrelevant or powerless. Widespread feelings of apocalyptic doom gave rise to feelings of self-pity and victimization among the survivors.

In all of this the clergy joined. The overwhelming pastoral needs of their parishioners made them very conscious of the public mood, and they in turn contributed to the widespread feeling that Germany, and the German race, was doomed. Despair reigned. Nevertheless, amongst the group of surviving leaders of the Confessing Church two other factors were uppermost in their minds. First, they saw the need to seize the opportunity to regain control of the whole Evangelical Church by evicting the German Christians who had so grievously misled the congregations and abused the gospel. Second, they needed to justify their position over the previous twelve years and prepare manifestos for the immediate future. After so many years of frustration, these men were now resolved to act decisively and with vigor.

In these tasks they received unexpected help from the occupation powers. Official Allied military policy in all of the occupation zones was predicated on reform and re-education, not on revenge. The mistakes of the Versailles treaty were not to be repeated. But such a task required the cooperation of the German people. In the eyes of Germany's new rulers, the churches provided possibly the only institutions that had managed to evade complete subordination to the Nazi regime. Several leading clergymen in addition to Martin Niemöller were known to have suffered im-

Ruins of the medieval city of Nuremberg, bombed heavily in World War II and site of the infamous Nuremberg rallies, captured in film by Leni Riefenstahl's *Triumph of the Will*. *Photo courtesy of the Archive of the A. R. Wentz Library, Lutheran Theological Seminary of Gettysburg.*

prisonment for their defiance of Nazi edicts. Others, like Clemens August Graf von Galen, the Catholic bishop of Münster, had preached fiery sermons against the Nazi's euthanasia program. On the basis of this record, the churches were therefore to be treated gently. They were to be allowed to denazify themselves. The occupation powers encouraged them to think in terms of rebuilding a new society, and they were given resources to do so when scarcity and dislocation were ever-present.[1]

As a result, the summer of 1945 saw some notable developments that were to have long-lasting effects. Thanks to Allied military cooperation, the occupation powers granted the request of Bishop Wurm of Württemberg, the senior bishop, that the remaining church leaders be enabled to meet to discuss the future. Church leaders arranged to meet in the central German town of Treysa, near Fulda, in late July 1945. It was to prove a significant meeting. It marked both the triumph of the Confessing Church and the continuance of deep theological rifts within its ranks.

Not the least of these was caused by the debate over how to come to terms with Germany's and the church's past.

Bishop Wurm dominated the Treysa meeting.[2] He had spent the previous two years pleading for reconciliation between the various factions within the Evangelical Church. Now was his opportunity to call all sides to collaborate on rebuilding their damaged institution. At the age of seventy-seven, and after long years of administering the church in Württemberg, Wurm enjoyed wide support. He was a staunch nationalist who therefore shared the pessimistic views about Germany's future. Nevertheless, he resolved to take advantage of the Allies' lenient policy to revitalize the church's administration for the task of reconstruction ahead. His model was clearly that of the pre-Nazi church, or rather of the kind of unified national structure that the Nazis had so cleverly taken over and distorted in 1933. His aim in broad terms was to "re-Christianize Germany," but from the top downward through the hierarchical institutions of the Lutheran tradition. This task was made easier by the fact that virtually nothing remained of the bloated pro-Nazi structures of the pre-1945 German Evangelical Church. The so-called Reich bishop, Ludwig Müller, had committed suicide. The German Christian officials still in office at the local level were easily enough evicted, and the national office had been eviscerated by the war's effects. There was therefore no need to take account of, or even to consider inviting, any of those who had so fulsomely praised Hitler from their pulpits.

At the same time, Wurm was aware that he had to contend with other survivors from the Nazi tyranny, especially the dogmatically intransigent members of the Dahlemite wing of the Confessing Church. This group, centered around the Reich council of brethren, was also intent on using the Treysa meeting to gain its own ends. Particularly, this group sought a very different church polity. They looked for a much more democratic, reform-minded, and gospel-based future. They were greatly assisted by the fact that their hero, Martin Niemöller, had not only survived eight years of concentration camp but had been liberated in time to return to Germany and was now ready to do battle again for his vision of the future church.

There was a third faction present at Treysa, namely, the followers of the bishop of Bavaria, Hans Meiser, who saw the future of the church in stricter denominational terms. In Meiser's view, the moment had come when the Lutherans should revoke the royal edicts of the early nineteenth century uniting both the Lutheran and the Reformed traditions in the single Old Prussian Union. Meiser wanted to pull together those who remained true to the pure Lutheran heritage and to dissociate from the Calvinist-tinged and obstreperously dogmatic northerners from the Union churches.

The scene was therefore set for a vigorous debate and even confrontation. By the time the meeting was held, a certain self-confidence had returned. All the clergy invited to attend claimed to speak for the Confessing Church. They now began to take credit for their survival and to stake out positions for the future. They could even express general satisfaction with their own conduct since 1933. Given the Nazi

From left, Martin Niemöller, Wilhelm Niesel, Theophil Wurm, Hans Mesier, Heinrich Held, Hanns Lilje, and Otto Dibelius gathered in Treysa, Germany, in 1945 to forge a new leadership for the German Protestant Church. *Photo courtesy of the Archive of the A. R. Wentz Library, Lutheran Theological Seminary of Gettysburg.*

state's unrelenting persecution of the church, they alleged, the Confessing Church had indeed acted commendably. As Hans Asmussen, one of the leading figures in the Schleswig-Holstein church, wrote in 1947, "We had then and we have now no regrets that we took such a stand. For one need have no regrets when one has done the right thing. God will certainly look upon it and let it serve as a permanent sign through the years to come that we were fully aware of the oneness of the body of Christ and that we were prepared to make sacrifices for it."[3] Now, they proclaimed, was "the hour of the church."

Such a stance, not surprisingly, invited a strong response from the more critical minority, who realized that much more was required. Karl Barth, Hermann Diem, and others from the Dahlemite wing joined Martin Niemöller in countering this postwar hubris with highly critical lectures and stinging public statements. These men acted as the conscience of the church and, as a consequence, many of their orthodox Lutheran colleagues treated them as pariahs.

Prior to the Treysa conference, the Meiser, Wurm, and Niemöller factions met separately to develop strategies that would give them the greatest influence at

Treysa.[4] All three groups regarded the conference as a crucial meeting because it was there that the postwar provisional church structure and leadership was to be decided. Despite their convening and forming a common leadership at Treysa (the twelve-member EKD council headed by Bishop Wurm), the tension between the leaders of these groups was evident throughout the period of reconstruction.[5] Niemöller defended the continued existence of the oppositional councils of brethren from the Nazi period and demanded that the new church be established on the theological foundation set down in Barmen.[6] He was especially unrelenting in his criticism of Wurm's organization of the conference, Meiser's attempt to lure the Lutheran churches into a united Lutheran federation, and Dibelius's decision to assume the title of "bishop."[7]

Widely divergent experiences under Nazism along with differences in political and theological convictions contributed to the disagreement as to how the recent past was to be represented to the church's various constituencies. The intensity with which they promoted their competing interpretations of the church's legacy under Nazism indicates that they understood all too well that the dominant interpretation would have a significant impact on the church's immediate and long-term future.

Conservatives Access the Recent Past

In pastoral letters, in private correspondence, in sermons, and in public statements, conservatives stressed the persecution of the church by the Nazi state and insisted that the Confessing Church had taken a united stance against Nazism. They defended the conservative, churchly nature of their resistance and used purposefully vague and obfuscating religious terminology to explain the rise of Nazism. In all of their statements they reminded the world that Germans had suffered horrendous treatment under the Nazis and were continuing to suffer under the Allies. Self-pity and self-praise were interwoven with predictions that the church would rise again from the rubble like a phoenix and rechristianize the German people.

To be sure, few from the Confessing Church wanted to deny entirely Germany's role in starting the war, the Nazis' inhumane treatment of particular domestic groups and foreign peoples, and the church's early naïveté regarding the Nazis' true intentions.[8] But conservatives in particular did not want to assign these facts or their own vacillation between consent and dissent under Nazism a prominent place in their postwar histories. While grudgingly conceding that the church should repent for its sins—vaguely defined as "forsaking the Lord"—most postwar church leaders identified the church with the German people and the victory over Nazism.[9] In most cases, church leaders did not identify with the *victors,* who churchmen increasingly accused of making German suffering worse, but rather with the *victory* against Hitler and with the "other Germany" that allegedly resisted Hitler's onslaught.

At the Treysa conference the conservative interpretation of the past dominated. The official church statement issued on behalf of all the church leaders at the conference, "Message to the Congregations," focused on the church's resistance, its captivity in the Nazi state, and its recent liberation from the shackles of Nazism (see appendix 3).[10] Although the "Message to the Congregations" alluded briefly to the Confessing Church's intermittent timidity, this was overshadowed by descriptions of men and women from all confessions who "took a stand against injustice" and "condemned concentration camps, mistreatment and murder of Jews and the sick, and sought to protect youth from the seduction of National Socialist propaganda."[11] The repression by the Nazis, the statement alleges, was so intense that it crushed the church's resistance. Only when the war was over and the Nazis were defeated could the church openly declare "what was prayed and planned behind walls and in seclusion."[12] The implication here is that it was too dangerous for church leaders to openly voice their opposition to the Nazis, so privately they prayed for the Nazis' defeat and planned for a future in which Christian virtues would be given a prominent place.

By means of such assertions and similar statements made at the local level or in their parishes, conservatives developed the myth of "conservative churchly resistance."[13] It was a myth created, in part, to assuage their consciences and cleanse an unimpressive resistance record. But at the same time, it was designed to prove to the Allies that these church officials had earned the right to define the future of their church without interference. To be sure, at various meetings before Treysa, these church leaders had received assurances to this effect from the Allied military government officials. But suspicions of the Allies' intentions were still rampant. The myth of conservative churchly resistance served therefore as a justification to both their current rulers and to their own congregations.

Like all myths, conservative churchly resistance was one part fact and many parts fiction. Conservatives insisted that in keeping with the Lutheran Church's apolitical, God-given commission to preach the gospel and administer the sacraments, their opposition to Nazism took place outside the political sphere—where it belonged. Their resistance, so the argument went, was not against Nazi politics per se but rather against those who would interfere in a pastor's right to preach the Word of God. They maintained that resisting a complete takeover of the church by the Nazi-backed German Christians and continuing to preach the Word of God as always was the responsible and appropriate response to Nazism for churchmen.

While it is certainly true that conservative churchmen rarely took a public or political stance against Nazism, it was not, as the myth of conservative churchly resistance implies, solely because they were men of the cloth. Rather, the infrequency of public protests by conservative churchmen can be attributed to their empathy for a nationalist, anticommunist, and antisemitic agenda.

Significantly, the orthodox Lutheran interpretation of Luther's doctrine of two kingdoms provided churchmen with a convenient theological trope for supporting their claim to having maintained a strict separation of religious and political spheres. Although conservatives rarely tried to stake a claim to a legacy of political resistance, they intimated that their conservative churchly resistance had politically detrimental effects for the Nazi regime. They were careful, however, not to draw attention to the church's politics during the Nazi period for fear of drawing attention to their initial enthusiasm for Hitler and their failure to speak out except when the church was under attack.

Emphasis on the conservative and churchly nature of their resistance allowed them to argue that as creatures of the religious sphere they had not contributed to the rise and sustenance of Nazi rule, which were political phenomena. Moreover, it allowed them to argue that they resisted without pointing to any particular act of resistance except that of being faithful to Jesus Christ or defending the church's traditional hierarchical structure. By defining their resistance as taking place in the religious sphere but having some influence on the eventual defeat of Nazism, church leaders pointed to their silent prayers as proof of both Nazi repression and the church's resistance.

Paradoxically, church leaders peppered their discourse of conservative churchly resistance with frequent remarks about making a new beginning in 1945. This suggests that they were aware of the need to placate those at home and abroad who listened with skepticism to the church's too-oft-repeated resistance discourse. The endless references to the church's new beginning and complete turnaround notwithstanding, there was no *Stunde Null* in the church. Just as antifascist committees were swept aside in favor of a conservative restoration in the political sphere, so too were alternative visions of the church in the religious sphere.

During the Third Reich, Hans Asmussen had been one of the strongest voices in favor of an alternative vision for the church. He had been a strong supporter of the Barmen-Dahlem line. He even coauthored a strong protest letter in 1936 that had been sent to Hitler. But after the defeat of the Nazis, Asmussen began a transformation toward a more conservative position. He eventually broke with Barth and Niemöller and identified with the moderately conservative group of Lutherans who believed, in good Lutheran fashion, that the church should confess its sins before God and then get on with business as usual.[14]

Asmussen's transformation began in June 1945 with a letter he addressed to Archbishop of Canterbury Geoffrey Fisher (1887–1972), seeking to re-establish the ecumenical connections that had been severed when the war began. It was also an attempt to win support from the established church in one of the occupying powers. For this reason Asmussen tried to put the best spin possible on the church's conspicuous silence about Nazi brutality. He assured the archbishop that the Confessing Church's silence and turning inward (*Verinnerlichung*) during the war years was due neither to agreement with Hitler's war aims nor to a spiritual flight from the reality of the times but rather was the result of severe repression by the Nazi state. Forced to toe the National Socialist Party line or relinquish the public sphere to Nazi authorities, the Confessing Church grudgingly chose the latter. Pastors sought to make the best of this situation, according to Asmussen, by enriching the church through intense self-reflection and prayer. Indeed, Asmussen emphasized that the church's *Verinnerlichung* had the salutary effect of molding a degree of spiritual cohesiveness previously unknown in the Protestant churches, thereby enhancing the church's witness and implicitly its churchly resistance.[15] Asmussen sought in his letter to counter a barrage of foreign radio broadcasts, many from Britain, which were lumping all Germans together as collectively guilty for the crimes committed under Nazi rule. If Germans were to receive a sympathetic hearing from any corner abroad, German churchmen believed it would come from the foreign churches. Therefore, it was imperative that foreign church leaders be convinced that German clergymen had vigorously combated Nazism in a manner appropriate to their calling.

It was wholly in keeping with the goals of conservative Confessing Church leaders to stress the church's unified resistance by minimizing or at least sanitizing past conflicts. In part, what lay behind the construction of an official church history that emphasized united resistance was power politics, pure and simple. Church leaders sought to guarantee themselves a leading role in the vital decisions about German reconstruction by convincing the occupation forces, the foreign churches in the ecumenical movement, and the German population itself that the Confessing Church—as a whole, not just certain individuals—had suffered great hardship for its opposition to the Nazi's inhumane and anti-Christian policies.

In order to give the impression that the church was more united in its antifascist stance than it was, prominent conservatives interpreted in a positive light the internal church struggles between the German Christians and the Confessing Church and downplayed the disagreements between the two wings of the Confessing Church. Conservatives characterized the split between the Confessing Church and German Christians as a unifying force that strengthened the "true" church's resistance to fascism.[16] In so doing, they used the capitulation of some churches to the National Socialist cause as a sign of their own resistance to the very same cause. They failed, however, to address the theological, political, and ecclesiastical reasons as to why large sections of the church had identified comfortably with the Nazis.

The political benefits of portraying the Confessing Church's unity in the Third Reich were palpable. The Allies knew of the resistance waged by churchmen like Martin Niemöller. As Dibelius pointed out after the war, Niemöller's name was symbolic of German resistance to the Nazi regime, and it was for this reason that church leaders at Treysa chose Niemöller to represent the church in foreign relations. "He alone could represent our church in a world still bitterly hostile to everything German."[17] In acknowledgment of such resistance records, the occupying powers showed respect to leaders of the Confessing Church by giving them some latitude for travel and public speaking. Nevertheless, the Allies were also well aware of the highly conservative and nationalist orientation of the Confessing Church. Although this conservative anticommunist orientation would later appeal to the Western Allies as the Cold War heated up, in the spring and summer of 1945 German nationalism was still the source of deep concern among the Allies. Even Niemöller, they noted, had offered to join the German war effort from his prison cell in 1939.[18] As it became clearer to church leaders that the Allies did not see them as liberated comrades but as defeated enemies, they maintained tenuous relations with the victors while still claiming the victory against Nazism for their own legacy.

Bishop Wurm of Württemberg, like Asmussen, also called attention to Nazi repression, confessional unity, and the church's opposition to Nazism in his statement, "A Message to Christianity Abroad," which he had prepared for consideration at the Treysa conference but which was never discussed there.[19] Wurm insisted that communication between German churches and churches abroad was impossible during the war because of the state's all-encompassing control. Now, in the summer and fall of 1945, he was taking the first opportunity to express the German church's desire to declare its solidarity with Christians outside Germany. He asked Christians abroad to refrain from drawing the conclusion that all Germans were pro-Nazi because no protest from within Germany was heard abroad during Hitler's dictatorship.[20] Those who did speak out, Wurm contended, ended up in concentration camps. To admit that nationalism and jingoism in both German and non-German churches caused the rift would have been more accurate, but it would not have served Wurm's goal of undermining charges of collective guilt.

Wurm, like many others, blamed the reparation burdens and mass unemployment caused by the Versailles treaty at the end of World War I for creating the conditions in Germany that allowed the Nazis to come to power. These conditions led to a mood of despair and in turn to extreme nationalism and the rise of the Nazis.[21] He acknowledged and condemned the suffering of others, namely, the mass murder of German and Polish Jews as well as the atrocities carried out by S.S. mobile units against the populations in German-occupied territories. But his emphasis was on the suffering and hardship endured by Germans as a consequence of National Socialism and, more recently, by the violations of law and lack of mercifulness on the part of the Allies. The church's conduct during the twelve years of Nazi rule never came up for criticism.

Bishop Wurm contended that the brutal acts perpetrated by both sides in World War II were the consequence of estrangement from God (*Gottesentfremdung*), enmity toward Christ (*Christusfeindschaft*), rampant greed (*Mammonismus*), and coarse materialism (*Materialismus*).[22] By emphasizing the general trend in post–World War I Europe away from religious-centered worldviews toward secularized human-centered ones, Wurm generalized away the particular origins of National Socialism and ultimately the specificity of the atrocities committed by the Nazis.[23] In Wurm's view, all of Europe was guilty of turning away from Christ. By claiming that the victorious powers were guilty of the same violations of human decency for which the world was correctly reproaching the National Socialist regime, Wurm equated the Allies with the Nazis.[24]

Wurm asked Christians abroad not to perceive the Nazi atrocities as representative of the German character. "Every people has its Jacobins, who under certain conditions attain power," he wrote.[25] By associating the Nazis with the Jacobins, Wurm accomplished two corresponding goals of the conservatives. He linked Nazism to Enlightenment thought and dechristianization, both characteristic of Jacobinism. And in so doing, he uncoupled Nazism from Germany's conservative traditions and tied it to mass politics and secularization, two trends conservative Lutherans found highly objectionable.

The use of grandiose and purposefully vague religious imagery and terminology was also evident in conservative explanations for the rise of National Socialism, the Holocaust, the barbarity of the Second World War, and Germany's collapse in 1945. Just as Lutherans sought to demonstrate that their actions had been in keeping with Luther's doctrine of two kingdoms, they relied on the Lutheran law-gospel dualism to explain Germany's defeat, destruction, and misery by saying all of it was a consequence of God's anger at his disobedient children. "God's angry judgment has broken out over us all," began Treysa's "Message to the Congregations."[26] This type of apocalyptic imagery suggested that human beings were responsible for the catastrophe but only because of their disobedience to God's Word. Now, so the argument went in the spring and summer of 1945, they could expect God's blessing and forgiveness. Church leaders at Treysa assured the population that their suffering was not in vain: "The peace of God also gives strength to those in sorrow, to the prisoners of war and their relatives, to the hungry and the cold, to the homeless and those injured in body and in soul."[27] Be patient, parishioners were told, God's mercifulness will bring respite. Thus, the law-gospel dualism provided an otherworldly explanation that allowed churchmen to shy away from concrete explanations and to comfort their highly demoralized congregations.

As the "Message to the Congregations" and other statements demonstrate, Confessing Church leaders were eager to explain that their wartime silence in the face of Nazism was not voluntary. At a time when the Allies were publicizing the full extent of German atrocities in the eastern territories, Wurm clearly saw a need to remind the world that Germans were victims twice over, first under the Nazis and now under the occupation forces. The suffering at home and abroad, the "Message to the Congregations" suggested, could have been lessened had more Christians throughout Europe taken their responsibility as Christians seriously by speaking out against all injustices—the gassing of Jews *and* the bombing of German cities. Protestant leaders attributed both victimizations to a turning away from God. The implication was that the Holocaust was just one manifestation of this larger phenomenon of secularization, which had its origins in the French Revolution.

Germans, so the argument suggested, had an excuse for not publicly condemning Nazi policy, namely, the terror tactics of the Nazi secret police. The Allies and Christians abroad, however, had no excuse for their silence regarding the atrocities committed against Germans. Christians, whether German or not, who ignored their responsibility were guilty of disloyalty to God and should, the statement advised, reassume Christian responsibility—understood broadly and vaguely as obedience to God.

It is revealing to examine the lengths to which pastors went to draw analogies between stories in the Bible and the church struggle. In a July 1945 sermon, Bishop Dibelius attempted to parallel the state's persecution of the Confessing Church to the persecution of the Jews in the Old Testament.[28] Drawing on a passage from Exodus, Dibelius claimed that the Confessing Church astonished Germans and others with its honorable conduct during the Third Reich just as the Israelites had caused astonishment by celebrating and ritualizing the event of Passover. In Exodus the angel of death "passes over" the children of Israel and kills "only" the firstborn of the Egyptians because the Israelites as commanded by God marked their homes with the blood from slaughtered lambs. Dibelius quotes the verse where a child asks "What does this mean?" that is, why do we perform this ritual, why do we act in this manner, why were we saved? The answer, of course, is that God keeps his promise to the faithful.[29] Devoting a third of his sermon to a commentary on the Confessing Church's struggle to carry on its work under totalitarian conditions, he verbally extolled the pastors in the concentration camps who conducted themselves in the most pious and unusual manner.

Dibelius went on to suggest that the church's resistance to the state was limited and hidden because Confessing Church leaders did not want to endanger innocent people. He compared the atmosphere in which the Confessing Church synods took place in Nazi Germany to that of the Babylonian captivity. And he dwelled on church synods that had resulted in Nazi interrogations, house-searches, and imprisonment until it became no longer possible to hold meetings. After this brief summary of the Confessing Church's oppositional stand, Dibelius declared, "And when someone looks at us with astonished eyes because we act differently than others, then joyfully the answer should come from our lips: the Lord with His mighty hand has delivered us from the power of the Devil and led us out of Egypt, out of the house of servitude."[30]

In comparing the Jews in Exodus to the churchmen and laymen in the Confessing Church in 1945, Dibelius linked the promises of redemption God had made to the Jews to a new covenant God made with the faithful, including the Confessing Church, through the crucifixion of Christ. In the difficult and dire circumstances of 1945, Dibelius called on the Confessing Church to continue to behave honorably as it had done during the last twelve years. Dibelius concluded that since the Confessing Church controlled the majority of congregations across Germany, its task was no longer to separate itself from others but to cooperate with others in establishing a church at peace with itself.[31]

Otto Dibelius, bishop of Berlin-Brandenburg and chairman of the Central Council of the German Evangelical Church in 1947. His fierce opposition to communism led to his banishment from East Germany by the Communist regime. *Photo courtesy of the Archive of the A. R. Wentz Library, Lutheran Theological Seminary of Gettysburg.*

What is truly astonishing about this sermon is that Dibelius could compare the conduct of German Protestants inside and outside the concentration camps to the Jews of ancient Israel without ever mentioning the Jews that Germans murdered in the camps. During the Nazi regime the Confessing Church never issued an official condemnation of the illegal and inhumane treatment of the Jews. Individuals spoke out, but the institutional antisemitism and anti-Judaism of the church was far too great for the Confessing Church to make an official protest. And Dibelius's voice was not among those that vigorously spoke out against the systematic murder of Jews.

From the very outset, conservative clergymen avoided a forthright explanation for the rise of Nazism and the subsequent misery Germans were enduring in 1945 by raising the discussion above the realm of human agency and responsibility to the general European trend of secularization and the work of God. Germany's bombed-out cities were not, they claimed, the result of German nationalism and territorial aggression, but rather they were God's response to man's worshipping and serving "the creature more than the creator."[32]

Helmut Thielicke, a renowned Lutheran theologian who preached anti-Nazi sermons in Stuttgart in 1944–45, stated explicitly that everything that had taken place in Germany needed to be understood in terms of its religious roots.[33] Like Wurm, he blamed the secularization of the modern world: "National Socialism is the last and most terrible product of secularization. Secularization means that man escapes from the hands of God and falls into the most fearful hands of men. It is the mystery of godless man that has broken out in Germany. Germany has had to experience this mystery and suffer because of it in the presence of the other peoples. That may have been its tragic mission."[34]

Thielicke relieved Germans from the burden of accountability for specific crimes but held them accountable and guilty for abandoning God. Consequently, the only corrective necessary was to return to the fold of the church. At one and the same time, conservatives admitted and universalized guilt—as Christians we are guilty before God, but then, of course, so is everyone. Thielicke even went so far as to imply in the above passage that Germany's uniqueness was not that the Nazis came to power in Germany and managed to stay in power until the Allies removed them; rather, Germany's uniqueness was in its exemplary degree of suffering that apparently was a part of the tragic mission assigned to Germany by God.

As the self-selected spokesmen for the defeated and demoralized population, many clergymen took advantage of the opportunity to win the trust of the population by licking their wounds. Despite the apparent contradiction in identifying the church at one and the same time with the victory against Hitler *and* with the defeated German people, church leaders saw no problem in this. They wanted to secure a minimum of support from the Allies in order to have a voice in Germany's future and to claim the role of spokesmen for the "other" Germany—those Germans who supposedly resisted National Socialism. Church leaders interpreted this role primarily as countering Allied accusations of collective guilt by stressing the severe hardship endured by the population at the hands of both the Nazi dictatorship and the Allied occupation.

Reformers Call the Church to Task

For their part, the churchmen associated with the councils of brethren at the Treysa conference wanted to issue a statement with teeth—one that would unambiguously address the church's guilt and call for repentance. In the days leading up to the conference, they drafted the "Message to the Pastors" (see appendix 2) to be issued at the same time as the "Message to the Congregations." But the majority turned them down. The Dahlemites were not only too wordy and too theological, but above all, they were too masochistic for the likes of Bishop Meiser and his colleagues.

In stark contrast to the conservatives' statement, the Dahlemite's "Message to the Pastors" explicitly pointed to the church's bloated bureaucracy and close relationship to the state as problems that had existed in the pre-Nazi church and made possible the debacle in the churches during the Nazi era.[35] The church's problems, they asserted, went deeper than merely the Nazi repression. Consequently, the council of brethren admonished pastors for rushing to restore the church to its pre-1933 condition as if a restoration would solve their problems. It was not enough "to simply overcome the destruction wrought by National Socialism," the Dahlemites insisted. "Our task goes further. A new church order must be created based on God's leadership" and the Barmen declaration.[36] By acknowledging that structural and theological flaws in the church led to its accommodating stance toward Nazism, "Message to the Pastors" recognized the need for fundamental reforms in the church's organization, leadership, and dogma.

The Dahlemites did more than just demand reforms; they also acknowledged the guilt of the German people and implicitly that of the pastorate. "Moral standards," the council of brethren declared, "are inadequate to measure the greatness of the guilt that our people have assumed. Fresh deeds of inhumanity are constantly coming to light. We confess our guilt and bow under the weight of its consequences."[37] Only by recommitting itself to faith in Jesus Christ could the German people provide a new foundation from which to build a new social life "based on the principles of freedom and justice." The pastorate was more important than ever because it could deliver the dual messages of God's judgment and forgiveness.

Although the "Message to the Pastors" was more forthright than the "Message to the Congregations," it did not mention the Jews by name. And there were critics like Karl Barth who expressed regret over references in it and in other church statements to the devil, demons, original sin, and the guilt of the other. In a letter to Niemöller, Barth singled out Hans Asmussen's evasive terminology for special criticisms, advising the Dahlemites against "Asmussensche Theologie."[38] Asmussen had, in fact, been extremely influential in drafting the "Message to the Pastors." Before Asmussen broke with the Dahlemites, he participated in their pre-Treysa meeting in Frankfurt. At the Frankfurt meeting he submitted the first draft of "Message to the Pastors" to members of the councils of brethren. Niemöller and others rejected it because of its overt Lutheranism, but the final draft still bore many signs of Asmussen's theological interpretation.[39] The claim in the first paragraph, for instance, that the German people were driven to commit atrocities by demonic powers was part of Asmussen's original draft and typical of much of his writing.[40] Elsewhere Asmussen had also referred to the satanic forces at work in the Nazi movement that successfully eliminated the natural gifts of reason and insight in many Germans.[41] That references to "demonic powers" and "apocalyptic manifestations" remained in the final draft after a series of revisions by various Dahlemites indicates that Asmussen was not the only one who considered this type of explanation for German atrocities acceptable.

Certainly it was appropriate for Christian leaders to employ explanations in keeping with the basic premises of Christian thought, but in avoiding altogether a discussion about the widespread support inside and outside the church for Nazi domestic and foreign policy, the "Message to the Pastors" failed to hold human beings and institutions like the church itself responsible for their concrete actions or inaction. Furthermore, emphasis on the abandonment of God as the most serious issue at hand served to divert attention from the actual role of churchmen and parishioners, whether it was one of anguished silence or professional complicity.

In a letter to Niemöller in late September 1945, Barth encouraged him to urge the German church to provide the ecumenical delegation visiting Stuttgart in October with a frank statement of German responsibility for the chaos and destruction that had engulfed Europe. Although the political and theological backgrounds of Niemöller and Barth could not have been more different, their experiences under the Nazis led them to similar conclusions about the underlying causes of the church's vacillation and irresolution when confronted by the German Christians and the Nazis. Of course, there is little doubt who was influencing who theologically. Barth towered over Niemöller—to the point that Niemöller's postwar theological proclamations resounded with Barthian expressions, concepts, and ideas.

As both an insightful critic and devoted friend of the German Protestant churches, Barth was uniquely placed to analyze the church's legacy under the Nazis, its reaction to the occupation forces, and the motivation behind many of the postwar statements. Earlier, in a lecture in January 1945, Barth warned a Swiss audience to keep a watchful eye on the German manipulation of religious rhetoric.

> We must reckon with the religious profundity of the Germans, which all too willingly avoids the acknowledgment of their own concrete guilt by pointing out the great truth that before God in the last resort all men and nations are alike guilty and alike in need of forgiveness for their sins: thus the bold conclusion is drawn that a particular German repentance is obviously unnecessary and absolutely uncalled for.[42]

Barth wanted every German to admit his responsibility, but he did not believe that Germans as a people were collectively guilty. He acknowledged that comparatively few Germans must have taken part in the crimes themselves. But all Germans were responsible because they directly or indirectly participated through either political indifference or errors of judgment.[43]

In an April 1945 essay written at the request of England's *Manchester Evening News,* patronizingly entitled "How Can the Germans Be Cured?" Barth likened Germany to a very sick patient.[44] Although all the nations of Europe were also likened to sick patients, Barth told the English that "some patients suffer from more serious diseases than others."[45] By distinguishing Germany from the rest of Europe, Barth separated himself from the apologists in the church who maintained that secularization was to blame for the rise of Hitler and the present state of affairs across Europe. Barth, in contrast, singled out what he saw as Germany's unique history to explain the origins of National Socialism. His focus on German history was a determining factor in his disagreements with many conservative churchmen, in particular, Hans Asmussen.

Barth's interpretation of German history was a negative variant of the classic *Sonderweg* thesis. In the nineteenth and early twentieth centuries, German historians had emphasized and often praised Germany's *Sonderweg* (special path) or uniqueness, comparing positively Germany's statism, *Kultur,* and early development of a welfare state with the parliamentarianism, *Zivilisation,* and laissez-faire economics of west European nations.[46] Barth, as well as many other postwar critics of Germany, challenged this positive variant of the German *Sonderweg* by maintaining that some of Germany's most celebrated national heroes, institutions, and intellectual movements contributed to the rise and positive reception of National Socialism. In a number of lectures to Swiss audiences in January and February 1945, entitled "The Germans and Ourselves," he drew a direct line in German history from the Prussian military and statist tradition to Hitler:

> The achievement of Frederick the Great and Bismarck could not be brought to a more logical conclusion nor to more complete destruction than it has been done by Adolf Hitler. . . . We have to reckon with the possibility that the great majority of Germans even now scarcely realize . . . what a responsibility they assumed when they supported first Bismarck, then Wilhelm II, and last of all, Adolf Hitler.[47]

Using similar logic in an open letter to French Protestants in 1939, Barth had maintained that conservative Lutheranism paved the way for the paganism of the German Christians in the 1930s:

> [Germany] suffers from . . . Martin Luther's error on the relation between law and gospel, between the temporal and spiritual order and power. This error has established, confirmed, and idealized the natural paganism of the German people, instead of limiting and restraining it.[48]

Here and elsewhere Barth asserted that Luther's doctrine of two kingdoms, the law-gospel dualism, and the divine orders, were responsible, in part, for Lutherans' easy accommodation with the German Christians and the Nazis. What Barth referred to here as errors—the Lutheran understanding of both the relation between law and gospel and church and state—Lutherans celebrated as key tenets of their tradition that distinguished them from Catholics and Calvinists. Barth believed that by separating the law from the gospel, the church from the state, and proclaiming that certain human institutions were divinely ordained, Lutherans relinquished the church's rightful and necessary role in promoting Christian values in the secular sphere.

As a result of his Swiss lectures Barth received a number of responses from belligerent Germans. These letters provide a foreshadowing of the responses protesting the October 1945 Stuttgart Declaration of Guilt and demonstrate the popular appeal of the ahistorical religious explanations supported by conservative theologians. For instance, a respondent from southern Germany asked Barth if the symptoms of Germany's illness were not "symptoms of a similar collective craze not unmistakably apparent among the Allies?"[49] He went on to say that the victors, no less guilty than the vanquished, were simply taking advantage of their superior military position to posit all the blame on German shoulders. "It is so pleasant to be able to avoid expurgation of oneself by flogging a suitable scapegoat."[50] And he concluded:

> May all at last realize that the third world war cannot be avoided by muzzling German science, by letting German children starve and by offering German babies, crying for want of food, the example of Auschwitz. People should be made to understand that German Hitlerism cannot be uprooted in the midst of world-Hitlerism, but only by trying to plant in all nations a spirit in which such monstrosities cannot survive.[51]

Many Germans accused the Allies of making Germany the scapegoat for all the barbarity of the Second World War and deliberately inflicting cruel and inhumane punishment on the innocent population. In fact, the author of this letter went so far as to assign a generic meaning to Hitlerism; the concept now required a hyphen and the adjectives German- or world- (or, one might assume, American-, French-, British-, and Russian-) to clarify which Hitlerism one was referring to. In referring to world-Hitlerism, Barth's correspondent denied the singularity of the crimes committed by Germans in Hitler's name.

Another letter writer accused Barth of lumping together murderers, heroes, and the general citizenry. Admittedly, he wrote, only a minority of "true heroes" had actively resisted, but, he pointed out, "such heroes are always and everywhere the exception rather than the rule."[52] He estimated that there were no more than 200,000 who participated in the inhumane treatment of Germans and non-Germans, and some 50,000 heroes. This left "99 percent of the Germans who are not guilty of actually committing crimes, without being worthy of the name of heroes."[53] The actions of this "trifling minority" of real criminals "is as unrepresentative of the

German people as the Schalburg-Corps is of the Danish."[54] In other words, every country had its racist and nationalist fanatics, and it was unfair to blame the entire population for the actions of extremists.

Barth responded that these figures were just "brain acrobatics." As far as he was concerned, the 99 percent of law-abiding Germans "took, each and all, the wrong train, after being warned in vain," and he believed it was a great disservice to Germans to encourage them to rebuild their nation on the premise that the vast majority of Germans were innocent:[55]

> How else could these 99 percent be helped if they do not decide to step forward this very day and partake in the responsibility for the future instead of trying to shove it on someone else? And why would they do that if they do not admit they were guilty yesterday of leading politically irresponsible lives? . . . Should these very people be given an alibi, and acquitted, or given the privilege of acquitting themselves, just because they were not present in person at Oradour, or perhaps never even heard of Oradour?[56]

While Barth acknowledged that comparatively few Germans must have taken part in the crimes themselves, all Germans were responsible because they directly or indirectly, through either support or indifference, participated in the rise of National Socialism. Germany did not need a nation of heroes, Barth retorted, but merely politically reasonable citizens ready to take responsibility for their actions if only by remaining in their places doing their jobs as they always had. Resistance would have arisen by itself, Barth maintained, if each civil servant had refused to carry out unconstitutional regulations; if each professor had stood by the scientific truth; if each minister had continued to preach the uncorrupted teaching of the gospel; if each officer had clung to what he considered his honor in the past; if each common man had insisted on his constitutional rights.[57]

Germany was not the only nation guilty of transgressions, Barth readily admitted, but the origins and nature of German transgressions were unique. He refused to equate the annihilation of the peasants of Oradour and the Jews at Auschwitz with the bombardment of the German industry and communications centers in the interest of winning the war.[58]

Since, according to Barth, the German people were the "most seriously ill," their cure required the most serious measures.[59] The prescriptive measures Barth recommended in April 1945 in the *Manchester Evening News*, however, were exactly the measures conservative theologians and most Germans hoped to avoid. What Barth proposed was a three-step cure. First, crushing military defeat. Barth did not want Germans to suffer unnecessarily, but he did fear that unless the nation experienced a resounding defeat it might quickly recover as it did after World War I and fail to draw the right lessons from its defeat.

Second, he called for the provision of positive role models. "Show them how gentlemen behave when they are in power," Barth smugly told the British.[60] At the same time, he counseled the Swiss to abstain from gloating over the Allied triumph. "What the Germans need now, at the dark turning point of their way, is, quite simply, *friends*" (Barth's italics).[61] Realizing that nations that had been occupied and abused by Germany would balk at offering the hand of friendship, Barth maintained that the Swiss must act differently. As Reformed Protestants, Barth argued, the Swiss understood Christianity to mean first the gospel and only after that the law.[62] The sequence gospel-law, which Barth had emphasized in his response to the conservative Lutheran critiques of the Barmen declaration, meant that the Swiss "would have to be their friends" first and unconditionally. Only later should the Swiss be "hard as iron" toward the Germans.[63] Although, to achieve diametrically opposite ends, both Barth and the conservative Lutherans applied their understandings of the relation between law and gospel to explain the past and set an agenda for the future. Many Lutherans stressed that the collapse of Germany was the manifestation of God's law and that now it was time for Germany to experience God's love and mercy, the message of the gospel.

The final element in Barth's cure was to "impose" on Germans a share of responsibility in public life. They had to learn that there was more to politics and public life than simply taking orders. Germans, he urged, must become open and honest in their civic dealings and assume responsibilities in the political arena, which meant taking responsibility for the nation's political institutions, practices, and programs.[64] Although it was not only the Germans who had to change, Barth believed, Germans should "have the grace to admit" that the guilt of others "does not concern them in the least."[65] Germans needed to be clear that it was their history, their actions and inaction that led directly to the destruction of their cities in 1945. And the Evangelical Church needed to do the same.

Most Germans resented Barth's probing criticisms. The conservatives, as can be seen in the "Message to the Congregations," were not ready to admit that the history, organizational structure, and theology of the church played a role in creating the conditions that led to the popularity of the German Christians and ultimately to the successful rise and sustained rule of the Nazis. These charges against Lutheranism prompted Asmussen to write an essay a couple of years later entitled, "Does Luther Belong before the Nuremberg Court?"[66] Clearly, conservatives were piqued that "radicals" were charging the church with having done too little and blaming the church's complacency and complicity on orthodox Lutheran theology and the church's hierarchical structure.

With admonishments like these, the Germans were not likely to see the Swiss or Barth as friends. In fact, at the Treysa conference many German church leaders thought Barth attended as a spy on behalf of the occupation forces. Although Barth was successful in provoking the conservatives and initiating a public discussion about the church's acquiescence during the Nazi era, ordinary Protestants were not convinced that fundamental changes were needed in the church.

But it was not only Barth and foreign churchmen who made frank and painful statements. A minority of German pastors heeded Barth's call for candid explanations unadulterated by nebulous theological vagaries. In precisely that spirit and with refreshing clarity, Pastor Gottlieb Funcke of Münster, in a lecture in late July, elucidated why God had unleashed his wrath and, not incidentally, why Hitler was so successful: "Because the majority [of Germans] cheered on the leadership of the Third Reich or actually gave it free rein as long as it seemed to offer successful results."[67] Funcke maintained that although many of the atrocities against Germans, Poles, Russians, and Jews were until recently relatively unknown, the inhumane treatment of German Jews had been known for a long time and that for this "we are all guilty."[68]

Typically, these reformers praised the work of the Confessing Church, especially the councils of brethren. At the same time, they also aimed for wider and more far-reaching reforms in the whole church. At the first postwar synod of the Berlin Confessing Church, Hans Böhm, a Lutheran pastor from Berlin-Zehlendorf and a leading figure in the Confessing Church's reform wing, described the councils of brethren as "the soul of the resistance" against the German Christians and the state.[69] Böhm's report, an official account of the Berlin Confessing Church during the church struggle, paid special tribute to Martin Niemöller as the symbol of the church's resistance to the state's effort to dechristianize the nation. Böhm portrayed the Confessing Church as a constant force of resistance ("exhorting and warning" Christians to "pull not the same yoke with unbelievers") and argued that its witness called for still more radical changes in the church.[70] He prodded his fellow Berliners not to shy away from serious housecleaning before carrying out an internal and external reordering of the entire church. But even he was not prepared to examine the Confessing Church's record too closely. The perceived positive legacy of the Confessing Church was rarely called into question—even by leading reformers.

Like Funke, Niemöller sought in his speech at Treysa a concrete explanation for all that had transpired in Germany and in particular within the church. As an Erastian church, a church beholden to the state, Niemöller contended, the Evangelical Church never considered that its public responsibility included passing critical judgment on the Nazi state and its policies. Rather than lay blame on a few Nazis or a general trend like secularization, Niemöller pointed to the structure of the Lutheran churches, their traditional subordination to the state, and the theology that undergirded these traditions.

He challenged the conservative Lutheran interpretation by emphasizing the responsibility of church leaders to openly criticize the state or its policy when they clash fundamentally with church doctrine. Although not citing the orthodox interpretation of Luther's doctrine of two kingdoms in this particular address, Niemöller directly challenged this central pillar of orthodox Lutheranism elsewhere. He was especially forthright in his critique of Lutheran orthodoxy in a 1946 address to the Confessing Church in Frankfurt when, in what sounded like a passage borrowed from a lecture by Barth, Niemöller said, "An error, which for a long time had a place in the Evangelical Church, consisted in the belief that the Evangelical Church does not have anything to do with public life."[71] The claims of God and the church, Niemöller asserted, encompass all areas of life, both the spiritual and the political worlds. Niemöller did not advocate that the church offer its official support for specific candidates in a political election but rather that Christians abide by Christian principles in the public sphere.

How churchmen understood the legacy of the church struggle and how they explained the twelve-year rein of Hitler was inexorably connected to the positions they took regarding the nature of confession, repentance, and forgiveness. Niemöller's forthright admission that the church's legacy from the church struggle and the Nazi period was a legacy of mistakes and missed opportunities—the fundamental causes of which he traced to deeply embedded organizational and theological traditions in Lutheranism—set the stage for a fierce showdown with conservatives over the practice and meaning of confessing guilt and acknowledging responsibility.

3

Guilt from Another World

Guilt, Repentance, and Forgiveness in the Year Zero

Nothing divided churchmen in 1945 more than the manner in which they interpreted the church's guilt for its conduct during the Third Reich. Although many in the pastorate and laity on the local level believed that any type of confession or apology was both unnecessary and undesirable, the majority of high-profile church leaders on the national level were in agreement that in one form or another the church should make a confession of guilt and do penance. How, for what, in whose name, and to whom one confesses and repents were—to say the least—contentious issues. Should a confession of guilt be issued by the church as a whole, or by individuals in the church? Should the confession be made to God, to other Christians, to the victims of the Third Reich, or to all three? Who were the victims? Was the church a victim? Should the confession be public or private? Do clergymen have a right to make a confession of guilt for the entire church, for the nation, or just for themselves? Should the confession be concrete, that is, for a particular act of commission or omission, or general, as in, "I have not been a faithful servant of Christ"? Should church leaders confess and accept guilt in the name of Germany, or in the name of the church? And finally, does repentance involve making practical changes in the way one lives or the manner in which the church operates?

Church leaders articulated two different yet overlapping conceptions of guilt. Conservative Lutherans interpreted it as religious guilt with its roots in the sinful nature of human beings, and they felt confession was a private matter between God and the individual. They considered a concrete confession of guilt by the church to be highly inappropriate because such a confession suggested uniformly guilty behavior within the church and implied that God delivered judgment on institutions as well as individuals, which, according to Lutheran doctrine, he did not. Thus, conservatives rejected the charge of collective guilt that the Allies articulated in the months immediately following the defeat of the Nazis. Guilt was by its very nature, conservatives argued, historically imprecise and a matter between the guilty individual and God. The only collective guilt conservatives were willing to discuss was the collective guilt of sinful humanity before God. Practically speaking, this meant that most conservatives opposed discussing the guilt or responsibility of the church as an institution while at the same time advocating that individual Christians confess and repent to God for having strayed from God's path.

Reformers conceived of guilt more concretely as culpability for historical actions. They maintained that the church and the Confessing Church *as institutions* were guilty of inaction when they failed to condemn antisemitism, the deification of Hitler, naked territorial aggression of the state, and systematic atrocities carried out against Jews, Slavs, and Gypsies from the eastern territories. Of course, as Christians, reformers concurred with conservatives in locating the ultimate source of sinful behavior in original sin. Nevertheless, they sought the specific causes of the church's concrete guilt in recent German history and politics, and particularly in the church's theology, structure, and relation to the state. Reformers also insisted on publicly confessing the church's guilt before Christians at home and abroad. Moreover, part and parcel with a confession of guilt was the necessity of making changes to ensure that the same mistakes would never happen again.

Message to the Congregations

As a confession of guilt, Treysa's "Message to the Congregations" is best understood as a compromise between these two positions, although a compromise clearly favoring a conservative understanding of guilt and forgiveness. After attributing Germany's collapse in 1945 to "God's angry judgment," the authors made the following confession:

> Today we confess: Long before God spoke in anger, He sought us with the Word of his love and we did not listen. Long before our churches became piles of rubble, our pulpits were restricted and our prayers were silenced. . . . Long before the sham government of our land collapsed, justice had been thwarted. Long before men were murdered, human beings had become mere numbers. . . .[1]

Who violated pulpits? Who silenced prayers? Who thwarted the law and murdered men? What begins as a confession using the first person plural "we" soon changes into a series of statements describing irresponsible, illegal, and murderous conduct but in which the "we" is dropped and the names of the responsible parties are never given. Instead of taking responsibility and saying, "Long before Germans murdered Jews, we churchmen mocked and disparaged Jewish life," the "Message to the Congregations" spoke in generalities and used the passive voice.

Except in the vague sense of not having been Christian enough, the church leaders at Treysa shied away from delegating concrete responsibility to pastors and church officials for contributing to the rise and sustained rule of the National Socialists through preaching nationalistic and antisemitic sermons. There were political and ecclesiastical reasons for this, namely, that a thorough reckoning with the church's long history of Christian antisemitism and devotion to the state would not only disrupt church unity and increase despair in the congregations but would also alienate parishioners from their church leaders. These leaders knew only too well how sensitive their people were to the imputation of guilt or responsibility—especially within the churches. The church did not want to discourage former or potential members by being too stern a judge. In view of the blanket accusation of guilt in the popular press of Germany's former enemies, church leaders contrived to make the church the "spokesman" or "champion" of the German people, to use the words of Pastor Wilhelm Halfmann from the north German state of Schleswig-Holstein.[2] When conservatives specifically discussed blame, it was usually directed at the former top-ranking Nazis. For instance, in Bishop Wurm's statement "A Message to Christianity Abroad," he wrote, "We do not refuse to share the guilt which leading men in the party and state have heaped on our people."[3] The implication is clear: as good Christians we must bear the guilt, but we are not guilty.

Although Treysa's "Message to the Congregations" conceded that during the Nazi era some Christians hid "behind men's orders" in order to "elude God's commands," the church as an institution never came under scrutiny for its early, and in many instances sustained, political support for Hitler and his policies. Conspicuously absent is any mention of the German Christians or practicing church members who enthusiastically joined the Nazi Party and cheered its successes even after it became indisputably clear in the 1930s that the Nazis were breaking laws, arresting opponents, and killing Jews. The Confessing Church's tenacious defense of the church against Nazi encroachments in the ecclesiastical sphere was consciously embellished by churchmen to include opposition to Nazism more generally.

The fact that the words *Schuld* (guilt) and *Buss* (repentance) never appear in the text goes a long way to explaining why church leaders at Treysa accepted "Message to the Congregations" but rejected the brethren council's less exonerating "Message to the Pastors," which included discussions of both guilt and repentance. It was one thing to discuss the church's guilt with other churchmen—even foreign churchmen—but German church leaders were ultracautious about alienating their parishioners by pointing to their complicity in, or complacency toward, a criminal regime.

Particularly revealing of conservatives' reluctance to make guilt a public issue was Bishop Meiser's effort to conceal the "Message to the Congregations" from the public. Whereas Bishop Wurm published the text in Württemberg's church newspaper and personally read the statement over Stuttgart radio in order to publicize it—it was, after all, an official church statement meant for the congregations—Meiser failed to mention it in his report on the Treysa conference to the pastors and parishes in Bavaria.[4] One can only conclude that if the watered-down confession in "Message to the Congregations" was too explicit for Meiser, then any confession of guilt intended for a German audience would indeed be too much for him. This was illustrated even more clearly in the conservatives' outright rejection of the brethren council's "Message to the Pastors."

Message to the Pastors

Unlike "Message to the Congregations," "Message to the Pastors" both provided concrete criticisms of the church and the Confessing Church, and openly confessed "our guilt" and the guilt of "our people." "Moral standards," the text read, "are inadequate to measure the greatness of the guilt that our people have assumed. . . . We confess our guilt and bow under the burden of its consequences."[5] Although the context alone was insufficient to specify which guilty activities reformers meant, conservatives wanted no part in the statement and obstructed its passage at the Treysa conference.

The admission of guilt was only one aspect of the brethren council's "Message to the Pastors" that provoked the Lutheran conservatives. There were other troublesome issues that conservatives found distasteful: it criticized the overwhelming influence of the bureaucracy in church matters; it emphasized the theology of the Barmen declaration; and it recommended substantive changes in the church's structure. The assertion that the church's traditionally close relationship to the state resulted in a predominance of church bureaucrats for whom the church's confessions and creeds were secondary complemented a corresponding emphasis on Barmen's alternative interpretation of, and emphasis on, the church's confessions and creeds.

The reformers who comprised the brethren council were quick to assure pastors that their critique of the church's 400-year tradition of close ties to the state was not a sign that the council was condemning the church's traditional relationship with the state altogether. But the council of brethren did suggest that the Reformation confessions had taken on new meaning at Barmen and that this new meaning should be the basis of the postwar church.[6] Indeed, "Message to the Pastors" criticized the church's proclamation and practice in the Third Reich for not living up to the theological declaration made at Barmen. Now, the reformers argued, it was the church's most pressing task to preach and practice the Barmen declaration. By acknowledging that structural and theological flaws in the church led to its accommodating stance toward Nazism, the "Message to the Pastors" recognized the need for fundamental changes in the church's organization and dogma.

Despite these positive aspects, as a confession of guilt the "Message to the Pastors" had two serious weaknesses. First, it lacked concreteness and was riddled with unwieldy Christian aphorisms. Second, and more importantly, the reformers did not distinguish themselves from their conservative colleagues by calling on pastors to condemn and abandon two thousand years of Christian contempt for Jews. By failing to see that two millennia of teaching contempt for Jews had provided modern antisemites with a foundation on which to build their racial justification for attacking Jews, the Dahlemites at Treysa missed an opportunity for desperately needed reform in the church's relationship to Jews and Judaism.

Similarly, the Berlin council of brethren's July 1945 "Statement of the Confessing Synod to the Pastors and Congregations" also begins with an instantly recognizable confession of the church's failure to live up to its Christian responsibilities but fails to maintain this critical edge throughout and to mention Christian antisemitism:

> Now God is calling us to repent. Our people, 90 percent of whom are baptized Christians, have allowed themselves with very little opposition to be robbed in very short order of their national and cultural life. For us Germans this is a shameful admission.
>
> The pastors and parish leaders who in this struggle were silent must face this fact: their refusal to speak out is now their condemnation. They are to blame for the conditions in the church and amongst our people. Often human fear outweighed the responsibility for the church, state, and people. Churchmen hid behind the words of the Bible in order to hide their submission to worldly powers. Only by submitting to the totalitarian claims of the state was it possible for the state to repress the Church's public role.

After acknowledging the truism that the majority of Christians mounted very little opposition to the Nazis, the leaders of the Confessing Church in Berlin placed blame squarely at the feet of pastors and parish leaders for providing a disgraceful example by silently acquiescing to the Nazi authorities. The Berlin statement went on to challenge the frequently stated claim that the Confessing Church was a resistance church. "Unfortunately," the text continued,

> the Confessing Church is not without guilt. To be sure many brothers and sisters witnessed in word and deed, but through lack of unanimity, through lack of courage in thought and deed, through falsely insisting on old ways, through our own failure and weakness, we spoiled the holy things God had entrusted us with. Compared with all these things we only suffered and resisted a little. We cannot be reproached with having been too radical, on the contrary, we reproach ourselves for having been silent when we should have spoken.
>
> As heavy as the passive guilt is upon the Christian Church, so deeply grateful are we that the Lord God has preserved the Church and allowed her to have a new start.[7]

Although more forthright than many declarations of guilt by church leaders, the statement, with its emphasis on the churchmen's silence and the unfortunate phrase "passive guilt," obscures the simple fact that leaders of the Berlin church, including the postwar bishop in Berlin-Brandenburg, Otto Dibelius, preached sermons and gave speeches that were zealous in their support for the Nazis in 1933.

Of all the Confessing churchmen to address the German people after the war,

Martin Niemöller was without equal in his emotional appeals for Christians to take seriously their obligation to confess and repent. His speech at the Treysa conference is a good case in point. As spokesman for the council of brethren at Treysa, Niemöller praised Wurm's call to reorganize the church along the lines set forth at Barmen but criticized the overall self-congratulatory tone of the conference.[8] Niemöller worried that despite the occasional lip service to Barmen by church leaders at Treysa, a real effort to implement Barmen would be shunted aside as it was during the Nazi period. This suspicion was well founded, given the conspicuous absence of Barmen theology from the text of "Message to the Congregations."

Niemöller believed that the Barmen declaration had overcome some of the most glaring theological defects in orthodox Lutheran theology and that the 1934 Dahlem resolutions had overcome organizational defects. After 1934, however, a combination of fear of challenging the Nazi state and support for particular Nazi policies had led the Confessing Church, especially the conservatives, to reverse those first forward-looking steps formulated at Barmen and Dahlem. Niemöller concluded that guilt lay primarily at the feet of the Confessing Church for not adhering to the declarations and resolutions it passed in 1934. Thus, in August 1945 Niemöller framed the question of guilt in the following manner:

> Certainly we are confronted by horrible deprivation and chaos. . . . We must ask ourselves, however, what brought this about. The disastrous situation in which we live is not a result of the fact that we lost the war. Who among us could wish that we had won? Where would we now be if Hitler had won? It is not difficult to imagine the chaos and catastrophe that would have caused.

He insisted that the primary blame for Germany's disastrous plight at the war's end lay, not with the Nazis or even the German people:

> No, the real guilt lies on the church because it alone knew that the way being taken would lead to disaster, and it did not warn our people, it did not unmask the injustice that had occurred, or only when it was too late. And here the Confessing Church bears a particularly large measure of blame, for it saw most clearly what was developing. It even spoke out about it, but then became tired and stood more in fear of human beings than of the living God. It is for this reason that the catastrophe has broken out over us and we are now pulled into the whirlpool. We, the church, however have to beat our breast and confess: my guilt, my guilt, my enormous guilt.[9]

Niemöller's address clearly was meant to challenge and provoke his conservative colleagues. Why else declare that the "real guilt" lay with the church because "it alone knew"? Obviously, the real blame lay with the Nazis, and the church could not have foreseen in 1933 or 1934 what would take place from 1941 to 1945. Niemöller's aim was to provoke his colleagues and at the same time provide an example for other churchmen to follow. After all, if he—the embodiment of church resistance, who had been held in a concentration camp from 1937 to 1945—could

Swiss Calvinist theologian and principal author of the Theological Declaration of Barmen, Karl Barth with his lifelong friend Martin Niemöller in 1946. *Photo courtesy of Special Collections, Princeton Theological Seminary Libraries on behalf of the Karl Barth Stiftung of Basel, Switzerland.*

publicly beat his breast and declare his guilt, then who in the church could possibly declare their innocence? Distressed by the self-righteousness he detected among his conservative colleagues, Niemöller hoped to block their primary goal of a quick and painless restoration by demonstrating that the church's errors during the Nazi period had deep roots in the Protestant Church—roots going back to the sixteenth century.

The church's close relationship to the state, Niemöller insisted, was at the root of its silence from 1933 to 1945. As an Erastian church (*Behördenkirche*), one that allowed state supremacy in ecclesiastical affairs, the church neglected its special God-given commission. In light of this, Niemöller called for a living church (*Lebendige Kirche*), one that "asks and hears" by actively soliciting the opinions and participation of the laity. To achieve such a church, fundamental changes were necessary: dismissal of compromised churchmen, elimination of the hierarchically organized church, organization of an inter-confessional church built from the ground up, and recognition that the church had a responsibility to critically engage in the public sphere.[10]

By public or Christian responsibility Niemöller meant that the church was responsible for more than only preaching the gospel and administering the sacraments. He attributed the church's failure to take this responsibility seriously to the Lutheran orthodox misinterpretation of Luther's doctrine of two kingdoms. It should fall to the church, Niemöller insisted, to criticize the state publicly when it failed to ensure each citizen his or her basic human rights. And for that reason, Niemöller declared, the church could not be "indifferent" to the form of the state or to its basic principles. Niemöller even went so far as to argue that Christianity and democracy had a special affinity, one that did not exist between Christianity and conservative authoritarianism.[11]

Preaching Divine Forgiveness

Whereas the reformers emphasized the admission of guilt and the implementation of practical changes in church organization, conservatives stressed the powerful message of God's forgiveness. In Pastor Halfmann's view, German Protestants were guilty and needed to repent, but exactly why and for what was never explicitly stated. Nor were conservatives clear as to whom a confession of guilt was to be made. As Hans Asmussen said in his June 1945 letter to the archbishop of Canterbury, "We preachers need greater wisdom in order correctly to deal with the question of guilt before God and man."[12] Sadly, this wisdom was not forthcoming from most church leaders whose role it was to provide direction to the pastors and laymen on how to confess and repent.

Pastor Halfmann was one who did take up the challenge in his May 1945 circular, "How Should We Preach?" in which he advised pastors in Schleswig-Holstein. A preacher, particularly one in war-weary Germany, he counseled, must keep four things in mind when delivering a sermon of repentance (*Busspredigt*). First, it must acknowledge that the German people were in a similar position to the Jews in the Book of Isaiah, that is, demoralized and alienated from God because they had forsaken the Lord.[13] Whereas Dibelius had compared the Jews in Exodus to the pastors and laymen in the Confessing Church, Halfmann compared God's punishment of the Jews for their disobedience and their subsequent suffering to God's punishment of the German nation. However, in view of the desperate and demoralized condition of most Germans, Halfmann advised against "throwing salt in their wounds" by being too severe in their sermons. Secondly, Halfmann counseled that all acts of confession and repentance should take place before God and not earthly judges. By confessing one's sins and repenting before God rather than before those persons against whom the offense was directed, Halfmann sought to avoid "any loss of dignity before the enemy (*Feind*)."[14] The confession was not meant to be made to the Jews or other peoples grievously mistreated by Germans—those Halfmann refers to as the enemy—but to God who was angry with German disloyalty. Thirdly, he warned against demonstrating any malicious satisfaction over the fate of the church's nemeses, the Nazis and German Christians. And finally, he cau-

tioned against linking the church too closely to the desperation and demoraliza-
tion of the total collapse, which he feared would only lead to further depression.
He advised pastors to emphasize how quickly and totally the present situation would
change, and to remain hopeful for a new future with Christ.[15] The most important
task of the pastor, according to Halfmann, was to stress God's mercy and love in
order to keep the German people from sinking into "the abyss of despair."

The sin of disobedience necessitated sermons of repentance, Halfmann contended. Since a Christian's guilt was a matter between him and the Lord and not
between himself and another human, Halfmann counseled against answering to
earthly accusers. By employing a conservatively defined religious notion of guilt
and forgiveness, Halfmann and his colleagues conveniently avoided concrete and
public discussions about the church's particular role in the Nazi period.

Asmussen repeated several of these themes in his June letter to the archbishop
of Canterbury. He asserted that the church had two pressing tasks in spring 1945:
to clarify the guilt question, and to fight against despair.[16] He explained that the
two tasks were not necessarily contradictory as long as the church approached the
guilt question sensitively. In fact, the two tasks, Asmussen suggested, would complement each other were it not for the Allies' espousal of the facile and banal notion of collective guilt.[17] The primary aim of Asmussen's letter was to convince the
archbishop that the accusations of Germany's collective guilt perpetrated by Allied, in particular British, radio broadcasts in the wake of the liberation of the concentration camps made it nearly impossible for churchmen to discuss guilt without appearing to side with the "enemy." Asmussen believed that the hesitation
among Germans to acknowledge their guilt was not because they considered themselves entirely innocent but because they did not accept the collective guilt thesis
and suspected that to admit a degree of guilt would be understood by the Allies as
an acceptance of that thesis. Asmussen complained to the archbishop that "the guilt
question is not as easy to solve as the foreign radio broadcasts suggest."[18]

Asmussen wanted to move the discussion of guilt to a higher "religious" plane.
"I am writing this, Reverend Father, in order to raise the question of guilt for all of
the atrocities to another level."[19] The guilt that Christians bore was a "guilt from
another world" because, he insisted, it was appropriate to speak of the guilt of all
Germans only if one understood this guilt as religious guilt, otherworldly guilt, guilt
between God and man. When man spoke of this type of guilt, he must tremble because it was guilt before the almighty God. Insisting that despair reigned in Germany because the wrong people (foreign radio announcers) discussed guilt in the
wrong context (over the air waves), Asmussen asserted, "We cannot excuse ourselves [for the Nazi years], but we can protect ourselves against those who want to
humanize (*vermenschlichen*) our guilt and in so doing make it unforgivable before
God."[20] Asmussen believed that by making guilt an issue solely between mortals,
radio broadcasters eliminated the possibility of reconciliation between Christians
in Germany and God. The implication was that Germans would react by refusing

to repent and would become defiant, thereby making forgiveness and reconciliation with God impossible. Asmussen warned the archbishop that if the radio broadcasts continued in the same vein, the German people would respond with defiance.[21]

For moderately conservative churchmen like Asmussen and Halfmann, their ultimate role was to assure Germans that God's forgiveness would bring about better times. The combination of wretched living conditions and the blanket accusations that Germans were collectively guilty of mass murder led many Germans to feelings of indignation and despair simultaneously. The role of the church, they felt, was to coax parishioners to repent while simultaneously comforting and consoling them with the reassurance that their God is a forgiving God. Guilt placed outside the context of God's mercy and love, they felt, leads people to become morbidly depressed with the burden of unforgivable guilt. One notices again the Lutheran emphasis on law and gospel. The law condemned and the gospel forgave. God's law or punishment had already been carried out, now was the time for comfort and forgiveness.

Whether conservatives deliberately employed religious rhetoric to blur the church's failings or sincerely sought to address the frightful situation by interpreting it through the lens of the law-gospel dualism is difficult to determine. Asmussen, Wurm, and other moderate conservatives as well as the reformers seem to have sincerely felt guilt for themselves, their church, and their nation. As churchmen they sought God's direction. As Lutherans they perceived that direction in a distinct way. Of course, the decision to discuss the guilt question at all was not entirely voluntary. The Allies forced church leaders into the uncomfortable position of having to respond to their collective guilt assertions. With some success, churchmen attempted to manipulate this discourse by stressing an interpretation of guilt in accordance with Lutheran doctrine—an interpretation that shied away from specific historical actions and emphasized the collective guilt of modern man for turning away from God. However, they assured their congregations, God does not turn his back on man. Although this particular understanding of guilt received approval among conservative clergymen and parishioners, it was not the only Lutheran interpretation.

Bonhoeffer's Critique of "Cheap Grace"

What many conservatives seemed to be seeking for themselves and the German people was what Dietrich Bonhoeffer had called "cheap grace" in his 1937 text *Nachfolge*: "Cheap Grace is the Grace we bestow on ourselves. . . . We Lutherans," Bonhoeffer reproached, "have gathered like eagles round the carcass of cheap grace."[22] True discipleship was hard work, it was costly. "When Christ calls a man, he bids him come and die."[23] Bonhoeffer did not mean that disciples of Christ were literally called on to die for Christ. But discipleship involved more than simply show-ing up to a church service once a week. Discipleship meant taking Christ's exam-ple, his sacrifice, seriously. In *The Cost of Discipleship* Bonhoeffer offered a poignant critique of those conservative church leaders who assured Christians of God's for-giveness but failed to give equal emphasis to repentance. Moreover, genuine con-fession and repentance involved genuine changes in the way one acts:

> The preaching of forgiveness must always go hand-in-hand with the preaching of re-pentance, the preaching of the Gospel with the preaching of the law. . . . It is the will of the Lord himself that the gospel should not be given to the dogs. . . . Nor is it enough simply to deplore in general terms that the sinfulness of man infects even his good works. It is necessary to point out concrete sins, and to punish and condemn them.[24]

The position of church conservatives was not necessarily in contradiction with Luther's writing on the justification of the sinner by faith through grace. But it did clash with Bonhoeffer and many of the reformers' interpretation of Luther's doc-trine of justification for which forgiveness was not cheap or unconditional. By re-penting for not having prayed more faithfully, conservatives were in effect agree-ing only to pray more faithfully in the future.

The centrality of the law-gospel dualism for Lutherans is one explanation for their tendency to espouse an easy form of forgiveness. If God's forgiveness, the gospel, is the automatic complement to God's judgment, the law, then it is only natural that God would forgive Germans after having judged them sinful. Ger-many's collapse was God's judgment, and now God was ready to forgive them. Sev-eral conservative Lutherans, such as Pastor Frick of the Bremen Inner Mission, em-phasized that "God's mercy is greater than our guilt."[25] The Asmussen-drafted "Message to the Pastors" also sought to assure pastors that God's justice was a "gra-cious justice" that might appear at first unduly harsh but that always brought with it God's promise of forgiveness and love. Although this in itself is not an unusual statement for a Protestant to make, it is problematic when not accompanied by any mention of repentance. Conservative Lutherans acted as if they agreed with Voltaire's quip that "God forgives because that is his business."[26] Niemöller strongly repudiated this notion by emphasizing the need to acknowledge one's sin and demonstrate a willingness, a desire, to change one's ways.

God's promise of forgiveness and mercy and the embodiment of this promise in the crucifixion of Christ is the cornerstone on which most Protestant doctrine rests. Part of the attraction of Luther's doctrine of the justification of the sinner by grace through faith is its apparent simplicity: through Christ's suffering on the cross, God absolved humanity of its sins. But the apparent simplicity is deceptive and can lead to varied or contradictory interpretations. There is no unanimity among Lutherans, let alone Protestants, about the correct meaning of this doctrine. What is generally accepted is that guilt deriving from sinful behavior divides human beings from God and that the reconciliation of humanity with God occurs only through God's forgiveness and mercy.

The great Reformation thinkers were not, however, in agreement as to whether there were preconditions for receiving God's forgiveness, and if there were any, what they consisted of. Even Luther himself revised his theory on how one receives salvation, ostensibly as a result of his tower experience (*Turmerlebnis*).[27] The early Luther argued that in order to be forgiven, the sinner must initiate the process by first recognizing his sinful behavior. An older Luther argued that the righteousness of God ensured that all sinners were forgiven regardless of whether or not they took the initiative in confessing and repenting their sins. In this revised view, repentance for one's sins is a result of, rather than a precondition for, receiving God's forgiveness. This is commonly interpreted to mean: good works do not make a good man, but a good man does good works.

Because Luther emphasized the free (unconditional) grace of God without an equal emphasis on improved Christian conduct, followers and critics alike interpreted Luther's doctrine to say that once a sinner was forgiven by God he was free to go on living as before. In rectifying this misinterpretation, Luther's Reformed contemporaries (Martin Bucer, John Calvin, and Huldrych Zwingli) tipped the balance in the other direction by emphasizing obedience to Christ and moral regeneration. They placed more emphasis on the moral renewal of the individual, institution, or society than on God's forgiveness.[28]

Although the links between these sixteenth-century doctrines of forgiveness and post–World War II notions of confession, repentance, forgiveness, and renewal are rarely explicit in church leaders' postwar statements, there is little doubt that these contradictory assumptions about forgiveness affected their thinking. How clergymen publicly interpreted or represented the church's guilt was motivated by political concerns as well. Since these churchmen wanted the EKD to play a prominent role in Germany's immediate and long-term plans, they were careful not to diminish these opportunities by offending their supporters or critics. Thus, political and theological convictions influenced the course of action or inaction. Disagreement over whether confession and repentance were the precondition or the outcome of God's justification was central to the acrimonious debates about how to come to terms with the Nazi past.

4

The Stuttgart Declaration of Guilt

Religious Confession, Freedom Charter,
or Another Versailles?

Considering the underlying animosities that lingered from the church struggle, the administrative unity achieved at the Treysa conference was a significant accomplishment. The new church leadership, however, enjoyed little respite. Critics from inside and outside the church bemoaned the lack of contrition by church leaders at Treysa. "You should have seen this self-satisfied church at Treysa," Niemöller rebuked a woman who had carped that he was placing too much blame on the church.[1] Some foreign observers came to similar conclusions as Niemöller. Robert Murphy, a political adviser to the American military government and a man sympathetic to the churches, reported to U.S. Secretary of State James F. Byrnes, "There is little evidence [at the Treysa conference] that the German Protestant Church repented Germany's war of aggression or the cruelties visited upon other peoples and countries."[2] Another American with close ties to the Confessing Church, Stewart Herman, concluded after the conference, "It cannot be said that the attitude of the church toward its political responsibility is as yet satisfactory, let alone clear."[3]

These sentiments were particularly common among foreign church leaders who in the spirit of Christian brotherhood sought reconciliation with the German churches. Willem Visser 't Hooft, a Dutch theologian and general secretary of the World Council of Churches (WCC), was one of several foreign churchmen who wanted the churches to lead the way in bridging the gap between former enemies. The first step in this process, they believed, was for the German church leaders to acknowledge their errors and publicly repent. To encourage such an outcome, a small delegation of mostly west- and north-European church leaders traveled to Stuttgart in mid-October 1945 to meet with the EKD leadership council.[4] An outpouring of warmth, compassion, and genuine contrition on both sides marked the meetings between the German church leaders and the European delegates from the WCC. This atmosphere of Christian fellowship, along with lobbying by foreign church leaders and Dahlemites on the EKD leadership council, culminated in the council's issuing the most controversial declaration of guilt in the immediate post-war years. On the morning of 19 October 1945, the EKD council presented the ec-umenical delegation with what has become known as the "Stuttgart Declaration of Guilt" (see appendix 4).[5]

Consisting of six brief paragraphs, the entire document filled just three quar-ters of a page. The declaration divides easily into two parts: the first part dealt with the Nazi past, and the remaining paragraphs with the postwar future. The first para-graph, one short sentence, merely welcomed the representatives of the WCC to the second meeting of the EKD council in Stuttgart.[6]

The second paragraph contained the now-famous confession stating that the church was in "a great solidarity of guilt" with the German people. "With great an-guish we state: Through us has endless suffering been brought upon many peoples and countries. . . . We accuse ourselves for not witnessing more courageously, for not praying more faithfully, for not believing more joyously, and for not loving more ardently." The authors do not mention the atrocities perpetrated against Jews or any specific actions by the church, such as its enthusiastic support for Hitler in the early years of the Nazi regime.

In fact, before vaguely mentioning German guilt, the declaration spoke of Ger-man suffering: "we know ourselves to be with our people in a great community of suffering, but also in a great solidarity of guilt." And before charging themselves with neglecting prayer, they tout their resistance to Nazism: "We have for many years struggled in the name of Jesus Christ against the spirit which found its ter-rible expression in the National Socialist regime of tyranny, but we accuse our-selves for not witnessing more courageously . . . ." After this rather ambiguous con-fession in the second paragraph, the Nazi past was not mentioned again in the declaration.

"Now a new beginning can be made in our churches" began the second half of the document. A necessary step in beginning anew was for the churches to "cleanse themselves from influences alien to the faith and to set themselves in order." They expressed the hope that God would grant the Protestant churches the authority to proclaim his word and encourage obedience to his will. German church leaders ex-pressed joy that a new beginning in Germany meant also the renewal of ecumeni-cal fellowship. They hoped that "tortured humanity" could find solace in the spirit of peace and love while avoiding the violence and revenge that was becoming pow-erful again throughout the entire world. The declaration ended with the sentence: "So in an hour in which the whole world needs a new beginning we pray: 'Veni Creator Spiritus' [Come, Creator Spirit]."

When Fritz Heuner, superintendent of the Dortmund church, declared that "in this declaration we feel the heartbeat of the Confessing Church," he expressed the pride some churchmen felt for the actions taken by EKD council.[7] Although Heu-ner's response was certainly an exception within the church, there were signs prior to the ecumenical visit that leaders of the Confessing Church recognized the need for confession and repentance.[8] The ecumenical delegation did not force the EKD council to make the confession. As far back as 1942, Asmussen had sent a letter to Visser 't Hooft acknowledging the guilt of the German people and churches. The disappointment Niemöller and his reform-minded colleagues had experienced when conservatives rejected their "Message to the Pastors" at Treysa prompted them over the coming months to publicly declare that confession, repentance, and reform were foremost on their agenda. This was made abundantly clear in the introductory remarks of Hans Asmussen, Martin Niemöller, and the representative of the German Reformed churches, Wilhelm Niesel, to the WCC delegates. They needed no prodding to express lament over their own and the church's failure to speak out loudly and clearly against Nazism. Nevertheless, the Stuttgart declaration was not simply an act of conscience. Persistent pressure by foreign church leaders for formal recognition of the German Church's inadequate response to Nazism played a significant role.

Pressure from Foreign Church Leaders

Although German church leaders were certainly grateful for the ecumenical visit and welcomed the opportunity to reestablish ties with their counterparts from abroad, they had not initiated the visit. In fact, the rather sudden appearance in Stuttgart of an ecumenical delegation of such size and prominence caught several members of the council by surprise.[9] For instance, Bishop Wurm, whose regional church hosted the meeting, had expected the visit to consist of Bishop George Bell of Chichester and his aide.[10]

Visser 't Hooft was largely responsible for organizing the visit and strongly encouraging a formal confession. In addition to such a declaration, the ecumenical delegation also expected a detailed statement explaining the course and actions taken by the church over the past twelve years.[11] A week before the Treysa conference, Visser 't Hooft assured Dibelius that the WCC would do everything it could to reestablish friendly relations with the German churches. But to do so, he wrote, would require overcoming the extremely strained relations between the churches as a result of the German occupation policy during the war. Visser 't Hooft suggested a brotherly conversation between church leaders as a precondition to reconciliation:

> This conversation will be very much easier if the Confessing Church of Germany would speak out openly—not only about the crimes of the Nazis, but also particularly about the sins of omission of the German people, including the church. The Christians of other countries do not wish to appear as Pharisees. But they require that

Dutch Reformed theologians Willem Visser 't Hooft and Hendrik Kraemer attended the meetings in Stuttgart in October 1945, when German church leaders issued the Stuttgart Declaration of Guilt. *Photo courtesy of the Archive of the A. R. Wentz Library, Lutheran Theological Seminary of Gettysburg.*

it be openly said . . . that the German people and the church too did not speak [against Nazism] with sufficient clarity and with sufficient emphasis.[12]

Visser 't Hooft also wrote Niemöller in late September that he thought a visit from a delegation of European Protestant Church leaders was in order, and he asked Niemöller to extend the invitations.[13] Far in advance of the meeting, Visser 't Hooft made it clear to Niemöller and other council members that the WCC delegates expected something in the way of a confession or admission of responsibility. In his subsequent report on the visit, Visser 't Hooft described the purpose of the delegation as follows,

It was agreed [beforehand by the WCC's delegation] that in order to make relations of full confidence between the German Church and the other churches possible, it would be necessary to have some expression from the German Church as to its atti-

Ruins of the nineteenth-century neo-Gothic Johanneskirche am Feuersee in Stuttgart. *Photo courtesy of the Archive of the A. R. Wentz Library, Lutheran Theological Seminary of Gettysburg.*

tude toward the acts which had been committed in the name of the German nation. On the other hand, it was also agreed that it would be impossible to present this desire as a condition, for that would mean that the declaration to be given by German Church leaders would not have the character of true spontaneity, and it was, therefore, decided that the first approach would be to say that the delegation had come to re-establish fraternal relationships but that there were still obstacles to be removed.[14]

Karl Barth was also instrumental in urging certain EKD council members to acknowledge past errors. After Barth heard that a meeting was planned, he rushed off a letter from Basel to Niemöller in Frankfurt, spelling out his thoughts on what should take place at such a meeting. Christians abroad, Barth said, were waiting for the German church to speak more clearly about German responsibility than what had been said at Treysa. Barth drafted a statement he thought appropriate, insisting that it must be clear and concise and avoid at all cost theological obfuscation, such as references to original sin, the general sinfulness of mankind, and demons or devils. The statement should say simply:

> The provisional leadership of the Evangelical Church in Germany recognizes and declares that the German people erred when they placed themselves in the hands of Adolf Hitler. It recognizes and declares that the misery, which has spread over Europe and Germany, is a consequence of that error. It recognizes and declares that through false statements and silence the Evangelical Church in Germany shares in the responsibility for this error.[15]

Barth regretted that whenever he lectured outside Germany about the German situation he was unable to provide the audience with any direct evidence of the German church's willingness to take responsibility and do penance: "I would give a kingdom for a text, for a text from which I could prove that clearly."[16] Barth was not the only one clamoring for something on paper.

At the first official discussion between the council of twelve and the ecumenical delegation on the afternoon of 18 October, Visser 't Hooft concluded his introductory comments by saying, "Help us to help you. That is the purpose of our conversation."[17] This was not blackmail. He was merely stating the reality of the situation. The German churches could not expect to be welcomed into the ecumenical movement without recognizing that their complacency and accommodation over the past twelve years had made it all that much easier for the Nazis to institute and enforce deadly policies throughout Europe.

Other members of the delegation also expressed their desire for something in writing that they could show the people at home. Following the moving introductory remarks by Asmussen and Niemöller, each of whom recognized verbally the guilt of the church, Hendrik Kraemer, representative of the Netherlands Reformed Church, said, "We have heard with deep sympathy what brothers Asmussen and Niemöller have said to us. If we can bring that back home as the voice of conscience of the Evangelical Church in Germany that would be like a reconciliatory act for the church in Holland."[18] And Alphons Koechlin, the president of the Swiss Protestant Church Federation, said in his report on the Stuttgart declaration that the delegates hoped "not to have to demand such a declaration but rather to receive it on the basis of the insight of the German Church alone."[19]

Without the letters from Visser 't Hooft and Barth prior to the meeting and the comments by Kraemer and Koechlin on the first day of the meeting, it is unlikely that a confession signed by the entire council would have been forthcoming. These European churchmen added weight to the voices of Asmussen, Niemöller, and Niesel, whose willingness to acknowledge the church's mistakes publicly was representative of neither the entire council nor those in positions of power in the church in the summer and fall of 1945.

Even Asmussen and Niemöller, who agreed wholeheartedly on the need for a confession of guilt, had very different understandings of what such a confession implied. Niemöller emphasized the guilt of the church: it failed to remain true to Christian doctrine, and it provided political support for many of Hitler's policies that ultimately made the crimes committed under his leadership possible. Asmussen, like his conservative colleagues, believed it was their duty as church leaders to accept responsibility in the name of the German people for what took place in the Third Reich. The church, to be sure, was guilty of complacency but not of complicity. Both pastors used every opportunity over the next few years to articulate these views in their responses to the dozens of lay and ecclesiastical critics of the Stuttgart Declaration of Guilt.

Interpreting the Stuttgart Declaration

After distributing a copy of the declaration to each member of the ecumenical delegation, Hans Asmussen, president of the church chancellery, immediately began the process of developing a nonpolitical interpretation of the document. "Do your best," he told them, "to make sure that this declaration is not misused politically but rather serves the purposes that we all desire."[20] This remarkable statement by Asmussen, coupled with the fact that the EKD council made no provisions to distribute copies to the German churches or the press, indicates that the authors feared the declaration might be regarded by Germans and non-Germans alike as an admission by the church that the entire catastrophe that beset Europe was the sole fault of Germans. Asmussen and his German colleagues knew that the meeting was, on the one hand, simply a gathering of German and sympathetic European churchmen—a congenial setting for speaking openly and honestly without having to watch one's every word. On the other hand, they also understood it was a meeting between representatives of the victors and the vanquished in which German church leaders spoke as representatives of the German nation. In the first sense, German church leaders felt they could relieve their consciences without fearing repercussions. As representatives of the nation, however, the victors could use their confession of guilt as justification for harsh punishment.

Pastor Pierre Maury, the representative of the Protestant Federation of France, thanked the members of the EKD council and praised their courage and faith in making such a difficult confession. He tried to assuage Asmussen's fears that the statement might be interpreted by Germany's former enemies as a confession of collective political guilt by remarking that he saw it as a religious confession made between Christian brothers in the name of Jesus Christ. Maury assured the council of twelve that the intention of the ecumenical delegation was not to vilify the German churches. All the churches of Europe, he maintained, stood before God's judgment and mercy: "Your declaration is a call to Christian life—also for us."[21] Bishop Wurm expressed relief at Maury's reassurances and received further guarantees from Dutch theologian Visser 't Hooft that the WCC would do everything it could to ensure that the declaration was not interpreted as an admission by Germany that it accepted sole political guilt for the ashes and ruins that lay across Europe.[22]

For the most part, Visser 't Hooft and Maury's sympathetic comments were indicative of the attitude of the entire ecumenical delegation.[23] The threat of a political interpretation came less from the churches abroad than from the pastors and laity at home. Asmussen, Wurm, and other German church leaders knew that the Stuttgart declaration represented a potential public relations bombshell at home should it be viewed abroad as an admission of Germany's collective political guilt. Hence, a deliberate decision was made to not circulate the declaration to the clergy and laity of the parishes. But in fact, the contents soon enough became known. Within days they were printed in the London press, followed quickly by publication in German newspapers.[24] What the declaration's authors had not foreseen was that even if the Stuttgart declaration were accepted abroad as a religious confession between Christian brothers, it would be seen at home as a confession of collective guilt by a prickly nation.

Responses at home vividly brought to mind reactions after the Ebert government signed the 1919 Treaty of Versailles, which declared that Germany bore sole guilt for the First World War.[25] Based on this charge, the victors had saddled Germany with an astronomical reparations bill and, among other punitive measures, took territory and reduced and limited the armed forces. Many Germans associated the hardship and humiliation that followed the signing of the treaty with the rising popularity of the ultranationalist and anti-Versailles platform of the Nazis in the 1920s and early 1930s. Some Germans were quick to compare the "sole war guilt" clause of the Versailles treaty with the acknowledgment at Stuttgart that the church and the German people were in "a solidarity of guilt" for bringing "endless suffering" to many peoples and countries. They feared that the victors would use this admission to once again punish Germany. The potent and painful memories of post-

Versailles economic hardship, political destabilization, and national humiliation did not bode well for an enthusiastic reception of the Stuttgart declaration.

Moreover, the phrase "solidarity of guilt" sounded too similar to "collective guilt" for many Germans. The collective guilt thesis espoused by some representatives of the Allies implied that all Germans who had not actively and publicly resisted the Nazi regime *in toto* were guilty of the crimes committed during the Nazi era—whether they had actually participated in the killings or not. The sensational and alarming nature of the collective guilt thesis caught the attention of many Germans even though it was subscribed to neither by a majority of the Allied representatives in Germany nor by the church leaders who authored the Stuttgart declaration. It seems probable, in fact, that many Germans focused their criticism on the collective guilt thesis because it was easier to refute than the more subtle argument, also prevalent in Allied circles, that all Germans were responsible to varying degrees for what took place in their country from 1933 to 1945. Although many Germans were just as hostile to discussing their collective responsibility as their collective guilt, there is no doubt that the references to *guilt* by Allied representatives hindered attempts to convince Germans to take *responsibility* for the Nazi government that they brought to power.

Some churchmen blamed the popular outcry over the declaration on a simple misunderstanding perpetuated by sensational and inaccurate press reports.[26] There was some truth to this. With the eye-catching headline, "Common Guilt for Endless Suffering: Protestant Church Discusses Germany's War Guilt," the *Ruhr-Zeitung* published an article that began, "For the first time leading men of the German church confessed Germany's war guilt, spoke of a common guilt for endless suffering, and a lack of resistance on the part of the church against the Nazi regime."[27] If leaders bothered to read beyond the misleading headline and lead sentence, they would have found the declaration itself, word for word, which says nothing about common guilt or war guilt. Many other such newspaper articles appearing at the same time contributed to the erroneous belief that the church's leadership acknowledged the collective guilt of the German people for the atrocities committed during the war. In contrast to the statements drafted at the Treysa conference, the Stuttgart declaration was intended primarily for a foreign audience. Thus, church leaders neither published the declaration in their church newspapers nor did they prepare a press packet explaining the context, background, and the church's interpretation of the declaration. The lack of a proactive stance, coupled with the presence of representatives of Allied countries who portrayed the German people as collectively guilty, inflamed a negative reaction at home.

Of course, German opposition to the Stuttgart declaration cannot be blamed wholly on poor packaging, Allied discussions of collective guilt, or the hostile climate in which it was issued. Pastor Wilhelm Niesel, a former doctoral student of Barth's and one of the two representatives of the German Reformed Church on the council of twelve, discerned a deeper cause behind the opposition: a general un-willingness among the German people to recognize, much less accept, responsibil-ity for the years of Nazi rule.[28] The righteous intermingling of self-justification and self-pity was as important a factor in creating a hostile atmosphere for a public con-fession as were postwar fears of another Versailles or Allied charges of collective guilt.

The *Menschlein* (Little People) and the Stuttgart Declaration

Grassroots Protestant objections to the Stuttgart declaration fell generally into two categories: practical and theological. Although the vast majority of critics re-lied more heavily on the former, a minority also raised theological issues in their critiques. The primary practical objection to a public acknowledgment of guilt was that the Allies would interpret it as recognition of collective political guilt and use it to justify harsh treatment in the occupation zones. Fear and defensiveness per-meated virtually all of the protests. Although some Protestants believed they were entirely innocent and had nothing to confess, most were willing to confess some degree of responsibility as long as their former enemies did so as well.[29] On the other hand, those protesters whose critiques were primarily theological defined their guilt as religious and maintained that a proper confession of guilt should be made be-fore God, not before other men. One critic reminded the Stuttgart authors that nei-ther the Allies nor the WCC "are our father confessor."[30]

A typical protest, written one week after the Stuttgart meeting, came from a long-winded, exasperated man from Hannover.[31] Herr D. warned church leaders that they were woefully out of touch with the mood on the street, which had become increasingly bitter due to the hardship endured over the past months. He expressed great disdain for Niemöller's sentence, "With great anguish do we state: through us has endless suffering been brought to many peoples and countries." This sen-tence, insisted on by Niemöller, was the only one in the declaration to acknowl-edge concretely the misery caused throughout Europe by Germany's armies, and it received much abuse from letter writers. For Herr D. this was masochism. He clearly had no hope or faith that mercy would be shown to Germany or that any-thing like the Marshall Plan, rearmament, or Germany's integration into the West were on the horizon. He feared a second Versailles. To emphasize his point, he appropriated the phrase "endless suffering" to describe the suffering the Allies inflicted on the German people.

> Have the authors of this confession of guilt completely forgotten the endless suffer-ing which the enemy brought on the German people, beginning with the hunger block-ade of the [First] World War and the persecution of Germans all over the world, to the phosphorous bombing raids (Dresden!!) and the millions of refugees from . . . the east who are crammed together in the remaining [western] territory and are un-able to sustain themselves . . . ?

If it had not been for the "crimes of Versailles," he continued, National Socialism and "its sins" would never have happened. Wrongdoing had occurred, but the real task of the church, he asserted, was to fend off the spirit of revenge among Germany's enemies.

In contrast to his treatment of Niemöller's sentence, Herr D. heaped praise on those passages that described the task of the church as defending the German people against unwarranted aggression from its neighbors. The overriding point of his protest was to emphasize that the task of the church was to protect and comfort its members, not to reproach them. It was a message repeated over and over in the spring and summer of 1945. For Herr D. the most resonant passage in the declaration was: "through the common service of the churches, the spirit of violence and revenge . . . may be brought under control." The authors of the Stuttgart declaration clearly meant "the spirit of violence and revenge" to refer to the vengeance of Germany's former enemies, and this was the sense in which most Germans understood it.

The writer went on to accuse "the enemy nations" of inflicting tremendous suffering on "millions of completely innocent Germans" by applying the Old Testament mentality of an eye for an eye, a tooth for a tooth. He consistently referred to the Allies as "the enemy" (*der Feind*), implying that although the war officially ended on 8 May 1945, this was not experienced as a liberation from Nazism but as a defeat, a defeat that he feared was far from over and would include future reprisals and retaliation on the part of the Allies. He proffered a veiled threat that the enemy's unrestrained "hate and frenzy of persecution" would only generate new hate and antisemitism among Germans, which would make everything that came before pale in comparison. The Allies, he warned, were mistaken if they thought terror, injustice, and revenge were going to foster a democratic spirit in Germany. Like many others, he urged that Germany's historical wrongs be righted through justice, including the punishment of war criminals and war profiteers. As for his warning of a renewal of antisemitism, one must wonder whether the writer really understood the roots of antisemitism and whether he associated the Allies with the Nazi stereotype of the Jew: an international conspirator and historical enemy of Germany.

In another letter, a seventy-eight-year-old man from Frankfurt on the Main, who claimed to have been thrown out of his parish for activities on the behalf of the Confessing Church, also blamed European policy toward Germany after World War I for the Nazi past. "A dreamer [*Phantast*] like Hitler," Herr S. contended, "would never have appeared without the Versailles treaty."[32] In a series of letters sent to the chancellery, Herr S. emphasized the continuity of Germany's mistreatment at the hands of the enemy from the end of World War I to the present. In contrast to vague and distant reference to Germany's crimes, he personalized the history of Germany's mistreatment at the hands of others by chronicling his own suffering as a result of the bombing raids. Even the heading on his stationery revealed his intention to emphasize his personal suffering. Next to his former address he typed "22–24 März 1944, ausgebombt [bombed out]." His meaning was clear: I am a victim, not a perpetrator. In fact, according to his letter, he was not a Nazi sympathizer but rather a victim of the Gestapo's reign of terror. Accordingly, he also called for an individual accounting for Nazi crimes. Like Herr D., he praised any action taken by the church in defense of the German people and against the Allies. His opposition to what he saw as the political nature of the declaration did not stem from an inflexible adherence to the doctrine of a strict separation of the earthly and spiritual kingdoms, of politics from religion, but from the belief that with the Stuttgart declaration the church had joined the political struggle on the wrong side. This position—that the church should engage politically in the defense of the German people—was evident in many letters. The tendency to see the church as a political institution that championed nationalist causes was directly in line with the strong nationalist tradition extant in Lutheran circles throughout the nineteenth and twentieth centuries.

Another letter from Herr S., dated February 1946, expressing satisfaction with an open and unreserved statement from church leaders charging occupation forces with the mistreatment of German prisoners of war, is evidence that his concern was not the church engaging in politics but the character of the church's politics. Millions, he claimed, found it incomprehensible that at the same time that German concentration camps and the persecution of Jews were under severe reproach by the Allies, the Allies were using Hitler-like methods (*Hitler Methoden*) against German prisoners of war.[33] He urged Germans not to forget the terrible suffering and countless deaths from the phosphorous bombing campaign, expulsions from the east, and starvation. It was only because of God's blessing, he believed, that the Allies did not use atom bombs against Germany as they did against Japan.

Typically, Herr S. did not believe that Germany was altogether innocent, nor did he think that Germany's crimes were more heinous than those of the Allies:

> Certainly repentance must be urged but we are not the only ones guilty [and] we should not be the only ones to roast on a spit. The fact is that the entire German people are guilty neither for the destruction of the synagogues, which for us were holy places of worship, nor for the atrocities of individual Nazi leaders. The world will only clearly recognize in the years to come who the real war criminals and war guilty were.

For someone who claimed to have been in opposition to Nazi rule, Herr S. ends his letter on a disappointingly equivocal note. "For us little people (*Menschlein*)," he claimed, there was no choice but to remain silent and pray.

A former Nazi Party member, Dr. K. of Nuremberg was extremely critical of the shameful pandering to the Allies. He accused Wurm and other church "dignitaries" of betraying the fatherland by acknowledging German guilt at all.[34] In his March 1946 letter Dr. K. assured Wurm that, although he was a former Nazi Party member, his deep Christian convictions remained intact throughout the years. While

Dr. K. expressed the deepest respect for Wurm's struggle on behalf of the church in the recent past, he expressed disgust with church leaders for recognizing German guilt in an international setting. The rumor that Wurm intended to discuss German guilt yet again at an upcoming conference of the WCC in Geneva infuriated him. He compared the behavior of Wurm and the EKD council to that of Matthias Erzberger, a liberal parliamentarian in the Center Party whom right-wing thugs murdered in 1921 for his support of the Versailles treaty. They (Wurm and Erzberger) spoke like nationalists, Dr. K. asserted, but betrayed the fatherland when it mattered most. "Wouldn't it be better in Geneva," Dr. K. asked rhetorically, "to insist that other nations open their secret archives and allow completely neutral institutions to examine the materials to determine who was really guilty in this war?" He then launched into an invective against the Allies, especially the "bloodthirsty Bolsheviks" and Churchill, who he described as a "characterless rag" for his opportunistic alliance with the Bolsheviks. He berated Wurm for doing a terrible disservice to himself and the church. "You may understand a little about first things (*den ersten Dingen*) but as a politician you're a big dilettante." Dr. K. concluded by harshly rebuking Wurm and his colleagues for failing to use their positions to defend the German people. "We haven't heard you raise objections because of the murder of tens of thousands by phosphor bombs. Shame on you Bishop." The simultaneous demand that Wurm stay out of politics and that he go to an international conference of church leaders in Geneva and accuse the Allies of war crimes was typical of many Germans who associated being a good Christian with being a good German.

Dr. M., a secondary-school teacher from Rendsburg on the Eider River in Schleswig-Holstein, recommended five ways to reverse the church's sullied reputation as a result of the declaration. First, some members of the council of twelve should resign their posts in light of their public and political shortcomings. Second, German church leaders should solicit a parallel declaration from the ecumenical delegation that visited Stuttgart and publish it in German newspapers. Third, if the publication of the Stuttgart declaration abroad did not bring about positive results within a short time, the EKD council should proclaim, as loudly as it confessed, that revenge and reprisals were unchristian. Fourth, German church leaders should impress upon the ecumenical delegation the importance in the Christian tradition of treating the defeated with humanity. And finally, the council should preach routinely and inform the media about efforts made on the part of the German churches to relieve German suffering. For example, they should publicize the protest by Bishop Meiser and Cardinal Michael Faulhaber of Munich to the American military government regarding the undifferentiated treatment of all Nazi Party members.

This letter from Dr. M., like others, displayed a popular misconception of the declaration, namely, that it addressed only Germany's guilt and failed to recognize German suffering and the Allied mood of revenge and retribution. Perhaps one source of this misconception was misleading press coverage. But it is more likely that the writer was blinded by the idea that a confession would not lead to forgiveness but rather would serve as a justification for revenge.

Paradoxically, it was Germans who interpreted the declaration as a confession of war guilt and projected this interpretation on their former enemies. Abroad, there was no doubt that Germany started the war, but the "Stuttgart Declaration of Guilt" was understood as a churchly declaration that recognized the suffering Germany caused its neighbors. The obsession of protesters with what they took to be the political, not churchly, thrust of the declaration and its political consequences can be traced back to German perceptions of the injustice of the Versailles treaty. Although none of them made a direct analogy between the EKD council and the so-called November Criminals, an epithet German nationalists used to describe the men who signed the Versailles treaty, there were many indirect associations made between the war-guilt clause in the Versailles treaty and the Stuttgart declaration.

Herr R. from Marktbreit in traditionally conservative Bavaria, called the Stuttgart declaration an act of "high treason" that would only prolong the suffering of the German people. He demanded that the declaration be revoked since it was an outrageous presumption on the part of church leaders, who represented only themselves.[35] If an individual council member, he continued, wanted to write a personal statement in which he accused all Germans of war guilt, then that was his right. He does not, however, have the right to claim that his personal opinion is that of the German people. Hence, Herr R. concluded, not only was the declaration illegal and invalid but "the action taken by church leaders is reminiscent of Nazi methods."[36] To accuse one's own church leaders of engaging in Nazi-like activity for issuing a declaration in the name of the German people not only suggests a refusal to acknowledge the murderous nature of Nazism but also accentuates the immense gulf that separated repentant church leaders and their unrepentant flock.

A woman from a Lutheran Confessing Church in Hann-Münden near Göttingen reported having first seen the wording of the declaration in the *Neuer Hannoversche Kurier* on 30 October 1945.[37] Frau E. praised churchmen who remained true to the church during the Nazi years and described the men on the recently formed EKD council as mountains of strength. Politely and articulately, she went on to express her dismay with the Stuttgart declaration. "You have in the name of the EKD recognized a guilt, which in no case the German people bear alone." What took place in the past twelve years in Germany, she claimed, could happen only because the victorious powers of 1918 did not see fit to end the war in 1918. The victors treated Germany with "hate and more hate" for the next fourteen years. They spoke the language of justice but treated Germany unjustly. When Hitler came in with his National Socialist ideas, she maintained, the German people clutched at these ideas as if they were a life raft. Even our enemies, she wrote, recognized the state established by Hitler. The guilt of the German people was that they allowed things to spin out of control and "did not scream loud enough against Hitler." Some people fought against Hitler and paid for it with their lives, but unfortunately not everyone did this. "That is our great guilt for which we must repent. But not only we bear the guilt of this war." How could you issue a declaration of guilt to a group of foreign clergymen, Frau E. wanted to know, when you are standing in a pile of rubble? Do you not see the mutilated bodies of German men, women, and children as a result of the air raids? she reproached.

In letter after letter the same cry of resentment is heard. To most Germans the suffering itself was more than enough punishment for whatever share of guilt Germans bore. The feeling was ever present that since the Allies also committed war crimes, this fact should somehow lessen the gravity of the crimes perpetrated by Germany.

Frau F., a pastor's wife from Lindau, took particular offense at a lecture Martin Niemöller had given in Heidelberg in which he repeated that as far as he was concerned, pastors, theologians, and church leaders were more guilty than anyone else, because of all people, they should have known that the Nazis were leading Germany down the wrong path.[38] Frau F. complained to Bishop Wurm, "The contention that we are all to blame (*mitschuldig*) for the sad events of the past years is something we Christians object to and in particular we relatives of pastors, for whom it is in no way clear that we in particular are guilty. . . . Pastor Niemöller had to understand," she continued, "that a good deal of resistance was mounted by pastors against the Third Reich and that the church and the parishes would not have been served, if all the pastors had gone to concentration camps." She then praised the Lutheran theologian Helmut Thielicke for recognizing God alone as the judge before whom all men and peoples were guilty.

The negative reaction by ordinary Protestants to the Stuttgart declaration can be understood only by considering their mind-set in the context of defeat and occupation. Confessions of guilt are hard even under the best of circumstances; typically they require the very difficult task of admitting one's responsibility for the physical and emotional pain suffered by another person or group. Conditions in Germany in autumn 1945 were, for three reasons, highly unpropitious for fostering a mentality of contrition or responsibility among Germans. First, many Germans who had supported the Nazis and participated in the atrocities were simply unrepentant. The war and the atrocities may have come to end in May 1945, but the racist and nationalist mentality of hundreds of thousands of Germans did not. In fact, defeat and occupation may have temporarily heightened these sentiments. Second, the extent of the atrocities committed by and in the name of the German people was difficult to comprehend even by those who had participated in them. No one, especially bystanders who made up the majority of Germans, was eager to take responsibility for barbarity of such magnitude. Third, German suffering was extensive as a result of their defeat, and naturally Germans prioritized their own suffering.

Images of the Allies liberating concentration camps intermingled in the minds of many Germans with images of Germans standing amidst piles of rubble that were once their homes. The two conflicting realities confronting Germans in 1945—of being perpetrators and of being victims—led many Germans to equalize and merge both perceptions and conclude that they were no more guilty of barbarous acts than the Allied armies who had reduced their homes to rubble.

Germans were indeed suffering horribly in 1945. Some 7 million Germans died in the war, approximately half of whom were civilians.[39] Approximately one million soldiers remained in prisoner-of-war camps, and another million were missing.[40] Millions of people had no news of their next of kin. Of the approximately 10 million Germans who fled behind the retreating German army or were expelled from German areas east of the Oder-Niesse line, between 1 and 2 million died.[41] Food, fuel, housing, transport, and other essentials were scarce or nonexistent in western Germany even before millions of poor, emaciated refugees arrived from the east. Allied soldiers raped tens of thousands of German women and girls, the majority of them in the Soviet zone.[42]

Many Germans could not see beyond their own suffering to that of their victims. Moreover, in the view of most Germans, the destruction and misery that surrounded them was not of their own making. As Karl Jaspers observed at that time, "One simply does not want to suffer any more. One wants to escape the misery [and] to live, but does not wish to ponder. The mood is as if one expects to be compensated after the terrible suffering or at least to be comforted; but one does not want to be burdened with guilt."[43]

Occupied by four enemy nations, Germans perceived the scarcity of food, the dismantling of industrial machinery by the military governments, and the denazification policies as victor's justice. British war reporter Alan Moorehead summed up the prevailing mood, noting that the Germans "had an immense sense, not of guilt, but of defeat."[44]

In their attempt to pull themselves out of this morass, many Germans, Christians and non-Christians alike, turned to the churches, the only institutions that had not collapsed, to intercede on their behalf.[45] Many church leaders reacted to this newfound prestige and popularity in the immediate postwar period by trying most earnestly to meet the needs of these potential constituents.[46] Why, the clergymen asked themselves, squander the "hour of the church" by admonishing and reproaching a population looking for comfort and support in their hour of need? This attitude helps explain Niemöller's unpopularity among both his colleagues and the general German population from 1945 to 1947. It also explains why church leaders never intended to publish the Stuttgart Declaration of Guilt in Germany. As the protest letters attest, Germans were furious that the very men in whom they had put their trust to help eliminate physical want and national humiliation would issue a declaration in the name of the German people that seemed to support the thesis that Germans were collectively guilty, and in so doing supposedly provide the Allies with the justification for inflicting the very suffering Germans looked to the church to alleviate.

Hans Asmussen (*left*), the controversial director of the EKD's chancellery, and Hanns Lilje, bishop of Hannover. Asmussen moved steadily into the church's conservative camp during the postwar years. *Photo courtesy of the Archive of the A. R. Wentz Library, Lutheran Theological Seminary of Gettysburg.*

Church Leaders Respond to Parish-Level Critics

Virtually every member of the council of twelve received critical letters or had irate pastors and parishioners demand answers to their questions and criticisms of the Stuttgart declaration. Although each council member responded in his own way to the criticism, a fairly clear division developed between the views of Niemöller and Niesel, on one side, and Asmussen, Dibelius, Lilje, Meiser, and Wurm, on the other. The division was not between those who defended it and those who did not, because at least initially, both reformers and conservatives provided impassioned defenses of the declaration and expressed exasperation with the unrepentant nature of their critics. Rather, the differences lay in how they interpreted the meaning of the confession and the degree of specificity they used to express their views.

Before examining the differences in tone and content of the various responses, the position of Hans Asmussen requires a brief explanation since he played such a central role in defending and interpreting the Stuttgart declaration. For the most part, as head of the church chancellery, Asmussen (or his assistant Dr. Jensen) responded to the protest letters sent to the chancellery in Schwäbisch Gmünd near Stuttgart. Asmussen also wrote a detailed commentary to counter the critics and explain the official position of the church.[47] With the blessing of Bishop Wurm, the chairman of the council, Asmussen distributed his commentary to pastors throughout Germany in November 1945. Although not everyone on the EKD council agreed with all aspects of Asmussen's interpretation of the Stuttgart declaration, parishes viewed the seven-page commentary as the church's official position. In many instances, Asmussen sent protesters both a copy of the commentary and a personal response to their queries and criticisms. Although some protesters found the commentary helpful, at least as many returned detailed critiques of the commentary itself, requiring yet another response by Asmussen or his assistant. The chancellery staff was not alone in taking this task seriously; every member of the council as well as other church leaders joined them in the fray.

By early 1946 there was a notable shift among conservative clergy who moved from defending the Stuttgart declaration, albeit from a conservative perspective, to public criticisms of the Allies' occupation policies. Asmussen was no exception. As the physical plight of Germans worsened and tension between the superpowers grew, church leaders had less patience for discussing German guilt. It was as if they were saying: We tackled the issue of German guilt in October '45, now we want to address the issues that matter most to us—increasing the quantity of material relief, addressing the problems in the Soviet zone, and relaxing the denazification policies of the military governments. For the most part, Niemöller and Niesel refused to give in to this shift in emphasis, although they did not hesitate to excoriate occupation policy when they felt it was unjust and made their task of encouraging repentance more difficult. Stewart Herman's quip that Niemöller might fight the occupation forces with the same tenacity as he had the Nazis had some truth to it.[48]

Conservatives Respond

Conservatives emphasized the separation between the political and religious spheres in their reading of the declaration and made a clear distinction between the guilt of the German nation during Hitler's dictatorship and the guilt of the church. They recognized that in the political sphere, which, they emphasized, the Nazis had governed and controlled for the last decade, Germans had caused terrible suffering. Some conservatives even acknowledged that Germans had started the war and killed millions of Jews. They insisted at the same time, however, that the church's confession of guilt was unambiguously religious in nature. The "us" in "through us has endless suffering been brought to many peoples and countries" was the German nation. The "we" in "we accuse ourselves for not witnessing more courageously, for not praying more faithfully, for not believing more joyously, and for not loving more ardently" was the church. To be sure, the church was a part of the German nation, but it was a unique part because it did not engage in political affairs. They maintained that politics, especially during the Third Reich, was not the sphere of the church, and thus the church was not politically accountable for Nazi aggression and racial policy. Of course, the church was present when the Nazis carried out their crimes and was therefore in "a solidarity of guilt" with the German people, but the church itself was not guilty of these crimes.

Asmussen explained in his commentary that the unusual semantics of the Christian language accounted for the popular misunderstanding of the declaration as a recognition of collective political guilt. The Christian community, he contended, spoke an entirely different language than the secular world—leading much of the world to misunderstand the religious nature of the confession.[49] The language that true Christians spoke to one another could be appreciated only by the faithful.[50]

By explaining the difference between a Christian understanding of guilt and a political understanding of guilt, Asmussen hoped to convince critics that church leaders acted as good Christians and consequently as good Germans. Christians did not speak of guilt, he admonished, in order to accuse other persons of having sinned. Accusations of guilt belonged to the political world; and in keeping with the conservative interpretation of the Lutheran doctrine of two kingdoms, Asmussen maintained in his commentary that "the church does not think to place itself in the service of political interests."[51] "We are not the judges of [other] nations."[52] Rather, a true Christian recognized that his own guilt, no matter how little, divided him from God and his Christian brothers. The only way to bridge that gap was through a confession and repentance.[53]

The Stuttgart declaration, the commentary continued, did this by saying to the Christian brothers of other nations, "I have sinned."[54] The "I" embraced both the speaker and those for whom he spoke, Asmussen explained. The specific sin, he continued, was the sin against the First Commandment that made other (worse) things possible.[55] Thus, Christian disobedience was the focus of the church's confession, not political misdeeds. Asmussen hinted that disregard for the First Commandment had political reverberations—which he did not describe—but then he declared the church innocent (*unschuldig*) of Nazism and its atrocities.[56] The only fault of the church was to sin against God.

In an unusually blunt passage that seems out of place in his overly theological commentary, Asmussen discussed German political guilt and reproached those at home who repeatedly pointed to the guilt of the Allies. If anyone was guilty of betraying the fatherland, Asmussen snapped at the protesters who called the declaration treasonous, it was those who hinder the church "from doing a right-about-face from its former sinful ways."[57] How can admitting that Germany caused tremendous suffering to many peoples and nations be an act of treason, Asmussen wanted to know.[58] He was quick to reassure his German audience that the council was aware of the dreadful state of affairs in Germany since the collapse and to remind them that the church was always the first to object to the misdeeds of the occupying forces. But to his credit, he was equally as quick to challenge those who continually grumbled about the guilt of the Allies:

> What does the injustice which is today being perpetrated against our nation have to do with the acknowledgment of our guilt? It means exactly nothing. It does not in the least change the evil that we Germans have done against the Poles, and in Greece and Holland. It in no way conceals our guilt towards the non-Aryans. It does not justify at all our silence or our cooperation in these past twelve evil years.[59]

He asked all the pastors, officials, and laymen within the church who had denounced the declaration whether they had the courage to stand behind the altar and in the name of Jesus Christ condemn the present mistreatment of Germans without beforehand asking Christ's forgiveness for past German injustices to others.[60] This brief yet no-nonsense statement on political guilt was certainly atypical of Asmussen. But he was not alone amongst his conservative colleagues to point out in sheer exasperation the obvious fact that Germans were responsible for war atrocities as well as for most of the hardship endured by Germany and its neighbors. It is worth noting in the above passage that Asmussen did not refer to the guilt of the church but of "we Germans." In fact, he frequently described the church as the institution that fought the hardest against "the sins of the last twelve years."[61] When Asmussen singled out the church for criticism, he kept the discussion entirely in the religious realm.

In a speech on the guilt question to pastors in Stuttgart in early December 1945, Bishop Wurm unambiguously recognized Germany's blame for starting the Second World War and murdering millions of Jews.[62] He did this to make a clear distinction between the Stuttgart declaration and the Versailles treaty, which was a legitimate target for invective. Whereas the Treaty of Versailles declared Germany's sole guilt (*Alleinschuld*) for launching a war that was, in fact, instigated by many nations, including Germany, the Stuttgart declaration merely acknowledged the indisputable fact that "through us has endless suffering been brought to many peoples and countries." Thus Wurm did not shy away from recognizing Germany's political guilt but was adamant that comparisons to the contemptible Versailles treaty—which the church had protested vocally in the 1920s—were entirely inappropriate. Like Asmussen, however, he avoided directly implicating the church in the nation's political guilt.

Wurm defended the concept of "a solidarity of guilt" by differentiating it from collective guilt and insisting that it was "a biblical concept from A to Z." Although participation by the church and Christian circles in events that took place under the Nazis had been minimal, the church had been present, and for this reason "we are partially to blame." Wurm concluded by restating that all the Allies, especially the Russians, were guilty of many of the same crimes that Germany was now being charged with. "I don't miss an opportunity," he assured his audience, "to bring this inconsistency to the attention of the Allies." It is all the more important, he pointed out, that we confess our guilt if we want our allegations against the Allies to be taken seriously.[63] For Wurm, it was important for the church to acknowledge Germany's misdeeds not only because it was Christian to do so but also because it gave the church greater leverage when it pointed a finger at the misguided and sometimes brutal policies of the Allies.

Other conservatives on the council also tried to depoliticize the confession, emphasizing that at Stuttgart, church leaders confessed the church's sins—namely, its weakness in confessing, praying, believing, and loving—and nothing else. Hanns Lilje, a prominent Lutheran leader and later the regional bishop in Hannover, responded to criticism by insisting: "I myself as a member of the council of the EKD never signed a declaration which said, 'the German people must admit its guilt for the war and its atrocities.'"[64] He maintained that the church had not spoken of its guilt because of political pressure, as several protesters charged, but rather because it was the right and duty of the church to speak as it did. If the world misinterpreted the statement as a political confession, Lilje contended, it was the fault of neither the council nor the ecumenical delegation. And Bishop Hans Meiser of Bavaria declared in a March 1946 statement entitled "We Confess Our Guilt" that the Stuttgart declaration was a statement by Christians to Christians and that from the beginning it was understood as such by the EKD council and the ecumenical delegation. It did not, Meiser insisted, take up the question of political war guilt.[65]

Bishop Otto Dibelius did not use the terms "political guilt" and "religious guilt" but instead distinguished between personal guilt (*persönliche Schuld*) and the guilt of mankind (*die Schuld der Gesamtheit*).[66] By limiting the types of guilt and categorizing criminal acts under National Socialism as personal, Dibelius eliminated the notion that Germans or the church as a whole were guilty or responsible. Individuals were guilty of specific acts, such as murder or theft, and humanity was guilty of disloyalty to God.

Dibelius maintained that a Christian guilty of committing a misdeed against another person must confess directly to that person, "I have treated you badly."[67] He even specified that any Christian who benefited from National Socialism at the expense of another person had the responsibility to confess and apologize to that person. In short, a personal offense required a personal confession. He did not address what the guilty Christian should do if he did not know the identity of his victim, if there were multiple victims, or if the victim was now dead or otherwise inaccessible, as were many of the victims of the Third Reich. The general tenor of his thought was nonetheless clear: individuals were responsible for the crimes committed under Nazi rule. Neither a nation nor an institution like the church could be collectively guilty.

But, the guilt of mankind, according to Dibelius, was inherent in all Christians.

The true Christian took this guilt as his own "without asking what percentage of it he was personally responsible for."[68] All Christians bore it equally. He saw the declaration issued at Stuttgart as a priestly duty not only because it confessed sinful behavior and called for repentance but also because it would help to free the church and its members from the straightjacket imposed by the Allies.

In his letters and commentary, Asmussen also addressed the question of whether it was appropriate for the church leadership to confess guilt in the name of the German people. Why, many protesters had asked, did the council presume to speak for the people? Asmussen responded with his theology of sacrifice.[69] As pastors and church leaders, the members of the council represented the people before God. Although the church leaders themselves were not guilty, they had a priestly duty to confess and accept the guilt on the part of their parishioners. "Was our statement a sacrifice?" Asmussen asked. "One would have to say that [it was]."[70] It was a pastor's duty to sacrifice. In the case of the Stuttgart declaration, the pastors' sacrifice consisted of taking the guilt of the people on their shoulders even though they themselves were innocent of the crimes of Nazism. Just as Christ sacrificed himself on the cross for mankind, the church leaders did the same at Stuttgart, intending to provide everyday Germans with a model. He also believed that the confession would soften the hearts of the Allies.

The Reformers' Response

In content and style, Martin Niemöller took a different approach in countering criticism of the Stuttgart declaration. Unlike Asmussen's commentary, which was lengthy and heavily theological, Niemöller responded with concrete and personal examples. He spoke to the ordinary German in words they would understand and he did not pander to their prejudices as conservatives did. Where Asmussen described the language of the church as the equivalent of a foreign language, which he then used in his commentary, Niemöller spoke simply and clearly about confession and forgiveness. When he talked about German suffering, he did it in the context of the suffering that Germans inflicted on others. When he criticized the Allies' concept of collective guilt, he did so not to assure the population that they were blameless, but to replace it with the concept of collective responsibility. Most important, he elaborated on the political consequences of the church's complacency.

Niemöller adamantly denied that he legitimized the Allies' collective guilt thesis—as many of his critics charged. In a letter to Frau F., an opponent of the declaration, he maintained that he never said that all Germans without differentiation were guilty of Nazi crimes. While he defended his claim that the German people have no right to place all the guilt onto the evil Nazis "as if we were innocent," he agreed that "certainly, we are not all murderers, thieves, and sadists." Nevertheless, he continued, the church was not without guilt, because it did little or nothing to warn the people of the ruinous direction the nation was taking. "I do not exclude myself from this guilt, rather I expressly include myself every time because I was also silent when I should have spoken."[71] The difference between this type of statement, which Niemöller made over and over in lectures, and Asmussen's theology of sacrifice clearly distinguishes the reform-minded and conservative approaches to defending and interpreting the Stuttgart declaration.

As the most vocal and visible proponent of the need for confession, repentance, and reconciliation, Niemöller received the brunt of hate mail from Protestants dissatisfied with the Stuttgart declaration. What angered people the most about Niemöller was that as a victim *and* opponent of Nazism he was in the position to speak to the world as a symbol of German victimization and resistance. He was the model German victim, but he refused to play the role. Where they wanted a champion for their cause to defend them against the real and perceived injustices of the Allies, they instead saw in Niemöller a virtual spokesman for the Allies. This was an unfair depiction—for Niemöller was no pawn, but neither was he a defender of the German people. On several occasions he declared that there was no collective *guilt* but collective *liability* (*Kollektivhaftung*).[72] He introduced the concept of collective liability to differentiate his position from those who stressed that only individuals who committed atrocities needed to take responsibility for their actions. Collective liability meant that German responsibility for past actions had to be borne by all Germans, just as all Germans benefited from past German glories. Every citizen was bound or tied to that which took place in his or her country. In Frankfurt in early January 1946, Niemöller told a lecture audience: "This guilt weighs heavily on the German people and on the German name and on Christianity. For these things happened in our world and in our name."[73]

In order to demonstrate to the German people how everyone was guilty in the sense of collective liability, Niemöller spoke of his own guilt. Since he had spent the years 1937–45 in a concentration camp, this admission must have had a tremendous impact on his countrymen. Frequently in 1946, Niemöller dramatically recounted the day he returned to Dachau with his wife to show her the cell where he had been imprisoned. He described how they saw for the first time a plaque commemorating the 238,756 inmates murdered by the Nazis from 1933 to 1945. His wife, he explained, nearly collapsed as they stood reading the plaque. What caused Niemöller to shudder, however, was not the number of dead—that he already knew—but the dates, 1933–45. "My alibi accounted for the years 1937–45 . . . [but] God was not asking me where I had been from 1937 to 1945 but from 1933 to 1945 . . . and for those first four years I had no answer."[74] During those early years of the Third Reich Niemöller behaved, as did most of his colleagues in the Confessing Church, very much like the conservative elite in the economy, the military, and the Catholic Church. He supported many of Hitler's policies, opposed a few that affected his or the church's independence, and was ambivalent about the rest. This was his guilt.

The Confessing Church too, Niemöller asserted, was not free of guilt; it failed on many occasions to speak out when it should have. It never spoke out when tens of thousands of Communists were thrown into the concentration camps in 1933. It never spoke out when the Nazis murdered the physically and mentally ill. The church only found its voice when the Nazis turned on it.

> Can we say we are not to blame? The persecution of the Jews, the manner in which we treated the occupied countries, the activities in Greece, in Poland, in Czechoslovakia, or in the Netherlands, all of which we could read about in the papers? That hundreds of hostages were simply lined up against the wall because of sabotage committed by others? . . . I think we Christians from the Confessing Church have lots of reasons for saying: My guilt, my guilt.[75]

Niemöller asked clergymen: "What would have happened if fourteen thousand Protestant pastors and their parishes across Germany had defended the truth with their lives in 1933 and 1934?" Perhaps thirty to forty thousand Protestants would have been killed, he continued, but they would have saved 30 to 40 million lives. He insisted that the church was not fit to preach the Word of God until it had made peace with God and man, not only by confessing but also by doing penance: "We owe it to our Savior that we change our ways; otherwise we will find no peace."[76]

Niemöller's confrontational style met with vocal opposition from students at Erlangen University in late January 1946. At the invitation of the Protestant student association, Niemöller gave an address to approximately 1,200 students. They booed, hissed, and stomped their feet in protest when he mentioned German guilt or condemned the atrocities against Poles and Russians.[77] Under fire, Niemöller responded with more fire. When the Nuremberg trials were making daily headlines, Niemöller declared in a sermon in Herford near Bielefeld in May 1946:

> Six million Jews, an entire people was cold-bloodedly murdered in our midst and in our name. How shall we deal with this fact? If I should ask one of you here, he would say: "Ask the local party head about that. What could I have done?" And the local party head will refer me to the district party head, and so on and so forth until we get to the [Nuremberg] courtroom with the 22 defendants. And what about them? Well, we can hear that every day—they blame it all on just three men. Three individuals who fortunately are no longer around: Hitler, Himmler and Goebbels. Yes, my dear friends, these three are dead. But the legacy of six million dead cannot be placed together with them in the grave. We have to accept the burden of that legacy; after all, we also accepted all those more favorable (or at least what seemed more favorable) legacies their actions bestowed on us over the course of the years.[78]

Niemöller, in stark contrast to Asmussen and the conservatives, concretized and personalized the processes of confession and repentance and tried to block attempts by others on the council to spiritualize the declaration. For Niemöller, the church's guilt was twofold: guilt before both man and God. He admitted that after the First

World War he nearly left the church when he heard pastors talking about war guilt. And he understood the fear that a confession of guilt might give the Allies an excuse to punish the Germans, but he insisted all the same that "we cannot find peace with God if we refuse to confess our guilt to the people we have harmed."[79] Niemöller maintained that by emphasizing only penance before God, Christians hindered the process of reconciliation between men. For the confession to be genuine, it had to be made publicly to those who suffered as a result of the church's complacency.

Conservatives accused Niemöller of leaning too far to the side of the political and neglecting his duties as a spiritual leader. Yet it was not that he spoke as a political rather than a spiritual man—he did not. In fact, he always tied a confession of one's political guilt to Jesus' death on the cross. True, he believed the church was politically guilty because it had acted politically irresponsibly. It did not speak out against the state, against its horror. But as a Christian, he believed that the church's political sins would be forgiven if confessed and that this forgiveness was necessary both for the church to continue preaching and to open the way for the church in the future. Niemöller extolled the Stuttgart declaration as the "Freedom Charter" of the EKD: by confessing its guilt and renouncing its past ways, the EKD became free to speak to the outside world and be listened to. As he pointed out, a public confession had important consequences for the stature of the church: it provided an opportunity for a dialogue and exchange of ideas with the churches abroad.[80] On this matter Niemöller agreed with his conservative colleagues.

Niemöller warned that the rejection of the Stuttgart declaration and the carping about the plight of Germans was symptomatic of a lack of faith. Indeed, he recognized that the lack of enthusiasm for an open and genuine confession of guilt was tantamount to a rejection of God's promise to forgive those who confess and repent. We grumble about confession and repentance, Niemöller explained, because we are not content with God. We think God is unjust toward us because we are suffering and unhappy. In reality, however, we are unjust toward him because he sent his only Son to bring us peace and forgive our sins and yet we refuse to acknowledge our sins.[81]

Conclusions

Attacked as treasonous at home and lauded as courageous abroad, the October 1945 Stuttgart Declaration of Guilt was simultaneously a public relations disaster and a stunning achievement for the leadership of the post-Nazi Protestant Church. Domestically, many Germans accused its authors of fostering the myth of German collective guilt for Nazi crimes and of thereby providing the occupation powers with a justification for their harsh policies. Internationally, foreign church leaders credited the Stuttgart declaration with paving the way for the reconciliation between Germany and its former enemies. Presented in Stuttgart by the church's national leadership council to an audience of west European church leaders, the Stuttgart declaration provided a foundation for the renewal of ecumenical relations between the Protestant churches of Europe and Germany. By confessing that the church was in "a solidarity of guilt" with the German people and "through us [Germans] has endless suffering been brought to many peoples and countries," German church leaders satisfied foreign church leaders who sought a confession. At the same time, it enraged a large segment of the German population. The ensuing public imbroglio over the guilt question eventually engulfed the entire church.

The contradictory nature of the Stuttgart declaration as well as the variety of interpretations by parishioners, pastors, and church leaders, are evidence of the dilemma facing churchmen in postwar Germany. As the only German institution to survive the war intact, the church was pressured by a number of different sources, foreign and domestic, to act and speak in a certain way. Many Protestants at the parish level wanted their church leaders to intervene on their behalf with the occupying powers to lessen the hardship brought about by harsh, impractical, and "vengeful" occupation policies. Although many clergy were sympathetic, they, as men of the cloth, also took seriously their responsibility to call the nation to repentance. And finally, there was pressure from foreign church leaders for their German counterparts to demonstrate in word and deed that the German population, including the church, recognized its responsibility for human and material losses brought about by the war and its consequences. The Stuttgart declaration was an attempt to negotiate a solution that would satisfy these conflicting political and religious demands.

The two wings of the postwar church never found common ground in their understandings of the Stuttgart declaration. The primary division between those churchmen who viewed the church's guilt as religious and those who recognized the political irresponsibility of the church's conservative nationalism increased in 1946 and 1947. The reformers, who were never pleased with the religious wording of the declaration, went on in 1947 to write the Darmstadt statement, which focused critically on the church's political history and urged the church to abandon its conservative nationalism in favor of a more progressive politics. The conservatives worked equally diligently within the church to restore and retain traditional values, order, and stability.

Despite the debate and protest surrounding the Stuttgart Declaration of Guilt, it was published for the entire world to see; and as such, the Protestant Church went on record for acknowledging its guilt and the guilt of the German people. After the Stuttgart meeting the Protestant churches of Western Europe recognized the German church as an integral part of the postwar ecumenical movement and in so doing began the process of German integration into the West. The church's role in the process of reconciliation and integration, however, was not entirely constructive, as Bishop Wurm's message "To the Christians in England" demonstrates.

5

The Guilt of the Others

Bishop Wurm's Letter to English Christians

In dramatic contrast to reactions to the Stuttgart declaration, domestic responses to Bishop Theophil Wurm's open message, "To the Christians in England," were warm and enthusiastic (see appendix 5).[1] Written two months after the Stuttgart meeting, Wurm's outspoken critique of the Allies' occupation policy and his comparison of it to the Nazis' occupation policy were, for many Germans, long overdue. By challenging the Allies to acknowledge the unnecessary suffering they had caused and were continuing to cause innocent Germans, Wurm came to represent, for many demoralized Germans, the fearless leader who stood up to the enemy. "You expressed exactly what the German people feel and for this the people are deeply grateful," a man from Düsseldorf wrote in a letter to Wurm.[2] Another man declared, "I can assure you that all respectable people stand solidly behind you."[3] A woman whose home had been destroyed by Allied bombs stated simply, "It gave us hope"; and a doctor from Karlsruhe was so elated that he described listening to the letter read on the radio as "the happiest minutes of my life."[4] Repeatedly describing Wurm's missive as "manly" and "courageous," letters from hundreds of men and women across Germany expressed profound gratitude for Wurm's intercession.

For the men and women who wrote the bishop of Württemberg, the broadcasting of his letter by the BBC in late January 1946 was seen as a turning point for the church and Germany. They expressed a sense of relief that finally a moral and courageous voice had spoken on behalf of the German people and was standing up to the cruel and dehumanizing policy of the Allies. They heralded his response as *the* new beginning that Germans had been waiting for—not the new beginning or zero hour (*Stunde Null*) frequently touted in association with the "liberation" of Germany from Hitler's Third Reich. To the contrary, the new beginning declared by Wurm's admirers was understood as an end to the years of suffering, deprivation, dishonor, and humiliation caused by the Allied bombardment and occupation. Many Germans viewed Wurm's stance against the perceived hypocrisy of the enemy and in defense of Christian values and German honor as the first step toward regaining control over their fate and reestablishing their honor.

The pronounced emphasis in Wurm's letter on the guilt of the Allies marked the beginning of a broader campaign among church leaders to shift some of the burden of guilt to the Allies. Representative of this new direction was Hans Asmussen's 1946 text, "The Guilt of the Others," which argued that acknowledgment of German guilt did not preclude the responsibility of church leaders to hold the Allies responsible for their misdeeds.[5] Helmut Thielicke, a widely respected Lutheran theologian inside and outside Germany, demonstrated his support for this new direction in his Good Friday sermon in 1947, which touched off a debate between himself and the reform-minded theologian Hermann Diem, published in 1948.[6]

Wurm had written his open letter in response to the archbishop of Canterbury's message to the German people broadcast by BBC in late November 1945, which many Germans found patronizing and self-righteous.[7] In his carefully crafted response, addressed to all Christians in England, Wurm attempted to do the impossible: to guide the German Church between an occupying power looking for genuine signs of contrition and a home population looking for a spokesman to confront their critics. Drafted in mid-December 1945, Wurm's letter received support from the EKD council after it cut one long paragraph and made other minor revisions. The final draft indicates that he must have feared a repetition of the negative reactions to the Stuttgart declaration more than he feared censure by the Allies. By condemning the expulsion of Germans from the eastern territories, the dismantling of German factories, and the indiscriminate internment of former Nazi Party members, Wurm left no doubt where his loyalties lay.

Grassroots responses to Wurm's letter were the mirror opposite of the responses to the Stuttgart declaration. Although letter writers were now championing the EKD council rather than disparaging it, they addressed the same themes that ran throughout their critiques of the Stuttgart declaration. Recognizing that they now had a sympathetic ear in the person of Bishop Wurm, letter writers launched into tirades against the occupation powers, lambasted Niemöller for preaching about German guilt, accused the rest of Europe of a long history of anti-German behavior, repeated old myths of how Germany was stabbed in the back by leftists and Jews in the First World War, bemoaned the unchristian behavior of the Allies, disparaged the democratic system of government, and worried about the fate of German POWs in Soviet camps.[8]

Despite efforts by German church leaders in fall 1945 to convince the Western Allies that a significant portion of the German population, especially Christians in Germany, accepted responsibility for the recent past, foreign church leaders, occupation authorities, and journalists from abroad were all keenly aware of German obstinacy. Official surveys by the military governments as well as everyday experience in the occupation zones confirmed that the spirit of repentance expressed in the Stuttgart declaration was the exception rather than the rule.[9] In the foreign—especially British—print and broadcast media, reports of unrepentant Germans were aired side-by-side with new disclosures of German barbarity and coverage of the Nuremberg trial of Germany's major war criminals. Calls for severe and lasting punishment of Germany were pervasive.

The more reproachful the Allied-controlled news media was, the more obstinate and defensive Germans became. According to German pastors and parishioners, the primary reason they could not adopt a policy of repentance was that the Allies refused to acknowledge their share of responsibility for the destruction and despair across Europe. As long as Germans continued to perceive the victors as unrepentant and vengeful, they would remain unrepentant themselves. These mutual recriminations made it nearly impossible for the German church hierarchy to convince pastors and parishioners that many Christians abroad, including Bishop of Chichester George Bell, had accepted the Stuttgart declaration as a confession between Christian brothers and that some had even responded with their own confessions.[10]

The Archbishop of Canterbury's Broadcast to the German People

The archbishop of Canterbury's highly publicized radio address on 28 November 1945 seemed to confirm German fears that the Stuttgart declaration was not having the desired effect of generating a spirit of Christian brotherhood and forgiveness among the Allies. To be sure, the archbishop, Geoffrey Fisher, addressed the German people, as Barth had in his lectures to Germans, as a fellow Christian rather than as an enemy. Nevertheless, Fisher's message contained a sharp critique of German self-righteousness and a stern warning that the English, as well as the rest of the world, were waiting for genuine signs of repentance from within Germany. The style and tone of the archbishop's statement, although far less abrasive than Barth's, was that of a religion instructor giving a lesson on how to be a good Christian. It was a lesson Germans resented. Although the archbishop empathized with German tribulations, he reminded them about the cause of their plight:

> I know well the terribly hard conditions that you are suffering; but you are not alone in that. In the evil days your armies brought destruction to your neighbors, and they, along with you, suffer from the harsh process by which their liberation and yours was achieved. . . . For many years, willingly or unwillingly, you have pinned your faith to one man, to one doctrine; and they have led you to the abyss.[11]

Already suspicious of English intentions and bitter after two defeats at their hands in the past thirty years, many Germans detected a subtext to Fisher's broadcast—that Germans were collectively guilty of supporting Hitler and destroying Europe and that their suffering was their own fault. This was not the message German

Archbishop of Canterbury Geoffrey Fisher. The archbishop's open letter to the German people and Bishop Wurm's response increased hostility between the English and Germans in 1945 and 1946. *Photo courtesy of the Archive of the A. R. Wentz Library, Lutheran Theological Seminary of Gettysburg.*

Protestants had hoped to hear from the spokesman for Christian England. As a result, Fisher's few sympathetic words fell on deaf ears.

Fisher assured them that England and the other victorious nations were doing everything possible to distribute the available resources to those in need, "friend and foe alike." "Believe us in this country, that it is our earnest desire that as rapidly as possible the physical sufferings of all shall be relieved. . . . The Christian Church knows no barriers of nationhood, race or blood." Needless to say, few in Germany believed nationalism and revenge were not influencing English occupation policy and that it had not found a home even in the Anglican Church. The archbishop advised the German people to make a positive contribution to the present situation by repenting and building a new society founded on Christian faith and love: "Look to your churches . . . seek the old faith again, the faith of Christ, man's Lord and Saviour."

Although the faith many Germans had placed in Hitler ended with his suicide and Germany's total collapse in spring 1945, it was still not at all clear who or what would fill the void in fall 1945. Fisher perceived correctly the danger inherent in a bitter and disillusioned population groping for direction. The German people had rejected Hitler and the Nazis, but Fisher knew they continued to hold strongly to the convictions that brought Hitler to power: they were drawn to nationalism; they desired strong and decisive leadership; and they believed hostile neighbors surrounded Germany. For Fisher, the solution was to steer Germans back to the church. It is ironic that many Germans accepted his advice, not to counter what Fisher saw as dangers, but because many church leaders were ultranationalist and many Germans shared their form of patriotism.

Due to the bitter resentment that many Germans harbored toward England, Fisher's address presented the EKD council with a dilemma. In a letter to his colleagues the day after the broadcast, Asmussen expressed the fear that the archbishop's address would only further inflame an increasingly frustrated and desperate German population. Germans would certainly want a forceful response, Asmussen believed. Patronizing advice from the very people who had months earlier relentlessly bombed German cities was not likely to receive a warm welcome from tired and hungry Germans. In his letter to church leaders, Asmussen sought advice on how the EKD should respond to an address by the prelate of the English church. "Does the speech mean that the policy of the [English] state is receiving support in a religious address? Or can one hope that here a beginning is being made to ban and to overcome the spirit of force and revenge through the spirit of the Gospel?" What should the German response be? Who should draft the response? Since there was no recognized spokesman for the German people, Asmussen believed it was the church that should respond in their name. Such a response had to be carefully crafted, however, since Germans were likely to interpret Fisher's speech as a sign that the English church and state were working together to subjugate the German people. Although Asmussen did not want to fan the flames of near-unanimous contempt for the English, neither did he want the council to appear too accepting of Allied interpretations of the German situation. The scathing responses to the Stuttgart declaration had made this point loud and clear:

> The conviction that English Christendom is hypocritical has worked itself deep into the German psyche, and not only since yesterday. This conviction must be destroyed. On the other hand, the occupation authorities do not make it easy for the people in Germany to hear the voice of Christ in this message of the Archbishop. We are not called, as churches, to gloss over the mistakes of the occupation authorities. Consequently, it is urgently necessary that the churches be clear regarding the position that they must take towards this address.

Asmussen concluded with the observation that Fisher's broadcast was clearly not a response to the Stuttgart declaration. In fact, Fisher never mentioned it. This silence, perhaps more than anything Fisher did say, affronted German church leaders, who had hoped that some good would come from the declaration of guilt issued a month and a half earlier. Asmussen acknowledged his disappointment to his colleagues: "We certainly cannot ask that there be a response so few weeks after [the Stuttgart meeting]. But Christians in Germany are waiting for such a response."[12]

In the northernmost regional churches of Schleswig and Holstein, the former bishop of Schleswig, Eduard Völkel, and the soon-to-be bishop of the Lutheran Church of Holstein, Wilhelm Halfmann, confirmed Asmussen's suspicion that Fisher's address would whip up harsh feelings toward England.[13] German Protestants, Völkel contended, associated the former archbishop of Canterbury, William Temple, with strong support for the Bolsheviks during the war, the bombing raids, and the barbarization of the war. The perception that English Christianity was fundamentally hypocritical was unlikely to subside as long the English maintained their malicious occupation policies and continued to give the German Communist Party freedom to develop in the British zone in Germany.

Seconding much of what Völkel stated, Bishop Halfmann described the popular view of English Christianity as the "embodiment of pharisaism." "The Pharisee," he wrote, "doesn't strike his own breast, but rather strikes the breast of the other." The perception of the English as always pointing the finger of blame at someone else, Halfmann contended, was reinforced by their constant demand for more breast beating by the Germans, and it led Germans to immediately dismiss as false and hypocritical whatever the English said.[14]

Just as the German church spoke with a new voice at Stuttgart, Halfmann declared, it was time for the English to speak with a new voice as well. Convinced that the religious confession made at Stuttgart had been misused politically by the English, Halfmann wanted the EKD council to make it clear to the English that Germans were understandably suspicious of the motives of the archbishop's call for further confessions:

> One must tell the English Church that it has no idea how difficult it was to speak as Christians [at Stuttgart] because their religious judgment that we are guilty agrees with the political judgment of the English government. In the address of the Archbishop it is impossible for the Christians of Germany to differentiate the voice of Christ from the voice of Caesar.

Halfmann also wanted English Christians to know that the anti-Christian spirit that reigned during the Second World War found its manifestation first in Bolshevism and later in the Allied leadership of the war and their postwar occupation policies. "Today in England they forget that the Germans who detested and fought National Socialism did so because they recognized it as a form of Bolshevism." In this statement he repeated a common theme among German conservatives, namely that National Socialism and Bolshevism were two sides of the same coin and that the majority of Germans despised both.[15] By Halfmann's logic, the coupling of National Socialism with Bolshevism and the Western Allies with the Bolsheviks through their alliance with the Soviet Union led to the implication that the Western occupation powers had more in common with these extremist ideologies than the German people.

Halfmann's and Völkel's views arrived too late to influence the EKD council's response, but Asmussen assured them that many of their concerns had been addressed.[16]

Bishop Wurm's Message to Christians in England

Wurm's open letter to English Christians was more tactful than Völkel's and Halfmann's but was nevertheless forceful and assertive. Parishioners were correct in reading Wurm's letter as a rebuttal of the archbishop's claims. Although the first part of Wurm's letter contained all the acknowledgments of German responsibility necessary to avoid outright accusations by the English that Germans remained unrepentant nationalists, it could not be mistaken for another confession. First, he thanked the archbishop for speaking to the German people as a brother and for not propagating black-and-white images of the victor as purely good and the vanquished as purely evil. Following the archbishop's lead, Wurm declared that Christians in Germany "affirm and accept in the same way [as English Christians] our responsibility and concern for the whole world." And Wurm claimed that "under the tyranny of National Socialism we refused to abandon this sense of responsibility and concern."[17]

Even at this early stage in his message one detects, as many English did, an attempt to portray Germany as one country among many responsible for the atrocities of World War II. This marked a slight retreat from the Stuttgart declaration, where the church acknowledged German responsibility for the "endless suffering" brought to "many peoples and countries." In contrast, the recognition of responsibility in Wurm's message was so general as to be virtually meaningless—acknowledging only "responsibility and concern for the whole world." The only mention of Nazi atrocities was an opaque reference that gave the impression that the church was on the front lines of the resistance movement: "It was a deep source of sorrow to us that we could not effectively prevent the gross ill treatment of other peoples and countries, and we were hated by the National Socialist leaders quite particularly because they were well aware of our condemnation of their misdeeds."

It is possible that Wurm felt it unnecessary to repeat what had been said at Stuttgart. But it is more likely that he viewed his message to English Christians as having an entirely different purpose from the declaration of guilt expressed in October. His purpose was to draw attention to the degree of suffering in Germany brought about by unjust Allied policies and to demonstrate that they were not significantly different from Nazi crimes.

Wurm's discussion of Allied misdeeds was part of a wider attempt by conservatives to interpret Nazism as one of many consequences of a general trend toward secularization in Europe. "We seek for the causes of what was done," Wurm declared, "not only in National Socialism, but also in a long history of estrangement from God and of backsliding from Christ, not least in the worldliness which more and more invaded our church." For this reason, Wurm readily agreed with the archbishop that the task ahead for Germany was to "return to God and His commandments."

In response to the archbishop's charge that Germany was responsible for its own misery by starting and conducting a brutal war, Wurm did acknowledge that Germany's misfortune was a consequence of its own transgressions, but he did so in a way that highlighted German suffering:

> We know that our cities would not be lying in ruins now, and our fellow countrymen would not be dying of hunger now, and our soldiers would not be languishing in the prisoner-of-war camps now, if millions of other human beings had not had to undergo the same suffering in earlier years. We know that there is no lack of people in other countries that think that whatever happens to the Germans cannot be bad enough. Far be it from us to attempt to make excuses for any act of injustice that was done to other peoples, far be it from us to attempt to explain it away.

Despite his promise not to make excuses or try to explain away German guilt, Wurm proceeded to do exactly that.

In the second half of his message, Wurm blamed the Allies for Germany's woes. He spelled out their anti-Christian behavior in some detail and likened it to the Nazis. "The military conquest and occupation of our country," Wurm stated, "was accompanied *by the very same acts of violence* against the civilian population about which such just complaint has been made in the countries of the Allies" (italics mine). He also criticized appeals by foreign authorities to the German people to work more vigorously to solve their own problems. These appeals "can only sound a mockery," Wurm maintained, when the Allies take away the limited raw materials and machines that would permit postwar German industry to move forward. Even more accusatory, Wurm continued, "To pack the German people into a still more narrow space, to cut off as far as possible the material basis of their very existence, is no different, in essentials, from Hitler's plan to stamp out the existence of the Jewish race." This type of treatment, he said, raised the serious danger that Germans would react as they did after Versailles:

> It has happened once before in history that the attempt has been made to secure peace by taking away from the vanquished the possibility of rising again by the imposition of enormous burdens of reparations and by the attempt to cut off territories of great economic importance. But experience shows that these measures only awakened the spirit of resistance and made the German people inclined to be a ready recipient of the ideology of National Socialism. If the political authorities of today act according to the same recipe, and seek to make Germany as small and weak as possible, and its

American churchmen Samuel McCrea Cavert (*left*) and Sylvester C. Michel-felder (*right*) with Bishop Theophil Wurm in 1945 on a trip to Germany to encourage reconciliation and to aid in the reconstruction of the churches. *Photo courtesy of the Archive of the A. R. Wentz Library, Lutheran Theological Seminary of Gettysburg.*

neighbors as great and strong as possible, then the evil spirits of revenge and retribution will not be banished from the world.

In the draft of Wurm's letter that the EKD council discussed at its third meeting in Frankfurt on 13 December 1945, there was an entire paragraph criticizing denazification policy and comparing the tactics the Nazis used to silence the churches with the tactics used by the occupation authorities to silence church leaders' objections to their policies. Although this section would certainly have pleased many Germans, church leaders feared it was too strong a critique of the Allied military governments and so cut it from the final draft.

As it was, Wurm's radio address caused no small reaction in England. The BBC aired a number of letters from English respondents, and a BBC commentator, Lindley Fraser, read his own response, titled "Wurming One's Way." After challenging point by point the historical accuracy of Wurm's understanding of Germany's place in European history and in particular his interpretation of the Versailles treaty,

Fraser accused Wurm of threatening the victorious powers with "revenge and reprisals." "I should have thought that a true Christian, if he needs help and forgiveness from his fellow men, would appeal to the Christian charity of the latter and would not try to frighten them into forgiving and forgetting." Fraser went on to say that Wurm's address only confirmed for many Englishmen that Germany was not to be trusted and that it must be kept weak and restrained.[18]

The BBC, in turn, received a flood of angry letters from Germans excoriating Fraser, as well as an official response from Asmussen contending that Fraser and much of the English population had misunderstood the intent of Wurm's message. Asmussen's measured response tried to spin Wurm's letter as a statement about the obligation of all Christians to accept and acknowledge their nation's guilt as a result of the war. He defended, however, Wurm's charge that occupation policy, in particular the dismantling of German industry, was unjust and would only lead to an increase in bitter feelings among Germans.[19]

In a long letter to the archbishop of Canterbury on New Year's Day 1946, Asmussen described Wurm's letter as "our response," indicating that the EKD council took responsibility for it. He gently explained to Fisher that every utterance by foreign church leaders to the German people was eagerly anticipated in the hope that it would carry a message of Christian charity and forgiveness. In that regard, Asmussen hinted that the archbishop's November message was disappointing because it was not understood by the German clergy or laity to carry a clear message of support or forgiveness. Asmussen maintained that the intent of Wurm's letter was simply to inform the English of indisputable facts: the German people's plight was extremely desperate, and the occupation powers were partially to blame for this. German church leaders, he contended, had a dual obligation to encourage confession and repentance *and* to alleviate physical want and despair. The Stuttgart declaration did the former and the letter to English Christians, the latter.[20]

Grassroots Protestants Applaud Their Bishop

Asmussen's diplomatic letters to the BBC and to the archbishop of Canterbury in no way mirrored the one-sided letters sent to Wurm by clergymen and laypersons across Germany. In fact, with the exception of a letter to the editor of the *Neue Hamburger Presse* by an astute student, the few critics—and there were very few—scolded Wurm for being too soft on the Allies. More typical was a letter of support from Herr R., who described himself as "a little man from the people." Herr R. expressed his great admiration for Wurm's frankness and honesty and expressed his hope that there were more men like Wurm in the church. "Today there are many people, who at first viewed the Allies as liberators, who now understand that the war was against all Germans not only against the Nazis." Yes, he conceded, the Nazi leadership needed to stand trial, but locking up thousands of former Nazi

Party members and "condemning millions to lifelong suffering" by denying them the necessities of life would only generate "eternal hate." He felt the current suffering was all the penance necessary from the German side. "I would like so much to speak with you about so many things because you enjoy my complete trust," Herr R. concluded.[21]

The admiration, respect, and awe evident in Herr R.'s letter and others had its origin in the belief that Wurm had taken a serious risk by speaking so openly. In the context of the Nuremberg trials, where the victors sat in judgment of the vanquished, many Germans perceived the Allies as doling out punishments indiscriminately. Herr H. from Herrsching applauded Wurm's courageous statement, noting that "the dangers that can follow from a simple listing of the facts is well known to all Germans." He saw Wurm's message as the beginning of a bold attempt by Germans to regain control over their fate and to fight hypocrisy and lies with truth and justice.[22] Several writers, including Herr H., compared Wurm's standing up to the Allies with standing up to Hitler and the Gestapo during the Third Reich. They portrayed Wurm, as he portrayed himself in letters and statements, as a great man who took a stand against injustice and lies, whether the origin of the abuse was the left Jacobinism of the Bolsheviks or right Jacobinism of the Nazis. By challenging the Allied interpretation of guilt and innocence and seeking to restore a sense of honor and dignity to the "trampled and tortured" German population, Wurm had earned the undying respect of many Germans.

Another common sentiment expressed by Wurm's supporters was disgust with the Western Allies for professing to be Christian nations when, in fact, they were only using Christianity as a veil behind which to carry out their oppressive occupation policies. Not surprisingly, the obvious contradiction in calling for German church leaders to intercede in the political sphere on behalf of the German population while at the same time accusing the Allies of masking their political agenda in religious trappings did not register with most letter writers. A woman from Wiesbaden, who wrote a very detailed three-page, single-spaced rebuttal of Lindley Fraser's broadside against Wurm, distinguished between the genuine Christian spirit evident in Wurm's letter and the *realpolitik* of the "so-called Christian nations."[23] Other letter writers specifically mention the broadcast of the archbishop of Canterbury as an example of the pulpit being used for political purposes. They resented that the leader of English Christianity would use biblical language to legitimize victors' justice.[24]

Some letter writers went so far as to portray a neat juxtaposition between the materialistic and godless Allies and the faithful Christians in Germany. The problem, however, with juxtaposing the bad Christians, who bombed Dresden and starved German children, with the good Christians in Germany was obvious. Germany was, after all, a Christian nation; and it was responsible for the mass slaughter of millions of innocent men, women, and children. It was one thing for Germans to appropriate for themselves the status of victim—they *were* suffering—but it was entirely another to continue to maintain the nineteenth- and early-twentieth-century notion that Germany's status as a Christian nation was unique and held a special place in God's salvation plan. To make this argument plausible one had to either deny the Nazi past, which some letter writers did, or blame the atrocities on a small group of brown-shirted fanatics who hijacked the country for twelve years, which most, following Wurm's example, did. To this latter argument Wurm and his supporters added the exculpatory caveat that had it not been for the abuse of Germany after the First World War, these fanatics would never have found support in a Christian nation. Thus, the blame ultimately lay at the feet of the Allies and their unchristian behavior over several decades.

Other letter writers combined their critiques of the professed Christianity of the Allies with a critique of European democracy. A refugee and former Nazi Party member from lower Silesia who wrote Wurm in early February 1946 began his letter in the typical praiseworthy manner:

> The Lord God blesses your courageous intercession on behalf of tortured humanity, especially those who are innocent of recent world events. With a feeling of liberation and a sigh of relief . . . suffering humanity . . . has heard your letter to Evangelical Christians in England. It is my firm opinion that thousands, if not millions, would express their thanks if they were in position to do so.

It was extremely unfortunate, the Silesian believed, that only the angry and vengeful occupying forces, especially the democracies, were heard on the radio and in the newspapers. After all, it was people living in democracies who were the most to blame: "They were the ones who had all the power. They could and should have stopped it. . . . Who then is more guilty in this last war, those who really knew and had all the powerful means at their disposal in a modern democratic state or the little German people (*die kleinen deutschen Menschen*), who at the time experienced an ever-worsening economic chaos?" Now, in the name of democracy, the Allies were using the same methods of torture against Germans, he contended, that had been used against the Jews. The voices of real Christians, who were filling the churches in Germany, were too afraid, he surmised, to openly oppose the policies of the military governments. For this reason he urged the "really important men," especially the clergy, to voice the concerns of ordinary people and bring about a remedy to the situation. In the name of Christianity, he called on the churches to bring this persecution to an end: "The hour of the Christian churches has arrived! God the Almighty blesses you in the struggle against injustice and inhumanity, against everything evil and for the benefit of justice."[25]

A school principal from a primarily Catholic region of Westphalia reported to Wurm that he and many of his neighbors had heard Wurm's letter on the radio and later read it in the local paper. Although a Nazi Party member since 1938, the headmaster described himself as "an inner opponent" (*innerer Gegner*) of National Socialism. Wurm's message gave him a great sense of relief, he explained, because he had begun to question the stance taken by the church since Germany's collapse. He was unhappy with church leaders for giving insufficient attention in their sermons and statements to the terrible costs Germans were paying for their liberation from Nazism. The church, he suspected, was involved in a quid pro quo with the Allies:

> The freedom and advantages, which the representatives of the church receive from the occupation authorities, and the church's close connection with them, gives one an embarrassing impression. Which side is the church on? Was Hitler right for opposing the church? I've heard many comments along these lines.

Even his students, he claimed, were so fed up with the church and the tone of the sermons since the collapse that they stopped attending mass. He asked rhetorically:

> Are the Germans alone to blame? Didn't Russia also take part in the attack on Poland and lead its own attack against tiny Finland? Weren't institutions similar to concentration camps established earlier by our eastern neighbors? Was it humane and Christian to pour fire from the sky onto German cities, especially when it had no military purpose whatsoever? Is the treatment of either our POWs, who are cut off from all contact with their homes, or the deportation of our comrades from the east humane or Christian?

For all these reasons, "it had been urgently necessary," he asserted "for the church, after its self-accusations and confessions of guilt to point to the guilt of the other." Not only would pointing out the faults of the Allies relieve Germans of some of the burden they were forced to carry, but it would also contribute to truthfulness and consequently peace. Wurm's letter, he declared, was "a beginning in this direction" and for that reason many Germans thanked him.[26]

A woman from Freiburg, Frau B., told Wurm that she had heard his address to the English by chance on the radio and was proud that someone from the educated class was willing to take the risk to proclaim to the rest of the world that the Germans, despite everything, still had their honor. Describing Wurm's efforts on behalf of the persecuted in Germany as a "Christian duty," she regretted that far too few Catholic and Evangelical clergymen were doing their duty. She felt it was an absolute scandal that the Allies treated all Nazi Party members as criminals and took from them their apartments, furniture, clothes, and jobs. Moreover, it was simply not fair that the Allies designated only those who had been in concentration camps as "victims of fascism." "Our soldiers also belong in this category," she concluded.[27]

Whether or not Frau B. was aware of Wurm's intercessions on behalf of Nazi Party members is not clear, but certainly many Germans knew of Wurm's critiques of the denazification process and in particular of his displeasure with the undifferentiated manner in which the Allies treated former Nazis. In early February Wurm had come under fire in the *Frankfurter Rundschau* for attempting to intercede on behalf of his son Hans, a doctor in Frankfurt, who had joined the NSDAP in 1922. Hans Wurm was sentenced to a one-year incarceration for failing to acknowledge his Nazi Party membership in the denazification questionnaire (*Fragebogen*), which the Allies required all Germans to fill out.[28] Wurm responded to the accusations by saying, "What I did for my son, has been nothing else than what I undertook in favor of a great many people of all ranks, namely, I requested that he was not judged by his party membership but by his real attitude and mind."[29] In order to stress that Nazi Party membership was a poor indicator of responsibility for Nazi crimes, Wurm insisted that even after his son joined the party his son's opinions and his own never differed significantly. Never a Nazi Party member himself, Wurm was sympathetic with many of its policies and thus could identify with men like his son who had joined and were now under scrutiny by the occupation forces.

While Wurm's defense of former Nazi Party members and his letter rebutting the archbishop of Canterbury increased his popularity with many Germans, a desire to elevate his stature was not his only motivation. An astute medical student, Richard Degkwitz, in a provocative letter to the *Neue Hamburger Presse* in late February 1946 perceived Wurm's real intentions. He charged the bishop with rewriting history by misrepresenting the facts and boldly shifting the burden of guilt by equating the lesser violations of the Allies with the greater violations of the Germans. Of the hundreds of archived responses to Wurm's letter to English Christians, Degkwitz's stands alone. Degkwitz wrote that Wurm's letter elicited in him both joy and shame: joy that someone was taking seriously the problems confronting Germany's reconstruction, and shame that the tone of Wurm's letter indicated his desire to gain popularity. Degkwitz even suggested that Wurm was writing, not to Christians in England, but to Germans at home, who were only too happy to applaud Wurm's mollifying message. Reaping praise from disgruntled Germans was as easy as it was unsightly; all one needed to do, charged Degkwitz, was to inaccurately describe the injustices of the Allies as greater than the injustices of the Nazis: "It seems to me . . . particularly bold, to characterize the measures against National Socialism as a greater injustice than the extermination of millions of men in German concentration camps." Degkwitz was equally critical of Wurm's claim that the Allies were intentionally denying Germans enough food to survive. The truth, he said, was that the English were forced to ration their supplies of food in order to provide for Germans. Degkwitz concluded by expressing regret that Wurm's letter had played into the hands of those in Germany who had the most to gain from distorting the facts and equalizing German and Allied misdeeds.[30]

The line of reasoning in Degkwitz's letter was analogous to that used by Karl Barth in a letter to a critic in 1945 in which Barth charged that it was a disservice to Germans to encourage them to rebuild their nation on the premise that they were primarily victims of the past years.[31] Not surprisingly, Degkwitz's accusation that Wurm distorted the facts in order to increase his popularity among unrepentant

Nationalists was not well received by Wurm's supporters. Some labeled him a traitor. Others chalked up his ignorance and disrespect to youthfulness and offered patronizing lessons in civics, history, and patriotism. One flag-waver from Hamburg began and ended his response to Degkwitz with the quote, "Right or wrong—my country!"[32]

Wurm's "To the Christians in England," marked a turning point in the church's thinking about how to publicly present the past and the church's role in that past. Although the revelations about Nazi barbarity continued to make front-page news around the world, the initial shock, which spurred churchmen to issue the Stuttgart declaration, had worn off. When pressed, church leaders could point to the Stuttgart declaration to prove that the church had fulfilled its task to encourage parishioners to confess and repent. Now was the time for the gospel, for forgiveness; the time for punishment, the law, had passed. "Ought we not," Wurm asked rhetorically, "in the presence and in the name of Him who died for our sins, to make a covenant to proclaim the word forgiveness rather than vengeance?"

Wurm was not the only church leader to claim that just as the church had taken a leading role in holding the state accountable during the Nazi period, now the church had an obligation to hold the military governments accountable in the postwar period. At the same time that Wurm's letter was causing a sensation in February 1946, Asmussen was circulating among members of the EKD council his twelve-page text, *Die Schuld der Andern* ("The Guilt of the Others"). As a member of the council and president of the church chancellery, he said he could no longer be silent about the injustices committed by the Allies. The Stuttgart declaration, Asmussen declared, was only half the truth. The other half he described vividly and graphically: the violent expulsion of the Germans from the eastern territories; brutal treks to the west by east German refugees in the middle of winter; the raping of German women and girls; starving and emaciated POWs scavenging for potato peels in Soviet concentration camps; starvation diets in the French zone consisting of 875 calories per day; Allied soldiers living comfortably in German homes; abuses of the Geneva Conventions; the intentional destruction of the German economy; and the indiscriminate internment of former Nazi Party members.[33]

A year later, in an infamous Good Friday sermon preached in the Church of St. Mark in Stuttgart, Helmut Thielicke, a professor of theology in Tübingen and director of the theological office of the Church of Württemberg, declared: "I can no longer accept the Church's public confession of sin, in which I myself unreservedly join, so long as this other thing is not said publicly, and as plainly and relentlessly as befits the speech of disciples of Christ." He went on to describe the Allies denazification program as "not only unjust" but "murder of the soul and of faith."[34] He contended that the injustices perpetrated by the Allies against German refugees, prisoners of war, and others were endangering the spiritual recovery of Germany and opening the way to nihilism. When Thielicke referred repeatedly in

Dismissed by the Nazis from his professorship at the University of Heidelberg in 1940, Helmut Thielicke, a renowned Lutheran theologian at the University of Tübingen after the war, became a prominent adversary of Karl Barth, Hermann Diem, and the Dahlemites. *Photo courtesy of the Archive of the Protestant Academy Bad Boll, Germany.*

his sermon to "the guilt of the church for its silence and complicity," he meant the church's silence and complicity in regard to the atrocities endured by Germans. Thielicke received hundreds of letters responding, most of them positively, to publication of his sermon.[35]

Wurm's letter, Asmussen's text, and Thielicke's sermon served one purpose: to initiate a more public and political role by the church in defending the German people against what conservatives perceived as victors' justice. Their reform-minded colleagues were also interested in developing a new political role for the church, but it became painfully obvious that their visions of the church and its role in society differed considerably.

6

On the Political Course of Our People

"The Confessing Church must have a political policy, we must have a political position as Christians, we need to say today that we are taking a new path."[1] The Lutheran churchman who made this clarion call was Hans Iwand, a member of the reform-minded council of brethren (*Bruderrat*) and an ally of the Dahlemite wing of the former Confessing Church. With the encouragement and assistance of Karl Barth and fellow reformers at the council of brethren's July 1947 meeting in Darmstadt, Iwand composed the first draft of the Darmstadt statement—officially entitled "Statement by the Council of Brethren of the Evangelical Church of Germany Concerning the Political Course of Our People" (see appendix 6).[2] The final draft, a product of much discussion and debate within the council of brethren, was both a confession of guilt for what they saw as the church's politically conservative past and a redefinition of the church's social and political mission in light of its accommodation with the Nazi regime. In the Stuttgart Declaration of Guilt the church had confessed its guilt, albeit vaguely and weakly; at Darmstadt the brethren council delineated where the church erred *politically* and resolved that that path would not be followed again. Although there had been some discussion within the brethren council about drafting a statement that would explicitly address the plight of Jews in Germany, neither Jews nor the "Jewish question" received mention in the one-and-a-half-page Darmstadt statement.[3]

Thus, the long-simmering debate among German Protestants over the relationship between the Protestant Church and politics reached a feverish pitch in August 1947 with the issuing of the highly controversial Darmstadt statement. The politically leftist nature of this statement as well as its theological challenge to traditional Lutheranism incurred the wrath of influential conservative churchmen and theologians such as Hans Asmussen and Walter Künneth. The polar responses within the church to the Darmstadt statement are highly significant because they provided the political and theological arguments that churchmen would use in staking out their positions in response to the Cold War.

Authored by the council of brethren, the leadership of the reformist wing of the postwar church, the Darmstadt statement brought to a head a tangle of irreconcilable political and theological differences that illuminated two different visions of the church in the postwar era. An early manifestation of Cold War polemics within the church, it set the stage for future showdowns between conservatives and reform-minded churchmen over German unification, East-West relations, and rearmament. The authors of the Darmstadt statement, all influenced by Swiss Reformed theologian Karl Barth, made a startling break with the traditional Lutheran practice of passive obedience to conservative civil authority. They asserted that the 400-year-old Lutheran tendency to back conservative and authoritarian political regimes contributed to the church's wholly inadequate response to Nazism. The council of brethren declared, "The alliance of the Church with the old and conventional conservative powers has taken heavy revenge upon us. . . . We rejected the right of revolution and tolerated and justified the evolution toward absolute dictatorship."[4] The choice of wording in all seven theses suggested that the men on the brethren council had no intention of building bridges to the conservative majority in the church.

Describing the recent political aims and actions of Germans as "false and evil," the first of the seven theses acknowledged that the German church had sinned and thereby alienated itself from God. In order to become reconciled with God, the church and the German people must seek absolution from their guilt by confessing their sins and following the call of Jesus Christ. Only after confessing, repenting, and receiving absolution could the church properly hear, receive, preach, and fulfill God's central message of reconciliation in the world.

Theses two through five explained how the German people and the church became separated from God by substituting nationalist ideals for God's message of forgiveness and reconciliation. Reconciliation between God and man, however, led to a practical commitment to the reconciliation between men of antagonistic nations and classes. As a consequence, the authors interpreted God's message as a call to action by engaging in social, political, and economic programs to benefit the poor and underprivileged. In fact, thesis five offered the very radical suggestion that, had the church not spurned Marxist economic theory, it would have been reminded of its obligations to the social and communal needs of society. And even more radical, the thesis strongly suggested that the Marxist ideal of a classless society designed to satisfy those needs was very much in accord with the gospel of God's coming kingdom.

In theses six and seven the authors resolved to bring about fundamental change in a politically conservative church by insisting on a new mission. The new mission was to promote measures that would ease the tension in domestic and international relations brought about by Nazi rule, the war, and its aftermath, and to fashion a new community of Christians with its socioeconomic and political needs taken fully into account. No longer was the church to remain passive in public affairs. "What we need is a return to God and to the service of our neighbor, through the power of the death and resurrection of Jesus Christ." The final thesis addressed the cynicism and despair prevalent in the post-1945 period that might revive a yearning for authoritarian political schemes of the past. The council of brethren urged a sober, responsible reconstruction of state institutions "that shall work for justice and for the welfare, peace and reconciliation of the nations."

The minutes of the brethren council's discussions and the highly critical responses to the Darmstadt statement attest to the highly polarized atmosphere within the Protestant Church two years after the end of the war.[5] By calling for fundamental changes in the church's theological and political convictions—changes resolutely opposed by the conservative majority—the council indicated it was willing to sacrifice the fragile unity established at Treysa in order to oppose a restoration of the church along politically conservative lines. Particularly contentious was the reformers' redefinition of the church's mission to include political activism in the public sphere. Although the reformers who issued the Darmstadt statement represented a minority in the church, they forced the conservative majority to respond publicly to their critique of Luther's doctrine of two kingdoms and their vision of a socially conscious and politically engaged church. By declaring that a truly rejuvenated and revitalized church must start with a forthright admission of the church's "false and evil ways," the Darmstadt statement refueled the unresolved debate begun at the end of the war between conservatives and reformers about the nature of confessing one's guilt and the nature of guilt itself.

The central message of the statement's seven theses, the need to foster reconciliation between God and man and between people of different nations, classes, and political orientations, appears, at first, uncontroversial. However, the reformers' contention that the church itself contributed to the alienation of man from God by virtue of its theological doctrine and conservative nationalist politics elicited strong condemnation in the conservative Lutheran camp. Moreover, the conservative majority was incensed by the council's assertion that dogmatic anticommunism and conservative Lutheranism had restricted the moral leadership of the church during the Nazi era and was jeopardizing the process of repentance, reconciliation, and reformation in the postwar period.

Churchmen from eastern Germany, such as Kurt Scharf and Gerhard Jacobi of Berlin, were no less displeased. Criticism from these easterners was especially alarming to Iwand and his colleagues since many of these churchmen had sided unequivocally with the Confessing Church during the Nazi era and now served on their regional councils of brethren. Having experienced the brutality of Soviet troops in 1945 and now living in close proximity to Soviet occupation forces, Scharf and Jacobi expressed shock over the council's defense of facile Marxist political and economic theory as well as disappointment that the council failed to recognize that the Soviet secret police were as insidious a threat to Christianity as the Gestapo had been. Thus, a broad range of churchmen, from theologians Hans Asmussen and Walter Künneth to former Dahlemites from the Soviet zone of occupation, subjected the radical statement to trenchant criticism for both political and theological reasons.

The authors of the Darmstadt statement contended that the new mission they championed was the logical outcome of the theology of the 1934 Barmen declaration.[6] In fact, the Darmstadt statement marked a significant radicalization of the fifth thesis of the Barmen declaration. It rejected the common interpretation of the Lutheran doctrine of two kingdoms according to which the mission of the church was to administer to people's spiritual needs, and the mission of the state was to maintain law and order in civil society. According to this interpretation, participation in the political sphere, especially as a critic of state policy, was not the domain of the church. The church should support the state in its task to maintain law and order but not actively campaign for one political party or another. For many of the reformers, the church-state dualism at the core of the doctrine of two kingdoms was partially to blame for the church's failure to condemn the Third Reich in toto. Building on Barth's Reformed theology, especially his assertion that obedience to Christ included rendering political judgments based on the gospel, the reformers resolved that the church must play a more active and critical role in civil society in the future. In short, they overcame the narrow definition of ethics espoused by orthodox Lutherans.

By spring 1947 it became abundantly clear to Niemöller and his reform-minded colleagues that their message of repentance, reconciliation, and reformation was being shunted aside by many Protestants and replaced by the jargon and slogans of Cold War politics. By shifting the debate away from guilt and responsibility for Nazi rule to the containment of Soviet communism, conservative Protestant leaders hoped to restore the church to its old role as the bulwark against communism. Intentionally or not, attention to the brutality of Soviet communism in the eastern territories had the effect of distracting attention away from Germany's wartime atrocities in eastern Europe.

The council of brethren feared that the church was not drawing the correct lessons from its mistakes during the Nazi era. In the context of the emerging Cold War and the receding concern for the Nazi past, the reformers believed a clear statement repudiating the church's inadequate response to Nazism was now necessary. Complementing a concrete confession of past errors, the Darmstadt statement represented a fundamental transformation in the church's mission—from one of private piety and conservative nationalism to one of reconciliation, social concern, and critical engagement in the political sphere.

Issued in the early days of the Cold War, the Darmstadt statement was seen by conservative Lutherans as both an abandonment of traditional Lutheranism and a strident call for the church to support radical left-wing political causes. For the reformers, political engagement and social activism were the only way to rectify the church's accommodation to policies that had led to Hitler's rise to power. While conservatives, on the other hand, admitted that the church had erred during the Hitler era and needed to confess, they did not believe it was necessary to change their political or theological commitments in light of those errors.

Ostensibly, the Darmstadt statement was a political tract. Its official title, "Statement by the Council of Brethren of the Evangelical Church of Germany Concerning the Political Course of Our People," suggested as much. Although much of its subject matter and rhetoric were political—and intentionally so—the bitter enmity that the statement elicited from conservatives was aimed as much at its underlying Reformed (Calvinist) theology as at its radical politics. The roots of this theological discord were firmly embedded in the centuries-old debates between Lutherans and Calvinists on the nature of salvation and the church's relation to the public sphere. The mutually supportive nature of theological doctrine and political practice emphasized by Barth in the immediate postwar years is particularly evident in the Darmstadt statement. By tying the spiritual reconciliation between God and individual Christians to the reconciliation of humanity on earth, the council of brethren redefined Protestant ethics.

Barth's Theological Influence

Although the suggestion that the council explicitly address the church's relation to the political sphere came from Iwand, the theological underpinnings of the Darmstadt statement undeniably lie in Barth's Reformed political theology.[7] By 1947 Iwand and the Dahlemites had concluded that in order to obstruct a political, organizational, and theological restoration of traditional Lutheran nationalism, they needed to construct a new political ethic. It was Barth's political and theological lectures, however, that ultimately gave them the confidence, the motivation, and most important, the theological foundation to act on these conclusions by challenging the conservative Lutheran establishment.[8] The influence of Barth's Reformed theology was so great on Iwand, the principle author of the Darmstadt statement, that Barth would later teasingly call him a "Reformed Lutheran."[9] That Barth, Iwand, and several other members of the council would later minimize the importance of the Swiss theologian's influence on the statement was the result of their concern that the statement would lose its appeal—as the Barmen declaration had—in Lutheran-dominated Germany if it was associated with Barth. Although Barth's affiliation with the document certainly gave conservative Lutherans additional cause to oppose it, the radical political ethic at its core was more than enough to bring about its condemnation.

The experience of Nazism led to a period of intense debate over the Lutheran doctrines of the divine orders and the two kingdoms and whether they should be preserved, revised, or abandoned entirely. Adherence to these two central doctrines of orthodox Lutheranism, both of which underscored a separation of church and state, was seen by many of Barth's supporters to have two unfortunate outcomes: first, an uncritical position by Christians toward the state; and second, the belief that the Christian ideal of reconciliation was a matter for the private (spiritual) sphere. In response to the first critique, conservative Lutherans enthusiastically defended the church's long history of allying itself with patriarchal conservative forces. Conservative Lutherans roundly rejected the implication of the second critique—that the church was devoid of a social ethic.[10] They defended themselves by saying that in addition to local parish work, Lutheran churches had been actively engaged for decades in providing charity for the needy, beds for the homeless, and care for the elderly and the sick through the work of its social welfare organization, the Inner Mission, and later, *Hilfswerk*.[11] But for the reformers this was not enough; they wanted to extend the church's mission beyond traditional social welfare work. Contending that God's gift of free unmerited grace was the equivalent of a divine call to human action, Barth and his supporters advocated progressive political engagement.

According to Barth, through the incarnation, death, resurrection, and exaltation of Jesus Christ we experience God's unconditional love and enter into a fellowship with God. This act of reconciliation of God and man in the spiritual kingdom, Barth contended, imparted to man the freedom to live according to God's message of reconciliation in the earthly kingdom. Christian freedom was the freedom to act in the world as a disciple of Christ. Thesis three of the Darmstadt statement criticized the church for failing to acknowledge and act on this freedom: "We have betrayed the Christian freedom which enables us and commands us to change the forms of life, when such a change is necessary for men to live together."

Insistence on the connection between spiritual reconciliation and temporal reconciliation distinguished Barth and his supporters from the conservatives both politically and theologically. In his critique of the dualism undergirding the Lutheran doctrines of the divine orders and the two kingdoms, Barth maintained that Christ's kingship encompassed both the spiritual and earthly kingdoms. By establishing a connection between the two kingdoms, Barth created the foundation for his political ethic. In the fifth thesis of the Barmen declaration, Barth had hinted at a political ethic; what had been implicit in his work twelve years earlier was explicit in his 1946 essay "The Christian Community and the Civil Community"— one might even say crudely explicit.[12]

Barth argued that because the state was part of the kingdom of God but ignorant of Scripture, it was first and foremost the Christian community's task to "remind" the state of the message of the Gospels by making political choices that suggested a "correspondence" to Christ's message. The goal of the church was neither to bring the kingdom of God into the political sphere nor to create a Christian state, but rather to guide civil society toward decisions and actions that acknowledge Christ's kingship. "The way Christians can help in the political sphere," Barth asserted, "is by constantly giving the State an impulse in the Christian direction." Most important, Barth insisted that the church could not be indifferent toward the form of the state since the state has its origin in a divine "ordinance" and belongs to the kingdom of God. Through the use of analogies with events from the Bible, Barth offered a surprisingly detailed and highly controversial account of the type of state a Christian should actively support.

In one of his more arcane analogies, Barth claimed that the political corollary of God's revelation of himself in Jesus Christ is that the church should oppose all secret policies and secret diplomacy. That is, since God revealed himself to man in the person of Jesus Christ, the state should reveal its policies to its citizenry in the public sphere. In a more accessible example, Barth drew an analogy between Christ's mission on earth to seek and save the most unfortunate, and the church's duty to support the state that stood for social justice. Drawing on numerous biblical verses, Barth asserted that the church stood in favor of constitutional states, social justice, political freedom, civil and individual responsibility, equality of races and classes, separation of powers, and equal access to the public sphere. Accordingly, the church stood against anarchy, tyranny, state secrets, naked power, peace at any price, nationalism, and revolution against a lawful state. Barth cautioned that these analogies should not be understood as the draft of a political constitution. "We used examples," he explained, "because we were concerned to illuminate the analogical but extremely concrete relationship between the Christian gospel and certain political decisions and modes of behavior." Although Barth maintained that the examples were merely illustrations of ways a Christian *might* make politically responsible decisions and choices, it was clear what type of political choices he thought Christians should make.

Protestants from many different traditions vociferously criticized Barth's analogical argument; the analogies were simply too politically explicit. It seemed to many laymen and clergy that Barth was saying that if you don't support social democracy, you're not a good Christian.[13] To say that God through his merciful forgiveness imparted to man the freedom to promote reconciliation on earth was one thing; to claim that God was against state secrets or in favor of parliamentary rule was entirely another. Moreover, as many critics pointed out, one can draw virtually any analogy one wants from the Bible. Certainly, conservatives could have easily matched Barth analogy for analogy with passages from the Bible that led one to different or opposite conclusions. Despite the general denunciation of Barth's use of analogies in "The Christian Community and the Civil Community," the underlying theological orientation—that the Bible provided guidance in political matters—survived relatively unscathed in the reform wing of the Confessing Church and provided the basis for the Darmstadt statement and later engagement in the political sphere.

Barth's 1947 lecture, "The Church—the Living Congregation of the Living Lord Jesus Christ," also resonated with many participants at the July meeting of the brethren council and had a major impact on the wording of the Darmstadt statement. In it Barth defined the church as a congregation (*Gemeinde*)—a gathering together of men and women for the purpose of acting as Christ's disciples in the world.[14] The mission of a congregation, according to Barth, was to spread the message of God's free grace, of the reconciliation of God and man, and to identify itself with the need and hope of the world.[15] He reproached the German Church for losing track of that message in its bureaucratic maze of ecclesiastical offices. Consistently from 1945 to 1947, Barth condemned the pronounced confessionalism and clericalism of the conservative Lutherans, their preoccupation with liturgy, and their desire to preserve the autonomy and rigidity of the regional churches. Later, Barth claimed that with this lecture he had "demolished the whole concept of church 'authority'—in both its episcopal and its synodal form—and constructed everything (rather like the Pilgrim Fathers) on the congregation."[16] Although the Darmstadt statement never directly addressed the church's ecclesiastical structure (episcopal, synodal, or congregational), it did define the church in terms of its "service to the glory of God and the welfare of mankind"—implying that the church had paid too much attention in the past to serving its own administrative and governing bodies.

Barth's emphasis on reconciliation and the church's mission in the world are explicit in the Darmstadt statement. Indeed, the first two sentences of the first thesis emphasized the central importance of reconciliation: "We have been given the message of reconciliation of the world with God in Christ. We must listen to this Word, accept it, act upon it, and fulfill it." To be sure, here the message of reconciliation refers to the spiritual reconciliation of God and man in Christ. But in addition to, and inextricably linked with, this spiritual reconciliation were concrete political and social dimensions of reconciliation for Barth and his disciples in the council of brethren. What the council envisaged in terms of reforms was never spelled out precisely. The lack of a concrete reform program, however, should not be seen as a sign of insincerity. The very fact that the Darmstadt statement called on Christians to participate as Christians in a socially conscious way in the economic, political, and social spheres was radical in itself.

Iwand's Emphasis on Reconciliation

In the context of divided and occupied Germany in 1947, the brethren council, and Iwand in particular, believed that part of the church's mission to serve God included fostering the spirit of reconciliation externally between nations and internally between classes. Despite the centrality of the theme of reconciliation, neither Barth nor the other members of the council insisted on the necessity of fostering reconciliation between Jews and Christians. Fear of resurgent German nationalism coupled with increasing friction between the East and West led the council to focus its attention on reducing Cold War tensions rather than to address the even more emotionally charged topic of Christian antisemitism and postwar Jewish-Christian relations. The second thesis of the Darmstadt statement candidly set the tone for the rest of the document.

> We went astray when we began to dream about a special German mission, as if the German character could heal the sickness of the world. In so doing we prepared the way for the unrestricted exercise of political power, and set our own nation on the throne of God. It was disastrous to lay the foundations of our state at home solely on a strong government, and abroad solely on military force. In so doing we have acted contrary to our vocation, which is to cooperate with other nations in our common tasks, and to use the gifts given to us for the benefit of all nations.

Iwand emphasized the disloyalty to the gospel inherent in nationalism even more forcefully in his own draft when he asserted that the church had exchanged God's justification of the sinner with the self-justification of nationalism.[17] Nationalist endeavors not only damaged the potential for reconciliation among men but—even more egregious—they elevated man to a position that was God's alone.

Perhaps more than any other churchman in the brethren council, Hans Iwand was troubled by the increasing tension between East and West Germany. Born in Silesia (which became a part of Poland after 1945) in 1899, the son of a pastor, Iwand studied theology at the University of Breslau and eventually taught at the University of Königsberg in East Prussia. Like many who eventually joined the Confessing Church, he praised National Socialism in 1933 but quickly changed his mind when the Hitler-backed German Christians took over the Prussian church and removed Iwand from his position at Königsberg. After teaching briefly at a university in Riga in 1934 where he was again forced out, he returned to East Prussia where he took over the leadership of the illegal seminary (*Predigerseminar*) of the Confessing Church. As a result of these experiences, Iwand became one of the Confessing Church's most radical proponents. During this period he declared, "A confessing church is always in the opposition, in every system, under every government, against every party." When the seminary was shut down in 1937, he left East Prussia and moved to Dortmund in the west, where he served as the pastor of St. Mary's parish.[18]

After the war East Prussia was ceded to Poland, causing the forced migration and the deaths of tens of thousands of Germans. Iwand acquired a position in 1945 teaching systematic theology at the University of Göttingen and worked tirelessly on the German refugee question and the reconciliation of East and West.[19] He was disturbed that many influential national church leaders—Bishops Wurm, Meiser, and Dibelius as well a number of reputable theologians and pastors such as Thielicke, Künneth, and Asmussen—sided unabashedly with the "Christian" West while demonizing the "Bolshevik" East. Gerard C. den Hertog, a scholar of Iwand's work explains:

> It was Iwand's conviction that at the base of history there lies a guilt, which blocked the way forward. In Stuttgart in 1945 guilt was confessed—but only to the representatives of the western churches. The greatest guilt lay, however, in the East. Because of the continuation after the Second World War of a simple friend-enemy mentality, a confession to the East was blocked.[20]

For Iwand the greatest danger facing the church was not Soviet repression in the East but the mentality that the West was a friend and the East an enemy. Iwand insisted that this friend-enemy mentality was implicit in the church's conservative Lutheranism, traditional nationalism, and rabid anticommunism. The sixth thesis of the Darmstadt statement addressed Iwand's concern that the church was siding with the West against the East: "It is not the phrase 'Christianity and Western Culture' that the German people, and particularly we Christians, need today. What we need is a return to God and to the service of our neighbor, through the power of the death and resurrection of Jesus Christ." Iwand feared that the postwar reconstruction of the German character (*das deutsche Wesen*), was developing along nationalist lines as it did after the First World War. In contrast to this direction, which had such disastrous results in the 1920s, Iwand advocated a rebirth of the church based on the gospel's message of reconciliation. And this, Iwand believed, required undermining nationalism within the church.[21]

Reconciliation between nations was just one aspect of temporal reconciliation advocated by Iwand. Holding that comfort and support for the poor and underprivileged was a crucial part of the message of God's kingdom, Barth and the Lutheran co-authors of the Darmstadt statement also maintained a link between the reconciliation of God with man and the reconciliation of men in the socioeconomic sphere. Thesis three ventures to describe Christian freedom as the freedom to pursue social change when socioeconomic inequalities preclude fellowship among men. The Darmstadt statement criticized the church for not recognizing as part of its mission the reconciliation of socioeconomic classes through the support of revolutionary changes in the social sphere. The official commentary on the Darmstadt statement, written primarily by Hermann Diem, left no room for mistaking who the reformers thought was to blame for the German church's failure to fulfill its obligation to engage actively in alleviating poverty and despair.[22] Diem accused the Lutheran Church establishment of serving its own institutional needs rather than meeting its responsibility to serve the community.

For the brethren council the message of God's free grace and the freedom it entailed meant that there was hope for *this world*. It meant primarily freedom to reform the church but also freedom to change the world: for example, to abolish poverty, to improve working conditions, and to provide medical care. Yet these types of concrete reforms were never made explicit in the Darmstadt statement.

Joachim Beckmann, Hans Iwand, Wilhelm Schneemelcher, and Karl Barth at a conference in Wuppertal in 1956. Iwand was the principal author of the controversial 1947 Darmstadt statement, and Beckmann co-authored the commentary on the statement along with other supporters of the council of brethren. *Courtesy of Special Collections, Princeton Theological Seminary Libraries on behalf of the* Karl Barth Stiftung *of Basel, Switzerland.*

One must investigate the activities of individual members of the council (Niemöller's vocal opposition to Adenauer's rearmament campaign is a case in point) to see how they interpreted the consequences of that God-given freedom. It was the established church's failure to grasp the temporal implications of Christian freedom that prompted the charges found in the third thesis:

> We went astray when we began to set up a "Christian Front" against certain new developments which had become necessary in social life. The alliance of the Church with the forces which clung to everything old and conventional has revenged itself heavily upon us. *We have betrayed the Christian freedom which enables us and commands us to change the forms of life, when such a change is necessary for men to live together.* We have denied the right of revolution; but we have condoned and approved the development of absolute dictatorship. (Italics mine)

Christian freedom enabled and commanded Christians to strive to improve relations between people through reforms or revolution if necessary. Thus, rather than

Charlotte von Kirschbaum, Hermann Diem, Karl Barth, and Helmut Gollwitzer near Locarno, Switzerland, in 1962. Barth was a powerful influence
on the Dahlemite wing of the Confessing Church, including German
theologians Diem and Gollwitzer. *Courtesy of Special Collections, Princeton
Theological Seminary Libraries on behalf of the* Karl Barth Stiftung *of Basel,
Switzerland.*

blame demons or God's angry judgment for Nazism, the war, and Germany's postwar plight, thesis three assigned culpability to the church's decision to eschew the
responsibility that comes with Christian freedom and instead to ally itself with conservative political forces. The reformers did not suggest that the church had condoned or approved of the Holocaust, but rather that the church's hostility to the
Weimar Republic and all the social, economic, and political reforms associated with
it contributed to the development of Hitler's "absolute dictatorship."[23] As Diem
and his colleagues argued in the council's official commentary on the Darmstadt
statement, "In the history of the Christian Church, and in particular in Germany
since the Reformation, one heard virtually only the commandment: one must submit to the unjust political and social order."[24]

By dismissing Weimar reforms as Communist inspired, thesis five implied, the church lost sight of its task to promote reconciliation among people of different classes and political orientations by actively engaging in radical social reform.

> We went astray when we failed to see that the economic materialism of Marxist teaching ought to have reminded the church of its task and its promise for the life and fellowship of men. We have failed to take up the cause of the poor and underprivileged as a Christian cause, in accordance with the message of God's Kingdom.

The reformers defined the church by its *service* to God and man—not by its confessions, offices, organizational structure, or alliance to the conservative state. Barth stated this forcefully in "The Christian Community and the Civil Community," when he declared, "As disciples of Christ, the members of His church do not rule: they serve."[25] Significantly, the Darmstadt statement portrayed the rejuvenation of the church in terms of both its new political responsibility *and* its obedience and witness to Jesus Christ. It tied Christian freedom inextricably to the political responsibility to make changes in institutional structures when they no longer served the needs of society. By succumbing to nationalist propaganda in the postwar period, the German church was threatening to squander again the opportunity to participate in the reconstruction of a responsible and humane government.

Political and Theological Critics

That conservatives, Hans Asmussen and Walter Künneth in particular, rejected the Darmstadt statement in light of its leftist politics and Barthian theology came as no surprise to the reformers. But when friends and colleagues from regional churches in eastern Germany harshly criticized it as well, the authors of the statement were taken aback. To the dismay of the reformers from the western zones, their eastern counterparts not only agreed with much of Asmussen and Künneth's critique but also felt betrayed by what they perceived as the brethren council's uncritical portrayal of life under communism and lack of sympathy for the churches in the eastern zone. All of the statement's detractors concurred that such a politically charged statement "was not a suitable statement for clergymen," as Berlin pastor and former Confessing Church leader Eitel-Friedrich von Rabenau stated to the brethren council in October 1947.[26] Eduard Putz, a pastor from Fürth in Bavaria, added quite appropriately that any statement that required a lengthy and detailed commentary to aid the reader's understanding of it was clearly problematic.[27]

The reformers' critique of Bismarck's use of blood and iron to found the German state in 1871 was the starting point for the conservatives' rebuttal. While acknowledging in retrospect that founding the German state, as Bismarck had, on an autocratic government and military force, created certain difficulties in domestic and foreign policy, Asmussen reproached the council of brethren for emphasizing only the negative side of the conservative nation-state. The "fatherland," he asserted, was one of the givens or instances (*Gegebenheiten*) through which the church received God's command. Although he avoided the terms "divine order" or "order of creation," which were often used by Lutherans to describe the state, the meaning was implied in *Gegebenheiten*. In fact, Asmussen argued that it was the duty of the church to remind Christians that the German state was one of the tools through which Christians received their God-given task in the world.[28]

Aggressive nationalism certainly had its dangers, but a conservative nationalism, he maintained, was justified in a world of nation-states. Asmussen pointed out that the occupation forces and all of Germany's neighbors, including the Swiss (a reference to Barth), were strongly nationalistic. Walter Künneth, a former member of both the Young Reformation movement and the Pastors' Emergency League during the Nazi era and a professor of systematic theology at the University of Erlangen afterwards, concurred with Asmussen in his critique in the *Evangelisch-Lutherische Kirchenzeitung*. He acknowledged that it was the church's duty to warn the German people about the dangers of an exaggerated nationalism. The reformers, however, were mistaken if they thought the task of the church was to denounce all national endeavors as precursors to National Socialism.[29]

Piqued by the reformers' assertion that the German nation had placed itself on the throne of God, Künneth warned, "One should take care not to understand all of German history as a direct preparation for National Socialism."[30] Just as all strong governments should not be associated with the work of the devil, he argued, neither should all weak governments be associated with God. The brethren council, he charged, was intentionally obfuscating the differences between the legitimate need for a strong government and a powerful military with the barbaric actions of the Nazis. Since the state was an emergency decree bestowed on the world by God in order to subdue chaos, it should not be identified automatically, argued Künneth, with the ungodly violence of National Socialism. Thus in true Lutheran fashion, Asmussen and Künneth defended the longstanding relationship between church and state based on the nineteenth-century notion of the state as an "order of creation" or "divine order" bestowed by God on the world to implement law and order. And in true conservative fashion, they separated their brand of nationalism from that of the Nazis.

For Künneth the immediate postwar years presented a unique situation for the church: it was the "Hour of the Gospel," which, rather than calling for revolutionary change, called for ever more stringent adherence to the church's God-given mission to preach the gospel.[31] While conceding that the church's alliance with the conservative establishment limited it in certain ways, he defended the Christian Front by citing numerous passages from the Bible allegedly confirming that God had bestowed conservative powers and institutions on man in order to tame lawlessness and avoid chaos. Thus, Künneth shared Asmussen's view that biblical authority and the Lutheran confessions supported the alliance of the church with conservative institutions. Under no circumstances would he accept the council of brethren's teleological argument that the Third Reich marked the culmination of Germany's long line of conservative rulers. After all, the church was proud of its country's conservative history.

Gerhard Jacobi, president of the Confessing Church in Berlin from 1933 to 1939 and a church leader there immediately after the war, offered some of the sharpest critiques of the statement. He maintained that the Darmstadt statement had met with 100 percent rejection by church leaders in Berlin despite the fact that 80 percent of the postwar Berlin church leadership was from the Confessing Church. The only supporters of the statement, he claimed, were the trade unions and the administration of the Soviet zone. "I don't think you understand the situation in the east," he told the council of brethren in Detmold in October 1947. "If you did, you would not have issued this statement in the form you did." It was inexplicable to Jacobi that his close colleagues could be so insensitive to the misery of most East Germans. What East Germans needed, Jacobi remonstrated, was a statement that offered some hope and comfort. Instead, the brethren council offered nothing but reproaches. "Has the Confessing Church forgotten what it means to suffer?" Jacobi asked.[32]

Particularly offensive to conservatives as well as to churchmen from eastern Germany was the reformers' charge that the church failed to support revolutionary changes and instead lent support to absolute dictatorship. In their statement, Iwand and his colleagues had challenged the conservatives' interpretation of the Nazi era, which held that during the Third Reich the church had chosen correctly to focus its energy on preserving the church's freedom to preach the gospel rather than offer political resistance. For Künneth and Asmussen, the church's role in the temporal world was to preach the gospel and leave politics to the politicians, lending support to neither absolute dictatorship nor a socialist revolution. The right to revolution, Künneth argued, was expressly denied in the gospel. In fact, by denying the right of revolutionary change in the past, the church had demonstrated its obedience to God's word.[33] Jacobi was also unconvinced by the council's logic regarding the right to revolution and accused it of masking their leftist politics with biblical phrases.

The critique of the Darmstadt statement extended beyond the political to the theological. Kurt Scharf, another close colleague of Niemöller's and a leader of the regional brethren council in Berlin-Brandenburg, contended that the council was practicing a form of self-absolution by saying in the sixth thesis, "In recognizing and confessing [our sins], we know that we are absolved as followers of Christ, and that we are now free to undertake new and better service to the glory of God and the welfare of mankind." The wording, Scharf charged, implied that whoever did not share the brethren council's historical view of the church's sins and its newly formulated mission would not receive absolution.[34]

For similar reasons, Künneth warned his conservative colleagues, "We are standing before a theological derailment, which carries the characteristics of a new German Christian theology but from the opposite political direction."[35] By comparing it to the Scottish Confession of 1560—a radical Reformed confession written by John Knox and other Scottish reformers—Künneth's and Asmussen's critiques of the Darmstadt statement drew attention to what they saw as a Reformed understanding of absolution.[36] In thesis one, Asmussen noted, the brethren council stated correctly that God's message cannot be properly received, lived, and preached *unless God absolves the church* of its sins through confession. But in thesis six, Asmussen pointed out, the council stated that by recognizing and confessing the church's sins in theses two through five, the church *knows* itself to be absolved. Asmussen, among others, found fault with this latter understanding of absolution. It suggested that recognizing and confessing the church's sins, as the council understood them, and redirecting the church's mission toward a more socially conscious activist role in society was itself a sign from God that the church was absolved.[37]

This type of thinking, Asmussen charged, was neither biblical nor based on the Lutheran confessions. He accused the brethren council of confusing faith and works. Believing God's forgiving grace was always present, regardless of whether there were any signs sent by God, Asmussen declared, "One can go astray as a believer and still be blessed. One cannot, however, be blessed by doing good works without faith."[38] He attributed the council's faulty rendering of absolution to its Reformed understanding of the gospel. In his critique, Künneth asked rhetorically, "Has everyone in the council of brethren overlooked the fact that the members of the Evangelical Church in Germany are overwhelmingly adherents to the Lutheran catechism?"[39]

How one is absolved (or justified) by God and what, if any, consequences absolution has was first and foremost a confessional—that is, denominational—dispute. Luther's doctrine of justification by faith alone excluded any role for good works in man's absolution. Lutherans believe that one is reconciled to God through one's faith. Faith, however, was not attributable to human work or action, because it is a gift from God. For Luther, the emphasis was on faith; for Calvin, the emphasis was on redemption or regeneration. Both Luther and Calvin agreed that justification was the work of God. The difference was where they placed the emphasis: for Luther, it was on man's inward condition of faith; for Calvin, on outward signs of justification. For Calvin, man need not concern himself with the perfection of his faith because faith was the work of Christ and therefore already perfect. Calvinists believed that God absolved man in order to free him to serve God. Although he denied that good works were a source of salvation, Calvin maintained that the works God did *through man* were signs of salvation.[40] Hence, it would follow that for the Reformed theologian, political actions reveal the grace of God working through man as signs of salvation.

Conclusion

With this fundamental distinction between Lutheran and Reformed confessions in hand, the critiques leveled by Asmussen, Künneth, and Scharf reveal a deeper level of concern than politics per se. They strongly suggest that the political differences between the Darmstadt authors and the conservative Lutherans are intelligible only when wedded to their theological counterparts. What stood in the way of a unified Protestant Church was not simply different political agendas but different theological orientations. The reformers, strongly influenced by Barth's Reformed theology, believed that a concrete confession of guilt necessarily entailed making concrete changes in the church's doctrine and mission to ensure that the same errors were not repeated in the future.

The authors of the Darmstadt statement attributed the Protestant Church's easy accommodation to Nazism to the church's adherence to conservative Lutheran theology and organization—in particular, to the Lutheran interpretation of the doctrine of two kingdoms. The Darmstadt statement confessed that the church was guilty of a conservative orientation that led to lending support to absolute dictatorship and to ignoring the economic and social needs of the lower classes. The reformers believed it was their Christian duty to participate in the public sphere in a socially and politically conscious way to ensure that the church would not, once again, be drawn into supporting inhumane causes. "[We] realize the responsibility," thesis seven read, "which rests upon us all to rebuild a better form of government in Germany that shall work for justice and for the welfare, peace and reconciliation of the nations." After acknowledging the church's political responsibility for past and future governments, the council of brethren turned its attention to the even more contentious issue of the church and the "Jewish question."

7

The Church and Antisemitism

For postwar Protestant Church leaders the "Jewish question" or "Jewish problem," which some clergymen had hoped to resolve in past decades through conversion and others through support for antisemitic legislation, consisted of three interrelated issues: the practical, the historical, and the theological.[1] The most immediate issue facing churchmen was practical: How should the church, in its day-to-day affairs, relate to and approach Jewish survivors of concentration and extermination camps? Considering the church's complacency toward the plight of Jews during the Nazi period, did it now have an obligation to demonstrate in practice that its indifference was a thing of the past?

Of course, the manner in which churchmen sought to resolve the practical dimension of the "Jewish question" depended to a large degree on how they would address the historical and theological dimensions. That is, how, in the wake of the Holocaust, should the church interpret the history of Jews in Germany, especially in the twentieth century? Would the antisemitic portrayal of Jews as treasonous and unethical still hold sway and influence the actions of most Protestants? Most important, the church had to confront the theological question of how it should understand the role of Jews in the Bible, in particular their role in God's salvation plan (*Heilsgeschichte*) since the time of Jesus. Was the traditional anti-Judaic interpretation that Jews were cursed by God for their rejection of Jesus as the Messiah still valid? If so, was it the church's obligation to continue to vigorously convert Jews to Christianity?

From the perspective of the twenty-first century, some of these questions might sound rhetorical—certainly they are offensive. To conceptualize Christian-Jewish relations as a "Jewish question" or "problem" is no longer acceptable. Nevertheless, in beleaguered Germany of the postwar period, they were serious, wrenching issues for leading members of the church. For some, the church's traditional answers—contempt, indifference, or conversion—were still acceptable. For others, the church struggle, the Holocaust, the founding of the State of Israel in May 1948, and finally, the beginnings of a postwar dialogue between Jewish and Christian leaders stimulated a reevaluation of traditional answers to the "Jewish question." Recognition by the clergy of the need for a fundamental transformation of the church's relationship to Jews and its understanding of Judaism was slow and halting, and at first, a minority view. Limited signs of progress, however, emerged after the war.[2] Among mainstream Protestants this recognition took decades, and to this day some continue to deny that the need exists.

Ascertaining the ways in which the Protestant Church responded to these issues and questions requires both an evaluation of statements by churchmen and a close look at the actual practices of the churches. In postwar Germany what was preached was not always practiced. Even though it took several years for church reformers to recognize that even their Confessing Church had been culpable and that changes were needed, the church did make progress in addressing its anti-Judaism and antisemitism in written and verbal proclamations. There were certain groups within the church that strove for friendly and mutually respectful relationships with Jews. Yet at the same time, many clergymen and laypersons, including some of the most powerful bishops and presidents of regional churches, maintained their ingrained prejudices, doing little to improve Protestant-Jewish relations. The EKD council and the church's chancellery repeatedly brushed aside a serious reconsideration of the "Jewish question" between 1945 and 1950 while national church leaders addressed what they said were more pressing concerns.

The most serious stumbling blocks to a rethinking of the church's doctrine and practice were deeply rooted in church theology and traditions, the manifestation of which could be seen in the prevalence of anti-Judaism and antisemitism in the church's leadership and congregations. By portraying Jews for nearly two thousand years as enemies of Christ and in more recent centuries as a subversive force within the German *Volk*, the church had created a legacy of anti-Judaism and antisemitism that continued, despite all the horrors of the Nazi-inflicted atrocities against the Jewish people, to influence the attitude and behavior of the majority within the church after 1945.

This chapter and the next address Christian-Jewish relations from 1945 to 1950. Chapter 7 examines the continued presence of antisemitism in the church and the misguided effort of the council of brethren in its 1948 "A Message Concerning the Jewish Question" to renounce the church's antisemitism while reaffirming its traditional anti-Judaism. While the reformers' forthright condemnation of antisemitism signaled a new direction in the church—despite the objections of conservatives—they undermined their own efforts by reinforcing the myth of supersessionism, which asserted that since the crucifixion of Christ the Christian church had superseded the Jews as God's chosen people.

The final chapter examines the debates within the church over its theological

anti-Judaism, in particular the myths of supersessionism and Christian triumphalism, which coalesced over the centuries into a teaching of contempt for Jews from
a Christian perspective. The realization that the church's widely accepted anti-Judaic
myths provided fertile ground for the growth of antisemitism in nineteenth- and
twentieth-century Germany culminated in the repudiation of supersessionism by
churchmen at the EKD's Berlin-Weissensee synod in April 1950.[3]

Lack of Concern and Denial of Need

The number of Protestant Church leaders in the postwar period who devoted
serious time and energy to addressing anti-Judaism and antisemitism within the
church was very small indeed. The number who actively provided assistance to surviving Jewish Christians—Jews who had converted to Christianity and had been
persecuted by the Nazis as Jews—amounted to a few dozen.[4] Even fewer *embraced*
Christians of Jewish descent as equal members of the Protestant community. Most
church leaders demonstrated little interest in addressing the "Jewish question" on
either a practical level or theoretical basis. They reluctantly acknowledged the Jewish suffering in their midst but quickly dismissed the idea that the church had been
in any way responsible or that it should have a role in making amends. Parishioners
across Germany were so resentful toward the remaining Jews, whom they perceived
as enjoying preferential treatment from the Allies, that they contested an annual
Sunday collection devoted to aid offices for Christians of Jewish descent and
Protestant missions that focused on proselytizing among Jews.

The same few names of mid-level church leaders appear over and over in the
archives in connection with their active concern for a new beginning in relations
with Jews from 1945 to 1950: Hermann Maas (1877–1970) in Heidelberg; Heinrich Grüber (1891–1975) in Berlin; Otto Fricke (1902–55) in Frankfurt; Adolf
Freudenberg (1894–1977) in London, Geneva, and later Heilsberg near Bad Vilbel;
Otto von Harling Jr. (1909–93) in the church chancellery; Otto von Harling Sr.
(1866–1953) in Celle near Hannover; and Karl Heinrich Rengstorf (1903–92) in
Münster. Missing from this list are the names of most of the leading figures in the
church, including Bishops Dibelius, Meiser, and Wurm of Berlin, Bavaria, and
Württemberg.

Although Martin Niemöller certainly did more than anyone else in the church
to publicly address the church's share of responsibility for fostering a context in
which the Nazis could come to power and initiate a campaign of discrimination
and terror against the Jews, he was not at the forefront when it came time for reforming the church's anti-Judaism. In fact, Niemöller's passivity in this regard led
those who were active to regard him as somewhat of a liability. In November 1947
Otto von Harling Jr., who had quite a bit of experience with Christian-Jewish re-

lations and had been appointed earlier that year to coordinate all matters having to do with the "Jewish question," counseled Niemöller and the brethren council not to rush into making a statement on the "Jewish question" because he felt they were unprepared and the church might regret it later.[5] Hans Asmussen, president of the church chancellery, was also relatively uninvolved in rethinking the church's historical and theological relationship with Jews. When the council of brethren finally issued its statement on Christian-Jewish relations, "A Message Concerning the Jewish Question," in April 1948, other members of the council, in particular the Reformed pastor Hermann A. Hesse (1877–1957), played prominent roles.[6]

Those most experienced with day-to-day Jewish and Jewish Christian concerns were the low-level pastors and staff who worked in the Jewish missions (*Judenmission*) and Jewish Christian aid offices, whose activities frequently overlapped.[7] In fact, missions often did both missionary and aid work, especially in the Lutheran regional churches. For example, the Jewish mission in Basel, directed by Robert Brunner, provided support for the mission work in Württemberg as well as sent care packages to the Jewish Christian aid office directed by Fritz Majer-Leonard in Stuttgart. In Hannover the Evangelical-Lutheran Central Federation for Mission to Israel, directed by Rengstorf and Harling Sr., included among its tasks both missionary work among Jews and aiding Jewish Christians. This was also the case with the Bavarian Lutheran mission.[8]

The overlap is significant because it suggests that the question of how to treat Christians of Jewish ancestry was understood within the church as part of the larger question of the relationship between Christians and Jews. Racial prejudice tied the "Jewish Christian question" to the "Jewish question." As the racial and religious "other," Jews received little attention from the church in the immediate postwar years except as potential converts. Jewish Christians had one less strike against them since they were baptized, but they were still viewed as outsiders on account of their race. The majority in the church directed their antisemitism toward both Jews and Christians of Jewish descent, forcing missionary work among the Jews and assistance work with Jewish Christians into a common struggle against this prejudice. The two groups of churchmen were in constant contact and had at least one common goal: to reform the church's racial interpretation of the "Jewish question." Neither endeavor could flourish as long as these deep-seated racial prejudices existed.

Both missionaries and aid workers complained frequently of the lack of support by regional and national church leaders. Although they did not explicitly accuse their superiors of antisemitism, the charge of antisemitism was often implicit in their criticisms of the church's indifference toward the plight of Jews and Jewish Christians. Gottfried Frohwein, a medical doctor in Bavaria and active for years in missionary work among Jews in Poland, maintained that there were three impediments to conducting successful missionary work among the Jewish displaced persons and refugees from Eastern Europe who were flooding the American zone of occupation in 1946 and 1947: the shortage of experienced and knowledgeable missionaries, antisemitism, and the indifference of the church leadership. He bemoaned both the "new antisemitism" taking root in Germany and the lack of compassion within the church for Jews from the East.[9] Harling Jr. confirmed Frohwein's assessment in a 1947 letter to a Bavarian pastor involved in missionary work: "It's just a fact, which is confirmed for me almost daily, that the understanding and interest in the churches for this work is extremely small."[10]

German missionaries believed that the Jews' "race" was no reason to exclude them from conversion to Christianity; not to preach the gospel to Jews would be a sign of antisemitism since it suggested that Jews were undesirable in the church for racial reasons. In fact, the men and women who staffed the missions were some of the most energetic in combating antisemitism, forthright in describing Germany's responsibility for the Holocaust, knowledgeable about Jewish history and Judaism, and concerned about the welfare of Jews in Germany after the war. Understanding perfectly well that the number of Jews who were likely to convert to Christianity was very small, they nonetheless held the deep conviction that it was their obligation as Christians to spread the gospel to all peoples, no matter how unpopular the work was within the Protestant community or among Jews. They received a good deal of criticism from their colleagues who did not want Jewish converts brought into the German Protestant Church.

The assumption behind missionary work among Jews was that the religious beliefs of the Jewish population were simply wrong and that conversion to Christianity was the way to salvation. Thus, the work of missionaries in post-1945 Germany was, by its very nature, anti-Judaic. But were the missionaries antisemitic? To be sure, racial antisemites opposed the work of missionaries. But it does not necessarily follow that missionaries did not also hold preconceived racial stereotypes of Jews. In fact, in the eyes of some outside observers, the attempt to solve the "Jewish problem" by converting Jews to Christianity is antisemitic because it is an attempt to rid the world of Jews, albeit by nonviolent means.[11]

Those working with Jewish Christians were especially disappointed that the church felt no sense of urgency about their relief work with racially persecuted Christians. Fritz Majer-Leonard, who directed an aid office in Stuttgart, believed that church leaders in Württemberg tolerated his work but never supported it enthusiastically. "Since the Central Leadership Council does not appear to be interested in this matter," he wrote to church leaders in 1947, "it is probably not necessary for me to send a copy of my report."[12] He also complained to Bishop Wurm that the Central Leadership Council in Württemberg displayed a meager interest in his work and offered little financial support.[13] Although it was unusual for reproaches to be sent directly to church leaders, there were many such complaints by missionaries and aid workers.

Church leaders underestimated the scale of the task of caring for Christians whose Jewish background subjected them to persecution. Estimates in 1947 of their numbers ranged from 50,000 to 60,000.[14] Although the number of Jewish Christians was therefore significant, church leaders lost sight of them, when they chose to, among the millions of other German DPs, refugees, and German Gentiles, who were also living in desperate conditions. In many cases it was the aid workers who had to draw the attention of church leaders to the situation of the Jewish Christians and to explain, for example, that the term "non-Aryan Christians" was an inappropriate and offensive term that defined Jewish Christians using Nazi racial terminology. They preferred to use instead, "racially persecuted Christians."

The Jewish Christians in Württemberg, Majer-Leonard explained in a letter to regional church leaders there, received aid from the church's Aid Office for Non-Aryan Christians (renamed the Aid Office for the Racially Persecuted in October 1946), which was a member of Heinrich Grüber's umbrella organization, the Association of Christian Aid Offices for the Racially Persecuted of non-Jewish Faith in Germany.[15] The Stuttgart office distributed care packages it received from Christian organizations abroad, provided legal advice and assistance to those who wanted to emigrate, and tried to address the spiritual needs of Christians of Jewish descent by fostering a sense of Christian brotherhood. Majer-Leonard emphasized that although it was a good thing that the church was providing some material and spiritual care to Jewish Christians, he believed that ultimately it was the state's obligation to provide financial and material reparations since the state had persecuted them. In an accompanying text, "On the Jewish Christian Question," Majer-Leonard stressed that although racially persecuted Christians deserved special care, a separate aid office established by the church, in all likelihood staffed by Jewish Christians, would ostracize them from other members of the Protestant Church.[16] He cited Paul's letter to the Ephesians to emphasize that there is no distinction between pagan converts to Christianity and Jewish converts. Moreover, he fiercely opposed the common perception that Jewish Christians owed the church some special commitment to serve as Christian ambassadors to the Jewish people.

Majer-Leonard contended that care for Jewish Christians was not just a matter of providing material needs but also about providing "lots of love" so that they would not become embittered. Although it was common for men and women in the missions and aid offices to encourage the church to show Jews and Jewish Christians more love, they never explained in any detail what expressing this entailed. One can surmise that it meant not only providing material and spiritual assistance—care packages and the message of the gospel that God, through his son Jesus Christ, offers salvation to all people—but also welcoming them into the congregation as regular members without superiority or condescension.

As Majer-Leonard indicated, there were no Protestant aid offices for Jews. Given the church's antisemitism and the scarcity of food, clothing, and housing in Germany, it is highly unlikely that it could or would have aided Jews in the immediate postwar years. Aid from Protestant churches was unnecessary, however, because Jewish relief agencies from the United States and elsewhere had enthusiastically taken on the job. Consequently, as early as the fall of 1945, exaggerated stories of Jewish abundance and opportunism began circulating within the church. The perception within the church that the Jewish standard of living was considerably higher than that of other Germans led many Christians to view Jews with bitter resentment. Even those Protestants who worked with Jewish Christians and were genuinely committed to resisting antisemitism within the church believed that Jews were doing quite well, thanks to the generous gifts "flowing lavishly from abroad," as Curt Radlauer, the chairman of Heinrich Grüber's Protestant aid organization for the formerly racially persecuted in Berlin observed.[17] That Jewish Christians and Gentile Christians had no equivalent provider was a source of overt dismay.

Perceptions among German Protestants notwithstanding, Jews in Germany lived a miserable existence in the immediate aftermath of the war.[18] Although inadequate food and housing was nearly a universal experience in postwar Germany, the mental and emotional anguish resulting from the Nazi racial policies of discrimination, deportation, and extermination was a plight German Gentiles did not experience. When the mayor of Frankfurt, Walter Kolb, gave a New Year's radio address in January 1947 in which he encouraged Frankfurt's Jewish émigrés to return, he received a flurry of letters from Jews remaining in Frankfurt, asking how he could make such an absurd statement considering the miserable conditions in which they lived amidst continuing signs of antisemitism.[19] Moreover, the flight from 1946 to 1948 of tens of thousands of Jews to Germany from eastern Europe, where fervent antisemitism had in some cases led to pogroms, meant that conditions for Jews in Germany remained hopeless. Not only had Jews lost virtually all their material possessions, they were often housed in former SS barracks and concentration camps and had virtually no prospects for finding employment. The vast majority of letters to the Jewish officials in charge of relief efforts were desperate pleas for bare necessities—food, housing, blankets, and medical attention—and for help with finding loved ones from whom they were separated.[20] Of course, Radlauer was correct in pointing out that Jewish Christians were excluded by Jewish aid organizations and consequently had to depend on meager church aid, but his description of Jewish aid for Jews as lavish was overblown, especially in late 1945 and early 1946 when he made these charges.

An unfortunate result of the perception of Jewish abundance and opportunism was that regional church leaders resisted asking their congregations to provide financial support for either the Jewish Christian aid organizations or the Jewish missions because they feared stirring up further resentment among their parishioners. As more Jews arrived from eastern Europe, Gentile Germans complained (although it was rarely true) that apartments had to be vacated for them, clothes provided for them, and necessities put aside for them.

This insular attitude disappointed missionaries and aid workers who hoped to support their work through a church collection. In the October 1945 announcement of their intent to resume the work of the Evangelical-Lutheran Central Federation for Mission to Israel, Otto von Harling Sr. and Karl Heinrich Rengstorf requested that the churches not only devote the traditional collection on the tenth Sunday after Trinity to the work of the Jewish mission but also the Good Friday collection in 1946.[21] Disappointed by the results of this appeal, they wrote a more detailed request in June 1947 that went to all regional church governments. For half a century, they pointed out, it had been the tradition of all the Lutheran churches to remember the Jewish mission on the tenth Sunday after Trinity. Now, they stressed, was not the time to allow this tradition to lapse. A month later Harling reported:

> The majority of regional churches did not react at all [to my appeal] and others responded that they were not proposing such a collection because the collection schedule was already set or for similar reasons. In many cases, this is certainly true. But from the tone of their writing one notices that the issue itself obviously causes feelings of discomfort.

Some of the regional churches preferred to donate directly to missions and aid offices rather than ask church members to contribute to a Sunday collection devoted to these "irksome" causes. The Central Church Council for Württemberg, under the jurisdiction of Bishop Wurm, was one that sent contributions directly to an aid office. "Here one has the very clear feeling," Harling continued, "that they would prefer to buy off their responsibility . . . than to confront the public on this matter."[22]

Although the Württemberg council finally gave in to the badgering of Majer-Leonard in fall of 1947 to devote future tenth Sunday after Trinity collections to his work, the council reneged in 1948, maintaining that the rise in antisemitism due to the Jewish refugees from the East made such a collection inopportune.[23] Although they raised no objection to that Sunday's sermons addressing the "Jewish question" and the church's responsibility to conduct missionary work among the Jews, they opposed requesting donations from parishioners for those purposes.[24]

The regional church in Hannover came up with a compromise. There would be no official collection stipulated by the church leadership in 1946, but the mission could make an informal request to pastors that they remember the mission's work in their collection on the tenth Sunday after Trinity. It was a compromise, Rengstorf explained in a letter to Pastor Friedrich Wilhelm Hopf of the Bavarian Jewish mission, which "places on us the burden of appealing to the pastors and congregations."[25] Rengstorf was not pleased to see the responsibility of the church thrown back on the private initiative of individuals such as himself and others in the mission.

Whereas some church leaders and congregations grudgingly supported the work of the Jewish missions and Jewish Christian aid stations, the churches nearly universally rejected direct contributions to Jewish communities and synagogues. In a rare case when the provisional church leadership in Bremen recommended that the 11 November 1945 church service address the pogrom of 9 November 1938 and devote the money collected that Sunday to the rebuilding of the synagogue and cemetery in Bremen, a debate broke out.[26] Pastor Denkhaus, a member of the regional council of brethren in Bremen, wrote a detailed opinion on the issue, recognizing the church's co-responsibility for the Nazis' attack on the Jews but maintaining that the church should play no role in providing financial support for the rebuilding of a synagogue in which Jesus would not be recognized as the Messiah. He believed that there was a considerable difference between the responsibility of the state to the Jews, which might include the rebuilding of the synagogue, and the responsibility of the church, which included acknowledging its failure to speak out during the Nazi period and preaching the gospel to the Jews.[27] The church's task was not to rebuild synagogues but rather to encourage Jews to see their misfortune and suffering as God's judgment and to accept Jesus' merciful forgiveness. "Whoever helps to rebuild a synagogue, helps bring about damnation," he wrote.[28] The national leadership council agreed with Denkhaus that it was inappropriate for Protestant churches to contribute to the rebuilding of a synagogue. Nevertheless, the provisional leadership of the church in Bremen went ahead with the collection.[29]

When word of Heinrich Grüber's intention, on behalf of the Evangelical Church in Berlin, to contribute 5000 DM to the rebuilding of a Berlin synagogue came to the attention of pastors and laypersons in Bavaria in late 1950, there was outrage.[30] A parishioner from Mühldorf asked what right Grüber had to spend the church's money on rebuilding a synagogue when so many Evangelical churches were in need of repair and renovation:

> I have absolutely nothing against using [the church's] surplus money for other matters, provided that all of the interests of the churches are already fulfilled, however certainly not for the building of Jewish synagogues. If the Berlin offices of the Evangelical Church really don't know what they should do with the church's money then first and foremost, again and again, thought must be given to the indescribable need of our brothers of Evangelical faith who are refugees [from the East].[31]

He concluded that as long as German refugees lived in wretched deprivation, and as long as the churches were not completely in order, then gestures such as that proposed by Grüber were unacceptable. Bavarian church leaders responded that since Grüber was not under their supervision they were in no position to challenge him. They presumed that the money must have come from voluntary donations by persons who felt some responsibility for the destruction of the synagogue and assured the parishioner that no Bavarian church money was involved.

Antisemitism toward Jewish Christians

The antisemitic attitude of the church toward Jewish Christians serves as a glaring example of the lethargic pace of their *metanoia*. The way the postwar church treated Jews who had converted to Christianity is especially relevant to the question of coming to terms with the church's antisemitism. The church during the Third Reich had done very little when the Nazis had persecuted Christians of Jewish origin as Jews, although certainly it did more than it had done for Jews.[32] The reality after the war was not much different.

Aid for Jewish Christians involved two interwoven issues: Who would provide and administer the aid, and would it consist of special assistance in light of their racial persecution? Initially, there was considerable controversy and confusion within the church over who would provide material assistance to Jewish Christians: relief agencies organized by the military (state) governments, the churches, or Jewish organizations. At first church leaders failed to see why racially persecuted Christians should fall under their purview. Since the Nazis had persecuted the Jewish Christians as Jews, not Christians, and the Jewish relief agencies such as the American Joint Distribution Organization (Joint) were better prepared to provide assistance than the church or state relief organizations, many within the church expected the bulk of material assistance for Jewish Christians to come from Joint and Jewish relief agencies in Germany.[33] However, the restrictive guidelines that governed the appropriations by Joint and Jewish community leaders were contrary to church leaders' expectations: care packages could not go to persons who did not practice the Jewish faith.

Stuttgart Jewish leaders Benno Ostertag and Josef Warscher informed Karl Hartenstein of the church in Württemberg in early August 1945 that Jewish Christians and "Jews of mixed race," who did not belong to the "Mosaic confession," had visited the Jewish aid office in Stuttgart seeking assistance. Although Ostertag and Warscher recognized that Jewish Christians had suffered as Jews during the Third Reich, they rejected the Nazis' racial designation of Jewish Christians as Jews. Since their relief organization provided aid only to practicing Jews, they could not care for Jewish Christians. Couldn't the Evangelical Church assume responsibility for Jewish Christians?[34] It was, in fact, this inquiry by the Jewish community, according to Majer-Leonard, that stimulated the church in Württemberg to set up in 1945 an aid organization within the Evangelical Society (*Evangelische Gesellschaft*) specifically geared toward Jewish Christians.[35]

As awareness spread that Jewish relief agencies were not providing for Jewish Christians, churchmen who had taken an active interest in their plight during the Third Reich again acted with compassion. During the fall of 1945, Heinrich Grüber in Berlin reopened his Protestant aid office for the racially persecuted, which had been closed down by the Nazi regime during the war, and Hermann Maas did the same in Heidelberg. Maas asked the American military government in Heidelberg in November 1945 for permission to provide racially persecuted Christians with material necessities and spiritual care. "We shall do it from a highly spiritual and religious point of view," he assured the authorities. There were also centers under the direction of Protestant churchmen and women in Bremen, Essen, Frankfurt, Karlsruhe, Kassel, and Mannheim. In some cases interconfessional organizations or the racially persecuted themselves established aid offices for persons persecuted by the Nuremberg laws. By 1948 relief centers could also be found in Braunschweig, Duisburg, Düsseldorf, Freiburg, Hamburg, Hannover, Köln, and in Schleswig-Holstein.[36] Bavaria was the exception in that it did not have a relief center designated solely to aid Jewish Christians; instead the Bavarian *Hilfswerk* in Nuremberg and the Inner Mission in Munich provided assistance.[37] Pastor Otto Fricke explained the goals of the Frankfurt office as follows:

> Our aim is to find the Jews and so-called "Mischlinge" (half-caste) hitherto persecuted who believe in Christ and who are in spiritual and material distress. We wish to give them advise [sic] in all questions regarding their struggle for existence, also to support them by giving material relief with regard to which, however, we depend entirely on the support of our Brothers and Sisters in the oecumene [ecumenical community]. Owing to the fact that most of this [sic] people who we care for have been uprooted mentally and spiritually we deem it our noblest task to do everything we can to make them feel at home in our parish and thus giving them that inner strength which they need. In particular, we wish to give them ministerial office so that they strengthen their faith in the word of God and in the true belief in JESUS CHRISTUS [sic] our Lord. The spiritual aim of our work is to overcome antisemitism by a spirit of real Christian brotherhood.[38]

Fricke estimated that the aid office, which extended its activities throughout the territory of Greater Hessen, provided assistance to approximately 3,500 Jewish Christians, 400 of whom were "full Jews" and 3,100 of "mixed race (*Mischlinge*)."

The mid-level churchmen like Fricke, Grüber, and Maas—as well as the men and women who staffed the aid offices and who initiated contact with Jews—were atypical Protestants. Concern for the plight of Jewish Christians much less fostering a spirit of repentance and reconciliation was far from the minds of most of their fellow Protestants.

For Grüber it was simply unacceptable that the church was leaving the Jewish Christian relief work to the initiative of a few individuals within the church. He suggested to Eugen Gerstenmaier (1906–86), the director of the Protestant relief agency *Hilfswerk,* that he establish a special branch dedicated to the care of Jewish Christians with someone like Hermann Maas as its director.[39] He reminded Gerstenmaier that during the Nazi period the church lacked the courage to intervene on behalf of Jewish Christians but that no such courage was necessary in the postwar period. It made no sense, Grüber continued, for individual churchmen to establish aid offices across Germany when the work of these tiny aid offices so clearly overlapped with the assistance provided by the more established *Hilfswerk.*

Gerstenmaier acknowledged the importance of providing relief for Jewish

Confessing Church pastor Heinrich Grüber, arrested by the Nazis in 1940 for aiding Jews and Christians of Jewish descent, spent nearly three years in Sachsenhausen and Dachau. After the war Grüber worked tirelessly on the behalf of persons persecuted by the Nazis for racial reasons. *Photo courtesy of the Archive of the A. R. Wentz Library, Lutheran Theological Seminary of Gettysburg.*

Christians but said that a special division within *Hilfswerk* would violate the organization's principle of providing assistance based on need without regard to race, confession, or political orientation.[40] *Hilfswerk* would certainly provide aid to Jewish Christians, but it would be nothing more or less than all Germans in need received. Frustrated by Gerstenmaier's obstinacy, Grüber founded an umbrella organization for Jewish Christian aid offices, the Central Committee of Christian Aid Societies for Racial Persecutes of non-Jewish Faith in Germany, which attempted to coordinate some of the relief effort.

Majer-Leonard was not as diplomatic in his critique of *Hilfswerk* as Grüber. He accused Gerstenmaier of expressing the "spiteful" opinion that Jewish Christians should feel privileged to be a part of the church and that their membership in the church came with certain costs.[41] Although Majer-Leonard never specified exactly what he meant by "costs," the implication was clear: he believed that central office of *Hilfswerk* and its director treated Jewish Christians as second-class Christians. In a letter to Christian Berg, an associate of Gerstenmaier's, Majer-Leonard concluded, "The Jewish question was the shibboleth of the church struggle. Should it again today obtain a similar meaning? The leadership of *Hilfswerk* would do good to examine this question seriously."[42] Although Gerstenmaier retaliated with a request for disciplinary action against Majer-Leonard for allegedly misrepresenting his comments, Majer-Leonard did not soften his criticism of *Hilfswerk* and its director.[43]

He maintained that Gerstenmaier's decision not to offer special aid to racially persecuted Christians had serious consequences. Jewish Christians, he told Bishop Wurm, were now taking a "hostile position" toward the German Protestant Church.[44] Whereas the Catholic Church's relief organization, Caritas, had named a reputable person to focus on the needs of Jewish Christians, *Hilfswerk* stood idly by. According to Majer-Leonard, this was having the unfortunate result of giving disreputable "sects" the opportunity to prey on Christians of Jewish heritage. For instance, the Hebrew Christian Synagogue in Los Angeles was sending care packets to Jewish Christians in South Germany hoping to gain a foothold there.[45]

The estrangement of the Jewish Christians from the Protestant Church was a popular theme among the critics of the church's meager relief effort. Rengstorf warned, "A new division threatens Christianity in our generation, a rift which has no precedent in the church's history: the division between those of her members from among the Gentiles and those from among the Jews."[46] Radlauer, who managed the Grüber bureau in Berlin, added, "Although persecution has ended, a great many of our Christian non-Aryans are being estranged from Germany and ardently wish to emigrate." "Hundreds" of Jewish Christians, Radlauer reported, are eagerly trying to join the Jewish community because they feel alienated from the Protestant community and know that they will receive better assistance if they become Jews of faith.[47] Robert Brunner, the director of the Basel mission, wrote a stinging critique of the German church's neglect of Jewish Christians and claimed that there was discussion among them of creating Jewish Christian churches or synagogues since they experienced little sense of brotherhood in the Protestant Church.[48] The final report for the meeting of the International Missionary Council's Committee on the Christian Approach to the Jews, held in Basel in 1947, read:

> We confess that the lack of love and understanding for the Hebrew Christians in many local churches is such that the setting up of local Hebrew Christian churches is unavoidable, but we would urge that no such step be ever taken unnecessarily, and that the existence of such a need should call the Church at large to penitence for its lack of love.
>
> We recognize with grief that the Hebrew Christian all too often does not feel at home in the Church of Christ, and we call on the Church at large to realize that the main reasons are our lack of love which cannot find room for the stranger and the latent root of antisemitism which often poisons the Church's life where it is least realized.[49]

In 1935 Marga Meusel, a church worker in Berlin, had asked, "Why must one always be told from the ranks of the non-Aryan Christians that they feel forsaken by the church and the ecumenical movement? . . . Why does the church do nothing? Why does it tolerate this unspeakable injustice?"[50] Why were Meusel's questions, asked two years into Hitler's regime, still appropriate two years after his demise? Why did the church neglect the Jewish Christians in the postwar period as they had during the Nazi period? Did the church learn nothing?

Many church leaders continued to perceive Jewish Christians as a racial and cultural entity different from German Gentiles. Yet they refused to acknowledge that the persecution Jewish Christians experienced as a consequence of these perceived differences required special physical and spiritual care. Recognition of the special needs of Jewish Christians would have meant recognition that not only had the Nazis persecuted Jewish Christians for racial reasons while the church did little to protect them, but also that the church itself had passed legislation during the Nazi era, the so-called Aryan paragraph, which barred "non-Aryans" from the ministry and forced Jewish Christian pastors into retirement.[51]

Although there had been a debate within the church over the Aryan paragraph—the church's version of the Nazis' April 1933 Civil Service Law—and there were some courageous voices that spoke publicly against this legislation, in particular Dietrich Bonhoeffer, the church passed the racist legislation in late September 1933, thereby applying, at least in theory, Nazi racial laws to the church. Despite this, a number of agencies throughout Germany connected with the Confessing Church did their best to provide support to "non-Aryan Christians,"[52] the most acclaimed being Heinrich Grüber's agency in Berlin. Other such offices existed in Nuremberg, Munich, and elsewhere.[53] But the isolated voices calling for a more active defense of Jewish Christians were drowned out by the deafening silence of men like Bishop Meiser of Bavaria, who never issued a statement on the Jews or Jewish Christians during the twelve years of Nazi rule. To be fair, the aid offices established in Munich and Nuremberg could not have operated without Meiser's approval. But his refusal and that of many others to publicly condemn antisemitism aided the Nazis' cause. After the passage of the Nuremberg Laws in September 1935, Meiser spoke against the suggestion that the church should address the "Jewish question": "I would like to raise my voice against a martyrdom that we bring upon ourselves. I look with some concern at the upcoming Prussian synod if it desires to broach such things as, for example, the Jewish question."[54]

That the church passed its own racial legislation directed against Jewish converts to Christianity reveals the uncontestable extent to which antisemitism had become embedded in the church. Churchmen could not argue, as they did with the persecution of the Jews, that the fate of Jewish Christians in the Third Reich was simply a consequence of Nazi racial policy, since Jewish Christians were also affected by church legislation and complacency. Nor could they argue that Jewish Christian suffering was the manifestation of God's curse against the Jews for rejecting Jesus as the Messiah. The only difference between Jewish Christians and the rest of the Protestant community was their "race," and it was this that made them outsiders within the church before and after 1945.

The failure of the church to defend Jewish Christians from 1933 to 1945 was both a failure to recognize the sacredness of the sacrament of baptism and a sign of support for Nazi racial doctrine. It meant that the church had insisted on the "primacy of race over grace."[55] As far as some in the church were concerned, baptism might make a Jew into a Christian, but it did not make a Jew into a German.[56] Although virtually every church leader agreed that the atrocities committed against the Jews and Jewish Christians were reprehensible, unchristian, and a stain on Germany's honorable history, it did not necessarily follow that antisemitism "within biblical limits" was unwarranted.[57] One could condemn the Nazis for murdering Jews and Jewish Christians, and at the same time, question Jewish loyalty to Germany, as Bishop Wurm and others in the church did.

As chairman of the EKD's leadership council and the grand old man in the church, Theophil Wurm had the opportunity to use his prominent position to provide the church as well as the world with a model of the repentant and reformed German Protestant. Unfortunately, Bishop Wurm did not distinguish himself from many of his fellow countrymen. He and they deeply regretted that more could not have been done to stop the systematic murder of hundreds of thousands of Jews, but they nevertheless continued to nurture the basic prejudices that allowed the Holocaust to happen. Although the atrocities committed against the Jews appalled Wurm, his image of the Jew as a corrupter of German values carried over from the first half of the century into the second half.[58] Like many in Germany, he held the fundamental belief that Jews and Judaism had a destructive effect on Germany and must be combated. Holding to this belief, he refused to condemn in its entirety the

National Socialist portrayal of Jews as avaricious, venomous, and intent on weakening the German *Volk.*

That Wurm refused to acknowledge unconditionally a distinction between, on the one hand, the systematic murder of the Jews planned and carried out by the state with the knowledge and assistance of the armed forces, and on the other hand, the Allied bombing campaign and occupation policies, can be attributed to his antisemitic and nationalistic views. In his October 1945 welcoming address to visiting ecumenical church leaders in Stuttgart, Wurm stated that the behavior of the occupying powers toward Germans was leading ordinary Germans to conclude that "we are being treated as our people treated the Jews, Poles, etc."[59] Although Wurm did not claim this opinion as his own at this time, he did not condemn it either. He simply said that German church leaders would continue to have difficulty convincing the German population to repent for the crimes of National Socialism as long as the occupying powers continued to mistreat Germans. Two months later the opinion Wurm had attributed to unrepentant Germans he now expressed as his own in his open letter to English Christians. "To pack the German people into a still more narrow space, to cut off as far as possible the material basis of their very existence, is no different, in essentials, from Hitler's plan to stamp out the existence of the Jewish race."[60] His insensitivity was further exposed two years later when, as the bishop of Württemberg, he could not even be bothered to be present in Stuttgart on 9 November 1947 when the Stuttgart Jewish Community dedicated a monument in memory of the Jews who were murdered nine years earlier in the infamous 1938 pogrom.[61]

Perhaps the most damning piece of evidence confirming Wurm's antisemitic attitude was his response to the council of brethren's April 1948 "A Message Concerning the Jewish Question."[62] Despite its continued reliance on theological anti-Judaism, the council's message demonstrated that there was a group of churchmen who took seriously their responsibility to speak publicly about the church's antisemitism and to encourage reform. It read, in part,

> It may rightly be said that after what has happened, after all that we allowed to happen in silence, we have no authority to speak now. We are distressed about what happened in the past, and about the fact that we did not make any joint statement about it. . . . It was a disastrous mistake when the Churches of our time adopted the secular attitude of mere humanity, emancipation and antisemitism toward the Jewish question. There was bound to be bitter retribution for the fact that antisemitism rose and flourished not only among the people (who still seemed to be a Christian nation), not only among the intelligentsia, and in governmental and military circles, but also among Christian leaders. And when finally this radical antisemitism, based on racial hatred, destroyed our nation and our Churches from within, and released all its brutal force from without, there existed no power to resist it—because the Churches forgot what Israel really is, and no longer loved the Jews. Christian circles washed their hands of all responsibility, justifying themselves by saying that there was a curse on the Jewish people. Christians no longer believed that the promises concerning the Jews still

held good; they no longer preached it, nor showed it in their attitude to the Jews. In this way we Christians helped to bring about all the injustices and suffering inflicted upon the Jews in our country.

In his response to a draft of this statement, Wurm asked rhetorically,

> Can one issue a statement on the Jewish question in Germany without mentioning the way Jewish literati, since the days of Heinrich Heine, sinned against the German people by mocking all that is sacred and how in many areas the peasants suffered as a result of Jewish profiteers? And if one wants to take action against today's rising antisemitism, can one be silent about the misfortune that the occupying powers have handed the reins of power to the Jews who have returned in order to placate their understandable bitter resentment?[63]

That the chairman of the national leadership council of the church could scold his reform-minded colleagues for failing to mention Jewish profiteers and opportunists in their long-awaited statement on the church's inadequate response to the roundup, deportation, and extermination of German Jews demonstrates that antisemitic stereotypes were held by the highest ranking members of the church hierarchy and parishioners alike. Wurm's 1952 tribute to the antisemitic Wilhelmine court chaplain Adolf Stöcker (1835–1909) confirms that his conservative antisemitism remained with him until his death in 1953.[64]

Wurm's distasteful prejudices did not go unnoticed by the Jewish community in Germany. In November 1949 the Jewish-German press excoriated Wurm for voicing the opinion, yet again, that Germans were victims of a smear campaign and vengeful policies by the occupation forces. Karl Marx, the Jewish editor and journalist who returned to Düsseldorf after the war from exile in England, reproached Wurm for calling for an end to the vengeful policies of the occupation powers, especially their denazification program, and comparing the crimes committed by the Allies to Hitler's crimes. Referring to Wurm as an influential "Church Prince," Marx accused him of propagating a new myth, similar to the stab-in-the-back legend after World War I, which emphasized the guilt of the Allies. Marx reminded Wurm that the rubble and ruins across Germany were not the first ruins to mark Germany's landscape. The earliest buildings reduced to rubble were the synagogues destroyed a year before the war began.[65]

As one might expect, Wurm's critique of the brethren council's "A Message Concerning the Jewish Question" made no objection to anti-Judaic theology. Although conservatives and reformers disagreed over the extent and implications of the church's antisemitism, they concurred—at least in 1948 when the brethren council issued its statement—that since the Jews had rejected Christ as the Messiah, the church had superseded them as God's chosen people. Until they accepted Christ and joined the church, Jewish people would continue to live under God's curse and be forced to wander the earth in exile.

The centuries-long acceptance of anti-Judaism in the church, especially evident in the theory of supersessionism, continued unchallenged after the war. Only after the founding of the State of Israel in May 1948 and two more years of reflection and debate about Christian-Jewish relations did churchmen acknowledge at their 1950 synod in Berlin-Weissensee the far-reaching theological implications of the Holocaust and the success of the Zionist project.

8

A Ray of Light in Their Darkness
The Church and Anti-Judaism

At its April 1948 meeting in Darmstadt, the brethren council (*Bruderrat*), which had so notably challenged Lutheran orthodoxy when debating Germany's political course a year earlier, still adhered to a theologically conservative position with regard to the Jews. The brethren council stated that "since Israel crucified the Messiah, it rejected its own election and its own destiny. . . . Through Christ and since Christ, the chosen people is no longer Israel but the Church."[1] Although church reformers demonstrated in their "A Message Concerning the Jewish Question" that they understood the disastrous effect of the church's institutional failure to take active steps to combat racism and antisemitism, they showed no awareness of the consequences of the church's anti-Judaic theology (see appendix 7).

The brethren council continued to rely on the established dogma that the new people of God, the church, superseded the Jews as God's chosen people. The council's four-page statement explicitly reaffirmed the theology of the nineteenth-century missionary movement by referring to Jews as the "straying children of Israel" who lived under God's judgment and would find salvation only by joining the church. They cautioned, "The fate of the Jews is a silent sermon, reminding us that God will not allow Himself to be mocked. It is a warning to us, and an admonition to the Jews to be converted to him, who is their sole hope of salvation."

Anti-Judaism was so deeply ingrained in church doctrine and tradition and so widely accepted by clergy and laity that it was virtually unthinkable in April 1948 that it might have played a role in the horrors that were coming to light daily. It was not exceptional, therefore, that the "Jewish question" message, issued one month before the founding of the State of Israel and only three years after the liberation of the camps, indicated no understanding on the part of the brethren council that these momentous events would have far-reaching significance for Protestant theology. Reflection and the passage of time were necessary before these churchmen would grasp the significance. In the meantime, the blindness in the German churches was not unique. Supersessionism, Christian triumphalism, and missionary thinking were orthodoxy in Protestant churches across Europe. The World Council of Churches declared in its 1948 statement, "The Christian Approach to the Jews," that "All of our churches stand under the commission of our common Lord: 'Go ye into the world and preach the gospel to every creature.' The fulfillment of this commission requires that we include the Jewish people in our evangelistic task."[2]

Even the 1950 Berlin-Weissensee statement (see appendix 8), which rejected the theory of supersessionism, was not, as one scholar claimed, the "Magna Carta" of the Evangelical Church on the "Jewish question."[3] Although it certainly marked a progressive transformation in the church's theology, it was not the radical *metanoia* it at first seems. It concludes by declaring, "We pray to the Lord of mercy that he may bring about the Day of Fulfillment (*Tag der Vollendung*) when we will be praising the triumph of Jesus Christ together with the saved Israel." The references to the "Day of Fulfillment" and the "triumph of Jesus Christ" indicate the belief that Judaism was not a way to salvation and that the church was waiting for the Jewish people to fulfill its destiny by joining in the triumph of the church.

Although Christian triumphalism and missionary thinking permeated the church in the immediate postwar years, these years were anything but static theologically.[4] The church struggle, the Holocaust, the founding of the State of Israel in 1948, and the nascent Christian-Jewish dialogue jarred some pastors and theologians into questioning traditional church doctrine on supersessionism and the relationship between Jews and Christians. Only after the profound political and theological shock of these events had had time to sink in were some reformist pastors and theologians prepared to abandon their former stance. They now recognized the need for a new approach, which was to lead them to adopt the controversial third sentence in the 1950 Berlin-Weissensee statement acknowledging the continued validity of God's promise to the Jewish people.

The process of challenging established doctrine on the "Jewish question" and institutionalizing tolerance was slow and intermittent. Thus, missionary thinking and practices continued in the 1950s and afterwards, although not always in the same manner as in the nineteenth and early twentieth centuries. The Berlin-Weissensee statement should be understood as a first step in challenging anti-Judaic theology. By the 1960s and 1970s, churchmen like Günther Harder (1902–78), Karl Heinrich Rengstorf, and Heinrich Vogel (1902–89), all of whom favored a new relationship with Jews based on dialogue and mutual respect, had succeeded in fostering a public debate within the church over the question "mission or dialogue?"[5] They all rejected traditional missionary work—defined as the conversion of Jews to Christianity through the efforts of trained missionaries—which sought to resolve the "Jewish question" through the elimination of Jews by baptizing them. As we shall see, the objection to traditional missionary work, however, did not entail a complete break with the theology that undergirded missionary thinking. Nevertheless it did take steps to promote dialogue between Protestant and Jewish theologians and to encourage a relationship based on mutual respect and learning. This new direction was especially evident in 1961 when the tenth postwar German Evangelical Church Rally (*Deutsche Evangelische Kirchentag*) met in Berlin and thousands of Protestants attended lectures and engaged in discussion on Christian-Jewish relations and Judaism.[6] Finally, in 1980 the Rhineland synod issued a statement explicitly condemning missionary work with Jews.[7]

In the immediate postwar years this transformation was in its infancy and barely detectable, especially at the level of the congregations. Discussion of the "Jewish question" continued to be dominated by churchmen with close ties to the Jewish missions. The vast majority of Protestant clergy and laity paid very little attention to the "Jewish question"—much less engaged in a debate over whether the Jews were still God's chosen people.

Missionary Thinking in Protestant Theology

Pointing to passages in the New Testament and to the example of Jesus for justification of their work, missionaries maintained that the church had an obligation to spread the gospel and draw as many non-Christians, especially Jews, into the church as possible. "Go therefore and make disciples of all nations," the gospel of Matthew reads, "baptizing them in the name of the Father and of the Son and of the Holy Spirit, and teaching them to obey everything that I have commanded you" (28:19–20 NRSV).[8] Many Protestants, and not only in Germany, considered conversion of Jews to be more important than other missionary work and more likely to succeed for several reasons: Jews believed in the same God as Christians, read the Old Testament, were often educated, and lived in Europe and the United States. At the World Missionary Conference held in Edinburgh in 1910, delegates concluded:

> The Jewish people have a peculiar claim upon the missionary activities of the Christian Church. Christianity is preeminently theirs by inheritance. The Church is under special obligation to present Christ to the Jew. It is a debt to be repaid, a reparation to be fully and worthy made.[9]

The near extermination of European Jewry and the founding of the State of Israel did not change this fact for missionaries. In a 1949 address at a conference on "The Church and the Jewish People in America," E. G. Homrighausen, a scholar at Princeton Theological Seminary, summed up the central role of missionary work among Jews:

> Evangelism is a "must." It is inherent in the Christian Faith, because God is an active, redeeming God. We have no choice in this matter. An unevangelistic Church or Chris-

tian is an impossibility. And we have no alternative but to take this Gospel to all men, and to the Jewish people in particular because they are so close to the Christian Faith. We ought to feel an especial sympathy for these spiritual kinsmen, for we have so much in common with them and we have received so much from their heritage.[10]

If approached with a good deal of Christian love and understanding, so the argument went, the Jews were more likely to see the light than the "godless pagans" in Africa or Asia, who had little in common with Western Christians.

These sentiments were only sharpened following the Second World War by the recognition that after the barbaric treatment of the Jews by the Nazis, the churches had an even greater responsibility to offer the consolation and love of the Christian gospel's message. As one ardent German supporter of missions argued:

> Just this fact [the murder of six million Jews] should compel us, out of our feelings of shame, to meet the Jews in the consciousness that we owe them our Christian witness, which alone can lead to Christ himself. Only this vital witness of committed Christians can restore the true relationship between synagogue and church, between Judaism and Christianity.[11]

But it was not merely a guilty conscience or the religious kinship between Jew and Christian that led a segment of Protestant missionaries to assign priority to missionary work among Jews. Jews, they argued, were central to God's salvation plan. Since the nineteenth century, Protestant missionaries, including Old Testament scholar Franz Delitzsch (1813–90)—himself of Jewish descent—argued that preaching the gospel to Jews was essential, since only when Jews accepted Jesus as the Messiah would God's promise of salvation come to fruition. Karl Heinrich Rengstorf, the postwar German director of the Institutum Judaicum Delitzschianum, reasoned that missionary work among the Jews was "occasioned by the fact that through the unbelief of His own people the fulfillment of God's work is delayed and hindered. His eternal purpose of salvation is not attained so long as His own people refuses to receive Him."[12] For Rengstorf the church remained incomplete until God's chosen people merged with the church by recognizing the new covenant manifested in Jesus of Nazareth. Jewish acceptance of the Messiah would mark the climax of God's purpose:

> The Church is unfaithful to itself . . . when it does not constantly pray for the redemption of the Jewish people as the people of the Old Testament election. Indeed, one must even say that the church rightly understands itself as the one universal Church of the divine salvation *only when it prays for the Jewish people* with deep sorrow and with earnest longing. (Italics mine)[13]

In the preceding passage, written in the early 1950s, Rengstorf did not advocate the use of missionaries to coax Jews to join the church, but he clearly believed that Jews would find salvation only when they joined the church. Thus it was the obligation of Christians to pray that Jews would accept their destiny. Rengstorf was at the forefront of the movement after the war to reshape the goals and methods of the Protestant missions to the Jews. Although the definition of missionary work was undergoing a transformation in the decade after the war, thanks in part to Rengstorf, as long as it continued to include the desire to convert Jews to Christianity, it relied on the notion that God's covenant with the church was in some way superior to his covenant with the Jews and that the act of conversion was an act of completion and fulfillment for Jews.

Protestant *Judenmission*

In a letter to church leaders across Germany in October 1945, the provisional leaders of the Evangelical-Lutheran Central Federation for Mission to Israel, Otto von Harling Sr. and Rengstorf, announced the reconstitution of the Central Federation and the Institutum Judaicum Delitzschianum, which had been founded in 1886 in Leipzig by Franz Delitzsch.[14] They acknowledged that after the Holocaust the context for missionary work had changed, and they made it clear that the task of the Central Federation was not to do traditional missionary work, at least not yet, but rather to study the "Jewish question."[15]

> The undersigned are clear that after all that has taken place, immediate evangelical work among the Jews by the German Church is at this time not possible. Thus it appears all the more important to us that the German Lutheran churches again have an office, which considers as its particular task to waken and encourage an understanding of the history and the present internal and external situation of Jewry, and to provide a hearing for and recognition of the words of the Holy Scriptures on the Jewish question and the meaning of Israel in God's plan. In this we see at the same time a contribution, which the Lutheran Church in Germany can make, to redressing the injustices done to Israel.

Significantly, their hesitation over approaching liberated Jews with the intention to convince them that the Messiah had come was practical not theological. The directors of the Central Federation did not question the theological underpinnings of missionary work among Jews, but they were sensitive enough to recognize that given the church's abandonment of Jews and neglect for Jewish Christians during the Third Reich—and throughout the history of the church for that matter—it was hypocritical and certainly unproductive to approach them now with the gospel.

For many German Protestants, especially those connected with missionary activities, the overthrow of Hitler's regime offered the possibility of starting again where they had been forced by the Nazis to leave off. It was hardly surprising, therefore, that many prewar attitudes reappeared and were given a renewed institutional form, as could be seen in the renewed activity of several local branches of the Jewish missions. These local branch offices did not demonstrate the same sensitivity in regard to proselytizing as Rengstorf's Central Federation. They did, to be sure, give lip service to the importance of studying Judaism and fostering a dialogue between Jews and Christians, but conversion was still the primary goal. The Central Federation's Bavarian contact, Pastor Friedrich Wilhelm Hopf of Mühlhausen near Nuremberg, delineated in a letter to Bavarian churchmen five tasks that the Bavarian mission would pursue, the first of which was the evangelization of Jews.[16] The other four tasks were fostering a spiritual discussion between church and synagogue, studying modern Judaism, caring for Jewish Christians, and developing a consciousness among church members of the church's partial responsibility for the antisemitic injustices during the Third Reich. Nowhere in Hopf's letter was there even the suggestion that the church had a responsibility to do something *for* Jews *as* Jews. Jews who had converted and Jews who might be converted were the Jews that most interested the Bavarians.

In August 1946 Pastor Hopf and Pastor Martin Wittenberg of Neuendettelsau, southwest of Nuremberg, asked pastors in Bavaria to remember the Jewish mission on the tenth Sunday after Trinity. It was common in many regional churches for pastors and theologians associated with missionary work or Jewish Christian assistance to present their colleagues with advice on how to conduct this service.[17] Along with the request for financial support, Hopf and Wittenberg provided a ten-point summary on how to conduct the church service.[18] Nearly three pages detailed an explanation of various biblical passages for the service with the recommended lead passage coming from Luke 19:43–44. In this passage, Jesus enters the temple in Jerusalem and drives out the traders. At the sight of the traders, he prophesies: "Indeed, the days will come upon you, when your enemies will set up ramparts around you and surround you, and hem you in on every side. They will crush you to the ground, you and your children within you, and they will not leave within you one stone upon another; because you did not recognize the time of your visitation from God" (NRSV). The message for mission Sunday was clear: the Jews had rejected the Son of God, in so doing had earned God's wrath, and suffering was the result.

No one better represented the missionary spirit than Bavarian layman and medical doctor Gottfried Frohwein. Frohwein's father had been a missionary doctor among the Jews in Vilnius, Poland, and Frohwein himself worked in Vilnius for a British mission to the Jews from 1934 to 1939.[19] Because of his firsthand experience, Frohwein was the resident expert that the Bavarian Jewish mission called on to lecture on its behalf and to write pamphlets for the education of pastors and laymen alike. In October 1946 at the meeting of the Working Committee for the Lutheran Jewish Mission in Nuremberg, he gave an extremely detailed report on the present situation of Jews in Germany, the influx of East European Jews into the American Occupation Zone in 1946, and the tasks of the church, and in particular the Jewish mission.[20] What stands out in this report is Frohwein's compassion for the plight of the Jews, his forthright recognition of the church's partial responsibility for the present situation of Jewish suffering, and most important, his conviction that, more than ever, the church had an obligation to approach Jews, especially those living in DP camps, with the message that Jesus was crucified for the salvation of all people.

At one point in his lecture he tells the story of a pastor who lived in an area, presumably in Bavaria, where in 1946 there was a particularly large "Jewish invasion" (*Judeninvasion*).[21] The pastor was concerned about the plight of the Jewish refugees and was also worried that his Protestant congregation was less than sympathetic toward these poor and hungry Jews from eastern Europe (*Ostjuden*). The pastor, so Frohwein explained, had his first experience with the Jewish refugees when he observed a man stealing apples from a tree in his garden. When asked by the pastor what he could do for him, the Jew answered very quietly that he sought the sacrament of the Holy Supper. The man was in fact a Jewish Christian who had been persecuted as a Jew and now lived among Jews but sought, without much success, contact and a sense of community from fellow Christians. Frohwein told his Bavarian audience that not only was this true of many Jewish Christians but that many Jews also sought Christian fellowship and that it was the role of the church to provide it. The Jews are waiting, Frohwein insisted, for an opportunity to come in contact with welcoming Christians. "Today and in all times, the Jew is very receptive to a real living Christianity of action. It is a ray of light in his darkness."[22]

The evidence suggests that for the vast majority of Jews in Germany, nothing could have been further from the truth.[23] According to the missionaries themselves, the missions were not even remotely successful in convincing Jews to join the church. In fact, the utter failure of the missions in the wake of the Holocaust and the success of the Zionist movement in Palestine played a significant role in the gradual process of undermining support within the church for the missions. Although Frohwein's pep talk to fellow Bavarian missionaries could do nothing to alter the Jewish perception of the church as hypocritical, diehard missionaries remained convinced that Jews needed, now more than ever, the hope and joy that came from knowing Christ's saving grace. Jews who had converted to Christianity in nineteenth-century Germany or in pre-Nazi Germany did so either to accelerate the process of assimilation or out of conviction. After experiencing twelve years of humiliation and terror by Germans and other Europeans who often professed to be Christians, few, if any, Jews considered converting to Christianity.

But it was not just the Jews that missionaries had trouble convincing. Theo Burgstahler, a pastor who worked in the Jewish mission in Ulm—where approximately 10,000 Jewish refugees lived in DP camps—reproached the church for forgetting that it was its obligation to preach God's word to Jews. "Missionaries by the thousands carry the gospel to the pagan world," he wrote in a short article in the Basel Jewish mission newsletter, but "Israel remains until today the stepchild of the mission."[24] Many Protestants, he pointed out, believed that Jews lived under the curse of God and Jews should first become church members before preaching to them. Since it was the case that Jews would not join the church spontaneously, Burgstahler insisted, the church must reach out to them. He also repeated Frohwein's claim, with no evidence to confirm it, that Jews reacted very positively to the Christian missionaries in the DP camps.[25]

As the DP camps disappeared from the German countryside in 1949–50 and Jewish communities began to spring up in Berlin, Frankfurt, Munich, and other large cities, the missions followed Jews to the cities. In 1952 Robert Brunner, a Swiss missionary, expressed interest in establishing a mission in Frankfurt (where 600 to 800 Jews lived), despite the presence of established English, American, and German missions. Adolf Freudenberg, a pastor of Jewish descent in the Frankfurt area, responded to Brunner that with Niemöller's blessing, he and some like-minded colleagues had founded an Evangelical Committee for Service to Israel in the Hesse-Nassau Church.[26] Although Freudenberg stressed that the committee was devoting its efforts to educating clergy, laity, and students about the central role Jews played in the history of Christianity, he said that they also encouraged Jews to take up the gospel. He concluded in his letter to Brunner that Jews in Frankfurt might become bitter if in addition to the Americans, English, and Germans, Swiss missionaries were to approach them as well.[27]

As the activities of Freudenberg and other Protestant pastors indicate, support for Jewish missions was not limited to professional Jewish missionaries alone. Even highly respected scholars and churchmen supported the missions. Hermann Diem and the Württemberg Theological Society issued a statement in April 1946 that severely criticized the church for antisemitism and racial arrogance during the Third Reich and also scolded the church for not contesting the Nazi's prohibition of the church's mission to the Jews.[28] When a group of reputable scholars and churchmen, including Pastor Hermann Maas, who had risked arrest in the 1930s for protecting Jews and Jewish Christians, gathered at the behest of the church chancellery in October 1947 in Assenheim to discuss the church's relationship to the Jews, they issued a nine-point statement that began by recognizing missionary work as an integral part of the church's service to the Jewish people.[29]

Although churchmen were careful to avoid causally linking the Jews' rejection of Jesus as the Messiah with their persecution in the Holocaust or the Jewish plight in postwar Germany, it was commonplace for churchmen to refer to the divine punishment or curse (*Fluch*) Jews brought on themselves for rejecting Jesus. It is not always clear what churchmen and theologians meant when they referred continually to God's judgment and punishment of Jews. When the council of brethren declared in its 1948 "A Message Concerning the Jewish Question" that "God's judgment still pursues Israel until today," were they equating God's punishment with the suffering Jews had experienced during the Third Reich and the continued hardships after the war? And when Rengstorf stated in the early 1950s that "God has always been compelled by the unfaithfulness of His people to punish them in order

Pastor Adolf Freudenberg, a Christian of Jewish descent, had been forced to emigrate from Germany in 1939 to England and later moved to Switzerland. In 1947 he returned to Germany as a pastor in Bad Vilbel-Heilsberg near Frankfurt, where he encouraged his parishioners and colleagues to acknowledge the church's antisemitism and to make amends. *Photo courtesy of the* Zentralarchiv der Evangelischen Kirche in Hessen und Nassau *(12-A/123 (iii/1), Darmstadt, Germany.*

to train them," does he mean that God used the Holocaust to convince Jews that the path they chose was the wrong one?[30]

Doubtless, neither the members of the brethren council nor Rengstorf wanted the Jews to bear the blame for their persecution during the Holocaust. In fact, the brethren council explicitly and repeatedly charged the German people, including church leaders, with succumbing to antisemitism. "Christian circles," admonished the authors, "washed their hands of all responsibility [for the antisemitic atrocities], justifying themselves by saying that there was a curse on the Jewish people." And Rengstorf even admitted that Gentiles were in part responsible for Jewish suffering when he acknowledged it was "connected with the fact that the peoples of the world feel strange and uncomfortable whenever they are confronted with the people of the divine election." Nevertheless, the theology of supersessionism, which the council of brethren, Rengstorf, and many other reputable church officials and theologians espoused in their statements, implied that the Jews' unfaithfulness was a cause, if not the primary cause, of Jewish suffering. This becomes abundantly clear when Rengstorf states, just a few lines after he recognized that the prejudice of Gentiles contributed to Jewish suffering, that

> the suffering of Israel has a further explanation, even more important than the first. . . . This further explanation arises from the fact that God has always been compelled by the unfaithfulness of His people to punish them in order to train them. . . . Thus the Jewish people and suffering belong together. . . . The greater their distress, the more certain they are of God's final victory, which will bring with it the honorable exaltation of His chosen people.[31]

Despite the broad acceptance of the theology underpinning Jewish missions there had been increasing signs that not all churchmen supported missionary theology unconditionally. Three months before the brethren council issued its "A Message Concerning the Jewish Question" in 1948, it met in Kassel to hear and discuss lectures on the "Jewish question" by Reformed pastor Hermann A. Hesse and Lutheran pastor Otto Fricke of Frankfurt.[32] Fricke caused a stir when he expressed the view that the church could no longer condone missionary work that expressly sought to convert Jews to Christianity. However, unlike Harling Sr. and Rengstorf in their 1945 announcement, Fricke's objections were theological not practical. Christians, he argued, could behave in model Christian fashion, and in so doing perhaps attract some Jews to the church. But since Jews put their trust and hope in the same God as Christians, the traditional missionary task of coaxing Jews to convert was inappropriate; Christians, said Fricke, should treat Jews as brothers. Hans Iwand, the principal author of the earlier (1947) brethren council statement "On the Political Course of Our People," agreed, saying that the church was sorely mistaken if it thought it could solve the "Jewish question" with the Jewish mission.[33]

Shocked by these critiques of the Jewish mission, Harling Jr. reminded the churchmen at Kassel that the missions were victims of antisemitism during the Nazi period, not advocates of it.[34] Niemöller also was in favor of preaching the gospel to the Jews: "Wherever I confront a Jew I must say to him that Jesus of Nazareth is the Christ."[35] Although Fricke and Iwand's opposition to traditional missionary thinking is evidence of the beginning of a theological critique of the mission to the Jews, these reservations did not find their way into the brethren council's "A Message Concerning the Jewish Question" three months later.

The founding of the State of Israel in May 1948 was a crucial factor in motivating further reflection. That the Jews had not only survived the Holocaust and nearly two thousand years of Christian hostility but were now establishing a state in the land God had promised them baffled churchmen. Had they not been taught that the Jews were condemned by God to wander the earth in exile until they recognized Jesus as the Messiah? Germans were not the only ones perplexed. At the founding meeting of the World Council of Churches in Amsterdam a few weeks after the May 14 founding of the Israeli state, delegates could only say, "We do not undertake to express a judgment" on the new nation.[36]

Karl Barth was less reticent. What does it mean, Barth asked in his 1949 essay, "The Jewish Problem and the Christian Answer," that God has remained faithful to the Jews? "How have they, all things considered, attained this surprising position of historical permanence, a permanence which increases rather than decreases [with the founding of a new state]?" The Christian answer was that the new state was a sign of God's continued love for the Jews. Christians, Barth explained, hated to hear that the Jews continued to be the chosen people because "we do not enjoy being told that the sun of free grace, by which alone we can live, shines not upon us, but upon the Jews, that it is the Jews who are elect and not the Germans, the French or the Swiss, and that in order to be chosen we must, for good or ill, either be Jews or else be heart and soul on the side of the Jews. 'Salvation is of the Jews.'"[37] Barth's insistence that the survival of Jews and the founding of a Jewish state were signs that the Jewish people were still the chosen people found favor with a small group of his supporters in Germany but was rejected by mainstream Lutherans.

Rengstorf's Committee on Service to Israel

More influential than Barth and more representative of the German Lutheran process of grappling with the church's theology of triumph, were the conferences organized by the German Evangelical Committee for Service to Israel (*Der Deutsche evangelische Ausschuss für Dienst an Israel*).[38] Founded in January 1948 in Hannover by Rengstorf, the Committee for Service to Israel was a branch of the International Missionary Council's Committee on the Christian Approach to the Jews (IMC-CAJ). Replacing the word "mission" with "service" (*Dienst*) indicated the intention of Rengstorf's Committee for Service to Israel to eschew promoting traditional missionary work. This was particularly evident in the regular conferences organized by the committee to address questions related to the church and the Jews. Between 1948 and 1982 the committee organized twenty-eight conferences in various West German cities devoted to the general theme "the Church and the Jews."[39] Despite Rengstorf's close relationship to the Jewish missions through his leadership of the Evangelical Lutheran Central Federation for the Mission to Israel, he opposed making the Jewish mission an explicit theme in the committee's conferences, in part because he wanted the conference to initiate a discussion with Jews, and to this end he hoped to include prominent Jewish speakers such as Rabbi Leo Baeck.[40]

Leo Baeck (1873–1956), an assimilated German Jew who served as a rabbi for the German army on the Eastern and Western fronts in the First World War, attended the committee's first conference in Darmstadt in October 1948, where he spoke about "Judaism on Old and New Paths."[41] Germany's most famous rabbi and a survivor of Theresienstadt concentration camp in Czechoslovakia, Baeck settled in England after the war and from there was a voice for reconciliation with Germany. He returned to Germany for the first time in October 1948. At a press conference a few days before his lecture in Darmstadt, Baeck explained that ever since his liberation from Theresienstadt he had set himself the task of visiting German Jews wherever German Jewish communities had taken root in the aftermath of the Holocaust.[42] This was his reason for visiting Germany, but he also wished to visit with his Christian friends, with whom he had remained friendly despite all that had happened. Although the Jews who remained in Germany deserved the support of Jews from abroad, Baeck believed that the history of Jews in Germany was over. To stay in Germany or emigrate was a decision each individual Jew would have to make for himself or herself; Baeck's decision to settle in London (until his death in 1956) made clear that he, for one, was not comfortable living in Germany.

At the conference Baeck spoke about the confrontation since the seventeenth and eighteenth centuries between the modern rational world and Jewish mysticism.[43] Modern European states emancipated Jews and gave rights to them in the eighteenth and nineteenth centuries, he acknowledged, but the Jewish soul suffered: "As a man of this mystical world it was hard for him [the Jew] to find a place in this rational world where he could understand and be understood. He must, it seemed, decide for one or the other. . . . A spiritual see-saw began, a struggle between the new world and the old religion." With the establishment of the State of Israel the problem was resolved by providing a place where "mysticism and ratio have been joined." Baeck emphasized the importance of the new state for the future of Judaism. "One thing is clear," he concluded, "the Bible has taken on a new life here [in Israel]."[44]

Baeck's only reference to National Socialism or the Holocaust was an opaque reference to "the unfortunate days when the crime (*Verbrechen*) was committed against the Jews of Germany and Poland."[45] He explicitly avoided an accusatory tone, although he did discuss the history of the persecution of Jews over the centuries. He emphasized the common roots of Judaism and Christianity and the need for Christians in Germany to rethink their theological attitude toward Jews: "The Christian Church should never forget that there can be no Bible without the Jewish Bible."[46] Christians who attempt to deny their Jewish roots, he warned, risk repeating Germany's recent past. In his only direct reference to the exculpatory statements by German Protestants regarding Jewish persecution, Baeck asserted that Christians who recognize Jews as God's chosen people will not "seek to justify something wrong which has been done or is about to be done by talking about the orders of creation." Nor will the true Christian, he continued, explain crimes against Jews with references to God's rejection of the Jews. Jewish suffering is no more a sign of God's rejection of them than is Christian suffering a sign of God's rejection of Christians. He concluded on the conciliatory note that Jews and Christians both look forward with the same hope and awe to the time of fulfillment. By stressing that Judaism and Christianity were different "ways of piety" and "ways of hope" that sought a common end, he made clear that Protestant efforts to convert the Jews to Christianity made no sense.

Although the conference itself was groundbreaking in that it brought together Jews and Christians for a dialogue in postwar Germany, Baeck was one of only four Jews present. Many in the audience were employed by or worked in Jewish Christian aid offices or Jewish missions in the western zones of occupation.[47] Despite the opportunity, none of the pastors or theologians explicitly condemned missionary work or called on the church to confess publicly its role for fostering a spirit in which the Nazis could come to power and carry out their antisemitic agenda.[48] Reports on the conference by churchmen emphasized the valuable exchange of information about the present situation of Jews and Jewish Christians in various regions in Germany and the world.[49]

The next conference in late February and early March 1950 in Kassel overcame some of these drawbacks. In his invitation to the conference, Otto Dibelius, who took over the chairmanship of the EKD council in 1949 from Wurm, set the tone by expressing his support for the conference because it was one way to encourage Christians in Germany to accept their share of responsibility for the behavior and attitude of the German people toward the Jews.[50] More important, the voice and presence of the missions was virtually nonexistent, and the conference was more accessible to the public, including an open roundtable discussion between a Protestant (Pastor Karl Janssen), a Catholic (Karl Thieme), and a Jew (Hugo Nothmann) as well as exposure to the conference proceedings through extensive media coverage.[51] Among the keynote speakers were well-known Jews and Jewish Christians: Rudolf Pechel, editor of *Deutsche Rundschau* and an inmate from 1942 to 1945 in Sachsenhausen and Ravensbrück concentration camps; Alfred Wiener, a German Jew who fled to Amsterdam when Hitler came to power and eventually founded the Wiener Library in London; and Hans Ehrenberg, a Jewish-Christian pastor from Westphalia who, after a short imprisonment in Sachsenhausen concentration camp, emigrated to England in 1939 with assistance from Dietrich Bonhoeffer.[52] The conference ended with a public discussion, which the local community was encouraged to attend, on the relationship between Christians and the new State of Israel.

That the conferences ignored traditional missionary views did not please mission participants. Wilhelm Grillenberger, a missionary from Munich, expressed disappointment in his report to church leaders in Bavaria that the Kassel conference never acknowledged the church's hope that the Jews would change their ways and recognize the Lord Jesus Christ.[53] For many churchmen like Grillenberger, the new emphasis on dialogue with Jews should not preclude missionary work.

Grillenberger's critique notwithstanding, other churchmen, such as Helmut Gollwitzer (1908–93), a former student of Barth's and a professor of systematic theology in Bonn and Berlin after his release from a Soviet POW camp in 1949, felt that the connection between the committee's conferences and the missions was too close and thus an obstacle to fostering a true dialogue. He advocated a new forum.[54] Although the missionary agenda was conspicuously absent from the conferences at Rengstorf's insistence, it was not because he believed that the Jews' rejection of Jesus was unproblematic. Rengstorf did not shy away from expressing, in his Kassel lecture "Israel and the Church in the Light of the Bible," the belief that although the Jews were still God's chosen people despite their rejection of Jesus as the Messiah, God punishes them, as he does all people, for their disobedience. "The real guilt of the Jewish people according to the New Testament," Rengstorf explained, "is that the Jews have not recognized God's goodness." But, he emphasized, only God had the right to punish the Jews. He insisted it was a misuse and misunderstanding of the New Testament to use its words to justify religious antisemitism and anti-Judaism.[55]

The message of the New Testament, according to Rengstorf, was that the relationship between Jews and the church must be based on the law of unlimited love:

> The mission of the Church to Israel can be based only on the love by which the Church itself lives, and in which it seeks to share its riches with the Jews. It is not enough to base this mission on a reference to the formal missionary command, for this might oblige us to a missionary activity, but could not assure us of its spiritual justification. At the same time, we ought to be clear about the fact that missions to the Jews will be carried out as unselfish service of the Church to Israel, and when they take place in the kind of relationship in which brother seeks and finds brother.[56]

Thus Rengstorf rejected the triumphalism of traditional missionary work, which implied that a perfect church sought to bring fulfillment and meaning to an imperfect people. Only when Jews recognize the traits of the Messiah—love, respect, and humility—*in the church* will they want to join it. "This means for the church in its relation to Judaism that, wherever it deliberately confronts the Jews with the gospel, it can do so only with humility and reverence."[57]

Rengstorf's Committee for Service to Israel had a decisive influence on the EKD's Berlin-Weissensee synod. Both the Kassel conference and the April 1950 synod took place in the midst of desecrations of Jewish cemeteries that received international attention in the press.[58] The committee agreed at its Kassel conference to send a letter to the chairman of the EKD council, Otto Dibelius, requesting that the council take some practical steps toward addressing the continued signs of antisemitism. One step was to encourage Protestant congregations to protect and care for Jewish cemeteries where the Jewish community was either very small or was no longer present. Moreover, Adolf Freudenberg, who had been frustrated for years by the EKD council's habit of putting off issuing a statement on the "Jewish question," wanted the committee to send the EKD council a draft of a hard-hitting statement on the "Jewish question" that he had written. He insisted that the church could not speak with integrity on the question "What can the church do for peace?"—the designated topic for the Berlin-Weissensee synod—without first acknowledging the church's complacency and complicity in the mistreatment of Jews.[59] Although the committee did not send Freudenberg's strongly worded draft statement, they did agree to send the president of the upcoming EKD synod, the laymen and former West German Minister of Interior Gustav Heinemann (1899–1977), a letter requesting that the synod make a statement on the "Jewish question."[60]

The Berlin-Weissensee Synod

Presumably the committee's letters to the EKD council and synod president, the rash of cemetery desecrations, and the dedication of a monument to the victims of Nazi racial persecution at the Weissensee Jewish cemetery on the Sunday that the synod opened (23 April 1950)[61] were all factors that prompted churchmen at the synod to address Christian-Jewish relations.[62] Certainly Bishop Dibelius's opening sermon on 23 April, when he declared the church's hope that Protestant congregations would take it upon themselves to protect Jewish cemeteries, suggests the influence of the committee's letter. On the following day, during the discussion on "What can the church do for peace?" the bishop of the Lutheran Church of Hannover, Hanns Lilje, was the first to say that it would be a great step toward peace if the church would issue a genuine statement of repentance in the name of the German people on the "Jewish question." It was left, however, to his colleague, Heinrich Vogel, a professor of systematic theology in Berlin and a friend of Karl Barth's, to call explicitly for the synod to issue a confession of guilt for the behavior of the church toward the Jewish people. The church in particular, he contended, must confess its guilt because the roots of the entire recent catastrophe lay in the church. Vogel criticized the authors of the Stuttgart declaration for dodging the issue of the church's guilt by referring to the church's "solidarity of guilt" with the German people as if the church *itself* was not guilty. The afternoon of the same day

Niemöller supported Vogel's call for a declaration of guilt saying it was long over-due and should have been made at Stuttgart in October 1945, but it would be bet-ter late than never. He strongly condemned the prevailing attitude in the church that the reprehensible behavior of the occupation powers somehow alleviated the Germans of their obligation to confess their guilt.[63]

At the end of the second day a committee was formed to draft a statement on "what can the church do for peace," which included Vogel, Niemöller, Joachim Beckmann, Theodore Dipper, and other churchmen actively interested in the "Jewish question." During the evening session of the fourth day, Dipper introduced the work of the committee. He explained that the committee members quickly came to the conclusion that the unresolved state of the church's relationship to the Jews, in particular the church's guilt toward the Jews, was a serious obstacle to complet-ing the committee's primary task of drafting a peace resolution. Thus a subcom-mittee was formed, headed by Heinrich Vogel, which drafted a statement on the "Jewish question."

Meeting, ironically, in the Adolf Stoecker Foundation headquarters, Vogel read a draft of the "Statement on the Jewish Question" to the synod, and for the rest of the evening and the next morning, the first official discussion of the "Jewish ques-tion" by a national body of elected Protestant Church leaders took place. Although some individuals articulated reservations about a public confession being misun-derstood by the world, nearly every churchman who spoke praised the statement and expressed deep gratitude and a sense of genuine relief that the church was finally issuing a statement that addressed the church's antisemitism and anti-Judaism.

The most significant area of disagreement was over point three of the statement, which addressed the continued validity of God's covenant with the Jews. Julius Jensen, a pastor from Lübeck and leading figure in the Inner Mission and *Hilfswerk* there, asked whether it was appropriate to speak of God's continued loyalty to the Jews without mentioning God's judgment of the Jews for their rejection of Jesus. Bishop Lilje, prelate Karl Hartenstein of Stuttgart, and Erlangen theologian Wal-ter Künneth all raised similar objections. Significantly, they did not challenge the notion that after the crucifixion of Jesus the Jews remained God's chosen people. This in itself was a sign that the reevaluation of the myth of supersessionism had come a long way. What Künneth and others wanted was to reformulate the sen-tence so that it addressed the "biblical fact" that since the crucifixion the Jews have stood under God's judgment—or, as Hartenstein put it, "an anti-Christian cloud of judgment." Künneth considered it an absolute necessity to mention this because year after year, on the tenth Sunday after Trinity, this fact was preached to the con-gregations and recognized by Christian churches.[64] Vogel agreed that if one were teaching a Bible lesson, God's promise to the Jews and judgment of them would certainly be taught together. But the "Statement on the Jewish Question" was a confession, and the mention of God's judgment of the Jews would send the wrong message—the message of Christian self-righteousness.[65] Vogel's argument must have found a sympathetic hearing because the final draft said nothing about God's judgment of his chosen people. In fact, the only mention of God's judgment was his judgment of Gentile Germany: "We caution all Christians not to balance what has come upon us as God's judgment against what we have done to the Jews." That all people, Christians and Jews, stood under God's judgment and mercy was implicit in the quote from Romans 11:32, which introduced the statement: "For God has consigned all men to disobedience, that He may have mercy upon all."

The decision to avoid explicit mention of God's judgment of the Jews and the subsequent need for Jewish repentance did not mean that the statement had no remnants of missionary thinking. In the final sentence the church prayed that the God of Mercy might "bring about the Day of Fulfillment when we will be praising the triumph of Jesus Christ together with the saved Israel." Presumably in reference to this sentence, Vogel said that he wanted to assure the pro-missionary critics of the statement that "it is a missionary statement."[66] But it was not a traditional missionary statement. The church, to be sure, still had an obligation to pray that the Jewish people would one day join the church and recognize Jesus as the Messiah, but as a prayer it did not involve coercion, pressure, threats, or even coaxing. Nevertheless, the sense of superiority and self-righteousness that undergirds missionary thinking was clearly present in this sentence.

Of course, the church's antipathy toward Jews was a consequence of both its anti-Judaism *and* antisemitism. The two were inextricably linked. To address one and not the other was to miss the undeniable link between teaching contempt for the people of the old covenant and violence against Jews. This had been the problem with the brethren council's 1948 statement. The Berlin-Weissensee synod did not make the same mistake; it addressed both the church's anti-Judaism and its antisemitism, although its repudiation of antisemitism was milder than the brethren council's. The Berlin-Weissensee synod declared:

> We state that *by omission and silence we became implicated* before the God of mercy in the outrage which has been perpetrated against the Jews by people of our nation. . . . We ask all Christians to disassociate themselves from all antisemitism and earnestly to resist it, whenever it stirs again, and to encounter Jews and Jewish Christians in a brotherly spirit. (Italics mine)

Indeed these sentences could be criticized for using the passive voice and for admitting to complacency and not complicity. The significance of the Berlin-Weissensee statement, however, is that the issuing body was an all-German synod. Unlike the council of brethren, which consisted of reform-minded churchmen from the old Dahlem wing of the Confessing Church, the synod was a broad coalition of churchmen and lay people of all theological persuasions. For such a group to admit to wrongdoing in their treatment of Jews was a vast improvement over previous official church statements.

A remarkable aspect of the Berlin-Weissensee statement was its call for action.

In an attempt to curb the growing number of attacks on Jewish cemeteries and to encourage German Protestants to take responsibility for their nation's murderous past, the authors of the statement called on Protestant congregations to protect and care for Jewish cemeteries. Although some congregations took up this challenge energetically, others ignored it or did very little. In May 1950 the church chancellery sent out a circular to regional church leaders stating that the words of the Berlin-Weissensee statement needed to be matched by deeds and that churches should not wait any longer to adopt a Jewish cemetery. Of the 715 Jewish cemeteries in Germany, the church chancellery reported 43 were entirely or partly in the care of Protestant communities in 1951.[67] Under the title "An Act of Atonement," the Jewish-German press applauded the efforts of the church in the Rhineland to protect and care for Jewish cemeteries there as an indication that the church intended to practice what it preached in Berlin.[68] It is one thing for the church to publicly proclaim an interest in Protestant Jewish reconciliation, the reporter wrote, but the integrity of the church will stand or fall on the degree to which churchmen put into practice the lofty words spoken in Berlin. Although the protection of Jewish cemeteries was a good start, the newspaper called on the church to do more in terms of teaching and preaching respect and tolerance for all human beings.

The Berlin-Weissensee synod's rejection of supersessionism was unprecedented and momentous. Although church leaders never explicitly tied the church's anti-Judaism to the Holocaust, they rejected the central tenet of Christian anti-Judaism and brought about a sea change in German Protestant theology. The unanimous acceptance of the Berlin-Weissensee statement by the synod brought to an end the church's shameful silence on the "Jewish question."

The Berlin-Weissensee statement could have been more critical and explicit about the church's complicity in the discrimination against Jews in the Third Reich. It could have addressed the centuries-long history of anti-Judaism and anti-semitism in the church. And it could have avoided altogether the notion that the Jews would remain lost sheep until they joined the church. Nevertheless, it was a victory for the small group of churchmen who had tirelessly and courageously struggled, some since 1933, for the church to rethink its historical, practical, and theological relationship to Jews and Judaism. And most important, it was the first step in a process that continues in the twenty-first century of reforming the church's understanding of, and relationship to, German Judaism.

Conclusion

In his 1959 essay "What Does Coming to Terms with the Past Mean?" the German philosopher and social critic Theodor Adorno (1903–69) expressed frustration and disdain with the German failure to face the Nazi past head-on. In the fourteen years since the end of the war, "no serious working through the past" had taken place. Instead, he detected a concerted effort to repress the past by "wiping it from memory."[1]

It was a rare Protestant churchman who sought to come to terms with the Nazi past by wiping it entirely from memory, but neither did churchmen confront it as Adorno had hoped by engaging in critical self-reflection. Instead, they sought to shape memories and interpretations by explaining the past through the lens of Protestant theology, traditions, and practices. Perhaps the Nazi past and Auschwitz were synonymous in Adorno's mind, but for most German churchmen Auschwitz did not embody the way they conceptualized or remembered the recent past. Although the pastors, theologians, and church leaders in this book came to different conclusions, they relied on Protestant doctrine and Christian teaching to conceptualize and interpret the tragedy of the Third Reich and the immediate postwar years. The dominant discourse of the church from 1945 to 1950 was borrowed from the Bible; to assuage present suffering, pastors and theologians invoked the traditional Christian concepts such as redemptive suffering, "God's righteous judgment," and "His unfathomable compassion"—concepts exemplified by the Brandenburg churchmen in their Repentance and Prayer Day declaration.

In their sermons, clergymen regularly employed empty exercises that did not require a serious working through of the recent past. Instead they drew on the crucifixion, suffering, and resurrection of Jesus Christ—images undeniably central to Christian teaching and thought. Jesus' suffering on the cross provided churchmen in postwar Germany with an analogy for the pervasive suffering around them. Churchmen not only compared Christ's suffering on the cross to the suffering in their midst, but they reminded parishioners that Christ died for them to take away their sins so they might live in the glory of God's loving forgiveness. In his Good Friday sermon in 1947, Lutheran theologian Helmut Thielicke told the parishioners of St. Mark's Church, "We are made to think of the multitudes who in our own day have suffered a kind of crucifixion—on the battlefield, in the concentration camps, in cellars destroyed as the bombs fell." But, he continued, there is another side to Good Friday and the crucifixion: "In spite of all, the heavens stood open over His pains and wounds. We too, coming to His Cross, can know this most consoling fact, that we may stand with Him under the opened heavens."[2] The sin-suffering-salvation discourse appealed to churchmen because it allowed them to discredit the judgment of "enemy" nations while calling on Germans to submit to the higher judgment of a merciful God.

Conservatives especially were reliant on this type of discourse. When they discussed the church's guilt, it was almost always construed as religious guilt, or guilt before God. Although there were variations and even contradictions in the way conservative Protestants viewed the years of the Third Reich, they generally agreed—though often reluctantly—that the church was guilty before God "for not witnessing more courageously, for not praying more faithfully, for not believing more joyously, and for not loving more ardently," as they declared in the Stuttgart Declaration of Guilt. Their adherence to conservative Lutheran theology and traditions obstructed the process of evaluating critically the church's conservative nationalism and antisemitism. They defended the limited nature of their conservative churchly resistance, which consisted primarily of defending the church against the storm-trooper tactics of the German Christians and the Nazis, as consistent with the Lutheran doctrine of two kingdoms. It was highly unusual for conservatives to express remorse for their complacency (and often complicity) in the Nazis' persecution of communists and socialists; the abolition of basic rights of association, assembly, and press; the elimination of parliamentary representation; the discrimination against, and persecution of, Jews; and the aggression toward, and occupation of, neighboring countries. Although they advocated a new beginning for the church in 1945, conservatives did not believe that such a rebirth entailed any fundamental changes in the church's theology, structure, or politics. Rather, the new beginning they sought meant confessing and repenting before God, restoring the established regional church authorities, renewing ecumenical ties, supporting a law-abiding conservative government, and ultimately, rechristianizing the German people.

Although the reformers were only slightly more forthcoming in examining the roots of their antisemitism, they did address the church's institutionalized conservatism, which had provided few incentives to oppose Nazism. Karl Barth, one year before his death, conceded that even the Dahlem wing of the Confessing Church, which he had provided with theological direction from 1934 to 1945, had been woefully inadequate in its opposition to Nazi political and racial policy. The Barmen

and Dahlem synods of 1934 had sought to protect the church theologically and ecclesiastically from the combined threats of the German Christians and the Nazis,
yet neither synod defended or promoted democratic rights, civil liberties, or, in
Barth's words, "common humanity" (*Mitmenschlichkeit*). Barth's admission, made
in a 1967 letter to Eberhard Bethge, the official biographer and a close friend of Dietrich Bonhoeffer, is quoted below at length because in it Barth acknowledged an
element of truth to the charge made by Manfred Jacobs, a professor of theology in
Münster, that Barth's decision to base the church's opposition in 1934 on the theological principle *Solus Christus* was a serious error since it failed to incorporate an
active defense of human liberty.[3]

> It was new to me that Bonhoeffer [as I read in your 1967 biography of him] in 1933
> viewed the Jewish problem as the first and the decisive question, even as the only one,
> and took it in hand so energetically. I myself have long felt guilty that I did not make
> this problem central, at least public, in the two Barmen declarations of 1934 which I
> had composed. In 1934, certainly, a text in which I said a word to that effect would
> *not* have found agreement either in the Reformed synod of January 1934 or in the
> General synod of May at Barmen—if one considers the state of mind of the confes-
> sors of faith in those days. But that I was caught up in my affairs somewhere else is
> no excuse for my not having properly fought for this cause [italics mine].
>   . . . Burdened with its problematic Lutheran tradition, [Germany] suffered pre-
> cisely because of the lack of . . . ethics, common humanity (*Mitmenschlichkeit*), the
> church serving the underprivileged, the cost of discipleship, socialism, peace move-
> ments—and, in all of this, just politics.[4]

As Barth rightly points out, he could have stressed a more political opposition based
on a concern for the basic rights of all human beings in 1933 and 1934. He could be
reproached for not doing so, but the assertion that his words would have fallen on
deaf ears rings true. Considering the emphasis Lutherans placed on obedience to
authority (*Obrigkeit*), a resistance movement within the Protestant Church based
on the defense of civil liberties was highly improbable at the time.

The problem was not only that Barth grounded the church's opposition in theological principles, as Manfred Jacobs contends, but rather that the political implications of these principles were never drawn out fully by Barth or the Confessing
Church. Barth himself—his Reformed theological background notwithstanding—
failed to see the link between his Christian convictions and political behavior. In fact,
in 1933 he insisted that politics was not the concern of the church. His role, he believed, was to provide theological direction at Barmen. The shortcomings of a strictly
theological approach became apparent in the mid-1930s when the Nazis stepped-
up their persecution of Jews and Christians. From this point on one can see in Barth's
writings and actions the gradual development of a political ethic—one that called
on followers of Christ to engage critically in political life based on their Christian
convictions.

Although the Dahlem wing of the Confessing Church pressed its opposition, both theological and political, further than the conservatives between 1935 and 1939, it never fully developed a political ethic during that period. The priority for them during the Nazi era always remained defending the church. Hermann Diem, Hans Iwand, Martin Niemöller, and other Dahlemites acknowledged this error immediately after the war when they declared at Treysa in 1945 and Darmstadt in 1947 that the church must draw on its religious convictions and apply them in the political sphere. The Darmstadt statement initiated that process by stating with surprising clarity where the church had failed and what new direction it should take. Even the 1945 Stuttgart declaration hinted that the church had a share in the responsibility to maintain peace and order—as the Barmen declaration had stated nine years earlier. These and the later statements on the "Jewish question" recognized that men and women, regardless of their race, nationality, or class were children of God and therefore required and deserved basic human rights. The basis of their defense of human rights was not natural law, which does not recognize the sinful nature of mankind, but rather the basic Christian premise that God bestowed dignity and intrinsic value on man by sacrificing his only Son on the cross. As Barth said in a 1953 address in Bielefeld, "Ethics has to make clear that every single step man takes involves a specific and direct responsibility toward God, who reached out for man in specific and direct encounter."[5]

In contrast to the placating measures and consoling steps advocated by conservatives, the reformers' route took the church in an entirely new direction. For the reformers, coming to terms with the past meant more than coming to terms with the church's behavior during the Nazi period. It meant coming to terms with the church's long history of a supportive relationship with the state, the nineteenth-century theology of the divine orders, the church's hierarchical structure, its lack of attention to the underprivileged, and its teaching of contempt for Jews. In short, it meant coming to terms with the absence of a progressive political ethic. Although too late to have a major impact on Nazi policy, the reformers, with Barth's assistance, did begin to develop a political ethic in the 1930s and proceeded to apply it in the public sphere in the postwar decades.

The legacy of Barmen and the church struggle for reform-minded clergy and laity was that they came to recognize their responsibility to both kingdoms, the earthly and the spiritual. No longer would the reformers allow Luther's doctrine of two kingdoms to be used as an excuse for pastors to compromise with the conservative or authoritarian governments in East and West Germany. The presence of clergymen in the fight to keep Germany unified, in struggles with the Communist authorities in East Germany, and in the anti-rearmament movement in the late 1940s and 1950s exemplifies the resolve of the reformers to break forever the alliance between throne and altar. In East Germany veterans from the Dahlem wing of the church struggle like Heinrich Grüber and Heinrich Vogel called on pastors to leap into the breach to defend the dignity of mankind against persecution and deception. In West Germany Niemöller, in particular, was a constant thorn in the side of Chancellor Konrad Adenauer. Niemöller's quip that Adenauer's administration was "conceived in the Vatican and born in Washington" and his inflexible opposition to rearmament earned Niemöller the epithet "enemy of the state" by the conservative chancellor.[6] The change in Niemöller's worldview appears all the more dramatic when one recalls his request in 1939 to be freed from his cell at Sachsenhausen concentration camp so that he could fight for the fatherland.

The motivation of reformers to urge the church and the German people to confront their past and to make fundamental changes stemmed from three complex factors: their theological principles; their experiences under Nazi rule; and their postwar political orientation, which was strongly influenced by their observation that few Germans showed signs of self-critical reflection and contrition.

Theologically, the reformers subscribed to—borrowing an expression from Barth—"Reformed Lutheranism."[7] The majority of the reformers were Lutherans and while they subscribed loosely to the Lutheran confessions, they were strongly influenced by Barth's Reformed (Calvinist) theology. Many of these "Reformed Lutherans" came from United churches, where strict Lutheran confessionalism had been tempered as a consequence of the administrative union of Reformed and Lutheran churches in the nineteenth century. The geographical center of the Dahlem wing of the Confessing Church was in the western territories of Prussia, especially in the Rhineland, where Reformed influences were historically the strongest.

Both the Barmen declaration, written by Barth, and the Dahlem resolutions provided the reformers with their theological and ecclesiastical direction after 1945. The Barmen position on the relationship between church and state was not radically different from the orthodox Lutheran interpretation of the doctrine of two kingdoms, but it did introduce minor modifications, which had great significance after the war. In describing the state's task as maintaining "justice and peace," Barmen provided the reformers with a starting point from which to challenge the conservative Lutheran view, which held that as long as the state provided order it was a Christian's duty to obey it. Barth's Reformed understanding of the relationship between church and state *and* his defense of the Jews as God's chosen people provided the reformers with the theological foundation for some of their most radical postwar statements.

After the war, many conservative Lutherans continued to subscribe to the orthodox interpretation of the doctrine of two kingdoms, law-gospel dualism, divine orders, and theory of supersessionism. They did not, however, completely reject the Barmen declaration; because the conservative faction interpreted Barmen differently, they simply attached less significance to it. The church's behavior during the Third Reich looked very different through the lens of orthodox Lutheranism than it looked through "Reformed Lutheranism." The church's compromises with the Nazi state were more difficult to criticize and easier to rationalize when relying upon orthodox Lutheran interpretations.

The second reason the Prussian-centered Dahlemites became reformers after the war was because these churchmen from "destroyed churches" shared similar experiences under the Nazis, including harassment, forced retirement, dismissal, arrest, and imprisonment. They had suffered greater injustices during the Third Reich and had compromised less, and as a result they were more likely to urge a detailed examination of the church's and their own personal roles during the Nazi era. They had less to explain and justify than church leaders from the "intact churches" who deliberately chose to compromise with the German Christians and the Nazis in the hope that it would save their churches from the fate of Prussian churches. As Niemöller explained after the war, it was his experience in the concentration camps—an experience Bishops Wurm and Meiser never had to endure—that led to the realization that communists and socialists were human beings too.[8]

The final factor that influenced how reformers interpreted the recent past was their ability to see beyond the present reality of a devastated and occupied Germany. Without exception, every church leader mentioned in this study criticized the occupation policies of the Allies for unnecessarily worsening the plight of German civilians. Reformers, however, maintained that these policies did not lessen the responsibility of German Protestants to confess and repent before God and man for their role in bringing Hitler to power, for supporting many Nazi policies, and for speaking out only when the church itself was threatened. Even after the war, conservatives, blinded by nationalist feeling, refused to distinguish the unprovoked and systematic murder of Jews and other groups from the Allies' ruthless bombing campaign and harsh occupation policies. Representative of conservative thinking was Bishop Wurm's contention that the Russian military campaign and the Allied occupation "cannot, in fundamental terms, be evaluated any differently than the extermination plans of Hitler against the Jewish race."[9]

The view that the monumental task of rebuilding Germany's economic, political, and social institutions after the Second World War afforded Germans little time or energy to confront the implications of widespread support for Nazism was held by many conservative churchmen in the decade following the war. In fact, it is still a common assumption held today. This myth should finally be put to rest in light of the extensive debate within the Protestant Church over the issues of guilt and responsibility for the Third Reich. The time and energy for critical self-reflection was there; what was missing was the will to examine thoroughly how the acceptance of political conservatism and orthodox Lutheran theology provided the motivation for churchmen to support many of Hitler's objectives. The predominant mood among church leaders after the war, as Niemöller had observed, was self-congratulatory. The churches were the only institutions to survive the Nazi period relatively intact, and the majority of church leaders were determined to use their privileged positions to reconstitute a conservative church and to champion the cause of their defeated people.

Although this conservative legacy survived into the postwar period and dominated church affairs in the decades to follow, the alternative vision of the church as the conscience of the people and champion of a new political ethic challenged the majority view and continues to influence a minority within the Protestant church today.

APPENDIX 1. Theological Declaration of Barmen

(Confessing Church, May 1934)

1. "I am the Way and the Truth and the Life; no one comes to the Father except through me" (John 14:6). "Truly, truly, I say to you, he who does not enter the sheepfold through the door but climbs in somewhere else, he is a thief and a robber. . . . I am the Door; if anyone enters through me, he will be saved" (John 10:1, 9).

Jesus Christ, as he attested to us in Holy Scripture, is the one Word of God which we have to hear, and which we have to trust and obey in life and in death.

We reject the false doctrine that the church could and should recognize as a source of its proclamation, beyond and besides this one Word of God, yet other events, powers, historic figures, and truths as God's revelation.

2. "Jesus Christ has been made wisdom and righteousness and sanctification and redemption for us by God" (1 Cor. 1, 30).

As Jesus Christ is God's assurance of the forgiveness of all our sins, so, and with equal seriousness, he is also God's mighty claim [Anspruch] upon our whole life. Through him befalls us a joyful deliverance from the godless fetters of this world for a free, grateful service to his creatures.

We reject the false doctrine, as though there were areas of our life in which we would not belong to Jesus Christ, but to other lords—areas in which we would not need justification and sanctification through him.

3. "Rather, speaking the truth in love, we are to grow up in every way into him who is the head, into Christ, from whom the whole body [is] joined and knit together" (Eph. 4:15–16).

The Christian Church is the congregation of the brethren in which Jesus Christ acts presently as the Lord in Word and sacrament through the Holy Spirit. As the church of pardoned sinners, it has to testify in the midst of a sinful world, with its faith as with its obedience, with its message as with its order, that it is solely his property, and that it lives and wants to live solely from his comfort and his direction in the expectation of his appearance.

We reject the false doctrine, as though the church were permitted to abandon the form of its message and order to its own pleasure or to changes in prevailing ideological and political convictions.

This translation of the six Barmen theses is a conflation of Arthur Cochrane's translation in *The Church's Confession* and Douglas S. Bax's translation in Eberhard Jüngel, *Christ, Justice and Peace.* Bax's translation first appeared in the *Journal of Theology for Southern Africa* 47 (June 1984). I found it necessary to use parts of each translation since both are somewhat awkward and hard to understand in certain sections. Each of the six theses has three parts: a quote from the Scriptures, an interpretation of the quote by the authors of the declaration, and a rejection of false doctrine by the declaration's authors.

4. "You know that the rulers of the Gentiles lord it over them, and their great men exercise authority over them. It shall not be so among you; but whoever would be great among you must be your servant" (Matt. 20:25–26).

The various offices in the church do not establish a dominion of some over the others; on the contrary, they are for the exercise of the ministry entrusted to and enjoined upon the whole congregation.

We reject the false doctrine, as though the church, apart from this ministry, could and were permitted to give to itself, or allow to be given to it, special leaders vested with ruling powers.

5. "Fear God. Honor the emperor" (I Peter 2:17).

Scripture tells us that, in the as yet unredeemed world in which the church also exists, the state has by divine appointment the task of providing for justice and peace. [It fulfills this task] by means of the threat and exercise of force, according to the measure of human judgment and human ability. The church acknowledges the benefit of this divine appointment in gratitude and reverence before him. It calls to mind the Kingdom of God, God's commandment and righteousness, and thereby the responsibility both of rulers and ruled. It trusts and obeys the power of the Word by which God upholds all things.

We reject the false doctrine, as though the state, over and beyond its special commission, should and could become the single and totalitarian order of human life, thus fulfilling the church's vocation as well.

We reject the false doctrine, as though the church, over and beyond its special commission, should and could appropriate the characteristics, the tasks, and the dignity of the state, thus itself becoming an organ of the state.

6. "Lo, I am with you always, to the close of the age" (Matt. 28:20). "The word of God is not fettered" (II Tim. 2:9).

The church's commission, upon which its freedom is founded, consists in delivering the message of the free grace of God to all people in Christ's stead, and therefore in the ministry of his own Word and work through sermon and sacrament.

We reject the false doctrine, as though the church in human arrogance could place the Word and work of the Lord in the service of any arbitrarily chosen desires, purposes, and plans.

APPENDIX 2. Message to the Pastors

(Brethren Council, August 1945)

The following translation with minor revisions is from *Ecumenical Press Service* 35 (September 1945).

In the face of our present collapse, we acknowledge all that has happened. We experienced how a political doctrine, which claimed to have a religious foundation, arose, asserted itself with unparalleled fanaticism, and treated its opponents worse than criminals. The empire, which rested on this political doctrine, collapsed in a violent catastrophe, and brought ruin to many peoples—not least our own. Inescapably trapped in this desperate situation, we are frightened by the manifestations of demons and apocalyptic powers that are bringing about this chaos. Demonic was the power that in the last few years drove the German people to atrocities before which we and the entire world shudder with horror. Apocalyptic were the manifestations of total war. The world trembles before the possibility that the tools of war could be used again in such a way that mankind would destroy itself.

Moral standards are inadequate to measure the greatness of the guilt that our people have assumed. Fresh deeds of inhumanity are constantly coming to light. Many cannot yet grasp the fact that all this can be true. In the darkness of our guilt death threatens both the body and soul of our people.

We confess our guilt and bow under the burden of its consequences. From the depths below we look up to Christ, the crucified one. He alone saves us and intercedes for us. From the depths below we look up to Christ, the risen one. He allows us to live in the midst of death. In his righteousness he opens for us the door to right and order. He allows us, as the free children of God, to serve his creation until the day when it too becomes free of serving the transitory nature of man's existence.

Because of this, we are commanded: "Wake up! Strengthen what remains and is about to die."[1]

The hearts of men are at the point of breaking because of the harsh reality around them. And yet it is God who in everything is punishing us with his merciful justice. He wants to provide us with assistance that is greater than all the distress that surrounds us and is seeking to overwhelm us. "Therefore the grave enlarges its appetite and opens its mouth without limit; into it will descend their nobles and masses with all their brawlers and revelers. So man will be brought low and mankind humbled, the eyes of the arrogant humbled. But the Lord Almighty will be exalted by his justice, and the holy God will show himself holy by his righteousness."[2]

The work of reordering the church also must take place in obedience to the merciful judg-

---

1. Revelation 3:2.
2. Isaiah 5:14–16.

ment of God. There is a great temptation to go back where we were before the persecution of the National Socialists. We must recognize, however, the fact that this way out, which would deny God's judgment, is forbidden us.

Not long ago we issued a statement at Barmen, and we are thankful we were able to. We also know, however, that the preaching and practice of the church in many respects fell short of this statement. We shall have to try harder to be true to it. Likewise, we know that at Barmen not everything could be said which must be said today.

We classify ourselves by our confession. We are not free to disregard our confessional classification. Each of us is called to be true to our confession. We have no right to say the differences between the confessions are irrelevant. However, at the same time we feel that God is at work bringing Christians of different confessions closer together than ever before.

Intact and destroyed churches are in the same condition today, in the sense that the harm done to the churches did not begin in 1933. Even earlier than this, a deplorable state of affairs arose—traceable to the confusion of church and state powers—that led to a predominance of bureaucracy in the church. Consequently it is not enough now merely to repair the damage caused by National Socialism. Our task goes further. A new order must emerge under the guidance of God and Biblical knowledge, church decisions, and spiritual enlightenment given to us by God.

In the midst of the distress of the last years God has opened anew men's ears to the message of the church. As evidence, pastors and congregations have not only pronounced their confession, but have also corroborated it with deeds and suffering. In this way it has again become clear that God's truth is not to be apprehended by the thinking process alone, but must also be acted upon. That has fallen to our lot, and it must not be overlooked in the ordering of the church.

For this reason, we do not think the teachings of the church are insignificant. We thank God for every right teaching which has been given to us and which will be further revealed to us. We hope that theological work by us will begin again which will rightly test all that happens in the church, investigating freely, and yet within the confines of the church. We thank God for the Reformation Confessions, and strive to understand them better. But we also recognize the significance of the confessions of the Old Church for today.

In the terrible years that lie behind us our congregations were brought together in growing numbers to celebrate the Holy Supper. There is a good deal of evidence for what this means for the life of the church and the congregation. We know that the congregation and the church are present only where the Lord Jesus Christ is present in our preaching and administering of the Holy Supper, and where Jesus Christ acts on us. Only from this type of congregation and church can a real church leadership emerge.

"God created man in his own image, in the image of God he created him."[3] The only man in whom we encounter the unveiled and undistorted image of God is the Son of God, our Lord Jesus Christ. When recognition of this is granted to us in our proclamation and administering of the Holy Supper, we learn to believe again that we and our neighbor are also created in the image of God. We learn also to oppose all powers that mock and distort God's likeness in order to destroy it. Without faith we can't love one another. Without faith and love, a pastor and representative of the church cannot serve his office.

---

3. Genesis 1:27.

We are aware that man today has abandoned belief in his divine origin and in his divine destiny, leading to an extravagant increase in his self-confidence. Now that man realizes what a terrible deception this was, he wallows in despair. No biological, historical, or moral value granted to man can provide a new foundation or certainty to his humanity. Only Jesus Christ can do that, the first-born of every creature, who we encounter in proclamation and the Holy Supper. "The first man was of the dust of the earth, the second man from heaven. As was the earthly man, so are those who are of the earth; and as is the man from heaven, so also are those who are of heaven. And just as we have borne the likeness of the earthly man, so shall we bear the likeness of the man from heaven."[4] Herein is the foundation of our true relationship to our neighbor. And here also is the foundation of our obligation to participate in the new ordering of our social life based on the principles of freedom and justice.

Last but not least, we give the world through our existence as a congregation all that we owe it. The congregation is the place in the world where the foundations of true community continue to exist when everything else falls to pieces. We cannot change the world. But when the influence of Christendom on public life ceases, the link binding freedom and justice is severed. We must ask ourselves: to what degree does the church bear responsibility for the whole of public life—state, society, and culture—and how far it has in fact carried out this responsibility. This question must be answered by the church for its members in light of our new knowledge and new spirit of obedience to Christ. Under the present circumstances, the pastor cannot be allowed to escape the necessity of cooperation in these matters. In this service the pastor should have the good conscience that he also acts in service to the Lord.

Amidst the unspeakable distress of our people and based on our love of God and our neighbor, the church's active assistance to those in need is bound to the pastors' and elders' task of caring for the soul. Our aid cannot be limited to the great work of helping those in physical need, but has to take place even moreso in our personal contact with the desperate plight of our neighbors.

But the important point is: Our collaboration in public life as well as our assistance of those in need will remain fruitless unless the Lord Christ is in our midst. Therefore the most important command given to us pastors is still to study Holy Scripture, to carry out theological work in the midst of our brethren, to preach and administer the Sacraments, and to glorify God and to beseech him for his Holy Spirit through prayer—and all this in the sure confidence that our Lord comes! Take care that this source of strength remains ever present. Let us make sure that the life of the congregation is directed inwards. "Therefore, my dear brothers, stand firm. Let nothing move you. Always give yourself fully to the Lord, because you know that your labor in the Lord is not in vain."[5]

The mercy of our Lord Jesus Christ is with us all.

---

4. Corinthians 15:47–49.
5. Corinthians 15:58.

APPENDIX 3. Message to the Congregations

(Treysa Conference, August 1945)

God's angry judgment has broken out over us all. God's hand is heavy upon us. It is only by the goodness of God that we are not completely destroyed. Those who knew God's Word feared His wrath and saw it coming, and consequently bore a heavy burden.

Today we confess: Long before God spoke in anger, He sought us with the Word of His love and we did not listen. Long before our churches became piles of rubble, our pulpits were restricted and our prayers were silenced. Shepherds allowed their flocks to languish, and congregations deserted their pastors.

Long before the sham government of our land collapsed, justice had been thwarted. Long before men were murdered, human beings had become mere numbers and human life trivialized. When a man's life becomes worthless, he thinks nothing of taking human life. He who rejects love will no longer strive for justice. He is no longer concerned about how people are misled and will pay no heed to the call for help of those who are in need. He lives and speaks as if such a need never existed. He will try to escape responsibility as Christians and non-Christians have done. He hides behind men's orders so as to elude God's commands. This lie has meant death to us. Cowardice in the face of suffering has brought upon us this immeasurable grief.

But in spite of all the failures of the church and the people, God provided men and women of all confessions, classes, and parties with the strength—even when it meant suffering and death—to take a stand against injustice and the arbitrary use of power. When the church took its responsibility seriously, it reminded the population of God's commandments and minced no words when it condemned concentration camps, mistreatment and murder of Jews and the sick, and sought to protect youth from the seduction of National Socialist propaganda. But churchmen were pushed into the remote sanctuaries of the church as if into a prison. Our people were separated from the church. The public was no longer allowed to hear its words; no one heard what it preached. Then came the wrath of God. God has taken from us that which men most desire to have.

Now the door is open once again. What was prayed and planned behind walls and in seclusion can now be brought out into the open. Many devout people, who sat in the darkness of a prison cell, have thought out the new order for the Church and the people. Those who decide as Christians to take over responsibility in the public sphere, do so to serve the public not for power. It takes a great deal of faith and self-denial to accept a public office in an hour of need.

The Church too has lost its fetters. It hopes for something new for its preaching and its order. Its erstwhile captivity has ended, and for that we rejoice. And so we stand before Evan-

This translation with minor modifications is from the *Ecumenical Press Service* 32 (September 1945): 144–56.

gelical Christianity and call upon our pastors and people to renew the life of the church. We call to our people: turn again to God!

Countless men and women who have suffered did not suffer in vain when they had faith in God. We bless those who have suffered. We bless those who would rather die than live without honor and engage in senseless destruction. We bless all who truly sought the welfare of their people. We thank God that in our Fatherland He has preserved people who sought His ways. We thank Him that He purifies consciences and saves sinners through the power of His Son. Those who feared God have felt His wrath, but He has also comforted them with His peace.

The peace of God also gives strength to those in sorrow, to the prisoners of war and their relatives, to the hungry and the cold, to the homeless and those injured in body and in soul. God's peace is your comfort. Remain patient even in your hour of trouble. Do not close your eyes and your heart to your needy brother beside you. With your feeble strength take part in the work of love, with which we are seeking to alleviate the worst suffering. Be merciful! Do not add to the uncharitableness of which there is too much in the world already! Avoid revenge and wicked talk. Let us seek God's Will in every rank and calling! Do not escape suffering and hunger by taking your life! "He who has faith will never flee!" Christ will refresh the weary and heavy-laden. He remains our Savior. No hell can be so powerful that God cannot overcome it. Fear not!

APPENDIX 4. Stuttgart Declaration of Guilt

(Evangelical Church of Germany council, October 1945)

The Council of the Protestant Church in Germany welcomes representatives of the World Council of Churches to its meeting on October 18–19, 1945, in Stuttgart.

We are all the more thankful for this visit, as we know ourselves to be with our people in a great community of suffering, but also in a great solidarity of guilt. With great anguish we state: through us has endless suffering been brought to many peoples and countries. What we have often borne witness to before our congregations, we now declare in the name of the whole Church. We have for many years struggled in the name of Jesus Christ against the spirit which found its terrible expression in the National Socialist regime of tyranny, but we accuse ourselves for not witnessing more courageously, for not praying more faithfully, for not believing more joyously, and for not loving more ardently.

Now a new beginning can be made in our churches. Grounded on the Holy Scriptures, directed with all earnestness toward the only Lord of the Church, they now proceed to cleanse themselves from influences alien to the faith and to set themselves in order. Our hope is in the God of grace and mercy that He will use our churches as His instruments and will give them authority to proclaim His word, and in obedience to His will to work creatively among ourselves and among our people.

That in this new beginning we may become wholeheartedly united with the other churches of the ecumenical fellowship fills us with deep joy.

We hope in God that through the common service of the churches the spirit of violence and revenge which again today tends to become powerful may be brought under control in the whole world, and that the spirit of peace and love may gain the mastery, wherein alone tortured humanity can find healing.

So in an hour in which the whole world needs a new beginning we pray: "Veni Creator Spiritus."

Bishop Wurm
Bishop Meiser
Superintendent Hahn
Bishop Dibelius
Professor Smend
Pastor Asmussen

Pastor Niemöller
Landesoberkirchenrat Lilje
Superintendent Held
Pastor Niesel
Dr. Heinemann

APPENDIX 5. To the Christians in England

Bishop Wurm, 14 December 1945

On November 28th His Grace the Lord Archbishop of Canterbury addresses a message to the German People. We, and as we hope many people in Germany, have received this message with great interest and close attention. It is perhaps the first time in history that the Primate of one people has addressed in brotherly terms another people, which has been defeated in war. England is the victor, Germany the vanquished, the English Archbishop speaks to us as a brother. We are filled with joy that, after the long monopoly of political propaganda, the voice of Christianity makes itself heard as well, and we gladly acknowledge it and answer this approach.

In his address to the German people His Grace the Archbishop of Canterbury makes it clear that the Church of England is well aware of her responsibility and concern for what happens to other nations, including the German people. We Christians in Germany affirm and accept in the same way our responsibility and concern for the whole world. Even under the tyranny of National Socialism we refused to abandon this sense of responsibility and concern. It was a deep source of sorrow to us that we could not effectively prevent the gross ill treatment of other peoples and countries, and we were hated by the National Socialist leaders quite particularly because they were well aware of our condemnation of their misdeeds.

The Lord Archbishop is absolutely right when he says that it is not humanly possible to undo the past; what's done cannot be undone. We know this only too well; we know that our cities would not be lying in ruins now, and our fellow countrymen would not be dying of hunger on the high roads now, and our soldiers would not be languishing in the prison of war camps now, if millions of other human beings had not had to undergo the same sufferings in earlier years. We know that there is no lack of people in other countries that think that whatever happens to the Germans cannot be bad enough. Far be it from us to attempt to make excuses for any active injustice which was done to other peoples, far be it from us to attempt to explain it away.

The Christians in England have heard our confessions of guilt, which the Council of the Evangelical Church in Germany expressed on the 19th of October 1945 in the presence of our Ecumenical Brothers. We seek for the causes of what was done not only in National Socialism but also in a long history of estrangement from God and of backsliding from Christ, not least in the worldliness which more and more invaded our Church. That is why we are in absolute agreement with His Grace the Archbishop of Canterbury that the return to God and His commandments, and the acceptance of the grace which is made plain to us in Christ, is absolute presupposition of any reconstruction in Germany. We are very thankful that the

---

This translation is from Stewart W. Herman, *The Rebirth of the German Church* (New York: Harper and Brothers, 1946), 275–79.

Lord Archbishop declares it to be a definite policy of Great Britain to work for the day in which Germany can again enter the Commonwealth of Nations, and that he proclaims the willingness of Christians in England to help to stem the flood of our outward tribulations. Permit me to speak a word quite plainly about how you, the Christians in England, could help us in our inner tribulation as well.

It is with a sense of serious responsibility and concern that we draw to your attention that the victory of the Allied powers was not simply the victory of good over evil. The military conquest and occupation of our country was accompanied by the very same acts of violence against the civilian population, about which such just complaint has been made in the countries of the Allies. What has happened since then in some of the occupation zones in the course of measures of de-Nazification has not always been well calculated to inspire the impression of a higher degree of justice and humanity. The many appeals which have been addressed to the German people to work out its own salvation and lift itself up again from its prone position can only sound a mockery when the last raw materials and machines are taken away even from branches of German industry which had nothing to do with the production of armaments. No one can say what is the scale of the tragedy which is now being played in the East of Germany. But it seems we must suppose it will claim victims numbered in millions.

We say this not with the intention of sending in, so to speak, one bill to balance another, but in order to draw attention to a serious danger which hangs over the world and us all. It has happened once before in history that the attempt has been made to secure peace by taking away from the vanquished the possibility of rising again by the imposition of enormous burdens of reparations and by the attempt to cut off territories of great economic importance. But experience shows that these measures only awakened the spirit of resistance and made the German people inclined to be a ready recipient of the ideology of National Socialism. If the political authorities of today act according to the same recipe, and seek to make Germany as small and weak as possible, and its neighbors as great and strong as possible, then the evil spirits of revenge and retribution will not be banished from the world. We know, on the authority of the Word of God, that in the sphere of politics one guilt draws another after it, and that according to the law of God the judge himself falls under the same condemnation, under which he sets out to condemn the evildoer. The calculations of those who thought they were obliged to inflict penalties upon the German people alone for the criminal negligence which led to the incendiarism of 1914, in which all the people of Europe had a certain share, were proved to be fundamental miscalculations. What happened in 1939 was, by contrast, a deliberate act of incendiarism. But if the intention is to inflict punishment still more severe for this, nobody will be benefited if injustice is paid back by still greater injustice. To pack the German people into a still more narrow space, to cut off as far as possible the material basis of their very existence, is no different, in essentials, from Hitler's plan to stamp out the existence of the Jewish race. One must believe that God will be an avenger— that is what we Christians in Germany preach to our embittered and indignant fellow-countrymen. Dear Christian brothers in England, may we beg of you to do the same? Ought we not, in the presence and in the name of Him who died for our sins, to make a covenant to proclaim the word forgiveness rather than vengeance, with all our power through the world? No one who really is guilty should escape his punishment, but to lock up hundreds of thousands of people in order to detect one hundred of the guilty is more than makes sense; to let millions of innocent men, women and children starve, in order to avenge millions equally innocent, only folly can consider that just.

The Lord Archbishop appeals to us to make a new beginning by shaping the life of Germany according to the commandments of Christ. We are fully convinced, and we never cease to say to our German people, that Germany must give up all trust in violence and put its trust in the power of the spirit and the power of justice once again. Nothing could help the German people more to do this than an object lesson in the behavior of the victor powers in the administration of justice and in the testimony of the spirit. To bring this about we send our appeal to the Christians in England and in all the world. It has been our misfortune and the misfortune of all Europe that for half a century England and Germany, in spite of honest attempts on both sides, have not been able to find each other and understand each other. If they could find each other now that would not be any menace to any other nation, but it might well be the salvation of Western Christendom.

May God, with His eternal treasure of riches, grant to the German people, by penitence, by faith and love, the possibility to make a new beginning. May He bless all peoples and give the whole world His peace.

(signed) D. Wurm
Bishop of Württemberg
(President of the Council of the
Evangelical Church in Germany)

Frankfurt, December 14, 1945

APPENDIX 6. Statement by the Council of Brethren of the Evangelical Church of Germany Concerning the Political Course of Our People

(Darmstadt Statement, August 1947)

1. We have been given the message of the reconciliation of the world with God in Christ. We must listen to this Word, accept it, act upon it and fulfill it. We are not listening to this Word, nor accepting it, nor acting upon it, not fulfilling it, unless we are absolved from our common guilt, from our fathers' guilt as well as our own, and unless we follow the call of Jesus Christ, the Good Shepherd, leading us out of all the false and evil ways into which we, as Germans, have strayed in our political aims and actions.

2. We went astray when we began to dream about a special German mission, as if the German character could heal the sickness of the world. In so doing we prepared the way for the unrestricted exercise of political power, and set our own nation on the throne of God. It was disastrous to lay the foundations of our state at home solely on a strong government, and abroad solely on military force. In so doing we have acted contrary to our vocation, which is to cooperate with other nations in our common tasks, and to use the gifts given to us for the benefit of all nations.

3. We went astray when we began to set up a "Christian Front" against certain new developments which had become necessary in social life. The alliance of the Church with the forces which clung to everything old and conventional has revenged itself heavily upon us. We have betrayed the Christian freedom which enables us and commands us to change the forms of life, when such a change is necessary for men to live together. We have denied the right of revolution; but we have condoned and approved the development of absolute dictatorship.

4. We went astray when we thought we ought to create a political front of good against evil, light against darkness, justice against injustice, and to resort to political methods. In so doing we distorted God's free grace to all by forming a political, social and philosophical front, and left the world to justify itself.

5. We went astray when we failed to see that the economic materialism of Marxist teaching ought to have reminded the Church of its task and its promise for the life and fellowship of men. We have failed to take up the cause of the poor and unprivileged as a Christian cause, in accordance with the message of God's Kingdom.

6. In recognizing and confessing this, we know that we are absolved as followers of Christ, and that we are now free to undertake new and better service to the glory of God and the welfare of mankind. It is not the phrase "Christianity and Western Culture" that the German people, and particularly we Christians, need today. What we need is a return to God and to the service of our neighbor, through the power of the death and resurrection of Jesus Christ.

This translation is from the *Ecumenical Press Service* 31 (12 September 1947), 215.

7. We have borne witness, and today we do so once again: "Through Jesus Christ we experience a joyous liberation from the ungodly fetters of this world for free and grateful service to all whom he has created." We therefore pray constantly: Do not let yourselves be overcome by despair, for Christ is the Lord. Say good-bye to the indifference of unbelief; do not be led astray by dreams of a better past or by speculations about another war; but in freedom and all soberness realize the responsibility which rests upon us all to rebuild a better form of government in Germany, that shall work for justice and for the welfare, peace and reconciliation of the nations.

APPENDIX 7. Message Concerning the Jewish Question

(Council of Brethren of the Evangelical Church, Darmstadt, April 8, 1948)

I

In obedience to our Lord Jesus Christ the council of brethren has come together to study what Holy Scripture says about the burning question of Judaism and the Christian Church, and we feel that we can no longer remain silent about this question, which lies on our hearts like a stone. It may rightly be said that after what has happened, after all that we allowed to happen in silence, we have no authority to speak now. We are distressed about what happened in the past, and about the fact that we did make any joint statement about it. We have not forgotten that a number of pastors and churches did speak out, and suffered for doing so; we thank God for it, and we thank them. We thank all who, in our own country and abroad, have helped us with old and new insights into the Word of God, and who have taken action by setting up warning signs.

Today when retribution is being meted out to us for what we did to the Jews, there is increasing danger that we may take refuge from God's Judgment in a new way of anti-semitism, thus conjuring up all the old devils once again. In this perilous situation and amid this temptation God's Word speaks to us and helps us to find the right attitude to the Jews. It is under the pressure of this Word that we speak, because we are filled with anxiety about the future and burdened by the past, and because we feel obligated to express our gratitude to all those individual people who spoke out, took action and suffered for doing so.

There is nothing final about our message. Its purpose is rather to ask you, pastors and congregations, to think about this question with us in the light of Holy Scripture, to help us and to ask God with us, that we may perceive things aright and be guided in the right way.

II

The Bible tells us, and the Creeds of our Churches confirm, that Jesus of Nazareth was a Jew, a member of the chosen people, Israel. When the eternal Word of God became man, it pleased God that he should enter human history as the son of Abraham and of David, and that he should die and rise again from the dead. But the Church is not allowed to teach that Jesus is a member of the Jewish people, just as it is not allowed to ascribe him to any other nation or race. For the relation of Israel to the Church this means:

This translation is from the WCC publication *The Relationship of the Church to the Jewish People: Collection of Statements by the World Council of Churches and Representative Bodies of Its Member Churches* (Geneva, 1964), 48–52.

1. That since the Son of God was born a Jew, the election and destiny of Israel found its fulfillment in him. The Church must oppose any other concept of Israel, including Judaism's understanding of itself as the prophet of an idea of human universality, or even as the savior of the world.
2. That since Israel crucified the Messiah, it rejected its own election and its own destiny. And thereby the resistance of all men and all nations to Christ becomes God's Event. We all share the guilt for the crucifixion of Christ. Therefore it is not permissible for the Church to brand the Jews as solely responsible for the crucifixion.
3. That through Christ, and since Christ, the chosen people is no longer Israel but the Church, which is composed of all nations both Jews and Gentiles. Christians (both Jewish and Gentile) are members of the Body of Christ and brethren. It is not permissible for the Church to separate Jewish Christians from Gentile Christians. At the same time, however, the Church is waiting for the erring Children of Israel to resume the place reserved for them by God.
4. That God remains true to Israel and does not abandon it, despite its disloyalty, despite its rejection of Christ. Christ was crucified and rose again, also for the Jews. That is the hope of Israel, since Golgotha. The fact that God's judgment still pursues Israel until today is a sign of His patience. The Church is guilty if for any other reason whatever it fails to testify to God's patience towards Israel.
5. That Israel under the judgment is the ceaseless confirmation of the truth, the reality of God's Word, and God's constant warning to His Church. The fate of the Jews is a silent sermon, reminding us that God will not allow Himself to be mocked. It is a warning to us, and an admonition to the Jews to be converted to him, who is their sole hope of salvation.
6. Because the Church recognizes the Jew as an erring brother destined for Christ, a brother whom it loves and calls, it is not permissible for the Church to regard the Jewish question as a racial or national problem, and let that determine its attitude towards the Jewish people, or towards individual Jews. Furthermore, the Church must show the world that the world is mistaken if it thinks it can settle the Jewish problem as if it were a racial or national one.

It was a disastrous mistake when the Churches of our time adopted the secular attitude of mere humanity, emancipation and anti-semitism towards the Jewish question. There was bound to be a bitter retribution for the fact that anti-semitism rose and flourished not only among the people (who still seemed to be a Christian nation), not only among the intelligentsia, and in governmental and military circles, but also among Christian leaders. And finally when this radical anti-semitism, based on racial hatred, destroyed our nation and our Churches from within, and released all its brutal force from without, there existed no power to resist it—because the Churches had forgotten what Israel really is, and no longer loved the Jews. Christian circles washed their hands of all responsibility, justifying themselves by saying that there was a curse on the Jewish people. Christians no longer believed that the promises concerning the Jews still held good; they no longer preached it, nor showed it in their attitude toward the Jews. In this way we Christians helped to bring about all the injustice and suffering inflicted upon the Jews in our country.

This is what the Word of God teaches us, so that we recognize with shame and grief what a great wrong we have done to Israel, and how deep our guilt is. As a Church we have failed to be the witness of salvation to Israel. Now we have to face the judgments of God which are coming upon us one after the other, so that we may bow beneath the mighty hand of God in sincere repentance, both as a Church and as a nation.

III

We therefore appeal to our churches and pastors, as members of God's people, to be aware of their special relationship with Israel. Remember again the mysterious link between Israel and the Church, created by God in His wisdom—and thus obey the testimony of the Old and New Testaments. Refrain from all forms of anti-semitism. Manifest the testimony of your faith and the signs of your love towards Israel with special care and with greater zeal. Tell them that the promises of the Old Testament are fulfilled in Jesus Christ. Assist those who are alone; help to atone for the wrong that has been done. Admittedly we realize that painful division which exists between us and those Jews who persist in rejecting their King, because we confess Christ Crucified. We will take care not to ignore that division, in our encounter with Israel. But realizing God's faithfulness to Israel, and in hope of His mercy, we will not grow weary in our intercession for Israel, and we will bear in mind the significance of its destiny. Let us accompany Israel on its way with biblical watchfulness and soberness, in humanity and love, and in hope of the day when Jews and Gentiles will all be one in Christ.

We appeal especially also to you, who are descended from the seed of Abraham, and who now through the goodness of God confess that Jesus Christ, the Crucified and Risen Lord, is the Savior, through whom you are blessed as children of God.

We ask you to fix your eyes on this miracle of God's mercy, and not to keep thinking about what has been done to you by people who were baptized with the same baptism as yourselves, and who are called with you to membership in the one Body of Christ.

We realize how difficult we have made it, through our silence and our lack of love, for you to believe that the time of salvation is at hand, in which the Jews and the Gentiles will praise God together, as the Father of our Lord Jesus Christ, for His truth and His mercy.

We realize how little cause you have at present to hope that the fraternal fellowship will be restored and made manifest through works of love, because you are rejected by the Jews on account of your Christian faith, and rejected by other Christians because of your racial origin, which throws you into special isolation and misery. But God, who has proved His faithfulness to you in your faith and your witness, will fulfill His work upon you and upon us. Through our suffering and our guilt He made us aware of His Word anew. We therefore beg you not to think any longer about the division for which we have been responsible. We beg you, for the sake of God's truth and for the sake of your vocation, not to shun our fellowship, not to leave us, and not to form your own Churches, but to stay with us, to listen with us to God's Word, to learn from it, and to teach us (so far as you are able) to praise God for His great deeds.

APPENDIX 8. Statement on the Jewish Question

(Synod of the Evangelical Church in Germany, Berlin-Weissensee, April 27, 1950)

For God has consigned all men to disobedience, that he may have mercy upon all (Rom. 11:32).

We believe in the Lord and Savior, who as a person came from the people of Israel.

We Confess the Church which is joined together in one body of Jewish Christians and Gentile Christians and whose peace is Jesus Christ.

We believe God's promise to be valid for his Chosen People even after the crucifixion of Jesus Christ.

We state that by omission and silence we became implicated before the God of mercy in the outrage which has been perpetrated against the Jews by people of our nation.

We caution all Christians not to balance what has come upon us as God's judgment against what we have done to the Jews; for in judgment God's mercy searches the repentant.

We ask all Christians to disassociate themselves from all antisemitism and earnestly to resist it, whenever it stirs again, and to encounter Jews and Jewish Christians in a brotherly spirit.

We ask the Christian congregations to protect Jewish graveyards within their areas if they are unprotected.

We pray to the Lord of mercy that he may bring about the Day of Fulfillment when we will be praising the triumph of Jesus Christ together with the saved Israel.

This translation is from *The Theology of the Churches and the Jewish People: Statements by the World Council of Churches and Its Member Churches,* with commentary by Allan Brockway, Paul van Buren, Rolf Rendtorff, and Simon Schoon (Geneva: WCC Publications, 1988), 47–49.

NOTES

Introduction

1. Quoted in Reinhard Rürup, ed., *Berlin 1945: A Documentation* (Berlin: Willmuth Arenhövel, 1995), 62.

2. *Ecumenical Press Service* 44 (November 1945): 218–19. The Lutherans who issued this statement were members of the Confessing synod of Berlin-Brandenburg.

3. Throughout this study I use the terms "Protestant" and "Evangelical" interchangeably. Some historians writing about German Protestantism in English have chosen to substitute "Protestant" for "Evangelical" in order to distinguish the German Evangelical churches from the Evangelical churches in the United States. Whereas in the United States "Evangelical" usually refers to churches associated with the conservative wing of Protestant Christianity, such as the Church of Christ or the National Baptist Church, in Germany "*evangelisch*" refers broadly to the three main Protestant traditions or denominations in Germany: Lutheran, Reformed, and United. Since many of the Protestant regional churches in Germany, such as the Evangelisch-Lutherische Kirche in Bayern, as well as the umbrella federation for the nation as a whole, the Evangelische Kirche in Deutschland, use "*evangelisch*" in their names, I retain Evangelical for reasons of accuracy and clarity.

4. The most important administrative union of Lutheran and Reformed churches took place in Prussia in 1817 during the reign of Frederick William III. In addition to the influence of Pietism and the Enlightenment, the Napoleonic consolidation of the approximately three hundred German principalities into thirty states with corresponding regional churches contributed to the development of Union churches. Napoleon's territorial consolidations brought Lutheran subjects under the rule of Reformed leaders, and Reformed subjects under the rule of Lutheran leaders. The easiest solution seemed to be the creation of United churches. Prussia's union was followed by unions in the Rhenish-Palatinate, Baden, Rhenish Hesse, and Württemberg in the decade from 1817 to 1827. Lutheran confessionalism was too strong elsewhere, especially in Bavaria, Saxony, and Hannover, for unions to take place. See Robert M. Bigler, *The Politics of German Protestantism: The Rise of the Protestant Church Elite in Prussia, 1815–1848* (Berkeley: University of California Press, 1972), 37; Daniel R. Borg, *The Old-Prussian Church and the Weimar Republic: A Study in Political Adjustment, 1917–1927* (Hanover, N.H.: University Press of New England, 1984), chap. 1; and Eckhard Lessing, *Zwischen Bekenntnis und Volkskirche: Der theologische Weg der Evangelischen Kirche der altpreußischen Union (1922–1953) unter besonderer Berücksichtigung ihrer Synoden, ihrer Gruppen und der theologischen Begründungen* (Bielefeld: Luther-Verlag, 1992).

5. *Statistisches Jahrbuch für das Deutsche Reich* (Berlin: R. Hobbing, 1934), 5–6.

6. Doris Bergen, *Twisted Cross: The German Christian Movement in the Third Reich* (Chapel Hill: University of North Carolina Press), 168 and 233, n. 12.

7. Ibid., 178.

8. Ernst Helmreich, *The German Churches under Hitler: Background, Struggle, and Epilogue* (Detroit: Wayne State University Press), 156.

9. Otto Dibelius, *In the Service of the Lord: The Autobiography of Bishop Otto Dibelius,* trans. Mary Ilford (New York: Holt, Rinehart & Winston, 1964), 7–8.

10. It is crucial that readers not confuse the terms "reformers," "reform-minded," and "reform wing" with the denominational designation "Reformed," i.e., Calvinist. The former with a small "r" refer to churchmen from Lutheran, Reformed, and United churches in the immediate postwar years in Germany who sought to *reform* the church's hierarchical structure and conservative theology in light of its easy accommodation with Nazism from 1933 to 1945. The latter with a capital "R" refers to the Protestant denomination that traces its roots to Martin Bucer (1491–1551), John Calvin (1509–64), and Huldrych Zwingli (1484–1531), among others. Karl Barth (1886–1968) was both a leader of the *reform wing* of the Protestant churches in postwar Germany and a Swiss *Reformed* theologian.

11. Harold Marcuse, *Legacies of Dachau: The Uses and Abuses of a Concentration Camp, 1933–2001* (Cambridge: Cambridge University Press, 2001), 74–77.

12. Protestants broke their silence regarding the church's antisemitism and anti-Judaism at the EKD's Berlin-Weissensee synod of April 1950. They admitted, "We through neglect and silence have been accomplices in the outrages that have been perpetrated by representatives of our people upon the Jews." Chapters 7 and 8 of this book address in detail the gradual and halting process that led to the Berlin-Weissensee statement.

13. For example, Niemöller collaborated with Bishop Wurm and Prelate Karl Hartenstein of Stuttgart on the "Memorandum by the Evangelical Church in Germany on the Question of War Crimes Trials before American Military Courts" (1949). See Marcuse, *Legacies of Dachau,* 106, 277–78; and, especially, Clemens Vollnhals, *Evangelische Kirche und Entnazifizierung 1945–1949: Die Last der nationalsozialistischen Vergangenheit* (Munich: R. Oldenbourg, 1989).

14. See Theodor Adorno, "What Does Coming to Terms with the Past Mean?" in *Bitburg in Moral and Political Perspective,* ed. Geoffrey Hartman (Bloomington: Indiana University Press, 1986), 114–29; Alexander and Margarete Mitscherlich, *The Inability to Mourn: Principles of Collective Behavior,* trans. Beverly R. Placzek (New York: Grove Press, 1975); Hermann Lübbe, "Der Nationalsozialismus im Deutschen Nachkriegsbewußtsein," *Historische Zeitschrift* 236 (1983): 579–99.

15. Robert G. Moeller, "War Stories: The Search for a Usable Past in the Federal Republic of Germany," *American Historical Review* 101, no. 4 (October 1996): 1009. Moeller published a book with the same title with University of California Press in 2001.

16. Karl Jaspers, *The Question of German Guilt,* trans. E. B. Ashton (New York: Capricorn Books, 1961); originally published as *Die Schuldfrage* (Heidelberg: L. Schneider, 1946).

17. For a thoughtful appraisal of the major studies on the Protestant churches under Nazi rule and a general understanding of the historiography until 1994, see Robert P. Ericksen and Susannah Heschel, "The German Churches Face Hitler: Assessment of the Historiography," *Tel Aviver Jahrbuch für deutsche Geschichte* 23 (1994): 433–59; also see the historiography section of Doris Bergen's essay, "Storm Troopers of Christ: The German Christian Movement and the Ecclesiastical Final Solution," in *Betrayal: German Churches and the Holocaust,* ed. Robert P. Ericksen and Susannah Heschel (Minneapolis: Fortress Press, 1999), 40–67.

18. Wolfgang Gerlach, *And the Witnesses Were Silent: The Confessing Church and the Persecution of the Jews,* trans. Victoria Barnett (Lincoln: University of Nebraska Press, 2000); originally published as *Als die Zeugen schwiegen: Bekennende Kirche und die Juden* (Berlin: Institut Kirche und Judentum, 1987).

19. Some of the studies I have found most useful include: Richard Evans, *In Hitler's Shadow: West German Historians and the Attempt to Escape from the Nazi Past* (New York: Knopf, 1989); Alf Lüdtke, "'Coming to Terms with the Past': Illusions of Remembering, Ways of Forgetting Nazism in West Germany," *Journal of Modern History* 65 (September 1993): 542–72; Norbert Frei, *Vergangenheitspolitik: Die Anfänge der Bundesrepublik und die NS-Vergangenheit* (Munich: Beck, 1996); Jeffrey Herf, *Divided Memory: The Nazi Past in the Two Germanys* (Cambridge, Mass.: Harvard University Press, 1997); Gesine Schwan, *Politik und Schuld: Die zerstörerische Macht des Schweigens* (Frankfurt am Main: Fischer Taschenbuch, 1997); Helmut Dubiel, *Niemand ist frei von der Geschichte: Die nationalsozialistische Herrschaft in den Debatten des Deutschen Bundestages* (Munich: Carl Hanser Verlag, 1999); Aleida Assmann and Ute Frevert, *Geschichtsvergessenheit/Geschichtsversessenheit: Vom Umgang mit deutschen Vergangenheiten nach 1945* (Stuttgart: Deutsche Verlags-Anstalt, 1999); Claudia Fröhlich and Michael Kohlstruck, ed., *Engagierte Demokraten: Vergangenheitspolitik in kritischer Absicht* (Münster: Westfälisches Dampfboot, 1999); A. D. Moses, "The Forty-Fivers: A Generation between Fascism and Democracy," *German Politics and Society* 17, no. 1 (Spring 1999): 94–126; Rudy Koshar, *From Monuments to Traces: Artifacts of German Memory, 1870–1990* (Berkeley: University of California Press, 2000); Marcuse, *Legacies of Dachau;* Hanna Schissler, ed., *The Miracle Years: A Cultural History of West Germany, 1949–1968* (Princeton, N.J.: Princeton University Press, 2001); Bill Niven, *Facing the Nazi Past: United Germany and the Legacy of the Third Reich* (London: Routledge, 2002).

20. Martin Greschat sets a very high standard with his study, *Die evangelische Christenheit und die deutsche Geschichte nach 1945: Weichenstellungen in der Nachkriegszeit* (Stuttgart: W. Kohlhammer, 2002). For more contributions to the literature on the Protestant churches and the Nazi past see note 27.

21. Chapters from the following books address these issues: Stewart Herman, *The Rebirth of the German Church* (New York: Harper and Brothers, 1946); Frederic Spotts, *The Churches and Politics in Germany* (Middletown, Conn.: Wesleyan University Press, 1973); Richard Gutteridge, *Open Thy Mouth for the Dumb! The German Evangelical Church and the Jews, 1879–1950* (New York: Harper and Row, 1976); Wolfgang Gerlach, *And the Witnesses Were Silent;* Victoria Barnett, *For the Soul of the People: Protestant Protest against Hitler* (New York: Oxford University Press, 1992).

22. For an introduction to the literature on the German Catholic Church and the Nazi past, see Konrad Repgen, "Die Erfahrung des Dritten Reiches und das Selbstverständnis der deutschen Katholiken nach 1945," in *Die Zeit nach 1945 als Thema kirchlicher Zeitgeschichte,* ed. Victor Conzemius et al. (Göttingen: Vandenhoeck and Ruprecht, 1988), 127–80; Michael Phayer, "The Postwar German Catholic Debate over Holocaust Guilt," *Kirchliche Zeitgeschichte* 8, no. 2 (1995): 426–39. Also see chapters 8–11 of Phayer's book *The Catholic Church and the Holocaust, 1930–1965* (Bloomington: Indiana University Press, 2000). Regrettably, there is at present no study that compares and contrasts the process of *Vergangenheitsbewältigung* in the Protestant and Catholic churches.

23. See, e.g., the books and collections of documents by Martin Niemöller's younger brother Wilhelm Niemöller, in particular, *Kampf und Zeugnis der Bekennenden Kirche* (Bielefeld: Bechauf, 1948) and *Die Bekennende Kirche sagt Hitler die Wahrheit: die Geschichte der Denkschrift der Vorläufigen Leitung von Mai 1936* (Bielefeld: Bechhauf, 1954).

24. See, e.g., Otto Dibelius, *In the Service of the Lord.*

25. There were some exceptions, such as Stewart Herman, Friedrich Baumgärtel, and Franklin Littlel, who challenged the use of a simple resistance-collaboration dichotomy to

describe the Protestant reaction to Hitler and criticized the failure of churchmen to learn from their mistakes. See Stewart Herman, *The Rebirth of the German Church;* Friedrich Baumgärtel, *Wider die Kirchenkampf-Legende* (Neudettelsau: Freimun Verlag, 1959); and Franklin Hamlin Littell, *The German Phoenix: Men and Movements in the Church in Germany* (Garden City, N.Y.: Doubleday, 1960).

26. John S. Conway, *The Nazi Persecution of the Churches, 1933–1945* (New York: Basic Books, 1968); Klaus Scholder, *The Churches and the Third Reich,* vol. 1: *Preliminary History and the Time of Illusions 1918–1934,* and vol. 2: *The Year of Disillusionment: 1934—Barmen and Rome,* trans. John Bowden (Philadelphia: Fortress Press, 1988); originally published *Die Kirchen und das Dritte Reich,* Band 1: *Vorgeschichte und Zeit der Illusionen, 1918–1934* (Frankfurt am Main: Ullstein, 1977), and Band 2: *Das Jahr der Ernüchterung 1934, Barmen und Rom* (Berlin: W. J. Siedler, 1985). Gerhard Besier recently wrote and published a third volume to the Scholder series covering the years 1934–37. See Gerhard Besier, *Die Kirchen und das Dritte Reich: Spaltungen und Abwehrkämpfe 1934–1937* (Munich: Propyläen, 2001).

27. Cited here are the books and articles this author found most useful. See the bibliography for more studies by the same authors. Victoria Barnett, *For the Soul of the People;* Gerhard Besier, Hartmut Ludwig, and Jörg Thierfelder, eds., *Der Kompromiß von Treysa: Die Entstehung der Evangelischen Kirche in Deutschland (EKD) 1945* (Weinheim: Deutscher Studien Verlag, 1995); Gerhard Besier, Jörg Thierfelder, and Ralf Tyra, eds., *Kirche nach der Kapitulation,* 2 vols. (Stuttgart: Verlag W. Kohlhammer, 1989–90); Gerhard Besier and Gerhard Sauter, eds., *Wie Christen ihre Schuld bekennen: Die Stuttgarter Erklärung 1945* (Göttingen: Vandenhoeck and Ruprecht, 1985); Armin Boyens, "Das Stuttgarter Schuldbekenntnis vom 19. Oktober 1945—Entstehung und Bedeutung," *Vierteljahrshefte für Zeitgeschichte* 19, no. 4 (October 1971): 374–97; Armin Boyens, "Treysa 1945—Die evangelische Kirche nach dem Zusammenbruch des Dritten Reiches," *Zeitschrift für Kirchengeschichte* 82, no. 1 (1971): 29–53; John S. Conway, "How Shall Nations Repent? The Stuttgart Declaration of Guilt," *Journal of Ecclesiastical History* 38, no. 4 (October 1987): 596–622; Martin Greschat, ed., *Die Schuld der Kirche: Dokumente und Reflexionen zur Stuttgarter Schulderklärung vom 18./19. Oktober 1945* (Munich: Kaiser, 1982); Martin Greschat, ed., *Im Zeichen der Schuld: 40 Jahre Stuttgarter Schuldbekenntnis. Eine Dokumentation* (Neukirchen-Vluyn: Neukirchener Verlag, 1985); Siegfried Hermle, *Evangelische Kirche und Judentum—Stationen nach 1945* (Göttingen: Vandenhoeck and Ruprecht, 1990); Kurt Jürgensen, *Die Stunde der Kirche: Die Ev.-Luth. Landeskirche Schleswig-Holsteins in den ersten Jahren nach dem Zweiten Weltkrieg* (Neumünster: Karl Wachholtz Verlag, 1976); Bertold Klappert, *Bekennende Kirche in ökumenischer Verantwortung: Die gesellschaftliche und ökumenische Bedeutung des Darmstädter Wortes* (Munich: Kasier, 1988); Franklin H. Littell and Hubert G. Locke, eds., *The German Church Struggle and the Holocaust* (Detroit: Wayne State University Press, 1974); Annemarie Smith-von Osten, *Von Treysa 1945 bis Eisenach 1948: Zur Geschichte der Grundordnung der Evangelischen Kirchen in Deutschland* (Göttingen: Vandenhoeck and Ruprecht, 1980); Hans Prolingheuer, *Wir sind in die Irre gegangen: Die Schuld der Kirche unterm Hakenkreuz* (Cologne: Pahl-Rugenstein, 1987); Christoph M. Raisig, *Wege der Erneuerung. Christen und Juden: Der rheinische Synodalbeschluss von 1980* (Potsdam: Verlag für Berlin-Brandenburg, 2002); Frederic Spotts, *The Churches and Politics in Germany;* Jörg Thierfelder, *Zusammenbruch und Neubeginn: Die evangelische Kirche nach 1945 am Beispiel Württembergs* (Stuttgart: Quell, 1995); Clemens Vollnhals, "Die Evangelische Kirche zwischen Traditionswahrung und Neuorientierung," in *Von Stalingrad zur Währungsreform: zur Sozialgeschichte*

des Umbruchs in Deutschland, ed. Martin Broszat, Klaus-Dietmar Henke, and Hans Woller (Munich: R. Oldenbourg, 1988).

1. The Church Struggle

1. Willem Visser 't Hooft, the first general secretary of the World Council of Churches (WCC), presented a similar interpretation of the church struggle immediately after the war in "The Situation of the Protestant Church in Germany," in *Kirche nach der Kapitulation: Die Allianz zwischen Genf, Stuttgart und Bethel,* ed. Gerhard Besier, Jörg Thierfelder, and Ralf Tyra (Stuttgart: W. Kohlhammer, 1989), 1:58–59. For discussions on the concept of the church struggle (*Kirchenkampf*), see Georg Kretschmar, "Die Auseinandersetzung der Bekennenden Kirche mit den Deutschen Christen," in *Kirche und Nationalismus: Zur Geschichte des Kirchenkampfes,* ed. Paul Rieger and Johannes Strauss (Munich: Claudius, 1969), 117–21; and Klaus Scholder, "The Church Struggle," in *A Requiem for Hitler and Other New Perspectives on the German Church Struggle* (London: SCM Press, 1989), 94–95.

2. There are several excellent studies in English on the church struggle. See John S. Conway, *The Nazi Persecution of the Churches, 1933–45;* Franklin H. Littell and Hubert G. Locke, eds., *The German Church Struggle and the Holocaust;* Ernst Christian Helmreich, *The German Churches under Hitler: Background, Struggle, and Epilogue;* Klaus Scholder, *The Churches and the Third Reich,* vol. 1: *Preliminary History and the Time of Illusions, 1918–1934,* and vol. 2: *The Year of Disillusionment: 1934—Barmen and Rome,* trans. John Bowden; Robert P. Ericksen, *Theologians under Hitler: Gerhard Kittel, Paul Althaus, and Emanuel Hirsch* (New Haven, Conn.: Yale University, 1985); Doris Bergen, *Twisted Cross: The German Christian Movement in the Third Reich;* and Robert P. Ericksen and Susannah Heschel, eds., *Betrayal: German Churches and the Holocaust.* In German the literature is voluminous. See the third volume of Scholder's series by Gerhard Besier, *Die Kirchen und das Dritte Reich: Spaltungen und Abwehrkämpfe 1934–1937;* Kurt Meier, *Der evangelische Kirchenkampf,* vol. 1, *Der Kampf um die "Reichskirche,"* vol. 2: *Geschichte Neuordnungsversuche im Zeichen staatlicher Rechtshilfe,* vol. 3: *Im Zeichen des Zweiten Weltkrieges* (Göttingen: Vandenhoeck and Ruprecht, 1976–84); Günther van Norden, *Der deutsche Protestantismus im Jahr der nationalsozialistischen Machtergreifung* (Gütersloh: Gütersloher Verlagshaus Mohn, 1979); Kurt Meier, *Die Deutschen Christen: Das Bild einer Bewegung im Kirchenkampf des Dritten Reiches* (Göttingen: Vandenhoeck and Ruprecht, 1964); Günther van Norden, *Der deutsche Protestantismus im Jahr der nationalsozialistischen Machtergreifung* (Gütersloh: Gütersloher Verlagshaus Mohn, 1979); Armin Boyens, *Kirchenkampf und Ökumene, 1933–1939: Darstellung und Dokumentation* (Munich: Christian Kaiser, 1969); and Eberhard Röhm and Jörg Thierfelder, *Juden, Christen, Deutsche 1933–45,* vol. 1: *1933–35,* vol. 2: *1935–38,* vol. 3: *1938–41* (Stuttgart: Calwer, 1990–95); Manfred Gailus, *Protestantismus und Nationalismus. Studien zur nationalsozialistischen Durchdringung des protestantischen Sozialmilieus in Berlin* (Cologne: Böhlau, 2001).

3. See Leonore Siegele-Wenschkewitz, "New Testament Scholarship and the Nazi-State: Christian Responsibility and Guilt in the Holocaust," in *Remembering for the Future,* vol. 3, ed. Yehuda Bauer et al. (New York: Pergamon Press, 1989), 2717–27, and her early groundbreaking book, *Neutestamentliche Wissenschaft vor der Judenfrage: Gerhard Kittels theologische Arbeit im Wandel deutscher Geschichte* (Munich: Kaiser, 1980); also see the collection of

essays on various theology faculties edited by Leonore Siegele-Wenschkewitz and Carsten Nicolaisen, *Theologische Fakultäten im Nationalsozialismus* (Göttingen: Vandenhoeck and Ruprecht, 1993). The standard text in English is Ericksen, *Theologians under Hitler*.

4. Friedrich Baumgärtel discusses this misinterpretation of the church struggle in *Wider die Kirchenkampf-Legenden* as does Conway, *The Nazi Persecution*, xvii–xviii.

5. Eberhard Bethge, "Troubled Self-Interpretation and Uncertain Reception in the Church Struggle," in *The German Church Struggle*, ed. Littell and Locke, 172–75.

6. Shelley Baranowski, "Consent and Dissent: The Confessing Church and Conservative Opposition to National Socialism," *Journal of Modern History* 59 (March 1987): 53–78.

7. Gerhard Besier, "The Stance of the German Protestant Churches during the Agony of Weimar, 1930–33," in *Die evangelische Kirche in den Umbrüchen des 20. Jahrhunderts: Gesammelte Aufsätze* (1994): 66.

8. Quoted in Richard Gutteridge, *Open Thy Mouth for the Dumb! The German Evangelical Church and the Jews, 1879–1950*, 72. Also see Marikje Smid's assessment of Meiser's 1926 essay, "Die evangelische Gemeinde und die Judenfrage," in *Deutscher Protestantismus und Judentum 1932/1933* (Munich: Kaiser, 1990), 340–45.

9. "Easter Message of the Old Prussian Union," 16 April 1933, in *The Third Reich and the Christian Churches: A Documentary Account of Christian Resistance and Complicity during the Nazi Era*, ed. Peter Matheson (Edinburgh: T. and T. Clark, 1981), 16–17.

10. See Robert P. Ericksen, *Theologians under Hitler: Gerhard Kittel, Paul Althaus and Emmanuel Hirsch*, 1985; Hans Tiefel, "The German Lutheran Church," *Church History* 41 (1972): 326–37; and Lowell C. Greene, "The Political Ethos of Luther and Lutheranism: A Reply to the Polemics of Hans Tiefel," *Lutheran Quarterly* 26, no. 3 (August 1974): 330–35.

11. For an analysis of Ludwig Müller's career, see Thomas Martin Schneider, *Reichsbischof Ludwig Müller: Eine Untersuchung zu Leben, Werk und Persönlichkeit* (Göttingen: Vandenhoeck and Ruprecht, 1993). Friedrich von Bodelschwingh, the conservatives' candidate for Reich bishop, had defeated Müller in the church elections in May 1933. But Bodelschwingh resigned after serving only one month on the grounds that he could no longer carry out his tasks when virtually the entire Prussian church was under police jurisdiction. As a result of Bodelschwingh's resignation, parish elections were held to elect regional and national synods, which in turn would elect a new Reich bishop. In the decisive parish elections of 23 July 1933, the German Christians, now with the active support of the Nazi state and party, gained control of all but three of the regional churches. In north Germany and much of Prussia the association of the German Christians with the Nazis increased their popularity and helped them win spectacular victories. Afterward, the first national synod elected Ludwig Müller as Reich bishop to the cheers of a number of delegates wearing their brown SA uniforms. See Shelley Baranowski, "The 1933 German Protestant Church Elections: *Machtpolitik* or Accommodation," *Church History* 49 (1980): 298–315.

12. It was a common phenomenon, as Ian Kershaw shows, for Germans to heap blame on Hitler's subordinates and the "fanatics" in the Nazi Party while maintaining a myth of Hitler as an exemplary and virtuous leader. See Ian Kershaw, *The "Hitler Myth": Image and Reality in the Third Reich* (Oxford: Oxford University Press, 1987).

13. "The Guiding Principles of the Faith Movement of the 'German Christians,'" 26 May 1932, in *The Third Reich and the Christian Churches: A Documentary Account*, ed. Peter Matheson, 5.

14. Arthur Frey, *Cross and Swastika: The Ordeal of the German Church* (London: SCM Press, 1938), 113.

15. Although German Christians would continue to hold the reins of power in these churches until 1945, by the end of 1934 the Nazi state had begun to withdraw much of its initial support for the movement because of the German Christians' incompetence at subduing opposition from the Confessing Church. Nevertheless, German Christian pastors remained committed to a racially pure church that synthesized Nazi ideology and Protestant theology. See Bergen, *Twisted Cross*, 15–20.

16. Klaus Scholder, *Churches and the Third Reich*, 1:550.

17. Ibid., 1:471.

18. The ninth thesis of the German Christians' guiding principles criticized missions to convert Jews to Christianity because conversion allowed "alien blood" into the body of the nation. On the Confessing Church and Jewish Christians, see Gerlach, *And the Witnesses Were Silent*, 11–86; Gutteridge, *Open Thy Mouth for the Dumb!* 91–151; Röhm and Thierfelder, *Juden, Christen, Deutsche 1933–45*, vol. 1; and Smid, *Deutscher Protestantismus und Judentum 1932/1933*, parts VI and VII.

19. See Peter Neumann, *Die Jungreformatorische Bewegung* (Göttingen: Vandenhoeck and Ruprecht, 1971), 108–14.

20. An excellent source on attitudes toward the "Jewish Question" held by prominent Protestant Church leaders and theologians in 1932 and 1933 is Smid, *Deutscher Protestantismus und Judentum 1932/1933*.

21. Kurt Meier, *Kirche und Judentum: Die Haltung der evangelischen Kirche zur Judenpolitik des Dritten Reiches* (Göttingen: Vandenhoeck and Ruprecht, 1968), 26.

22. Kurt Meier, *Der evangelische Kirchenkampf*, 1:92–93. For the platform of the Young Reformation, see Wilhelm Niemöller, *Handbuch des Kirchenkampfes* (Bielefeld: Bechauf, 1956), 82–83.

23. There were exceptions in the church, such as Dietrich Bonhoeffer. See "The Church and the Jewish Question," in his *No Rusty Swords: Letters, Lectures and Notes 1928–1936*, ed. Edwin H. Robertson (New York: Harper and Row, 1965), 221–29. Eberhard Busch and Mark Lindsay argue that Karl Barth should also be considered an exception; see Busch, *Unter dem Bogen des einen Bundes: Karl Barth und die Juden 1933–1945* (Neukirchen-Vlyun: Neukircher Verlag, 1996); and Lindsay, *Covenanted Solidarity: The Theological Basis of Karl Barth's Opposition to Nazi Antisemitism and the Holocaust* (New York: Peter Lang, 2001). On Martin Niemöller and antisemitism, see Robert Michael, "Theological Myth, German Antisemitism and the Holocaust: The Case of Martin Niemöller," *Holocaust and Genocide Studies* 2, no. 1 (1987): 105–22.

24. Paul Douglass, *God among the Germans* (Philadelphia: University of Pennsylvania Press), 133.

25. The figure 50,000 is an estimate by Julius Richter, a missionary and advocate for Christians of Jewish descent. Approximately two to four hundred Jews converted to Protestantism each year from 1900 to 1939, except in 1933 when more than nine hundred converted. See Röhm and Thierfelder, *Juden, Christen, Deutsche*, 192–99.

26. See Gerlach, *And the Witnesses Were Silent*, 11–49.

27. Quoted in Ruth Zerner, "German Protestant Responses to the Nazi Persecution of the Jews," in *Perspectives on the Holocaust*, ed. Randolph L. Braham (Boston: Kluwer-Nijhoff, 1983), 62–63. Künneth's essay, "Das Judenproblem und die Kirche," in *Die Nation vor Gott:*

Zur Botschaft der Kirche im Dritten Reich, ed. Walter Künneth and Helmut Schreiner (Berlin: Wichern, 1934). For further discussion of this essay, see Röhm and Thierfelder, *Juden, Christen, Deutsche 1933–1945*, 1:155–59, and Smid, *Deutscher Protestantismus und Judentum 1932/1933*, 364–69.

28. Zerner, "German Protestant Responses," 62.

29. "The Church and the Jewish Question," in Dietrich Bonhoeffer, *No Rusty Swords*, 221–29. Also see Röhm and Thierfelder, *Juden, Christen, Deutsche 1935–45*, 1:174–81.

30. Bonhoeffer, *No Rusty Swords*, 226–27.

31. On Bonhoeffer's understanding of a Christian's obligation to Jews, see Röhm and Thierfelder, *Juden, Christen, Deutsche 1933–45*, 1:174–78; Gerlach, *And the Witnesses Were Silent*, 25–30; Eberhard Bethge, *Dietrich Bonhoeffer: A Biography*, revised and edited by Victoria J. Barnett (Minneapolis: Fortress Press, 1999), 304–23; Eberhard Bethge, "Dietrich Bonhoeffer and the Jews," in *Ethical Responsibility: Bonhoeffer's Legacy to the Churches*, ed. John D. Godsey and Geoffrey B. Kelly (New York: Edwin Mellen Press, 1981); Smid, *Deutscher Protestantismus und Judentum*, 415–56; Ruth Zerner, "Dietrich Bonhoeffer and the Jews: Thoughts and Actions, 1933–1945," *Jewish Social Studies* 37 (Summer and Fall 1975): 235–50; Stanley R. Rosenbaum, "Dietrich Bonhoeffer: A Jewish View," *Journal of Ecumenical Studies* 18 (Spring 1981); Kenneth C. Barnes, "Dietrich Bonhoeffer and Hitler's Persecution of the Jews," in *Betrayal*, ed. Ericksen and Heschel, 110–28; and Robert E. Willis, "Bonhoeffer and Barth on Jewish Suffering: Reflections on the Relationship between Theology and Moral Sensibility," *Journal of Ecumenical Studies* 24, no. 4 (Fall 1987): 598–615.

32. Barth, *Theological Existence Today!* (London: Hodder and Stoughton, 1933), 64.

33. Ibid., 67–68.

34. Karl Barth, "The Church's Opposition in 1933," in *The German Church Conflict* (Richmond, Va.: John Knox Press, 1968), 16.

35. Cochrane, *The Church's Confession under Hitler* (Pittsburgh: Pickwick Press, 1976), 109.

36. This number fell as divisions in the Confessing Church grew after 1934. Wilhelm Niemöller, the brother of Martin Niemöller, estimates that approximately 21 percent of the pastors in Germany were "in long-term, active cooperation" with PEL. See Wilhelm Niemöller, "The Niemöller Archives," in *The German Church Struggle*, ed. Littell and Locke, 53.

37. The noteworthy churchmen elected to the (Reich) council of brethren were President Karl Koch of Bad Oeynhausen near Minden, Bishop Hans Meiser of Munich, Bishop Theophil Wurm of Stuttgart, Pastor Joachim Beckmann of Düsseldorf, Pastor Karl Immer of Barmen, Pastor Gerhard Jacobi of Berlin, Pastor Martin Niemöller of Berlin-Dahlem, Pastor Hans Asmussen of Altona, and Pastor Hermann Hesse of Wuppertal-Elberfeld as spokesman of the Reformed churches. Over the next few years the membership of the council of brethren would change dramatically, increasingly including more and more Confessing churchmen from the radical or Dahlem wing of the Confessing Church. See Gerhard Niemöller, *Die erste Bekenntnissynode der Deutschen Evangelischen Kirche zu Barmen*, vol. 2: *Text, Dokumente, Berichte* (Göttingen: Vandenhoeck and Ruprecht, 1959), 204.

38. Klaus Scholder, "The Church Struggle," in *A Requiem for Hitler*, 102. As will become clear later in this section, many Lutherans dispute Scholder's positive assessment of the Barmen declaration.

39. Sasse asserted in 1936, "He who recognizes the Theological Declaration of Barmen as a doctrinal decision has thereby surrendered the Augsburg Confession and with it the

confession of the orthodox Evangelical Church. What is pure and false doctrine, what is and is not to be preached in the Lutheran Church can only be decided by a synod which is united in the confession of Lutheran doctrine, and not an assembly at which Lutherans, Reformed, Consensus United, Pietists, and Liberals were all equal participants, as was the case in Barmen." See Sasse's essay "Against Fanaticism," in Hermann Sasse, *The Lonely Way: Selected Essays and Letters*, vol. 1: *1927–1939* (Saint Louis: Concordia Publishing House, 2002). The original German, "Wider die Schwarmgeisterei," was published in *Lutherische Kirche* (1 August 1936): 237–40.

40. See appendix 1 for an English translation of the declaration.

41. Scholder, *Churches and the Third Reich*, 2:137.

42. Karl Barth, *Church Dogmatics* (Edinburgh: T. and T. Clark, 1936–62), 2.1: 172–82.

43. Quoted in Jüngel, *Christ, Justice and Peace: Toward a Theology of the State in a Dialogue with the Barmen Declaration* (Edinburgh: T. and T. Clark, 199), 223. Also see Scholder, *Churches in the Third Reich*, 2:13–14, and Susannah Heschel, "Nazifying Christian Theology: Walter Grundmann and the Institute for the Study and Eradication of Jewish Influence in German Church Life," *Church History* 63, no. 4 (December 1994): 587–605.

44. Werner Elert, *Law and Gospel*, trans. Edward H. Schoeder (Philadelphia: Fortress Press, 1967), 8.

45. Karl Barth, "Gospel and Law," in *Community, State and Church*, with an introduction by Will Herberg (Garden City, N.Y.: Anchor Books, 1960), 71.

46. The Ansbach Memorandum is reprinted in Wilhelm Niemöller, *Kampf und Zeugnis*, 128–29.

47. Gerhard O. Forde, *The Law-Gospel Debate: An Interpretation of Its Historical Development* (Minneapolis: Augsburg, 1969), 138. As Forde points out, Barth's understanding of gospel and law as unified was not simply a reaction to German Christian theology but was a "consistent Barthian theme" extending back to the early 1920s.

48. Elert, *Law and Gospel*, 4.

49. See in particular Sasse's "Against Fanaticism," in *The Lonely Way*, 307–10.

50. In *The Encyclopedia of the Lutheran Church* (Philadelphia: Fortress Press, 1965), Heinz Brunnote concludes his entry on the Barmen declaration with the following commentary: "Barmen proved that churches of differing theological positions can present a common declaration in a concrete situation when they take their stand on the Word of God. But 'Barmen' has remained an event of history and did not achieve the character of a 'confession' of a new church; the reason is that the theological discussion concerning the individual theses was not sufficiently serious to bring about the necessary 'deep consensus of the church'" (194). For a more detailed analysis of Barmen from a Lutheran perspective in the immediate postwar era, see Christian Stoll, *Die theologische Erklärung von Barmen im Urteil des lutherischen Bekenntnisses* (Munich: Verlag der Evang.-Luth. Kirche in Bayern, 1946) and Heinz Brunotte, *Die theologische Erklärung von Barmen, 1934, und ihr Verhältnis zum lutherischen Bekenntnis* (Berlin: Lutherisches Verlagshaus, 1955).

51. See Niemöller's July 1945, "The Position and Prospects of the Evangelical Church," ZEKHN-Darmstadt 62/1016.

52. In addition to the Reich council of brethren (*Reichsbruderrat*) elected at Barmen, councils of brethren were often elected at the local and regional level to administer to the affairs of the Confessing Church communities throughout Germany.

53. Douglass, *God among the Germans*, 261.

54. Ibid.

55. Eberhard Busch, *Karl Barth: His Life from Letters and Autobiographical Texts*, trans. John Bowden (Philadelphia: Fortress Press, 1976), 254.

56. Röhm and Thierfelder, *Juden, Christen, Deutsche 1933–45*, 1:337.

57. See Besier, *Die Kirchen und das Dritte Reich*, 82–96.

58. Röhm and Thierfelder, *Juden, Christen, Deutsche 1933–45*, 1:337–46.

59. Besier, *Die Kirchen und das Dritte Reich*, 83.

60. Busch, *Karl Barth*, 261.

61. Ibid. Barth consistently maintained that the Confessing Church's lack of clarity was an inevitable consequence of its willingness to compromise with moderate German Christians. As Barth said in the summer of 1935, "The story of the Confessing Church in the National Socialist Germany of these years [1933–35] is no glorious chronicle, . . . no heroic or saintly story. . . . We can and must reproach this Confessing Church for not recognizing the enemy early on in its real dangerousness and for not unambiguously and forcefully opposing to him early on the Word of God, which judges human deceit and injustice, as was her duty as the Church of Jesus Christ. Her path . . . has been . . . almost a continuous series of errors, confusions, and disappointments" (*German Church Conflict*, 45–46).

62. Besier, *Die Kirchen und das Dritte Reich*, 396–423.

63. Matheson, *The Third Reich*, 56.

64. Otto Dibelius, "Die Staatskirche ist da! Ein Wort zur gegenwärtigen kirchlichen Lage." In *Dokumente des Kirchenkampfes II: Die Zeit des Reichskirchenausschusses 1935–1937*, ed. Kurt Dietrich Schmidt (Göttingen: Vandenhoeck and Ruprecht, 1964).

65. Besier, *Die Kirchen und das Dritte Reich*, 423–29.

66. Ibid., 427.

67. See Scholder, "Political Resistance or Self-Assertion as a Problem for Church Governments," in *A Requiem for Hitler*, 135–37.

68. Busch, *Karl Barth*, 273.

69. Besier, *Die Kirchen und das Dritte Reich*, 431, 482–87; Cochrane, *The Church's Confession*, 275–77. The entire letter is translated and reprinted in Cochrane, appendix X, 268–79.

70. Cochrane, *The Church's Confession*, 277.

71. Bethge, "Troubled Self-interpretation," 174.

72. Martin Niemöller, *From U-Boat to Pulpit* (London: W. Hodge, 1936). On Niemöller's career, see Dietmar Schmidt, *Martin Niemöller: Eine Biographie* (Hamburg: Rowohlt, 1959); Jürgen Schmidt, *Martin Niemöller im Kirchenkampf* (Hamburg: Leibniz-Verlag, 1971); James Bentley, *Martin Niemöller, 1892–1984* (New York: Free Press, 1984); John S. Conway, "The Political Theology of Martin Niemöller," *German Studies Review* 9, no. 3 (October 1986): 521–46; Hubert Locke and Marcia Sachs Littell, eds., *Remembrance and Recollection: Essays on the Centennial Year of Martin Niemöller and Reinhold Niebuhr, and the Fiftieth Year of the Wannsee Conference* (Lanham, Md.: University Press of America, 1996); Hermann Düringer and Martin Stöhr, *Martin Niemöller im Kalten Krieg: die Arbeit für Frieden und Gerechtigkeit damals und heute* (Frankfurt am Main: Haag und Herchen, 2001).

73. Conway, "Political Theology of Martin Niemöller," 524.

74. Martin Niemöller, *Here I Stand*, trans. Jane Lymburn (Chicago: Willett, Clark and Company, 1937), 223.

75. There has been much debate about why Niemöller made this request. Patriotism was certainly one motive, but it is also clear that his wife and lawyer believed he would have a better chance of surviving the war years in the navy than in a concentration camp. For this debate, see Conway, "Political Theology of Martin Niemöller," 537.

76. Kurt Meier, *Der evangelische Kirchenkampf,* 3:43–53.

77. Quoted in Helmreich, *German Churches under Hitler,* 230.

78. Scholder, "Political Resistance or Self-Assertion," 137.

79. Busch, *Karl Barth,* 289.

80. Conway, *The Nazi Persecution,* 230.

81. Ibid., 231.

82. The statistics come from *The Encyclopedia of the Third Reich,* ed. Christian Zentner and Friedemann Bedurftig (New York: Macmillan, 1991), 1:515.

83. Röhm and Thierfelder, *Juden, Christen, Deutsche 1933–45,* 3.1:19–61. On Gollwitzer and von Jan's sermons, see 62–68 and 69–92 respectively. Also see Gerlach, *And the Witnesses Were Silent,* 141–52; Barnett, *For the Soul of the People,* 142–43.

84. See Franklin H. Littell, *The Crucifixion of the Jews: The Failure of Christians to Understand the Jewish Experience,* 3rd ed. (Macon, Ga.: Mercer University Press, 1996).

85. Röhm and Thierfelder, *Juden, Christen, Deutsche 1933–45,* 3.1:93–133. Gerlach, *And the Witnesses Were Silent,* 154–62. Gerlach emphasizes that the "Grüber office" was "explicitly commissioned by the second Provisional Church Administration," i.e., the leadership body of the Dahlem wing of the Confessing Church after 1936 (p. 155).

86. On Barth, see Eberhard Busch, *Unter dem Bogen des einen Bundes,* 313–58; and Mark Lindsay, *Covenanted Solidarity,* 261. On Bonhoeffer, see Eberhard Bethge, *Dietrich Bonhoeffer: A Biography,* 607; and Kenneth C. Barnes, "Dietrich Bonhoeffer and Hitler's Persecution of the Jews," in *Betrayal,* ed. Ericksen and Heschel, 110–28.

87. Barnes, "Dietrich Bonhoeffer and Hitler's Persecution of the Jews," 124–25.

88. Ibid., 125–26.

89. Stewart Herman, *It's Your Souls We Want* (New York: Harper and Brothers, 1943), 208.

90. Gutteridge, *Open Thy Mouth,* 238.

91. Ibid., 248.

92. Ibid., 354. The entire letter is translated in appendix VI, pp. 353–55. Also see David J. Diephouse, "Antisemitism as Moral Discourse: Theophil Wurm and Protestant Opposition to the Holocaust" (paper presented at the 30th Annual Scholars' Conference on the Holocaust and the Churches, Philadelphia, March 2000).

93. Gutteridge, *Open Thy Mouth,* 120.

94. See Theodor Dipper, *Die Evangelische Bekenntnisgemeinschaft in Württemberg 1933–1945,* Arbeiten zur Geschichte des Kirchenkampfes, vol. 17 (Göttingen: Vandenhoeck and Ruprecht, 1966); and Jörg Thierfelder, *Das Kirchliche Einigungswerk des württembergischen Landesbischofs Theophil Wurm,* Arbeiten zur Kirchlichen Zeitgeschichte, vol. 1 (Göttingen: Vandenhoeck and Ruprecht, 1975).

95. See Dipper, *Die Evangelische Bekenntnisgemeinschaft,* 284–85; and *Kirchliches Jahrbuch* (1933–45), 441–43.

96. Jörg Thierfelder, *Zusammenbruch und Neubeginn,* 37.

97. Responses to a 1947 letter from Hans Asmussen, president of the church chancellery, asking each regional church leader to characterize the doctrinal foundation of his regional church provide evidence of the bitter dispute over the Barmen declaration and the doctrinal basis of the postwar church. Asmussen wanted to know, among other matters, the meaning and import of the Barmen theological declaration in the twenty-seven regional churches. The responses varied significantly. The questionnaire can be found in the *Amtsblatt der Evangelischen Kirche in Deutschland* 1, no. 5 (15 February 1947): 9–12. Many of the responses

can be found in the Evangelisches Zentralarchiv in Berlin, file 2, folder 12 (hereafter cited as EZA 2/12).

98. For the position of Meiser and the Lutheran council on the Barmen declaration and the *Vereinigten Evangelische-Lutherische Kirche Deutschlands* (VELKD), see Wolf-Dieter Hauschild, "Vom 'Lutherrat' zur VELKD," in . . . *und über Barmen hinaus: Studien zur Kirchlichen Zeitgeschichte*, ed. Joachim Mehlhausen (Göttingen: Vandenhoeck and Ruprecht, 1995), 451–70; "Erklärung des Rates der Evang.-Luth. Kirche Deutschlands vom 27. August 1945," *Kirchliches Jahrbuch* (1945–48): 7–8; and "Der Kampf um die Neuordnung der EKD (1946–47)," 66–94; Christian Stoll, "Die Lage der Lutherischen Kirche innerhalb des deutschen Gesamtprotestantismus," in *EKiD oder nicht? Eine Aufsatzreihe, zusammengestellt von Ev.* Vortragsdienst in der Mark (Dortmund-Hombruch, n.d.), 3–7; Hans Meiser, "Theolog. Erklärung von Barmen im Ordinationsgelübde," EZA 2/12, 2–6; and Hans Meiser, "Vor der Verwirklichung der Vereinigten Evang.-Luth. Kirche Deutschlands," *Evangelische-Lutherische Kirchenzeitung* 2, no. 14 (31 July 1948): 127.

99. See Niemöller's speech at the 21 August 1945 meeting of the councils of brethren in Frankfurt and the resolution presented at the Treysa conference by the councils of brethren in Gerhard Besier, Hartmut Ludwig, and Jörg Thierfelder, eds., *Der Kompromiß von Treysa: Die Entstehung der Evangelischen Kirche in Deutschland (EKD) 1945* (Weinheim: Deutscher Studien Verlag, 1995), 142–59.

100. Martin Niemöller to Wilhelm Niemöller, 10 November 1945, in Niemöller, *Die deutsche Schuld,* 21 and 28.

101. See Martin Niemöller to Wilhelm Niemöller, 20–28; Martin Niemöller, "Von einer neuen Aufspaltung der evangelischen Christenheit in Deutschland?" in *EKiD oder nicht?* 16–19; Hans Iwand, "Ende der EKiD?" in *EKiD oder nicht?* 8–14; Hans Iwand, "Lutherische Kirche? Warum ich als lutherischer Theologe grundsätzlich Gegner der Vereinigten Evangelisch-lutherischen Kirche Deutschlands bin," *Evangelische Theologie* 1946–47: 385–88.

102. See Martin Niemöller, "The Positions and Prospects of the Evangelical Church," July 1945, ZEKHN-Darmstadt 62/1016.

103. Bishop Wurm to Rat der Ev.-Luth. Kirche Deutschlands, 10 July 1946, EZA 2/12, 1–6.

104. Armin Boyens, "Treysa 1945—Die evangelische Kirche nach dem Zusammenbruch des Dritten Reiches," *Zeitschrift für Kirchengeschichte* 82, no. 1 (1971): 36–37.

105. For an insightful overview of these activities, see Stewart Herman's *Rebirth of the German Church.*

106. Clemens Vollnhals, *Evangelische Kirche und Entnazifizierung 1945–1949,* 52–60.

107. These accusations continued after the war. See Niemöller to Asmussen, 28 November 1946, ZEKHN-Darmstadt 62/539; and Bogner to Niemöller, 15 March 1946, LKA Nuremberg LKR 1, 102h (new number 303).

2. Representations of the Nazi Past in Early 1945

1. Major Earl L. Crum, a religious affairs officer with the U.S. forces in Germany, was an advocate of the German churches playing a leading role in the reconstruction of the country. In his report on the August 1945 Treysa Conference he stated, "It remains for the Mil-

itary Government, with a watchful eye, to offer sufficient latitude to the Church to establish a sound moral basis for the new Germany. If the Church is unable to accomplish this, it is doubtful whether any other agency can do it." See Clemens Vollnhals, ed., *Die evangelische Kirche nach dem Zusammenbruch: Berichte ausländischer Beobachter aus dem Jahre 1945* (Göttingen: Vandenhoeck and Ruprecht, 1988), 129–33.

2. There are a number of excellent studies and document collections on the Treysa conference. See Fritz Söhlmann, ed., *Treysa 1945: Die Konferenz der evangelischen Kirchenführer 27–31. August 1945* (Lüneburg: Heliand, 1946); Annemarie Smith-Von Osten, *Von Treysa bis Eisenach 1948;* Jörg Thierfelder, "Theophil Wurm und der Weg nach Treysa," *Blätter für württembergische Kirchengeschichte* 85 (1985): 149–74; Ralf Tyra, "Treysa 1945: Neue Forschungsergebnisse zur ersten deutschen Kirchenversammlung nach dem Krieg," *Kirchliche Zeitgeschichte* 2 (1989): 239–76; Gerhard Besier, Hartmut Ludwig, and Jörg Thierfelder, eds., *Der Kompromiß von Treysa.* And most recently, Martin Greschat, *Die evangelische Christenheit und die deutsche Geschichte nach 1945,* 96–131.

3. Hans Asmussen, "Gehört Luther vor das Nürnberger Gericht?" *Nachrichten für die evangelisch-lutherischen Geistlichen in Bayern,* 2, nos. 19–20 (1947): 123–28.

4. See Hartmut Ludwig, "Tagung der Bekennenden Kirche in Frankfurt/M," and the accompanying documents on the pre-Treysa meeting of Martin Niemöller and his colleagues from the councils of brethren in *Der Kompromiß von Treysa,* ed. Besier et al., 1:9–20; and Gerhard Besier, "Auf dem Weg zur Bildung einer Lutherischen Kirche" and the accompanying documents on the meeting organized by Hans Meiser and the conservatives in *Der Kompromiß,* 21–31. Also see Smith-von Osten, *Von Treysa.*

5. The provisional EKD council established at Treysa consisted of six churchmen from Lutheran churches, four from United churches, and two from Reformed churches. The twelve members were: Bishops Theophil Wurm, Hans Meiser, and Otto Dibelius of Württemberg, Bavaria, and Berlin-Brandenburg; Hanns Lilje of the executive council of the church in Hannover; Superintendents Heinrich Held of Essen-Rüttenscheid and Hugo Hahn of Stuttgart; Pastors Hans Asmussen, Martin Niemöller, and Wilhelm Niesel of Schwäbisch Gmünd, Darmstadt, and Reelkirchen; Professor Rudolf Smend of Göttingen; layman Gustav Heinemann of Essen; and Johann Peter Meyer of Hamburg-Altona.

6. See Niemöller's speech at the 21 August 1945 meeting of the councils of brethren in Frankfurt and the resolution presented at the Treysa conference by the councils of brethren in *Der Kompromiß,* ed. Besier et al., 1:142–59.

7. Martin Niemöller, "The Position and Prospects of the Evangelical Church," July 1945, ZEKHN-Darmstadt 62/1016; Niemöller to Asmussen, 22 June 1946, ZEKHN-Darmstadt 62/539; Dibelius to Niemöller, 1 August 1946, LKA Stuttgart D1/225.

8. Greschat, ed., *Die Schuld der Kirche,* 54, says: "Daß es eine solche deutsche Schuld gab, daran zweifelte in diesen ersten Wochen und Monaten nach Kriegsende in Deutschland praktisch kaum jemand."

9. The Protestant Church repented in the October 1945 Stuttgart Declaration of Guilt "for not witnessing more courageously, for not praying more faithfully, for not believing more joyously, and for not loving more ardently." The Stuttgart declaration is discussed in detail in chapter 4.

10. "Message to the Congregations," *Ecumenical Press Service* 32 (September 1945): 155–56. For the original, see "Wort an die Gemeinden," in *Die Protokolle des Rates der Evangelischen Kirche in Deutschland,* 1:5–7.

11. "Message to the Congregations," 156.

12. Ibid.

13. The term "conservative churchly resistance" is mine, not theirs. For a discussion of myths regarding the church struggle, see Baumgärtel, *Wider die Kirchenkampf-Legenden.*

14. Dibelius reports that very shortly after Asmussen assumed the directorship of the church chancellery, the friendship between Niemöller and Asmussen turned into "bitter antagonism." This becomes particularly clear in the correspondence between the two after the EKD Council issued the Stuttgart Declaration of Guilt in October 1945. See Dibelius, *In the Service of the Lord,* 218.

15. Hans Asmussen to archbishop of Canterbury, 16 June 1945, in *Die Schuld,* ed. Greschat, 64.

16. See Hans Böhm, "Rechenschaftsbericht des Bruderrates der Bekennenden Kirche Berlins, 29 July 1945," in *Treysa 1945,* ed. Söhlmann, 117–27.

17. Otto Dibelius, *In the Service of the Lord,* 217.

18. Various representatives of the occupation forces and foreign churches questioned Niemöller about his decision. Stewart Herman, the American Lutheran representative, reported, "I suggested he [Niemöller] confine his comments to a simple declaration that he made a mistake in September 1939 and that he regrets his action. He told me that he acted on the advice of his lawyer, who thought that he was helping to save Niemöller's life at the outbreak of war. He was also moved by the fact that his sons, whom he had always wanted to send to England for their education, would be forced to fight and that he felt he should stand with them." See Vollnhals, *Die evangelische Kirche nach dem Zusammenbruch,* 75.

19. Bishop Wurm, "Ein Wort an die Christenheit im Ausland," LKA Stuttgart D1/210. According to Greschat, Wurm had prepared this text for discussion at the August Treysa meeting but it never came up for discussion. It was published in an undated newsletter. See Greschat, ed., *Die Schuld,* 55 and 62, n. 3.

20. Wurm, "Ein Wort an die Christenheit im Ausland," LKA Stuttgart D1/210.

21. Ibid.

22. Bishop Wurm, "Bericht über die kirchliche Entwicklung der letzten zwölf Jahre," in Söhlmann, *Treysa 1945,* 20.

23. For an examination of the concept *secularization* in Protestant theology after 1945, see Wolfgang Lück, *Das Ende der Nachkriegszeit: Eine Untersuchung zur Funktion des Begriffs der Säkularisierung in der "Kirchentheorie" Westdeutschlands 1945–1965* (Bern: Herbert Lang, 1976). Wurm in *Kirche nach der Kapitulation,* ed. Besier et al., 246.

24. Wurm, "Ein Wort an die Christenheit im Ausland," LKA Stuttgart D1/210.

25. Ibid.

26. "Message to the Congregations," 155.

27. Ibid., 173.

28. Otto Dibelius, "Das Fragen um die Christen her," in *Treysa 1945,* ed. Söhlmann, 111–17.

29. The opening scriptural quote for Dibelius's sermon was from Exodus 13:14: "In days to come, when your son asks you, 'What does this mean?' say to him, 'With a mighty hand the Lord brought us out of Egypt, out of the land of slavery.'"

30. Dibelius, "Das Fragen um die Christen her," in *Treysa 1945,* ed. Söhlmann, 114.

31. Ibid., 115.

32. Quoted in Carins, "The German Reaction," in Vollnhals, *Die evangelische Kirche nach dem Zusammenbruch,* 167.

33. Helmut Thielicke, "Die Kirche inmitten des deutschen Zusammenbruchs. Ihre Beurteilung der Lage und ihre Ziele," ZEKHN-Darmstadt 62/722. Also available in *Kirche nach der Kapitulation,* ed. Besier et al., 1:203–209.

34. Thielicke, "Die Kirche," in *Kirche nach der Kapitulation,* ed. Besier et al., 204.

35. "Message to the Pastors," *Ecumenical Press Service* 35 (September 1945): 173–74. For the original, "Wort an die Pfarrer," see *Die Protokolle des Rates der Evangelischen Kirche in Deutschland,* ed. Nicolaisen and Schulze, 1:173–76.

36. "Message to the Pastors," 173–74.

37. Ibid., 173.

38. Barth to Niemöller, 28 September 1945, in Ludwig, "Karl Barths Dienst," 319. For a fuller treatment of the testy relationship between Barth and Asmussen, see Gerhard Besier, "Die Auseinandersetzung zwischen Karl Barth und Hans Asmussen: Ein Paradigma für die konfessionelle Problematik innerhalb des Protestantismus?" in *Die evangelische Kirche in den Umbrüchen des 20. Jahrhunderts, Gesammelte Aufsätze,* 1:121–42.

39. For the critique of Asmussen's draft, see Besier, Ludwig, and Thierfelder, *Der Kompromiß von Treysa,* 108–109.

40. For Asmussen's draft, see Besier, Ludwig, and Thierfelder, *Der Kompromiß von Treysa,* 172–76.

41. Asmussen to the archbishop of Canterbury, in *Die Schuld,* ed. Greschat, 65, 67.

42. Karl Barth, "The Germans and Ourselves," trans. Ronald Gregor Smith in Karl Barth, *The Only Way* (New York: Philosophical Library, 1947), 106.

43. Barth to First Letter Writer, in *The Only Way,* 38–39.

44. Karl Barth, "How Can the Germans Be Cured?" trans. Marta K. Neufeld, in *The Only Way,* 3–20.

45. Ibid., 3.

46. See Jürgen Kocka's article, "Asymmetrical Historical Comparison: The Case of the German Sonderweg," *History and Theory* 38 (February 1999): 40–50.

47. Barth, "The Germans and Ourselves," 83.

48. Karl Barth, "First Letter to French Protestants," December 1939, in Karl Barth, *The Christian Cause* (New York: Macmillan, 1941), n.p.

49. Barth did not disclose the identity of the two letter writers. Second Letter to Karl Barth (1945) in Barth, *The Only Way: How Can the Germans Be Cured?* (New York: Philosophical Library, 1947), 44.

50. Ibid., 44 and 46.

51. Ibid., 47.

52. First Letter to Barth, 27.

53. Ibid., 29.

54. Ibid., 30. The Schalburg-Corps was a pro-Nazi Danish group.

55. Barth to First Letter Writer, 33.

56. Ibid., 37. Oradour was a French village in the Limoges area known for its partisan activity in 1944. On 10 June 1944 an SS unit entered Oradour, rounded up all the residents (634 men, women, and children), forced them into a church, and burned the church, killing everyone inside. Oradour became a symbol of Nazi brutality. See "Oradour-sur-Glane," in *Encyclopedia of the Holocaust,* ed. Israel Gutman (New York: Macmillan, 1990), 3:1091.

57. Barth to First Letter Writer, 38–39.

58. Barth to Second Letter Writer, 53.

59. Barth, "How Can the Germans Be Cured?" 3.

60. Ibid., 6.

61. Barth, "The Germans and Ourselves," 91.

62. Ibid., 96–97.

63. Ibid., 104.

64. Barth to Second Letter Writer, 52.

65. Barth, "How Can the Germans Be Cured?" 10.

66. Hans Asmussen, "Gehört Luther vor das Nürnberger Gericht?" 123–28; see also Asmussen's "Sollen wir unser Vaterland lieb haben?" *Schriftendienst der Kanzlei der Evangelischen Kirche in Deutschland,* no. 2 (1946).

67. Gottlieb Funcke, "Unsere Ehre darf nicht verloren sein," 31 July 1945, *Die Schuld,* ed. Greschat, 70.

68. Ibid., 70.

69. Böhm, "Rechenschaftsbericht," 120.

70. Ibid., 120.

71. Martin Niemöller, "Ansprache an die Vertreter der Bekennenden Kirche," 6 January 1946, in *Die deutsche Schuld, Not und Hoffnung* (Zollikon-Zürich: Evangelischer Verlag, 1946), 12.

3. Guilt from Another World

1. "Message to the Congregations," 155.

2. Wilhelm Halfmann, "Wie sollen wir predigen?" in *Die Stunde der Kirche,* ed. Jürgensen, 263. Halfmann was elected Bishop of Holstein in 1946.

3. Wurm, "Wort an die Christenheit im Ausland," LKA Stuttgart D1/210.

4. Smith-von Osten, *Von Treysa,* 137.

5. "Message to the Pastors," 173.

6. Ibid.

7. "Wort der Bekenntnissynode an die Pfarrer und Gemeinden," in *Treysa 1945,* ed. Söhlmann, 139–40. For the English translation that I have used with minor revisions, see *Ecumenical Press Service* 35 (August 1945): 150–53.

8. Niemöller, "Rede auf der Kirchenversammlung in Treysa," 28 August 1945, in *Die Schuld,* ed. Greschat, 78–81.

9. Ibid., 79.

10. Ibid., 79–80.

11. Ibid., 81.

12. Asmussen to archbishop of Canterbury, in *Die Schuld,* ed. Greschat, 65.

13. Halfmann cites Isaiah 1:2–7. In these passages God spoke to the people of Judah saying, "I reared children and brought them up, but they have rebelled against me. . . . Ah, sinful nation, people laden with iniquity, offspring who do evil, children who deal corruptly, who have forsaken the Lord, who have despised the Holy One of Israel, who are utterly estranged! Why do you seek further beatings? Why do you continue to rebel? . . . Your country lies desolate, your cities are burned with fire; in your very presence aliens devour your land; it is desolate, as overthrown by foreigners."

14. Halfmann, "Wie sollen," 262.

15. Ibid., 262.

16. Asmussen to archbishop of Canterbury, 65.

17. Ibid.

18. Ibid., 67.

19. Ibid. "Ich schreibe dies, hochwürdiger Vater, um die Frage nach der Schuld an alle dem Furchtbaren auf eine andere Ebene zu heben."

20. Ibid., 68. "Wir können uns nicht entschuldigen, aber wir können uns dagegen wehren, daß man uns unsere Schuld vermenschlicht und sie damit vor Gott unvergebbar macht."

21. Wurm made a similar point but with even stronger language. In his statement "A Message to Christianity Abroad," Wurm wrote: "Wenn die Völker jetzt nicht lernen, ihre Beziehungen auf Vergebung und Vertrauen zu gründen statt auf Rache und Vergeltung, ist eine letzte Weltkatastrophe unvermeidlich" (Wurm, LKA Stuttgart D1/210).

22. Dietrich Bonhoeffer, *The Cost of Discipleship*, trans. R. H. Fuller (New York: Touchstone, 1995), 44, 53; originally published as *Nachfolge* (Munich: Christian Kaiser, 1937).

23. Ibid., 89.

24. Ibid., 287–88.

25. Pastor Constantin Frick, "Wir sind nach heldenhaftem Kampf besiegt," in *Die Schuld*, ed. Greschat, 71.

26. Quoted in Gregory L. Jones, *Embodying Forgiveness: A Theological Analysis* (Grand Rapids, Mich.: Eerdmans, 1995), 19.

27. Luther has claimed that his theological breakthrough took place in a tower of the Augustinian monastery at Wittenberg.

28. Alister E. McGrath, *Reformation Thought: An Introduction* (Oxford: Blackwell, 1993), chapters 5 and 6.

4. The Stuttgart Declaration of Guilt

1. EZA 2/35, 162.

2. See Murphy's report in *Die evangelische Kirche nach dem Zusammenbruch*, ed. Vollnhals, 120–22.

3. See Gerhard Besier, ed., "Ökumenische Mission in Nachkriegsdeutschland: Die Berichte von Stewart W. Herman über die Verhältnisse in der evangelischen Kirche 1945/46, part 1," *Kirchliche Zeitgeschichte* 1, no. 1 (1988): 335.

4. The ecumenical delegation consisted of Willem Visser 't Hooft, general secretary of the WCC; Samuel McCrea Cavert, the general secretary of the federal council of Churches of Christ in America; George Bell, the Anglican bishop of Chichester as representative of the archbishop of Canterbury; Alphons Koechlin, the president of the Swiss Protestant Church Federation; Hendrik Kraemer, representative of the Netherlands Reformed Church; Sylvester Clarence Michelfelder, the leader of the American section of the Lutheran World Convention in Geneva; and Pierre Maury, representing Marc Boegner of the Protestant Federation of France. The Norwegian representative was unable to arrive in time.

5. Eleven of the twelve members of the EKD council signed the final version that Asmussen distributed to the ecumenical delegation. Dr. Meyer of Hamburg, one of the twelve men elected to the EKD council at Treysa, was not present and therefore did not sign the document. For a complete list of EKD council members see chapter 2, note 5.

6. The EKD council's first official meeting took place at Treysa in late August 1945 immediately following the creation of the council at the Treysa conference organized by Bishop Wurm.

7. Quoted in *Kirche im Ruhrgebiet: ein Lese-und Bilder-Buch zur Geschichte der Kirche im Ruhrgebiet von 1945 bis heute*, ed. Günther Brakelmann et al. (Essen: Klartext, 1991).

8. John S. Conway emphasizes this point in his very informative article "How Shall Nations Repent? The Stuttgart Declaration of Guilt, October 1945," *Journal of Ecclesiastical History* 38, no. 4 (October 1987): 596–622. He argues that the declaration of guilt was primarily a voluntary act by the EKD council and not the result of blackmail by the ecumenical delegation. "The accusation that the German Churchmen were forced to issue the Stuttgart Declaration in return for the promise of material aid is without foundation. . . . The decisive initiatives taken by Asmussen and Niemöller derived from their earlier reflections and from their acute disappointment that their message ["Word to the Pastors"] had not already been accepted at the Treysa conference." In addition to Asmussen's 1942 letter to Visser 't Hooft, Conway cites other personal statements by leaders of the Confessing Church and the public statements made in the summer of 1945 at Berlin-Spandau, Frankfurt, and Treysa. For Asmussen's 1942 letter, see Greschat, *Die Schuld*, 25–26. Stewart Herman also argues, almost forty years before Conway, that at Stuttgart the church had "adopted a policy of repentance even if all their members had not." See Herman, *Rebirth of the German Church*, 141.

9. Willem A. Visser 't Hooft, Report on the Visit of a Delegation from the World Council of Churches to Germany in *Die evangelische Kirche nach dem Zusammenbruch*, ed. Vollnhals, 196; Besier, "Zur Geschichte," 29.

10. Greschat, *Die Schuld*, 92.

11. Ibid., 91–92.

12. Quoted in Conway, "How Shall the Nations Repent?" 608.

13. Visser 't Hooft's 27 September 1945 letter to Niemöller is reprinted in full in Ludwig, "Karl Barths Dienst," 317–18.

14. Visser 't Hooft, Report on the Visit, in *Die evangelische Kirche nach dem Zusammenbruch*, ed. Vollnhals, 194.

15. Barth to Niemöller, 28 September 1945, in Ludwig, "Karl Barths Dienst," 318. This letter is also reprinted in *Dokumente zur Bonhoeffer-Forschung 1928–1945* (Munich: Chr. Kaiser Verlag, 1969), ed. Jørgen Glenthøj, 339–40.

16. Ludwig, "Karl Barths Dienst," 319.

17. Visser 't Hooft in *Die Schuld*, ed. Greschat, 96.

18. Ludwig, "Karl Barths Dienst," 323.

19. Quoted in *Die Schuld*, ed. Greschat, 91.

20. Quoted in Gerhard Besier, "Zur Geschichte der Stuttgarter Schulderklärung vom 18./19. Oktober 1945," in Gerhard Besier and Gerhard Sauter, eds., *Wie Christen ihre Schuld bekennen: Die Stuttgarter Erklärung 1945* (Göttingen: Vandenhoeck and Ruprecht, 1985), 32.

21. Quoted in Besier, "Zur Geschichte," 32–33. Moreover, Bishop George Bell of England laid great emphasis on the significance of Maury's statement in his report on the meeting in Stuttgart and his trip to Germany. See "Bericht George K. A. Bells über seine Deutschlandreise vom 18. bis 30. Oktober 1945," in Vollnhals, ed., *Die evangelische Kirche nach dem Zusammenbruch*, 224.

22. Besier, "Zur Geschichte," 33.

23. The WCC's October 1945 newsletter reported, "The [WCC] delegation expressed its deep gratitude for this truly Christian message. A new basis for fellowship had thus been laid. It accepted the message in all humility and considered it as a call to the other churches to redouble their efforts to help the German Church and the German nation in their great

suffering and to work towards the removal of injustices." For examples of the responses to the Stuttgart declaration by European churches, see Greschat, *Die Schuld,* 302–308.

24. Greschat, *Die evangelische Christenheit,* 148.

25. See Daniel Borg, "German Protestants and the Ecumenical Movements: The War-Guilt Imbroglio, 1919–1926," *Journal of Church and State* 10, no. 1 (Winter 1968): 51–71.

26. At a meeting of pastors in Stuttgart in early December 1945, Wurm blamed the "political press." See Ansprache des Herrn Landesbischof im Stuttgarter Pfarrkonvent am 4. Dezember 1945 über die Schuldfrage, LKA Stuttgart D1/210.

27. The entire article, "Gemeinsame Schuld für endlose Leiden," from the 27 October 1945 *Ruhr-Zeitung* was reprinted in *Kirche im Ruhrgebiet,* 98.

28. Pastor Wilhelm Niesel, Abschrift, EZA 2/36, 20.

29. Stewart Herman, Report on German Reaction to the Stuttgart Declaration, in Gerhard Besier, ed., "Ökumenische Mission in Nachkriegsdeutschland: Die Berichte von Stewart Herman über die Verhältnisse in der evangelischen Kirche 1945/46," *Kirchliche Zeitgeschichte* 2, no. 1 (1989): 312–15.

30. Superintendent Hoppe to Wurm, 9 November 1945, EZA 2/34, 31.

31. K. D. to Wurm, 3 November 1945, EZA 2/34, 21.

32. E. S. to Wurm, 20 November 1945, EZA 2/34, 34.

33. E. S. to Asmussen, February 1946, EZA 2/35, 9.

34. F. K. to Wurm, 13 March 1946, LKA Stuttgart D1/211.

35. R. S. to Kongress, 26 October 1945, EZA 2/34, 1.

36. Ibid.

37. M. E. to Rat der EKD and Wurm, 1 November 1945, EZA 2/34, 18.

38. A. F. to Wurm, 10 March 1946, EZA 2/35.

39. V. R. Berghahn, *Modern Germany: Society, Economy, and Politics in the Twentieth Century* (Cambridge: Cambridge University Press, 1987), 177.

40. Estimates on the number of German POWs in Soviet camps vary considerably. See Moeller, *War Stories,* 37–38. Also see Dennis L. Bark and David R. Gress, *From Shadow to Substance 1945–1963* (Oxford: Basil Blackwell, 1989), 41.

41. Moeller, *War Stories,* 34–35, 40; Bark and Gress, *From Shadow,* 35–36.

42. Norman M. Naimark, *The Russians in Germany: A History of the Soviet Zone of Occupation, 1945–1949* (Cambridge, Mass.: Harvard University Press, 1995), 83–90.

43. Quoted in Berghahn, *Modern Germany,* 185.

44. Quoted in Dagmar Barnouw, *Germany 1945: Views of War and Violence* (Bloomington: Indiana University Press, 1996), 17.

45. Frederick Spotts, *Churches and Politics in Germany,* 51.

46. See John S. Conway, "Die Rolle der Kirchen bei der 'Umerziehung' in Deutschland," in *Das Unrechtsregime. Internationale Forschung über den Nationalsozialismus,* vol. 2, ed. Ursula Büttner (Hamburg, 1986).

47. Hans Asmussen, Kommentar, ZEKHN-Darmstadt 62/1016.

48. Herman, Memorandum on Conversation with Pastor Niemöller in Frankfurt on July 31, 1945, in Vollnhals, ed., *Die evangelische Kirche nach dem Zusammenbruch,* 75.

49. Asmussen, Kommentar, ZEKHN-Darmstadt 62/1016.

50. Asmussen to U. W., 1 March 1946, EZA 2/35, 94.

51. Asmussen, Kommentar.

52. Asmussen quoted in Herman, *Rebirth,* 130.

53. Asmussen to U. W., 1 March 1946, EZA 2/35, 95.

54. Ibid.

55. Ibid.

56. Ibid.: "Wir haben ein Recht . . . uns unschuldig zu wissen am Nazismus und an seinen Greueln. . . ."

57. Quoted in Herman, *Rebirth*, 139.

58. Hans Asmussen, "Die Stuttgarter Erklärung: Ein Rundgespräch zur Schuldfrage," *Verordnungs-und Nachrichtenblatt. Amtliches Organ der Evangelischen Kirche in Deutschland* 6 (February 1946): 1–2.

59. Asmussen, Kommentar.

60. Ibid.

61. Asmussen, "Die Stuttgart Erklärung," in *Verordnungs-und Nachrichtenblatt*, 4.

62. LKA Stuttgart D1/210.

63. Ibid.

64. Lilje, Antwort an S., in Greschat, ed., *Die Schuld*, 225.

65. Hans Meiser, *Kirche, Kampf und Christusglaube: Anfechtungen und Antworten eines Lutheraners*, ed. Fritz and Gertrude Meiser (Munich: Claudius-Verlag, 1982), 176.

66. Otto Dibelius, Etwas von Schuldbekenntnissen, in Greschat, ed., *Die Schuld*, 254.

67. Ibid.

68. Ibid.

69. Ludwig, "Karl Barths Dienst," 301.

70. Asmussen, Kommentar.

71. Niemöller to F., 10 November 1945, EZA 2/35, 162.

72. Martin Niemöller, Die Erneuerung unserer Kirche, 1946, in Greschat, ed., *Die Schuld*, 207.

73. Martin Niemöller, Ansprache an die Vertreter der Bekennenden Kirche in Frankfurt a.M., 6 January 1946, in Niemöller, *Die deutsche Schuld*, 5.

74. Niemöller, Der Weg ins Freie, 3 July 1946, in Greschat, ed., *Die Schuld*, 202–203.

75. Niemöller, Ansprache an die Vertreter, 6.

76. Ibid., 6–7.

77. This lecture is reprinted in Greschat, *Die Schuld*, 188–92.

78. Quoted in Frank Stern, *The Whitewashing of the Yellow Badge: Antisemitism and Philosemitism in Postwar Germany*, trans. William Templer (Oxford: Pergamon Press, 1992), 307–308.

79. Niemöller, Ansprache an die Vertreter, 7.

80. Ibid., 14–15.

81. Ibid., 4.

5. The Guilt of the Others

1. For Wurm's letter, see Herman, *Rebirth*, 275–79.

2. J. S. to Wurm, 17 February 1946, LKA Stuttgart D1/211.

3. K. R. to Wurm, 1 February 1946, LKA Stuttgart D1/210.

4. B. D. to Wurm, 2 February 1946, LKA Stuttgart D1/210; and H. Z. to Wurm, 2 February 1946, LKA Stuttgart D1/210.

5. Hans Asmussen, "Die Schuld der Andern," ZEKHN-Darmstadt 62/539.

6. Hermann Diem and Helmut Thielicke, *Die Schuld der Anderen: Ein Briefwechsel zwischen Helmut Thielicke und Hermann Diem* (Göttingen: Vandenhoeck and Ruprecht, 1948).

7. The archbishop's broadcast to the German people is reprinted in Herman, *Rebirth*, 273–75.

8. The hundreds of letters to Wurm praising his "To Christians in England" are housed with his papers at the regional church archive in Stuttgart, LKA Stuttgart D1/210 and 211.

9. Both OMGUS (Office of Military Government, United States) surveys and reports by the British Foreign Office reported critically on the attitudes of Protestants on German guilt and responsibility. Barbara Marshall sums up this evidence in "German Attitudes to British Military Government 1945–47," *Journal of Contemporary History* 15 (1980): 655–84.

10. Stewart Herman also thought that at least one of the reasons the Stuttgart declaration was such a "sore spot" for Germans was that the Christian declarations of guilt and repentance by Germany's enemies, in particular by the United States and Great Britain, were unknown in Germany. "Invariably, when mention of these statements is made to them [German pastors], earnest pastors straighten up as though a great weight had been lifted from their own shoulders. It is the weight of worry as to how German expressions of guilt will be used abroad" (Herman, *Rebirth*, 136).

11. Archbishop Fisher, Broadcast by his Grace the Archbishop of Canterbury, 273.

12. Asmussen to various church leaders, 29 November 1945, EZA 2/164.

13. Halfmann to EKD Rat, 27 December 1945, EZA 2/164. Halfmann's letter quoted Bishop Völkel at length.

14. Halfmann to EKD Rat, 27 December 1945, EZA 2/164.

15. Ibid.

16. Asmussen to Vorläufige Kirchenleitung der Ev.-Luth. Landeskirche Schleswig-Holsteins, 6 January 1946, EZA 2/164.

17. Wurm, "To the Christians in England," 14 December 1945, reprinted in full in Herman, *The Rebirth*, 275–79. See appendix 5 for the text.

18. Lindley Fraser, "Wurming One's Way," 14 February 1946, EZA 2/35, 189.

19. Asmussen to BBC, 15 February 1946, in *Die Protokolle des Rates der Evangelischen Kirche in Deutschland*, ed. Nicolaisen and Schulze, 1:311–15.

20. Asmussen to Fisher, 1 January 1946, ZEKHN-Darmstadt 62/539.

21. K. R. to Wurm, 1 February 1946, LKA Stuttgart D1/210: "Hierzu möchte ich Ihnen als ein kleiner Mann aus dem Volke folgendes mitteilen."

22. G. H. to Wurm, 10 February 1946, LKA Stuttgart D1/210.

23. Ellen Badoglio, Tatsachen gegen "Scharfer Wind aus London," 12 March 1946, LKA Stuttgart D1/211. On 6 March 1946 the *Wiesbadener Kurier* published an article, "Scharfer Wind aus London," which quoted from Fraser's "Wurming One's Way" broadcast at length. Badoglio's piece was a response to both Fraser and the article.

24. F. S. to Wurm, 17 February 1946, LKA Stuttgart D1/242.

25. Ostflüchtling to Wurm, 2 February 1946, LKA Stuttgart D1/210.

26. Oberstudiendirektor to Wurm, 2 March 1946, LKA Stuttgart D1/211.

27. C. B. to Wurm, 19 February 1946, LKA Stuttgart D1/211. For more on the church and denazification, see Vollnhals, *Evangelische Kirche und Entnazifizierung 1945–1949;* and Ronald Webster, "Opposing 'Victors' Justice': German Protestant Churchmen and Convicted War Criminals in Western Europe after 1945," *Holocaust and Genocide Studies* 15, no. 1 (Spring 2001): 47–69.

28. Gerhard Besier and Gerhard Sauter, eds., *Wie Christen Ihre Schuld bekennen: Die Stuttgart Erklärung 1945* (Göttingen: Vandenhoeck and Ruprecht, 1985), 51, n. 64.

29. Wurm to the editor of *Frankfurter Rundschau,* 8 February 1946, LKA Stuttgart D1/242.

30. Richard Degkwitz, "Zu Bischof Wurm: 'An die Christen in England,'" *Neue Hamburger Presse,* 23 February 1946.

31. Barth to First Letter Writer, in *The Only Way,* 37.

32. Herr H. M., "An den Briefkasten der N.H.P.," LKA Stuttgart D1/211.

33. Asmussen, "Die Schuld der Andern," 4–11.

34. Thielicke's sermon is reprinted in Diem and Thielicke, *Die Schuld der Anderen: Ein Briefwechsel zwischen Helmut Thielicke und Hermann Diem,* 11.

35. Hermann Diem, a Lutheran theologian close to Barth and a scathing critic of apologists for the church's accommodation with Nazi racial policy, was not one of those positive respondents. He said that he too was dismayed by the treatment of German prisoners of war but that he went to the occupation authorities to complain rather than preach a sermon to Germans that encouraged their apologist tendencies. See Diem's and Thielicke's exchange of letters in *Die Schuld der Anderen,* 16; and in Diem, *Haben wir Deutsche etwas gelernt?* (Zürich: Evangelischer Verlag, 1948).

6. On the Political Course of Our People

1. Protokoll über die Sitzung des Bruderrates der EKD in Darmstadt, 6 July 1947, in *"Zum politischen Weg unseres Volkes" Politische Leitbilder und Vorstellungen im deutschen Protestantismus 1945–1952, Eine Dokumentation,* ed. Dorthee Buchhaas-Birkholz (Düsseldorf: Droste Verlag, 1989), 92.

2. See appendix 6 for a full translation of the Darmstadt statement, originally published as "Ein Wort des Bruderrates der Evangelischen Kirche in Deutschland zum politischen Weg unseres Volkes," *Flugblätter der Bekennenden Kirche* 8 (August 1947). The Ecumenical Press Service (EPS) of the World Council of Churches (WCC) printed an English translation, "Statement Concerning the Political Course of Our People," in its 12 September 1947 newsletter. The translation in the appendix is the EPS translation with some minor revisions of my own. For two contrasting historical interpretations of the Darmstadt statement, see Hartmut Ludwig, "Die Entstehung des Darmstädter Wortes," *Junge Kirche* supplement to 8/9 (1977): 1–15; and Erwin Wilkens, "Zum 'Darmstädter Wort' vom 8 August 1947," in Günther Metzger, ed., *Zukunft aus dem Wort* (Stuttgart: Calwer Verlag, 1978), 151–69.

3. On the discussions within the church about drafting a statement on the "Jewish question" in 1946 and 1947, see Siegfried Hermle, *Evangelische Kirche und Judentum—Stationen nach 1945,* 195–202 and chapter 5. I address the "Jewish question" in detail in chapters 7 and 8 of this book.

4. This is from the third thesis of the Darmstadt statement.

5. The minutes of the council of brethren's 5–6 July 1947 meeting at which they discussed the necessity of a public statement on the church's role in the public sphere are reprinted in *"Zum politischen Weg,"* ed. Buchhaas-Birkholz, 77–103. Of the several critiques of the Darmstadt statement appearing in 1947, the two most significant from the conservative side are Hans Asmussen's 28 August 1947 letter to the council of brethren, "Schreiben

des Leiters der Kirchenkanzlei der EKD Asmussen an den Bruderrat der EKD," reprinted in *"Zum politischen Weg,"* ed. Buchhaas-Birkholz, 106–10; and Walter Künneth, "Zum politischen Weg unseres Volkes: Eine theologische Antwort an den Bruderrat der EKD," *Evangelisch-Lutherische Kirchenzeitung* 2/3 (15 November 1947): 13–16. At the 15–16 October 1947 meeting of the council of brethren in Detmold, the Darmstadt statement received further criticism from several churchmen from eastern Germany, including Eitel-Friedrich von Ranenau, Kurt Scharf, and Gerhard Jacobi. For these criticisms, see Protokoll über die Sitzung des Bruderrates der EKD am 15./16.10.1947 im Diakonissenhaus Detmold, ZEKHN-Darmstadt 62/1026. For an excellent analysis of the Darmstadt statement, especially in its ecumenical context, see Bertold Klappert, *Bekennende Kirche in ökumenischer Verantwortung: Die gesellschaftliche und ökumenische Bedeutung des Wortes* (Munich: Chr. Kaiser, 1988).

6. In the commentary on the Darmstadt statement, Hermann Diem and his colleagues quote from the second thesis of the Barmen declaration: "Through him [Christ] befalls us a joyful deliverance from the godless fetters of this world for a free, grateful service to his creatures." They recognized in their commentary that during the Nazi era the church failed to take up the freedom given to them by Christ for the service or benefit of mankind. The Darmstadt statement was the council of brethren's attempt to give concrete meaning to what that service might be in the postwar period. See the commentary in Joachim Beckmann, *Hoffnung für die Kirche in dieser Zeit* (Göttingen: Vandenhoeck and Ruprecht, 1981), 85.

7. Particularly influential were Barth's 1946 essay, "The Christian Community and the Civil Community," and the lecture he delivered at the council's July 1947 Darmstadt meeting, "The Church—The Living Congregation of the Living Lord Jesus Christ." The first essay is available in Karl Barth, *Against the Stream: Shorter Post-war Writings 1946–52*, 15–50; for the lecture, see "Die Kirche—die lebendige Gemeinde des lebendigen Herrn Jesus Christus," in *"Zum politischen Weg,"* ed. Buchhaas-Birkholz, 77–82. The lecture, which Barth presented in various versions across Germany, was a draft of the lecture he gave at the 1948 Amsterdam meeting of the WCC. An English translation of the Amsterdam lecture, "The Church—The Living Congregation of the Living Lord Jesus Christ," is available in *Man's Disorder and God's Design: The Amsterdam Assembly Series* (New York: Harper and Brothers, 1949), 67–76. Another printed version is available in the German periodical *Unterwegs* 4 (1947): 6–26. My quotes are from Buchhaas-Birkholz's compilation of Darmstadt documents. Also relevant for an understanding of Barth's political ethics, see Karl Barth, *Church and State,* trans. G. Ronald Howe (London: SCM Press, 1939); *The Church and the Political Problem of Our Day* (New York: Charles Scribner's Sons, 1939); *The Christian Cause: A Letter to Great Britain from Switzerland* (London: Sheldon Press, 1941); and *The Church and the War,* trans. Antonia H. Froendt (New York: Macmillan, 1941).

8. See Klappert, *Bekennende Kirche in ökumenischer Verantwortung,* 43–46, esp. 46.

9. Barth's friendly quip to Iwand that there was nothing finer than a "Reformed Lutheran" was made in 1951 (Busch, *Karl Barth,* 372).

10. On the political and social role of German Protestantism, see Ernst Troeltsch, *The Social Teaching of the Christian Churches,* trans. Olive Wyon (London: George Allen and Unwin, 1956), 2:523–69; Fritz Fischer, "Der deutsche Protestantismus und die Politik im 19. Jahrhundert," *Historische Zeitschrift* 171 (1951): 473–518; William O. Shanahan, *German Protestants Face the Social Question,* vol. 1: *The Conservative Phase 1815–1871* (Notre Dame, Ind.: University of Notre Dame Press, 1954); Robert M. Bigler, *The Politics of German Protestantism;* Conway, "The Political Role," 819–42.

11. See, e.g., Asmussen's 19 August 1947 response to the Darmstadt statement in *"Zum politischen Weg,"* ed. Buchhaas-Birkholz, 108.

12. Barth, "The Christian Community," in *Against the Stream,* 15–50.

13. One is reminded of Bonhoeffer's controversial comment during the *Kirchenkampf* that "whoever knowingly cuts himself off from the Confessing Church in Germany cuts himself off from salvation." See Dietrich Bonhoeffer, "On the Question of Church Community," 22 April 1936, in *A Testament to Freedom: The Essential Writings of Dietrich Bonhoeffer,* ed. Geffrey B. Kelly and F. Burton Nelson (San Francisco: Harper, 1990), 173.

14. Barth, "Die Kirche—die lebendige Gemeinde," 77–78.

15. Ibid.

16. Busch, *Karl Barth,* 343.

17. Iwand's draft can be found in *Bekennende Kirche in ökumenischer Verantwortung,* ed. Klappert, 115–16.

18. Hans Joachim Iwand, *Frieden mit dem Osten,* ed. Gerard C. den Hertog (Munich: Kaiser, 1988), foreword, I.

19. Ibid.

20. Gerard C. den Hertog in foreword to *Frieden mit dem Osten,* III.

21. Protokoll, 92.

22. Joachim Beckmann, Hermann Diem, Martin Niemöller, and Ernst Wolf, "Das Wort des Bruderrates der Evangelischen Kirche in Deutschland zum politischen Weg unseres Volkes," in Joachim Beckmann, *Hoffnung für die Kirche in dieser Zeit,* 78.

23. Ibid., 79.

24. Ibid., 78.

25. Barth, "Christian Community," 40.

26. Rabenau at the October 1947 council of brethren meeting in Detmold, ZEKHN-Darmstadt 62/1026.

27. Putz at the October 1947 Detmold meeting, ZEKHN-Darmstadt 62/1026. The council of brethren agreed to write a detailed commentary after the statement received considerable criticism, which many on the council believed was due to misunderstandings.

28. Asmussen to *Bruderrat,* 28 August 1947, in *"Zum politischen Weg,"* ed. Buchhaas-Birkholz, 106–107.

29. Walter Künneth, "Zum politischen Weg unseres Volkes: Eine theologische Antwort an den Bruderrat der EKiD," *Evangelische-Lutherische Kirchenzeitung* 1, no. 2/3 (15 November 1947): 13–16.

30. Ibid., 14.

31. Ibid., 13.

32. Protokoll über die Sitzung des Bruderrates der EKD am 15./16.10.1947 im Diakonissenhaus Detmold, ZEKHN-Darmstadt 62/1026.

33. Künneth, "Zum politischen Weg," 14.

34. Protokoll über die Sitzung des Bruderrates der EKD am 15./16.10.1947 im Diakonissenhaus Detmold, ZEKH Darmstadt, B. 62/1026.

35. Künneth, "Zum politischen Weg," 16.

36. Asmussen to Bruderrat, 28 August 1947, in *"Zum politischen Weg,"* ed. Buchhaas-Birkholz, 107.

37. Ibid., 109. The council of brethren tried to clarify this statement in its commentary on the Darmstadt statement written a few months later. The commentary on thesis six read: "That the freedom was given to us to recognize and openly to confess [theses two through

five] is for us the most hopeful sign that God is allowing us to make a new beginning in His church." See Beckmann, *Hoffnung für die Kirche*, 83.

38. Asmussen to *Bruderrat*, 28 August 1947, in *"Zum politischen Weg,"* ed. Buchhaas-Birkholz, 110.

39. Künneth, "Zum politischen Weg," 14.

40. Ralph C. Hancock, *Calvin and the Foundations of Modern Politics* (Ithaca, N.Y.: Cornell University Press, 1989) 123–40.

7. The Church and Antisemitism

1. The literature on the "Jewish question" or "Jewish problem" in Germany in the nineteenth and twentieth centuries is extensive. Some that I have found most helpful include: Reinhard Rürup, "Kontinuität und Diskontinuität der 'Judenfrage' im 19. Jahrhundert. Zur Entstehung des modernen Antisemitismus," in *Sozialgeschichte Heute. Festschriften für Hans Rosenberg zum 70. Geburtstag*, ed. Hans-Ulrich Wehler (Göttingen: Vandenhoeck and Ruprecht, 1974), 388–415; Franklin Littell, *The Crucifixion of the Jews*, 1996; Uriel Tal, *Christians and Jews in Germany: Religion, Politics, and Ideology in the Second Reich, 1870–1914* (Ithaca, N.Y.: Cornell University Press, 1975) and his article, "On Modern Lutheranism and the Jews," *Leo Baeck Yearbook* 30 (1985): 203–14; Donald L. Niewyk, "Solving the 'Jewish Problem': Continuity and Change in German Antisemitism, 1871–1945," *Leo Baeck Yearbook* 35 (1990): 335–70.

2. Paul van Buren, a former professor of religion at Temple University and author of the three-volume *Theology of the Jewish-Christian Reality* (Lanham, Md.: University Press of America, 1980–95) argues persuasively that the Holocaust and the foundation of the Israeli state brought about a "repudiation . . . of what the church has said and taught [regarding Jews] from the second century until the twentieth." See his essay "Changes in Christian Theology," in *The Holocaust: Ideology, Bureaucracy, and Genocide*, ed. Henry Friedlander and Sybil Milton (Millwood, N.Y.: Kraus International Publications, 1980), 285–93.

3. The Berlin-Weissensee statement, "Wort an die Judenfrage," is translated as "Statement on the Jewish Question," in *The Theology of the Churches and the Jewish People: Statements by the World Council of Churches and its member churches* (Geneva: WCC Publications, 1988), 47–48. The brethren council's statement "Ein Wort zur Judenfrage" is translated by the WCC as "A Message Concerning the Jewish Question," in *The Relationship of the Church to the Jewish People*, edited by the WCC (Geneva, 1964), 48–52. See appendix 7 and 8 for translations.

4. Despite the racial underpinnings of the terms "Jewish Christians" and "baptized Jews"—both of which the Nazis and German Christians used to describe Jews who converted to Christianity and their offspring—I use these terms or similar variants because they are useful in describing a group singled out and persecuted by racial legislation passed by both the state and the church.

5. Harling Jr. to Niemöller, 8 November 1947, LKA Stuttgart D1/222, 1.

6. The brethren council's statement on the "Jewish question" is analyzed in some detail later in this chapter and the next.

7. Although the Protestant missions to the Jews tended to include aiding Jewish Christians as part of its work, Jewish Christian aid offices did not consider missionary work to be one of their tasks.

8. The theological and practical dimensions of the church's mission to Israel are discussed in detail later in this chapter.

9. In September 1946 Frohwein placed his medical practice in the hands of a colleague in order to devote himself full-time to missionary work among the Jews in Bavaria. He described the obstacles facing missionaries in a lecture, "Der zeitiger Stand des Evangeliumsdienstes unter Israel in Deutschland unter besonderer Berücksichtigung der amerikanischen Zone," LKA Nuremberg V. III/51, 2, n.d. (presumably late 1946 or early 1947).

10. Harling Jr. to Hopf, 8 August 1947, LKA Nuremberg V. III/51, 3.

11. See, e.g., Allan R. Brockway's contention that evangelizing Jews is a form of anti-semitism, "Should Christians Attempt to Evangelize Jews?" http:www.abrock.com/Attempt.html.

12. LKA Stuttgart A126/658, 166.

13. Majer-Leonard to Wurm (27 March 1947), LKA Stuttgart A126/658, 168.

14. See the newsletter of the Basel Jewish mission, Der Freund Israels 74, no. 6 (December 1947). Also see H. L. Ellison's report "The Racially Persecuted Christians in Germany: Report on a Journey—May 5 to June 25, 1948," ZEKHN-Darmstadt 36/81.

15. Majer-Leonard to Oberkirchenrat Schauffler (30 October 1946), LKA Stuttgart A126/658, 139.

16. The text is entitled, "Zur judenchristlichen Frage," LKA Stuttgart A126/658, 141.

17. Curt Radlauer, "What the Protestant assistance-work begs from London, 30 Jan. 1946," LKA Stuttgart HR/Büro Grüber.

18. One of President Truman's own aides, Earl G. Harrison, came to the conclusion after visiting DP camps in Germany in late summer 1945 that "many Jewish displaced persons . . . are living under guard behind barbed-wire fences, including some of the most notorious concentration camps, amidst crowded, frequently unsanitary and generally grim conditions, in complete idleness, with no opportunity, except surreptitiously, to communicate with the outside world, waiting, hoping for some word of encouragement and action on their behalf." Harrison's report goes on for several pages describing the dismal conditions in which Jews lived in the months immediately following the end of the war. Also see Angelika Königseder and Juliane Wetzel, Waiting for Hope: Jewish Displaced Persons in Post–World War II Germany, trans. John Broadwin (Evanston, Ill.: Northwestern University Press, 2001); Michael Brenner, After the Holocaust: Rebuilding Jewish Lives in Postwar Germany (Princeton, N.J.: Princeton University Press, 1997), 1–77; Jael Geis, Übrig sein—Leben "danach": Juden deutscher Herkunft in der britischen und amerikanischen Zone Deutschlands 1945–1949 (Berlin: Philo, 2000); Frank Stern, "Breaking the 'Cordon Sanitaire' of Memory: The Jewish Encounter with German Society," in Thinking about the Holocaust: After Half a Century, ed. Alvin H. Rosenfeld (Bloomington: Indiana University Press, 1997), 213–32; and Atina Grossman, "Home and Displacement in a City of Bordercrossers: Jews in Berlin 1945–1948," in Unlikely History: The Changing German-Jewish Symbiosis, 1945–2000, ed. Leslie Morris and Jack Zipes (New York: Palegrave, 2002), 63–99. An excellent archival source on the conditions of Jews in postwar German is the Central Archive of the History of Jews in Germany, Zentralarchiv für die Geschichte der Juden in Deutschland in Heidelberg (ZAJD-Heidelberg), in particular the activity reports and correspondence of the Jewish aid office (Betreuungsstelle) in Frankfurt and the correspondence of Julius Dreifuss, the chairman of the Jewish community in Düsseldorf.

19. ZAJD-Heidelberg 1/13 A. 740.

20. Ibid.

21. Following the precedent set in the Bible, "Israel" in the title of Harling Sr. and Rengstorf's organization refers to the Jewish people, not to the state of Israel. LKA Stuttgart A126/658.

22. Harling Jr. to Hopf, 30 July 1947, LKA Nuremberg V. III/51, 3. "Hier hat man sehr deutlich das Gefühl, dass man sich gern von der Verantwortung und vor allem von der lästigen Notwendigkeit, in dieser Angelegenheit an die Öffentlichkeit heranzutreten, loskaufen möchte."

23. Draft of Oberkirchenrat response to Hartenstein, February 1948, LKA Stuttgart A126/658, 248. Also see Hermle, *Evangelische Kirche und Judentum,* 143.

24. LKA Stuttgart A126/658, 292. This is particularly interesting in light of the fact that the Stuttgart Jewish mission was in debt 3,700 DM in November 1948 to the Basel Jewish mission. See "Bericht über die zweite Sitzung der Geschäftsstelle Stuttgart," 16 November 1948, LKA Stuttgart A126/659, 8–10.

25. Letter from Rengstorf to Hopf, 24 January 1946, LKA Nuremberg V. III/51.

26. See *Die Protokolle des Rates der Evangelischen Kirche in Deutschland,* Band 1: *1945/46,* 121 and 199–200; and Hermle, *Evangelische Kirche und Judentum,* 269–70 and 291–96.

27. Hermle, *Evangelische Kirche und Judentum,* 295.

28. Denkhaus quoted by Dibelius, *Die Protokolle,* 199.

29. *Die Protokolle des Rates der Evangelischen Kirche in Deutschland,* Band 1: *1945/46,* 122 and 199–200. It is unclear whether the EKD council's opposition to the collection was made explicit to the provisional church leadership of Bremen.

30. In which newspapers and radio reports the Bavarian churchmen learned of Grüber's contribution is unclear, but *Saat und Hoffnung: Vierteljahresschrift für das Gespräch zwischen Christentum und Judentum* 73, no. 1 (1950) and *Freiburger Rundbrief* no. 10/11 (January 1950) reported that Grüber presented the Jewish community in Berlin, on behalf of the Evangelical Church in Berlin, 5,000 DM for the reconstruction of their synagogue and that the Berlin Jewish leader and Auschwitz survivor Heinz Galinski expressed his gratitude for the donation.

31. G. G. to Evangelische Landeskirchenleitung München, 13 January 1951, LKA Nuremberg LKR XIV, 1608a.

32. See Eberhard Röhm and Jörg Thierfelder, *Juden, Christen, Deutsche 1933–1945,* vol. 1: *1933 bis 1935* (Stuttgart: Calwer, 1990); Wolfgang Gerlach, *And the Witnesses Were Silent;* Richard Gutteridge, *Open Thy Mouth for the Dumb;* and Robert Ericksen and Susannah Heschel, *Betrayal: German Churches and the Holocaust.*

33. On Joint, see Ronald Webster, "American Relief and Jews in Germany, 1945–60: Diverging Perspectives," *Leo Baeck Yearbook* 38 (1993): 293–321.

34. LKA Stuttgart A126/658, 215.

35. Hartenstein to Ostertag, 9 August 1945, LKA Stuttgart A126/658, 128.

36. This list was compiled from reports by Fritz Majer-Leonard and H. L. Ellison. Although the two reports essentially concur, they diverge on whether to label the relief centers in Mannheim and Karlsruhe as directed by churchmen or by Jewish Christians themselves. Majer-Leonard to Kanzlei der EKD, 24 February 1948, LKA Stuttgart D23/29; and H. L. Ellison, "The Racially Persecuted Christians in Germany: Report on a Journey—May 5 to June 25, 1948," ZEKHN-Darmstadt 36/81.

37. See Hermle, *Evangelische Kirche und Judentum,* 158–62.

38. Fricke et al. to Our Brothers and Sisters in Christ, December 1946, ZEKHN-Darmstadt 36/81.

39. Grüber to Gerstenmaier, 6 April 1946, ADW ZB 842. In addition to Grüber, several

churchmen from the ecumenical movement also contacted Gerstenmaier. See Adolf Freudenberg to Robbins W. Barstow, 19 December 1946, ADW ZB 842, 74–76; Heinz Kloppenburg to Zentralbüro des Hilfswerkes, 1 January 1948, ADW ZB 842, 169; J. Hutchinson Cockburn to Gerstenmaier, 4 April 1946, ADW ZB 842; and Stewart Herman to Gerstenmaier, 12 August 1946, ADW ZB 842. Also see Siegfried Hermle, "'Wo ist dein Bruder Israel?' Die Impulse Adolf Freudenbergs zur Neubestimmung des christlich-jüdischen Verhältnisses nach 1945," *Kirche und Israel: Neukirchener theologische Zeitschrift* 4 (1989): 42–59.

40. Gerstenmaier to Grüber, 29 April 1946, ADW ZB 842.

41. Majer-Leonard to Berg, 31 July 1947, ADW ZB 442b. Majer-Leonard claimed that Gerstenmaier made these comments at the 6 June 1947 meeting on the situation of refugees and Jewish Christians held in the Central Office of *Hilfswerk* in Stuttgart. The alleged comments do not appear in the minutes of the meeting; see Protokoll, ADW ZB 442B. Majer-Leonard repeated this charge in several letters to various colleagues. See Majer-Leonard to Berg, 22 August 1947, ADW ZB 442b; Majer-Leonard to Hilfswerk der Evang. Landeskirche in Württemberg, 22 January 1948, ADW ZB 842, 167; Majer-Leonard to Harling, 24 February 1948, LKA Stuttgart D23/29; and Majer-Leonard to Wurm, 31 May 1948, LKA Stuttgart D1/222, 1.

42. ADW ZB 442B.

43. On the disciplinary proceedings, see ADW ZB 442B.

44. Majer-Leonard to Wurm, 31 May 1948, LKA Stuttgart D1/222, 1.

45. For more on the founder of the First Hebrew Christian Synagogue in Los Angeles, Arthur U. Michelson, see his autobiography, *Out of the Darkness into the Light: Life Story of Arthur U. Michelson* (Los Angeles: Jewish Hope Publishing House, 1955).

46. Quoted in Eva Fleischner, *Judaism in German Christian Theology since 1945: Christianity and Israel Considered in Terms of Mission* (Metuchen, N.J.: Scarecrow Press and American Theological Library Association, 1975), 57. The quote is from Rengstorf's 1948 lecture, "Die eine Kirche aus Juden und Heiden."

47. Radlauer, "What the Protestant assistance-work begs from London," 30 January 1946, LKA Stuttgart HR/Büro Grüber.

48. Robert Brunner, "An unsere Deutschen Freunde," *Der Freund Israels* 74, no. 6 (December 1947): 84.

49. Quoted from H. L. Ellison, "The Church and the Hebrew Christian," in *The Church and the Jewish People,* ed. Göte Hedenquist (London: Edinburgh Press, 1954), 160. For the minutes of the June 1947 Basel meeting of the IMCCAJ, see LKA Stuttgart A12/658.

50. Quoted in Gerlach, *And the Witnesses Were Silent,* 85. The entire text is reprinted in appendix 13 in Röhm and Thierfelder, *Juden-Christen-Deutsche,* 1:391–96.

51. The Nazis persecuted Jewish Christians as they persecuted all other Jews. In April 1933 the Nazis passed the "Law for Restoration of the Professional Civil Service," which led to the dismissal of "non-Aryans" from the civil service. Although this law did not affect the clergy, religion teachers, or theology faculty, it obviously did affect "non-Aryan Christians" who held positions in the civil service. The Nazis defined a "non-Aryan" as anyone who descended from one parent or grandparent who was "non-Aryan." It was not long before the German Christians (*Deutsche Christen*) called for a church resolution that would bar non-Aryans (Jewish Christians) from the ministry. The German Christians proposed the so-called Aryan paragraph in September 1933 and in so doing sparked the church struggle (*Kirchenkampf*). On the debate over the Aryan paragraph, see Röhm and Thierfelder, *Juden, Christen, Deutsche 1933–35,* 1:190–223; Wolfgang Gerlach, *And the Witnesses Were Silent,* 30–48;

Richard Gutteridge, *The German Evangelical Church and the Jews,* 91–151; and for the case of Bavaria, see Johannes Zwanzger, "Betreuung der nichtarischen Christen," 25 August 1945, LKA Nuremberg LKR XIV, 1624b (new number 2595).

52. See Gutteridge, *Open Thy Mouth for the Dumb,* 212, and chapter 6 in general.

53. See Johannes Zwanzger's report cited above on the activities in Munich.

54. Gerlach, *And the Witnesses Were Silent,* 96. Also see Besier, *Die Kirchen und das Dritte Reich,* 847–49.

55. The quip is Doris Bergen's from *Twisted Cross,* 88, although she uses it in reference to the German Christians.

56. Doris Bergen quotes a Berlin clergyman at a German Christian rally in 1934 saying, "They say that everyone is equal before God. But baptism never made a Jew into a German, nor did it ever straighten a crooked, hook-nose. . . . The Jew has no scruples. Even now he would manage to let himself be baptized outwardly in order to get into the top positions. We want a Christianity that is true to our race" (ibid., 22).

57. Barnett quotes a pastor saying, "Anti-Semitism is justified but this anti-Semitism must remain within biblically set limits" (*For the Soul of the People,* 125).

58. David Diephouse, "Antisemitism as Moral Discourse."

59. Die Protokolle des Rates der EKD, 1:40.

60. LKA Stuttgart D1/210.

61. LKA Stuttgart D1/222, 1.

62. "Ein Wort zur Judenfrage," ZEKHN-Darmstadt 62/1026. The brethren council's statement is translated as "A Message Concerning the Jewish Question," in *The Relationship of the Church to the Jewish People,* ed. WCC (Geneva: WCC, 1964), 48–52. See appendix 7 for the text.

63. Wurm to Mochalski, 17 January 1948, LKA Stuttgart D1/222, 1. "Kann man in Deutschland ein Wort zur Judenfrage reden, ohne zu erwähnen, was das jüdische Literatum am deutschen Volk gesündigt hat durch Verspotten des Heiligen seit den Tagen Heinrich Heines und was in manchen Gegenden das Bauerntum zu erleiden hatte durch jüdischen Wucher? Und wenn man gegen den heute sich regenden Antisemitismus vorgehen will, kann man verschweigen daß es ein Unglueck ist, wenn die Besatzungsmächte emigrierten Juden das Heft in die Hand gegeben haben, um ihre begreiflichen Rachegefühle abzureagieren?"

64. Wurm's 14-page tribute, "Adolf Stöckers Kampf für Kirche and Volk," is available at the LKA Stuttgart D1/3, 2. Also see Diephouse, "Antisemitism as Moral Discourse."

65. Karl Marx, "'Schluss mit der Abrechnung' Altlandesbischof Wurm setzt sich ein," *Allgemeine Wochenzeitung der Juden in Deutschland* 4, no. 30 (4 November 1949), 1. After returning to Düsseldorf from England in 1946, Marx founded the *Jüdisches Gemeindeblatt für die Nord-Rheinprovinz und Westfalen,* which eventually became the *Allgemeine Jüdische Wochenzeitung in Deutschland.* See *After the Holocaust,* 59, and Brenner's interview with Karl Marx's wife, Lilli Marx, 125–29.

8. A Ray of Light in Their Darkness

1. Following the practice in the Bible, churchmen used the term "Israel" to refer to the Jewish people. In order to avoid confusion, I refer to the country of Israel as the state of Israel.

2. This statement was in fact a bold one. It was directed against the pro-Nazi German Christian movement, which excluded Jews from missionary work for racial reasons. Today the WCC statement looks old-fashioned, but at the time it was specifically aimed at those sections of the German church that still believed that no Jews belonged in the EKD and were disgruntled by the prospect of worshipping next to Christians of Jewish descent. See *The Theology of the Churches and the Jewish People: Statements by the World Council of Churches and Its Member Churches* (Geneva: WCC Publications, 1988), document 2.

3. Renate Maria Heydenreich, "Erklärungen aus der Evangelischen Kirche Deutschlands und der Ökumene zur Judenfrage 1932–1961," in *Der Ungekündigte Bund: Neue Begegnung von Juden und christlicher Gemeinde,* ed. Dietrich Goldschmidt and Hans-Joachim Kraus (Stuttgart: Kreuz Verlag, 1962), 255.

4. See Eva Fleischner, *Judaism in German Christian Theology since 1945;* Paul Aring, *Christliche Judenmission* (Neukirchen-Vluyn: Neukirchener Verlag, 1980); John Conway, "Protestant Missions to the Jews 1810–1980: Ecclesiastical Imperialism or Theological Aberration?" *Holocaust and Genocide Studies* 1, no. 1 (1986): 127–46.

5. See Dietrich Goldschmidt and Hans-Joachim Kraus, eds., *Der ungekündigte Bund.* Günther Harder was a founder of both the Arbeitsgruppe für Juden und Christen and the Institut Kirche und Judentum at the Kirchliche Hochschule in Berlin. His contribution to the above-mentioned collection, "Kirche und Synagoge: Nicht Mission sondern Gespräch," prompted considerable debate. See also Harder's "Christen vor dem Problem der Judenfrage: Evangelisch-jüdisches Gegenüber seit 1945," in *Christen und Juden: Ihr Gegenüber vom Apostelkonzil bis heute,* ed. Wolf-Dieter Marsch and Karl Thieme (Mainz: Matthias-Grünewald-Verlag, 1961), 251–69. On the differences between Harder and Rengstorf, see Eva Fleischner, *Judaism in German Christian Theology since 1945,* 74–78, 101, and 112. Heinrich Vogel was a professor of theology at the Kirchliche Hochschule and Humboldt University in Berlin. He was also the primary author of the 1950 Berlin-Weissensee statement.

6. On the 1961 *Kirchentag,* see Goldschmidt and Kraus, eds., *Der ungekündigte Bund.* Founded in August 1949, the *Kirchentag* was an annual rally of Protestant laity organized by a layman, Dr. Reinhold von Thadden-Trieglaff. Its purpose was to involve everyday Protestants in discussions about contemporary issues from a Christian perspective. See Franklin Littell, *The German Phoenix: Men and Movements in the Church in Germany,* chapter 4.

7. See *The Theology of the Churches,* 175; and John Conway, "The Changes in Recent Decades in the Churches' Doctrine and Practice towards Judaism and the Jewish People," in . . . *und über Barmen hinaus: Studien zur Kirchlichen Zeitgeschichte,* ed. Joachim Mehlhausen (Göttingen: Vandenhoeck and Ruprecht, 1995), 552.

8. Matthew 28:19. Some missionaries cited other passages from Matthew and Romans to make the point that missionary work among the Jews should be prioritized, e.g., "Go nowhere among the Gentiles, and enter no town of the Samaritans, but go rather to the lost sheep of the house of Israel. As you go, proclaim the good news, 'The kingdom of heaven has come near'" (Matt. 10:5–7 NRSV). And from Romans 1:16 they cite, "For I am not ashamed of the gospel; it is the power of God for salvation to everyone who has faith, to the Jew first and also to the Greek (NRSV).

9. Quoted in Conway, "Protestant Missions to the Jews," 132.

10. Elmer G. Homrighausen, "Evangelism and the Jewish People," *International Review of Missions* 39 (July 1950): 320.

11. Quoted in Conway, "Protestant Missions to the Jews," 139.

12. Karl Heinrich Rengstorf, "The Spiritual Basis for Jewish Evangelism," *International*

Review of Missions 40 (April 1951): 149. Also see Rengstorf's brief history of the institute, *Das Institutum Judaicum Delitzschianum 1886–1961* (Munster: Achendorff, 1963).

13. Karl Heinrich Rengstorf, "The Jewish Problem and the Church's Understanding of Its Own Mission," in *The Church and the Jewish People*, ed. Göte Hedenquist (London: Edinburgh, 1954), 27–36.

14. While the Evangelical-Lutheran Central Federation for Mission to Israel acted as an umbrella organization for the Jewish missions tied to Lutheran regional churches, the Berlin Federation for Mission to the Jews provided guidance to the north-German United churches; and the Swiss Basel Jewish Mission was associated with the missionary work in Württemberg, Baden, Pfalz, and Hessen. See Bericht über die zweite Sitzung der Geschäftsstelle Stuttgart des Vereins der Freunde Israels, 16 November 1948, LKA Stuttgart A126/659, 8.

15. Evangelisch-Lutherischer Zentralverein für Mission unter Israel to Evangelischen Oberkirchenrat, 24 October 1945, LKA Stuttgart A126/658, 132.

16. Hopf to H. Sasse, G. Schmidt, H. Kressel, K. Krodel, and T. Poehlmann, 3 January 1946, LKA Nuremberg V. III/51, 1.

17. For more examples of the efforts of church leaders and pastors to advise their colleagues on the tenth Sunday service, see Hermle's discussion of a letter from Bishop Julius Bender of Baden to the pastorate, *Evangelische Kirche und Judentum*, 339–44. A similar letter from Bender is reprinted in *Judaica* V (1949): 309–10. Also see the 21 February 1948 letter from Heinrich Riedel, a member of the leadership council of the Bavarian church, to pastor Hopf asking if he would provide his thoughts on possible sermon topics for the next tenth Sunday after Trinity service. Reidel offered to publish Hopf's ideas in the Bavarian church newspaper so that other pastors could use his suggestions. He also reminded Hopf that the tenth Sunday after Trinity service "is held collection-free" (LKA Nuremberg V. III/51, 3).

18. Letter from Hopf and Wittenberg to Alle Pfarrämter der Evang.-Luth. Kirche in Bayern, January 1946, LKA Nuremberg V. III/51, 1.

19. Hopf, "Bestätigung," LKA Nuremberg V. III/51, 2. Hopf considered Frohwein's experience to be crucial to the success of the mission in Bavaria. He also indicated that Frohwein's international contacts would help foster working relationships with English organizations like Christian Relief Work for Victims of Racial Laws and the British Society for Propagation of the Gospel among the Jews.

20. Gottfried Frohwein, "Auszug aus dem Referat in Nürnberg am 25. Oktober 1946 auf der Arbeitsgemeinschaft für Judenmission," LKA Nuremberg V. III/51, 1.

21. Frohwein estimates that of the 120,000–150,000 Jewish refugees who fled from East European countries to the American zone, 60 to 70 percent were in Bavaria.

22. Frohwein, "Auszug aus dem Referat in Nürnberg," LKA Nuremberg V. III/51, 1.

23. See "Bericht des Herrn Pfarrer Grillenberger über die Judenmission in Bayern beim Landesmissionsfest in Nürnberg Juli 1949," LKA Nuremberg V. III/51, 1.

24. Theo Burgstahler in *Der Freund Israels* 74:6 (December 1947): 83.

25. Theo Burgstahler in *Der Freund Israels* 74:3 (July 1947): 40.

26. Freudenberg to Brunner, 12 January 1953, ZEKHN-Darmstadt 155/794. Martin Niemöller was the church president of the Evangelical Church of Hesse-Nassau from 1947 to 1964.

27. Freudenberg to Majer-Leonard, 25 November 1952, ZEKHN-Darmstadt 155/794.

28. Gerlach, *And the Witnesses Were Silent*, 227–28.

29. LKA Stuttgart D1/222, 1. In addition to Hermann Maas and Karl Heinrich Rengstorf, the other signatories of the Assenheim statement were Dr. Günther Harder of Berlin's Kirch-

liche Hochschule, Prof. Jannasch of the University of Mainz, Dr. Med. and missionary Gottfried Frohwein, Pastor Theo Burgstahler from Ulm, and Harling Jr.

30. The quote comes from Rengstorf's essay, "The Jewish Problem and the Church's Understanding of Its Mission," 34.

31. Ibid. 34–35. Catholics espoused similar thoughts on Jewish suffering. Michael Schmaus, a leading Catholic theologian in Germany wrote in 1949 that "God has . . . great plans for the people chosen by him. . . . God's purpose in his judgments upon the chosen people is not destruction, but salvation. . . . Only because God cannot forget his people, only because he is willing to let it be lost, does he punish it hard and frequently." Quoted in Eva Fleischner, *Judaism in German Christian Theology since 1945,* 157. For the entire article, see Michael Schmaus, "Das Verhältnis der Christen und Juden," *Judaica* V (1949): 182–91.

32. Protokoll über die Sitzung des Bruderrates der EKD am 7–8 January 1948 in Kassel, ZEKHN-Darmstadt 62/1026, 3.

33. Ibid.

34. Ibid., 6.

35. On Niemöller's antisemitism and anti-Judaism, see Robert Michael, "Theological Myth, German Antisemitism and the Holocaust: The Case of Martin Niemöller," *Holocaust and Genocide Studies* 2, no. 1 (1987): 105–22.

36. See Allan Brockway's essay "The Theology of the Churches and the Jewish People," http://www.abrock.com.

37. Karl Barth, "The Jewish Problem and the Christian Answer," in *Against the Stream: Shorter Post-War Writings, 1946–52* (New York: Philosophical Library, 1954), 200.

38. Hermle covers the founding of the Committee for Service to Israel and the early debates about its purpose very thoroughly. See Hermle, *Evangelische Kirche und Judentum,* 205–209; and Otto von Harling Jr., "Kirche und Israel," *Kirchliches Jahrbuch für die Evangelische Kirche in Deutschland* (1953): 324–28.

39. Karin Haufler-Musiol, "125 Jahre Zentralverein: Ein historischer Überblick," in *Auf dem Wege zum christlich-jüdischen Gespräch: 125 Jahre Evangelisch-lutherischer Zentralverein für Zeugnis und Dienst unter Juden und Christen,* ed. Arnulf H. Baumann (Münster: Lit verlag, 1998): 36.

40. Hermle, *Evangelische Kirche und Judentum,* 214–15.

41. Leo Baeck, "Das Judentum auf alten und neuen Wegen," *Judaica* VI (1950): 133–48.

42. "Pressekonferenz mit Herrn Rabbiner Dr. Baeck," 14 October 1948, ZAJD-Heidelberg 1/13, A. 722.

43. In addition to Baeck, the speakers included, among others, Martin Niemöller, who welcomed the conference participants; Conrad Hoffmann, the director of the International Committee on the Christian Approach to the Jews; Curt Radlauer from Grüber's Berlin aid office for Jewish Christians; Martin Wittenberg of the Bavarian Jewish mission; and Rengstorf.

44. Baeck, "Das Judentum," 138–39.

45. Ibid., 144.

46. Ibid., 146.

47. Hermle, *Evangelische Kirche und Judentum,* 221–22.

48. Ibid., 223; Niemöller's brief introductory remarks were an exception; he stressed that the present suffering in Germany was a consequence of German guilt for the atrocities committed against Jews.

49. See two reports on the Darmstadt conference by Otto von Harling Jr. and John Witt, a Swiss pastor from Zurich, ZEKHN-Darmstadt 155/792.

50. Otto Dibelius, "Einladung zu einer Studientagung 'Kirche und Judentum,'" January 1950, in Rolf Rendtorff and Hans-Hermann Henrix, eds., *Die Kirchen und das Judentum. Dokumente von 1945 bis 1985* (Munich: Chr. Kaiser Verlag, 1988), 545–46.

51. Hermle, *Evangelische Kirche und Judentum*, 224–27. The meeting was also reported on positively by the Jewish press. See E. G. Lowenthal, "Um den Glauben an das Menschliche," *Allgemeine Wochenzeitung der Juden in Deutschland* (10 March 1950).

52. Grillenberger to Oberkirchenrat Riedel, "Studientagung in Kassel über 'Kirche und Judentum,'" 21 June 1950, LKA Nuremberg LKR XIV, 1608a. Also see Adolf Freudenberg's report "Studientagung 'Kirche und Judentum,'" *Bekennende Kirche auf dem Weg* (15 March 1950): 7–10. On the plight of pastor Ehrenberg in the Third Reich, see Röhm and Thierfelder, *Juden, Christen, Deutsche 1933–45*, 1:182–89, and 2:35–58; Barnett, *For the Soul of the People*, 134–35; and Gerlach, *And the Witnesses Were Silent*, 24–25. Ehrenberg was the author in 1933 of the "Seventy-Two Guiding Principles on the Jewish Christian Question." Gerlach writes, "Ehrenberg had set the standard for his church in thesis 59: 'The Church of the Reformation in Germany stands or falls in 1933 on the temptation to separate the Jewish Christians—completely or in part—from itself. In the final phase of the church conflict, the Jewish Christian question will be the symbol and heart of that conflict.'"

53. Grillenberger to Oberkirchenrat Riedel, "Studientagung in Kassel über 'Kirche und Judentum,'" 21 June 1950, LKA Nuremberg LKR XIV, 1608a.

54. Hermle, *Evangelische Kirche und Judentum*, 261–62.

55. See the passage of Rengstorf's lecture quoted by Grillenberger in his report, LKA Nuremberg LKR XIV, 1608a.

56. Rengstorf, "The Jewish Problem and the Church's Understanding of Its Mission," in *The Church and the Jewish People*, ed. Hedenquist, 42.

57. Rengstorf, "The Spiritual Basis for Jewish Evangelism," 151.

58. The leading German-Jewish newspaper, *Allgemeine Wochenzeitung der Juden in Deutschland*, devoted considerable space to reports on the desecration of Jewish cemeteries.

59. The draft of Freudenberg's statement "Sätze zur Judenfrage als Friedensfrage," is reprinted at the end of his report "Studientagung 'Kirche und Judentum,'" in *Bekennende Kirche auf dem Weg* (15 March 1950): 9–10. On the committee's letters to the EKD council and the president of the Berlin-Weissensee synod, see Grillenberger, 21 June 1950, LKA Nuremberg LKR XIV, 1608a; Hermle, *Evangelische Kirche und Judentum*, 233–34; Otto von Harling Jr., "Kirche und Israel," *Kirchliche Jahrbuch* (1953): 305.

60. Harling, "Kirche und Israel," 305.

61. The monument reads: "dedicated to the memory of our murdered brothers and sisters of 1933–45, and to the living who should fulfill the legacy of the dead." Some 115,000 Jews from working and lower-middle-class families are buried in the Weissensee cemetery, which was founded in 1880.

62. See Heydenreich, "Erklärungen aus der Evangelischen Kirche Deutschlands und der Ökumene zur Judenfrage 1932–1961," 254–55; and Hermle, *Evangelische Kirche und Judentum*, 348–51.

63. See Berlin-Weissensee 1950 Bericht, 14, 102, 116, 131–32.

64. Ibid., 341.

65. Ibid., 323.

66. Ibid., 327.

67. See Hermle, *Evangelische Kirche und Judentum*, 363–64; and LKA Nuremberg Kreisdekan München/223. Harling Jr. reported in the 1953 *Kirchliches Jahrbuch für die evangelis-*

che Kirche in Deutschland that approximately seventy cemeteries were under the care of church communities.

68. "Ein Akt der Wiedergutmachung," *Allgemeine Wochenzeitung der Juden in Deutschland,* 4 (30 June 1950): 1.

Conclusion

1. Theodor W. Adorno, "What Does Coming to Terms with the Past Mean?" 115.

2. Helmut Thielicke, *Die Schuld der Anderen,* 6–7.

3. Manfred Jacobs, "Konsequenzen aus dem Kirchenkampf: Kirchengeschichtliche und theologische Aspekte," *Lutherische Monatshefte* 8 (1969): 561–67. In contrast to Jacobs, Klaus Scholder maintains that "the Confessing Church, in focusing on the confession, cannot be accused of having made the wrong issue its theme. The church could not have attacked National Socialism as a political religion more effectively than at the place where in God's name it denied the total claim of National Socialism on the whole of human life. In this sense the struggle for the freedom and purity of the proclamation of the gospel was at the same time a political battle against the forces which supported National Socialist rule" ("The Church Struggle," 104). In addition to Bethge's article, "Troubled Self-Interpretation and Uncertain Reception in the Church Struggle," in *The German Church Struggle and the Holocaust,* ed. F. H. Littell and Hubert G. Locke (Detroit: Wayne State University Press, 1974), see his essay "Geschichtliche Schuld der Kirche," in *Christliche Freiheit im Dienst am Menschen, Zum 80. Geburtstag von Martin Niemöller,* ed. Karl Herbert (Frankfurt am Main, 1972), 136; and Gutteridge, *Open Thy Mouth for the Dumb!* 277–80.

4. Bethge, "Troubled Self-Interpretation," 167.

5. Karl Barth, "The Gift of Freedom: Foundation of Evangelical Ethics," in *The Humanity of God* (Richmond, Va.: John Knox Press, 1966), 86.

6. Spotts, *Churches and Politics in Germany,* 240–41, 251, and 330. See also Harry Noormann, *Protestantismus und politisches Mandat 1945–1949,* 2 vols. (Gütersloh: Gütersloh Verlag Gerd Mohn, 1985); Johanna Vogel, *Kirche und Wiederbewaffnung: Die Haltung der Evangelischen Kirchen in Deutschland in den Auseinandersetzungen um die Wiederbewaffnung der Bundesrepublik 1949–1956* (Göttingen: Vandenhoeck and Ruprecht, 1978); and Wolf Werner Rausch and Christian Walther, eds., *Evangelische Kirche in Deutschland und die Wiederaufrüstungsdiskussion in der Bundesrepublik 1950–1955* (Gütersloh: Gütersloh Verlag Gerd Mohn, 1978).

7. Barth referred to Hans Iwand as a "Reformed Lutheran" in 1951 (Busch, *Karl Barth,* 372).

8. Niemöller, "Ansprache an die Vertreter," in *Die deutsche Schuld,* 12–13.

9. Wurm, "To Christians in England," 278.

BIBLIOGRAPHY

Archival Sources

Archiv des Diakonischen Werkes der EKD, Berlin (ADW)
Bestand: Zentralbüro (ZB) Hilfswerk der EKD, Stuttgart
ZB 192A (Zentralbüro-Ost, vol. 1)
ZB 442B (Inländische Presse, vol. 2)
ZB 840 (Politische Angelegenheiten: Allgemeines)
ZB 842 (Nichtarier-Betreuung)
Evangelisches Zentralarchiv in Berlin (EZA)
Bestand 2: Kirchenamt der EKD 1929–86
2/12 (Lutherrat)
2/34, 35, 36, 37, 38 (Schuldfrage)
2/39 (Kirchenversammlung in Treysa 1945)
2/66, 67 (Berliner Stelle)
2/90, 91 (Bekennende Kirche)
2/93 (Berliner Bekenntnissynode 1945)
2/111 (Amtsblätter der Landeskirchen)
2/161 (Schriftwechsel mit dem Kirchlichen Außamt)
2/164 (Öffentliche Erklärungen)
2/176 (Austausch von Theologiestudenten)
2/271, 272, 273, 274, 275, 276, 277, 278 (Kirche und politisches Leben)
2/309 (Rundfunk)
2/784 (Präsident Asmussen)
Zentralarchiv der Evangelischen Kirche in Hessen und Nassau (ZEKHN-Darmstadt)
Bestand 36: Akten des Reichsbruderrates
36/73 ("Ein Wort zur Judenfrage"—Schriftwechsel und Stellungsnahmen)
36/81 (Christlich-jüdische Zusammenarbeit)
Bestand 62: Nachlass Martin Niemöller
62/14 (Kirche und Politik)
62/539 (Korrespondenz mit Hans Asmussen)
62/565a (Korrespondenz mit Hermann Diem)
62/592 (Korrespondenz mit Heinrich Grüber)
62/722 (Korrespondenz mit Helmut Thielicke)
62/742 (Korrespondenz mit Theophil Wurm)
62/1016 (Material zur Neugestaltung der EKD)
62/1026, 1027 (Reichsbruderrat der EKD)
Bestand 155: Kirchenverwaltung der EKHN
155/792 (Judenfrage 1947–51)
155/793 (Judenfrage 1948–58)
155/794 (Evan. Arbeitskreis für den Dienst an Israel in Hessen und Nassau, Band 1, 1951–58)

Zentralarchiv zur Erforschung der Geschichte der Juden in Deutschland (ZAJD-Heidelberg)
    Bestand 1/5: Jüdische Gemeinde Düsseldorf
        1/5/74–94 (Allgemeine Korrespondenz, A–Z, 1945–48)
        1/5/113–21 (Allgemeine Korrespondenz, A–Z, 1949–51)
        1/5/227 (Ansprache Sieradz, 1949–51)
    Bestand 1/13, A.: Jüdische Gemeinde Frankfurt
        1/13, A. 65 (Betreuungsstelle, 1945–49)
        1/13, A. 66 (Betreuungsstelle, 1946–47)
        1/13, A. 98 (Betreuungsstelle, 1946–47)
        1/13, A. 111–13 (Landes-und Stadtbehörden Korrespondenz, 1948–49)
        1/13, A. 151 (Betreuungsstelle, 1945–46)
        1/13, A. 154 (Betreuungsstelle, 1945–46)
        1/13, A. 159 (Betreuungsstelle, 1946)
        1/13, A. 256 (Betreuungsstelle, 1946)
        1/13, A. 390 (Betreuungsstelle, 1946)
        1/13, A. 256 (Betreuungsstelle, 1946)
        1/13, A. 258 (Betreuungsstelle, 1946)
        1/13, A. 531 (Betreuungsstelle, 1946)
        1/13, A. 554 (Betreuungsstelle, 1946)
        1/13, A. 632 (Max Meyer, Allgemeine Korrespondenz, 1946–50)
        1/13, A. 578–79 (Max Meyer, Allgemeine Korrespondenz, 1946–49)
        1/13, A. 593–99 (Max Meyer, Allgemeine Korrespondenz, H–Q, 1945–50)
        1/13, A. 600–606 (Max Meyer, Allgemeine Korrespondenz, A–G, 1945–50)
        1/13, A. 632 (Rabbi Leopold Neuhaus, Korrespondenz, 1946–47)
        1/13, A. 708 (Handakte von Max Meyer, 1947–49)
        1/13, A. 722 (Wilhelm Stern, Korrespondenz, 1947–48)
        1/13, A. 740 (Betreuungsstelle, 1946)
        1/13, A. 745 (Max Meyer, Allgemeine Korrespondenz, 1947–51)
        1/13, A. 746 (Zentralrat der Juden, 1951–54)
        1/13, A. 783–90 (Fritz Stein, Korrespondenz, 1946–48)
        1/13, A. 1002–12 (Einladung, Max Meyer, 1946–49)
        1/13/2169 (Rabbi Leopold Weinberg, Korrespondenz)
        1/13/2023 (Hermann Maas, Korrespondenz)
    Bestand 1/15: Jüdische Gemeinde Nordrhein
    1/15/136 (American Joint Distribution Committee, 1948–60)
    1/15/190 (American Joint Distribution Committee, 1945–61)
    1/15/218 (Allgemeine Korrespondenz, K, 1948–54)
    1/15/296 (Allgemeine Korrespondenz, M, 1948–55)
    1/15/522 (Wiedergutmachung, 1946–53)
Landeskirchliches Archiv Nürnberg (LKA Nuremberg)
    Bestand: Kreisdekan München (KdM)
        KdM 223 (Judenbetreffend)
    Bestand: Landeskirchenrat (LKR)
        LKR z. 1, 102h (new no. 303) (Rat der EKD)
        LKR 1, 102 (AA) (new no. 442) (Kirchliches Aussenamt der EKD, 1939–52)
        LKR XIV, 1608a (Judentum, 1933–63)
        LKR XIV, 1624b (new no. 2595) (Seelsorge an nichtarischen Christen 1938–48)

Bestand: Evangeliumsdienst unter Israel (Vereine III [V.III])
V.III/51, 1 (Vermischtes)
V.III/51, 1 (Schriftwechsel A–G)
V.III/51, 2 (Schriftwechsel H–Z)
V.III/51, 4 (Vermischter Schriftwechsel A)
Landeskirchliches Archiv Stuttgart (LKA Stuttgart)
Bestand D1: Nachlass Landesbischof Wurm
D1/2 (Predigten und Kasualreden von LB Wurm, 1943–51)
D1/3, 1 (Vorträge, Ansprache und Hirtenbriefe von LB Wurm, 1903–50 s.d.)
D1/3, 2 (Vorträge, Ansprache und Hirtenbriefe von LB Wurm, 1903–49 s.d.)
D1/222, 1 (EKD. Kirche und Judenfrage)
D1/222, 2 (EKD. Kriegsdienstverweigerung und Wiederbewaffung)
D1/210 (Schuldfrage, 1945–81)
D1/211 (Schuldfrage, 1945–50)
D1/224, 1 (Reichsbruderrat 1945–50)
D1/224, 2 (Reichsbruderrat 1945–50)
D1/245 (Allgemeine Korrespondenz 1945, A–Z)
D1/246 (Allgemeine Korrespondenz 1946, A–F)
D1/242 (Allgemeine Korrespondenz 1945–48)
Bestand D23: Nachlass Hartenstein
D23/7 (EKD Schriftwechsel)
D23/68 (Vorträge und Ansprachen)
D23/77 (Briefwechsel M–Q)
D23/78 (Briefwechsel R–Z)
Bestand 126: Allgemeine Kirchenakten
A126/658 (Mission und Seelsorge an Juden und Armeniern)
A126/659 (Mission und Seelsorge an Juden)
A126/661 (Mission und Seelsorge an Juden)
A126/672 (Mission und Seelsorge an Juden)
Bestand: Hilfsstelle Akten (HA)
HA/Büro Grüber

Published Documents and Collections

Besier, Gerhard, Hartmut Ludwig, and Jörg Thierfelder, eds. *Der Kompromiß von Treysa: Die Entstehung der Evangelischen Kirche in Deutschland (EKD) 1945*. Weinheim: Deutscher Studien Verlag, 1995.

Besier, Gerhard, and Gerhard Sauter, eds. *Wie Christen ihre Schuld bekennen: Die Stuttgarter Erklärung 1945*. Göttingen: Vandenhoeck and Ruprecht, 1985.

Besier, Gerhard, Jörg Thierfelder, and Ralf Tyra, eds. *Kirche nach der Kapitulation*. 2 vols. Stuttgart: Verlag W. Kohlhammer, 1989–90.

Boyens, Armin. *Kirchenkampf und Ökumene 1933–1939: Darstellung und Dokumentation*. Munich: Kaiser, 1969.

Buchhaas-Birkholz, Dorthee, ed. *"Zum politischen Weg unseres Volkes": Politische Leitbilder und Vorstellungen im deutschen Protestantismus 1945–1952, Eine Dokumentation*. Düsseldorf: Droste Verlag, 1989.

Glenthøj, Jørgen. *Dokumente zur Bonhoeffer-Forschung 1928–1945.* Munich: Kaiser, 1969.

Greschat, Martin, ed. *Die Schuld der Kirche: Dokumente und Reflexionen zur Stuttgarter Schulderklärung vom 18./19. Oktober 1945.* Munich: Kaiser, 1982.

———. *Im Zeichen der Schuld: 40 Jahre Stuttgarter Schuldbekenntnis: Eine Dokumentation.* Neukirchen-Vluyn: Neukirchener Verlag, 1985.

Heidtmann, Günter, ed. *Hat die Kirche geschwiegen? Das öffentliche Wort der evangelischen Kirche aus den Jahren 1945–64.* Berlin: Lettner-Verlag, 1964.

Merzyn, Friedrich, ed. *Kundgebungen: Worte und Erklärungen der Evangelischen Kirche in Deutschland 1945–1959.* Hannover: Verlag des Amtsblattes der Evangelischen Kirchen in Deutschland, 1959.

Nicolaisen, Carsten, and Nora Andrea Schulze, eds. *Die Protokolle des Rates der Evangelischen Kirche in Deutschland.* Vol. 1. Göttingen: Vandenhoeck and Ruprecht, 1995.

———. *Der Weg nach Barmen: Die Entstehungsgeschichte der Theologischen Erklärung von 1934.* Neukirchen-Vluyn: Neukirchener Verlag, 1985.

Niemöller, Gerhard, ed. *Die erste Bekenntnissynode der Deutschen Evangelischen Kirche zu Barmen.* Vol. 2: *Text—Dokumente—Berichte.* Göttingen: Vandenhoeck and Ruprecht, 1959.

The Relationship of the Church to the Jewish People. Edited by the World Council of Churches. Geneva: WCC, 1964.

Rendstorff, Rolf, and Hans-Hermann Henrix, eds. *Die Kirchen und das Judentum: Dokumente von 1945 bis 1985.* Munich: Chr. Kaiser Verlag, 1988.

Schmidt, Kurt Dietrich, ed. *Dokumente des Kirchenkampfes: Die Zeit des Reichskirchenausschusses (1935–1937).* Arbeiten zur Geschichte des Kirchenkampfes, vols. 13 and 14. Göttingen: Vandenhoeck and Ruprecht, 1964.

Söhlmann, Fritz, ed. *Treysa 1945: Die Konferenz der evangelischen Kirchenführer 27.–31. August 1945.* Lüneburg: IM Heliand Verlag, 1946.

The Theology of the Churches and the Jewish People, Statements by the World Council of Churches and Its Member Churches. Commentary by Allan Brockway, Paul van Buren, Rolf Rendstorff, and Simon Schoon. Geneva: WCC Publications, 1988.

Vollnhals, Clemens. *Die evangelische Kirche nach dem Zusammenbruch: Berichte ausländischer Beobachter aus dem Jahre 1945.* Göttingen: Vandenhoeck and Ruprecht, 1988.

Published Sources

Adorno, Theodor W. "What Does Coming to Terms with the Past Mean?" In *Bitburg in Moral and Political Perspective,* edited by Geoffrey Hartman. Bloomington: Indiana University Press, 1986.

Ahlers, Rolf. *The Barmen Theological Declaration of 1934: The Archeology of a Confessional Text.* Lewiston, N.Y.: Edwin Mellen Press, 1986.

———. "The Confession of Altona." *Harvard Theological Review* 77, nos. 3–4 (1984): 377–94.

Allgemeine Wochenzeitung der Juden in Deutschland (1949–55).

Althaus, Paul. *The Divine Command: A New Perspective on Law and Gospel.* Philadelphia: Fortress Press, 1966.

———. *Theologie der Ordnungen.* Gütersloh: Verlag C. Bertelsmann, 1934.

Amtsblatt der Evangelischen Kirche in Deutschland. Edited by the Rat der EKD. Stuttgart, 1946–47.

Arendt, Hannah. *Essays in Understanding 1930–1954.* Edited by Jerome Kohn. New York: Harcourt Brace and Company, 1993.

Aring, Paul. *Christliche Judenmission.* Neukirchen-Vluyn: Neukirchener Verlag, 1980.

Asmussen, Hans. "Die Bedeutung der Synode von Dahlem." *Fluglätter der Bekennenden Kirche* 2 (1946).

———. "Gehört Luther vor das Nürnberger Gericht?" *Nachrichten für die evangelisch-lutherischen Geistlichen in Bayern* 2, nos. 19–20 (1947): 123–28.

———. *Sollen wir unser Vaterland lieb haben?* Schriftendienst der Kanzlei der Evangelischen Kirche in Deutschland, no. 2. Schwäbisch Gmünd: Carl Nagel, 1946.

———. "Die Stuttgarter Erklärung." *Die Wandlung* 3, no. 1 (1948): 17–27.

———. "Die Stuttgarter Erklärung: Ein Rundgespräch zur Schuldfrage," *Verordnungs-und Nachrichtenblatt. Amtliches Organ der Evangelischen Kirche in Deutschland* 6 (February 1946): 1–2.

———. *Zur Jüngsten Kirchengeschichte: Anmerkungen und Folgerungen.* Stuttgart: Evangelisches Verlagswerk, 1961.

Assmann, Aleida, and Ute Frevert, *Geschichtsvergessenheit/Geschichtsversessenheit: Vom Umgang mit deutschen Vergangenheiten nach 1945.* Stuttgart: Deutsche Verlags-Anstalt, 1999.

Baeck, Leo. "Das Judentum auf alten und neuen Wegen," *Judaica* VI (1950): 133–48.

———. "Some Questions to the Christian Church from the Jewish Point of View." In *The Church and the Jewish People,* edited by Göte Hedenquist. London: Edinburgh Press, 1954.

———. "Why Jews in the World: A Reaffirmation of Faith in Israel's Destiny." *Commentary* 3 (June 1947): 501–507.

Baranowski, Shelley. "Consent and Dissent: The Confessing Church and Conservative Opposition to National Socialism." *Journal of Modern History* 59 (March 1987): 53–78.

———. "The 1933 German Protestant Church Elections: *Machtpolitik* or Accommodation." *Church History* 49 (1980): 298–315.

Bark, Dennis L., and David R. Gress. *From Shadow to Substance 1945–1963.* Oxford: Basil Blackwell, 1989.

Barnes, Kenneth C. "Dietrich Bonhoeffer and Hitler's Persecution of the Jews." In *Betrayal: German Churches and the Holocaust,* edited by Robert P. Ericksen and Susannah Heschel. Minneapolis: Fortress Press, 1999.

Barnett, Victoria. *For the Soul of the People: Protestant Protest Against Hitler.* New York: Oxford University Press, 1992.

Barnouw, Dagmar. *Germany 1945: Views of War and Violence.* Bloomington and Indianapolis: Indiana University Press, 1996.

Barth, Karl. *Against the Stream: Shorter Post-war Writings 1946–52.* Edited by Ronald Gregor Smith and translated by Stanley Godman. London: SCM Press, 1954.

———. *This Christian Cause.* New York: Macmillan, 1941.

———. "The Christian Community and the Civil Community." In *Against the Stream: Shorter Post-war Writings 1946–52,* edited by Ronald Gregor Smith and translated by Stanley Godman. London: SCM Press, 1954.

———. "The Church—The Living Congregation of the Living Lord Jesus Christ." In *Man's Disorder and God's Design.* The Amsterdam Assembly Series. New York: Harper and Brothers, 1949.

———. *Church and State.* Translated by G. Ronald Howe. London: SCM Press, 1939.

———. *The Church and the Political Problem of Our Day.* New York: Charles Scribner's Sons, 1939.

———. *The Church and the War.* Translated by Antonia H. Froendt. New York: Macmillan, 1944.

———. *Church Dogmatics.* 5 vols. Edinburgh: T. and T. Clark, 1936–62.

———. *Eine Schweizer Stimme 1938–1945.* Zollikon-Zürich: Evangelischer Verlag, 1945.

———. "The First Commandment as a Theological Axiom." In *A Karl Barth Reader,* edited by Rolf Joachim Erler and Reiner Marquard and translated by Geoffrey W. Bromiley. Grand Rapids, Mich.: Eerdmans, 1986.

———. *The German Church Conflict.* Richmond, Va.: John Knox Press, 1968.

———. "The Germans and Ourselves." In *The Only Way,* translated by Ronald Gregor Smith. New York: Philosophical Library, 1947.

———. "The Gift of Freedom: Foundation of Evangelical Ethics." In *The Humanity of God.* Richmond, Va.: John Knox Press, 1966.

———. "Gospel and Law." In *Community, State and Church,* edited and with an introduction by Will Herberg. Garden City, N.Y.: Anchor Books, 1960.

———. "How Can the Germans Be Cured?" Translated by Marta K. Neufeld, in *The Only Way,* 3–20. New York: Philosophical Library, 1947.

———. "The Jewish Problem and the Christian Answer." In *Against the Stream: Shorter Postwar Writings, 1946–1952.* New York: Philosophical Library, 1954.

———. *Die Kirche zwischen Ost und West.* Zürich: Evangelisches Verlagshaus, 1949.

———. *The Only Way: How Can the Germans Be Cured?* New York: Philosophical Library, 1947.

———. *Theological Existence Today!* London: Hodder and Stoughton, 1933.

Barth, Karl, and Johannes Hamel. *How to Serve God in a Marxist Land.* New York: Association Press, 1959.

Baumgärtel, Friedrich. *Wider die Kirchenkampf-Legenden.* Neudettelsau: Freimund, 1959.

Beckmann, Joachim. *Hoffnung für die Kirche in dieser Zeit.* Göttingen: Vandenhoeck and Ruprecht, 1981.

Beintker, Michael. "Die Schuldfrage im Erfahrungsfeld des gesellschaftlichen Umbruchs im östlichen Deutschland." *Kirchliche Zeitgeschichte* 4, no. 2 (1991): 445–61.

Bentley, James. *Martin Niemöller, 1892–1984.* New York: Free Press, 1984.

Benz, Wolfgang. "Warding Off History: Is This Only a Problem for Historians and Moralists?" *Holocaust and Genocide Studies* 3, no. 2 (1988): 137–50.

Bergen, Doris L. *Twisted Cross: The German Christian Movement in the Third Reich.* Chapel Hill: University of North Carolina Press, 1996.

Berghahn, V. R. *Modern Germany: Society, Economy, and Politics in the Twentieth Century.* Cambridge: Cambridge University Press, 1987.

Besier, Gerhard. "Die Auseinandersetzung zwischen Karl Barth und Hans Asmussen: Ein Paradigma für die konfessionelle Problematik innerhalb des Protestantismus?" In *Die evangelische Kirche in den Umbrüchen des 20. Jahrhunderts, Gesammelte Aufsätze,* vol. 1. *Kirche am Übergang vom Wilhelminismus zur Weimarer Republik.* Neukirchen-Vluyn: Neukirchen Verlag, 1994.

———. "In der Kirche neu anfangen. Historisch-theologische Überlegungen am Bespiel der Nachkriegszeit und aktueller Probleme." In *Die evangelische Kirche in den Umbrüchen des 20. Jahrhunderts, Gesammlte Aufsätze.* Vol. 1. Neukirchen-Vluyn: Neukirchen Verlag, 1994.

———. *Die Kirchen und das Dritte Reich: Spaltungen und Abwehrkämpfe 1934–1937.* Berlin: Propyläen, 2001.

———. "Ökumenische Mission in Nachkriegsdeutschland: Die Berichte von Stewart Herman über die Verhältnisse in der evangelischen Kirche 1945/46." Edited by Gerhard Besier. 3 parts. *Kirchliche Zeitgeschichte* 1–2 (1988–89).

———. "The Stance of the German Protestant Churches during the Agony of Weimar, 1930–33." In *Die evangelische Kirche in den Umbrüchen des 20. Jahrhunderts, Gesammelte Aufsätze,* vol. 1. Neukirchen-Vluyn: Neukirchen Verlag, 1994.

———. "Zur ekklesiologischen Problematik von 'Dahlem' (1934) und 'Darmstadt' (1947)." In *Die evangelische Kirche in den Umbrüchen des 20. Jahrhunderts, Gesammelte Aufsätze,* vol. 1. Neukirchen-Vluyn: Neukirchen Verlag, 1994.

———. "Zur Geschichte der Stuttgarter Schulderklärung vom 18./19. Oktober 1945." In *Wie Christen ihre Schuld bekennen. Die Stuttgarter Schulderklärung 1945,* edited by Gerhard Besier and Gerhard Sautter. Göttingen: Vandenhoeck and Ruprecht, 1985.

Besier, Gerhard, Hartmut Ludwig, and Jörg Thierfelder, eds. *Der Kompromiß von Treysa: Die Entstehung der Evangelischen Kirche in Deutschland (EKD) 1945.* Weinheim: Deutscher Studien Verlag, 1995.

Bethge, Eberhard. *Dietrich Bonhoeffer: A Biography.* Revised and edited by Victoria J. Barnett. Minneapolis: Fortress Press, 2000.

———. "Dietrich Bonhoeffer and the Jews." In *Ethical Responsibility: Bonhoeffer's Legacy to the Churches,* edited by John D. Godsey and Geoffrey B. Kelly. New York: Edwin Mellen Press, 1981.

———. "Geschichtliche Schuld der Kirche." In *Christliche Freiheit im Dienst am Menschen, Zum 80. Geburtstag von Martin Niemöller,* edited by Karl Herbert. Frankfurt am Main, 1972.

———. "Troubled Self-Interpretation and Uncertain Reception in the Church Struggle." In *The German Church Struggle and the Holocaust,* edited by Franklin H. Littell and Hubert G. Locke. Detroit: Wayne State University Press, 1974.

Bettis, Joesph. "Political Theology and Social Ethics: The Socialist Humanism of Karl Barth." In *Karl Barth and Radical Politics,* edited and translated by George Hunsinger. Philadelphia: Westminster Press, 1976.

Bigler, Robert M. *The Politics of German Protestantism: The Rise of the Protestant Church Elite in Prussia, 1815–1848.* Berkeley: University of California Press, 1972.

The Blackwell Encyclopedia of Modern Christian Thought. Edited by Alister E. McGrath. Oxford: Basil Blackwell, 1993.

Bock, Gisela. "Racism and Sexism in Nazi Germany: Motherhood, Compulsory Sterilization, and the State." *Signs* 8, no. 3 (1983): 400–21.

Bodenstein, Walter. *Ist nur der Besiegte schuldig? Kritischer Rückblick auf das Stuttgarter Schuldbekenntnis.* Ascndorf: MUT-Verlag, 1985.

Bonhoeffer, Dietrich. *The Cost of Discipleship.* Translated by R. H. Fuller. New York: Touchstone, 1995. Originally published as *Nachfolge.* Munich: Christian Kaiser, 1937.

———. *Ethics.* Edited by Eberhard Bethge. New York: Collier Books, 1955.

———. *No Rusty Swords: Letters, Lectures and Notes 1928–1936.* Edited by Edwin H. Robertson. New York: Harper and Row, 1965.

———. *Spiritual Care.* Translated by J. C. Rochelle. Philadelphia: Fortress Press, 1985.

———. *A Testament to Freedom: The Essential Writings of Dietrich Bonhoeffer.* Edited by Geffrey B. Kelly and F. Burton Nelson. San Francisco: HarperCollins, 1990.

Borg, Daniel. "German National Protestantism as a Civil Religion." In *International Perspectives on Church and State,* edited by Menachem Mor. Omaha: Creighton University Press, 1993.

———. "German Protestants and the Ecumenical Movements: The War-Guilt Imbroglio, 1929–1926." *Journal of Church and State* 10, no. 1 (Winter 1968): 51–71.

———. *The Old-Prussian Church and the Weimar Republic: A Study in Political Adjustment, 1917–1927.* Hanover, N.H.: University Press of New England, 1984.

———. "*Volkskirche,* 'Christian State,' and the Weimar Republic." *Church History* 35, no. 2 (June 1966): 186–206.

Bornkamm, Heinrich. *Luther's Doctrine of the Two Kingdoms in the Context of His Theology.* Translated by Karl H. Hertz. Social Ethics Series, no. 14. Philadelphia: Fortress Press, 1966.

———. *Luther's World of Thought.* Translated by Martin H. Bertram. Saint Louis: Concordia Publishing House, 1958.

Bower, Tom. *The Pledge Betrayed: America and Britain and the Denazification of Post-war Germany.* New York: Doubleday, 1982.

Boyens, Armin. "Das Stuttgarter Schuldbekenntnis vom 19. Oktober 1945—Entstehung und Bedeutung." *Vierteljahrshefte für Zeitgeschichte* 19, no. 4 (October 1971): 374–97.

———. "Treysa 1945—Die evangelische Kirche nach dem Zusammenbruch des Dritten Reiches." *Zeitschrift für Kirchengeschichte* 82, no. 1 (1971): 29–53.

Braaten, Carl. "God in Public Life. A Rehabilitation of the Lutheran Idea of the 'Orders of Creation.'" *Lutheran Theological Seminary Bulletin* (Winter 1990): 34–53.

Brakelmann, Günter, Traugott Jänichen, and Karin Celen. *Kirche im Ruhrgebiet: Ein Lese-und Bilder-Buch zur Geschichte der Kirche im Ruhrgebiet von 1945 bis heute.* Essen: Klartext Verlag, 1991.

———. "Verhängnis—Versagen—Irrtum—Schuld: Anmerkungen zum Umgang mit kirchlicher Zeitgeschichte." *Kirchliche Zeitgeschichte* 4, no. 2 (1991): 522–32.

Brenner, Michael. *After the Holocaust: Rebuilding Jewish Lives in Postwar Germany.* Princeton, N.J.: Princeton University Press, 1997.

Brockway, Allan. "For Love of the Jews: A Theological History of the International Missionary Council's Committee on the Christian Approach to the Jews, 1927–1961." Ph.D. diss., University of Birmingham, 1992.

———. "The Theology of the Churches and the Jewish People." http://www.abrock.com (accessed 23 January 2004).

Brunner, Robert. "An unsere Deutschen Freunde." *Der Freund Israels: eine Zeitschrift der Stiftung für Kirche und Judentum* (1945–50) 74, no. 6 (December 1947): 84.

Brunotte, Heinz. *Bekenntnis und Kirchenverfassung: Aufsätze zur kirchlichen Zeitgeschichte.* Göttingen: Vandenhoeck and Ruprecht, 1977.

———. *Die Evangelische Kirche in Deutschland: Geschichte, Organisation und Gestalt der EKD.* Gütersloh: Gütersloher Verlagshaus Mohn, 1964.

———. *Die theologische Erklärung von Barmen, 1934, und ihr Verhältnis zum lutherischen Bekenntnis.* Berlin: Lutherisches Verlagshaus, 1955.

Buren, Paul van. "Changes in Christian Theology." In *The Holocaust: Ideology, Bureaucracy, and Genocide,* edited by Henry Friedlander and Sybil Milton. Millwood, N.Y.: Kraus International Publications, 1980.

————. *Theology of the Jewish-Christian Reality.* 3 vols. Lanham, Md.: University Press of America, 1980–95.

Busch, Eberhard. *Karl Barth: His Life from Letters and Autobiographical Texts.* Translated by John Bowden. Philadelphia: Fortress Press, 1976.

————. *Unter dem Bogen des einen Bundes: Karl Barth und die Juden 1933–1945.* Neukirchen-Vlyun: Neukirchener Verlag, 1966.

Chandler, Andrew. *Brethren in Adversity: Bishop George Bell, the Church of England and the Crisis of German Protestantism 1933–1939.* Suffolk: Boydell Press, 1997.

————. "The Death of Dietrich Bonhoeffer." *Journal of Ecclesiastical History* 45, no. 3 (July 1994): 448–59.

Cochrane, Arthur C. *The Church's Confession Under Hitler.* Pittsburgh: Pickwick Press, 1976.

Conway, John S. "The Changes in Recent Decades in the Churches' Doctrine and Practice towards Judaism and the Jewish People." In . . . *und über Barmen hinaus: Studien zur Kirchlichen Zeitgeschichte,* edited by Joachim Mehlhausen. Göttingen: Vandenhoeck and Ruprecht, 1995.

————. "Christian-Jewish Relations during the Fifties." *Kirchliche Zeitgeschichte* 3, no. 1 (1990): 11–27.

————. "The German Churches and the Jewish People Since 1945." In *Antisemitism in the Contemporary World,* edited by Michael Curtis. Boulder, Colo.: Westview Press, 1986.

————. "How Shall Nations Repent? The Stuttgart Declaration of Guilt." *Journal of Ecclesiastical History* 38, no. 4 (October 1987): 596–622.

————. *The Nazi Persecution of the Churches 1933–45.* New York: Basic Books, 1968.

————. "The Political Role of German Protestantism, 1870–1990." *Journal of Church and State* 34, no. 4 (Autumn 1992): 819–42.

————. "The Political Theology of Martin Niemöller." *German Studies Review* 9, no. 3 (October 1986): 521–46.

————. "Protestant Missions to the Jews 1810–1980: Ecclesiastical Imperialism or Theological Aberration?" *Holocaust and Genocide Studies* 1, no. 1 (1986): 127–46.

————. "Die Rolle der Kirchen bei der 'Umerziehung' in Deutschland." In *Die Unrechtsregime. Internationale Forschung über den Nationalsozialismus,* vol. 2: *Verfolgung—Exil—Belasteter Neubeginn,* edited by Ursula Büttner. Hamburg: Hans Christians Verlag, 1986.

Dahm, Karl-Wilhelm. "German Protestantism and Politics, 1918–39." *Journal of Contemporary History* 3 (January 1968): 29–49.

Dähn, Horst. "Kirchen und Religionsgemeinschaft." In *SBZ-Handbuch: Staatliche Verwaltungen, Parteien, gesellschaftliche Organisationen und ihre Führungskräfte in der Sowjetischen Besatzungszone Deutschlands 1945–1949,* edited by Martin Broszat and Hermann Weber. Munich: R. Oldenbourg Verlag, 1990.

————. *Konfrontation oder Kooperation? Das Verhältnis von Staat und Kirche in der SBZ/DDR, 1945–1980.* Opladen: Westdeutscher Verlag, 1982.

Dibelius, Otto. *Die Ernte Des Glaubens: Kriegsnöte und Kriegserfahrungen.* Berlin-Lichterfelde: Edwin Runge, 1916.

————. *In the Service of the Lord: The Autobiography of Bishop Otto Dibelius.* Translated by Mary Ilford. New York: Holt, Rinehart and Winston, 1964.

————. *Das Jahrhundert der Kirche: Geschichte, Betrachtungen, Umschau und Ziele.* Berlin: Furche-Verlag, 1926.

————. *Reden—Briefe, 1933–1967.* Edited by Jürgen Wilhelm Winterhager. Stuttgart: Eugen Rentsch Verlag, 1970.

———. "Die Staatkirche ist da! Ein Wort zur gegenwärtigen kirchlichen Lage." In *Dokumente des Kirchenkampfes II: Die Zeit des Reichskirchenausschusses 1935–1937,* first part (1935 bis 28. Mai 1936), edited by Kurt Dietrich Schmidt. Göttingen: Vandenhoeck and Ruprecht, 1964.

Diem, Hermann. *Haben wir Deutsche etwas gelernt?* Zollikon-Zürich: Evangelischer Verlag, 1948.

———. *Karl Barths Kritik am deutschen Luthertum.* Zollikon-Zürich: Evangelischer Verlag, 1947.

———. *Kirche und Entnazifizierung: Denkschrift der Kirchlich-Theologischen Sozietät in Württemberg.* Stuttgart: W. Kohlhammer, 1946.

———. *Die Kirche zwischen Rußland und Amerika.* Munich: Kasier, 1948.

———. *Restauration oder Neuanfang in der Evangelischen Kirche?* Stuttgart: Franz Mittelbach Verlag, 1946.

———. *sine vi—sed verbo: Aufsätze, Vorträge, Voten.* Munich: Kaiser, 1965.

Diem, Hermann, and Helmut Thielicke. *Die Schuld der Anderen: Ein Briefwechsel zwischen Helmut Thielicke und Hermann Diem.* Göttingen: Vandenhoeck and Ruprecht, 1948.

Diephouse, David J. "Antisemitism as Moral Discourse: Theophil Wurm and Protestant Opposition to the Holocaust." Paper presented at the 30th Annual Scholars' Conference on the Holocaust and the Churches, Philadelphia, 6 March 2000.

———. *Pastors and Pluralism in Württemberg 1918–1933.* Princeton, N.J.: Princeton University Press, 1987.

Dipper, Theodor. *Die Evangelische Bekenntnisgemeinschaft in Württemberg 1933–1945.* Arbeiten zur Geschichte des Kirchenkampfes, vol. 17. Göttingen: Vandenhoeck and Ruprecht, 1966.

Douglass, Paul. *God Among the Germans.* Philadelphia: University of Pennsylvania Press, 1935.

Drummond, Andrew Landale. *German Protestantism since Luther.* London: Epworth Press, 1951.

Dubiel, Helmut. *Niemand ist frei von der Geschichte: Die nationalsozialistische Herrschaft in den Debatten des Deutschen Bundestages.* Munich: Carl Hanser Verlag, 1999.

Düringer, Hermann, and Martin Stöhr. *Martin Niemöller im Kalten Krieg: Die Arbeit für Frieden und Gerechtigkeit damals und heute.* Frankfurt am Main: Haag und Herchen, 2001.

Ecumenical Press Service (1944–50).

EKiD oder nicht? Eine Aufsatzreihe, zusammengestellt vom Evangelischen Vortragsdienst in der Mark. n.d.

Elert, Werner. "The Concept of the Orders of Creation." In *Faith and Action: Basic Problems in Ethics: A Selection of Contemporary Discussions,* edited by H. Schrey. Edinburgh: Oliver and Boyd, 1970.

———. *Law and Gospel.* Translated by Edward H. Schoeder. Philadelphia: Fortress Press, 1967.

Ellison, H. L. "The Church and the Hebrew Christian." In *The Church and the Jewish People,* edited by Göte Hedenquist. London: Edinburgh Press, 1954.

Encyclopedia of the Holocaust. Edited by Israel Gutman. New York: Macmillan, 1990.

Encyclopedia of the Lutheran Church. Edited by Julius Bodensieck. 3 vols. Minneapolis: Augsburg Publishing House, 1965.

The Encyclopedia of the Third Reich. Edited by Christian Zentner and Friedemann Bedurftig. 3 vols. New York: Macmillan, 1991.

Erickson, Robert P. "A Radical Minority: Resistance in the German Protestant Church." In *Germans Against Nazism: Nonconformity, Opposition and Resistance in the Third Reich. Essays in Honour of Peter Hoffmann*, edited by Francis R. Nicosia and Lawrence D. Stokes. New York: Berg, 1990.

———. *Theologians under Hitler: Gerhard Kittel, Paul Althaus and Emanuel Hirsch.* New Haven, Conn.: Yale University Press, 1985.

Ericksen, Robert P., and Susannah Heschel, eds. *Betrayal: German Churches and the Holocaust.* Minneapolis: Fortress Press, 1999.

———. "The German Churches Face Hitler: Assessment of the Historiography." *Tel Aviver Jahrbuch für deutsche Geschichte* 23 (1994): 433–59.

Evangelische Kirche in Deutschland, Kirchenkanzlei, Berlin. *Berlin-Weissensee Synod 1950: Bericht über die zweite Tagung der ersten Synode der Evangelischen Kirche in Deutschland vom 23.–27. April 1950.* Hannover: Schlütersche Verlagsanstalt, 1950.

Evans, Richard. *In Hitler's Shadow: West German Historians and the Attempt to Escape from the Nazi Past.* New York: Knopf, 1989.

Fischer, Fritz. "Der deutsche Protestantismus und die Politik im 19. Jahrhundert." *Historische Zeitschrift,* 171 (1951): 473–518.

Fischer, Hans Gerhard. *Evangelische Kirche und Dokumente nach 1945.* Lübeck, 1970.

Fleischner, Eva. *Judaism in German Christian Theology since 1945: Christianity and Israel Considered in Terms of Mission.* Metuchen, N.J.: Scarecrow Press and American Theological Library Association, 1975.

Flugblätter der Bekennenden Kirche. Edited by the Bruderrat der EKD. Stuttgart, 1946–48.

Forde, Gerhard O. *The Law-Gospel Debate: An Interpretation of Its Historical Development.* Minneapolis: Augsburg Publishing House, 1969.

Forell, George W. "Luther's Conception of 'Natural Orders.'" In *Lutheran Church Quarterly* 18, no. 2 (April 1945): 160–77.

Forstman, Jack. *Christian Faith in Dark Times: Theological Conflicts in the Shadow of Hitler.* Louisville, Ky.: Westminster/John Knox Press, 1992.

Freese, Karl Friedrich. "Zum Verhältnis zwischen Staat und Kirche in der Deutschen Demokratischen Republik." *Wissenschaftliche Zeitschrift* 33, no. 4 (1984): 283–92.

Frei, Norbert. *Vergangenheitspolitik: Die Anfänge der Bundesrepublik und die NS -Vergangenheit.* Munich: Beck, 1996.

Der Freund Israels: Eine Zeitschrift der Stiftung für Kirche und Judentum. Basel: Stiftung für Kirche und Judentum, 1945–50.

Frey, Arthur. *Cross and Swastika: The Ordeal of the German Church.* Translated by J. Strathearn McNab. London: SCM Press, 1938.

Friebel, Thomas. *Kirche und politische Verantwortung in der sowjetischen Zone und der DDR 1945–1969: Eine Untersuchung zum Öffentlichkeitsauftrag der evangelischen Kirchen in Deutschland.* Gütersloh: Gütersloher Verlagshaus Mohn, 1992.

Friedlander, Saul. *Memory, History, and the Extermination of the Jews in Europe.* Bloomington: Indiana University Press, 1993.

Friedmann, W. *The Allied Military Government of Germany.* London: Stevens and Sons, 1947.

Fröhlich, Claudia, and Michael Kohlstruck, eds. *Engagierte Demokraten: Vergangenheitspolitik in kritischer Absicht.* Münster: Westfälisches Dampfboot, 1999.

Fulbrook, Mary. *The Divided Nation: A History of Germany 1918–1990.* New York and Oxford: Oxford University Press, 1992.

Gailus, Manfred. "Overwhelmed by Their Own Fascination with the 'Ideas of 1933':

Berlin's Protestant Social Milieu in the Third Reich." *German History* 20, no. 4 (2002): 462–93.

———. *Protestantismus und Nationalsozialismus: Studien zur nationalsozialistischen Durchdringung des protestantischen Sozialmilieus in Berlin.* Cologne: Böhlau, 2001.

Geis, Jael. *Übrig sein—Leben "danach": Juden deutscher Herkunft in der britischen und amerikanischen Zone Deutschlands 1945–1949.* Berlin: Philo, 2000.

Gerhardy, Gordon J. "Hermann Sasse: Confessor." *Lutheran Theological Journal* 29, no. 1 (May 1995): 11–19.

Gerlach, Wolfgang. *And the Witnesses Were Silent: The Confessing Church and the Persecution of the Jews.* Translated and edited by Victoria J. Barnett. Lincoln: University of Nebraska Press, 2000.

———. "The Attitude of the Confessing Church Toward German Jews in the Third Reich, and the Way After." In *The Barmen Confession: Papers from the Seattle Assembly,* edited by Hubert G. Locke, Toronto Studies in Theology, vol. 26. Lewiston/Queenston: Edwin Mellen Press, 1986.

Germino, Dante L. "Two Types of Recent Christian Political Thought." *Journal of Politics* 21 (1959): 455–86.

Geyer, Michael, and John W. Boyer. *Resistance Against the Third Reich 1933–1990.* Chicago: University of Chicago Press, 1992.

Gimbel, John. *The American Occupation of Germany.* Stanford, Calif.: Stanford University Press, 1968.

Goeckel, Robert F. "Church-State Relations in the Post-Communist Era: The Case of East Germany." *Problems of Post-Communism* (January/February 1997): 35–48.

———. "The GDR Legacy and the German Protestant Church." *German Politics and Society* 31 (Spring 1994): 84–108.

———. *The Lutheran Church and the East German State: Political Conflict and Change under Ulbricht and Honecker.* Ithaca, N.Y., and London: Cornell University Press, 1990.

Goldschmidt, Dietrich, and Hans-Joachim Kraus, eds. *Der ungekündigte Bund: Neue Begegnung von Juden und christlicher Gemeinde.* Stuttgart: Kreuz-Verlag, 1962.

Green, Clifford, ed. *Karl Barth: Theologian of Freedom.* Minneapolis: Fortress Press, 1991.

Greene, Lowell C. "The Political Ethos of Luther and Lutheranism: A Reply to the Polemics of Hans Tiefel." *Lutheran Quarterly* 26, no. 3 (August 1974): 330–35.

Greschat, Martin. *Die evangelische Christenheit und die deutsche Geschichte nach 1945: Weichenstellungen in der Nachkriegzeit.* Stuttgart: W. Kohlhammer, 2002.

———. "Kirche und Öffentlichkeit in der deutschen Nachkriegszeit (1945–1949)." In *Kirchen in der Nachkriegszeit: Vier zeitgeschichtliche Beiträge,* edited by Armin Boyens, Martin Greschat, Rudolph von Thadden, and Paolo Pombeni. Göttingen: Vandenhoeck and Ruprecht, 1979.

———. "'Rechristianisierung' und 'Säkularisierung': Anmerkungen zu einem europäischen konfessionellen Interpretationsmodell." In *Christentum und politische Verantwortung,* edited by Jochen-Christoph Kaiser and Anselm Doering-Manteuffel. Stuttgart: Verlag W. Kohlhammer, 1990.

———. "Weder Neuanfang noch Restauration: Zur Interpretation der deutschen evangelischen Kirchengeschichte nach dem Zweiten Weltkrieg." In *Die Unrechtsregime: Internationale Forschung über den Nationalsozialismus,* vol. 2: *Verfolgung—Exil—Belasteter Neubeginn,* edited by Ursula Büttner. Hamburg: Hans Christians Verlag, 1986.

———. "Zwischen Aufbruch und Beharrung: Die evangelische Kirche nach dem Zweiten Weltkrieg." In *Die Zeit nach 1945 als Thema kirchlicher Zeitgeschichte,* edited by Victor Conzemius, Martin Greschat, and Hermann Kocher. Göttingen: Vandenhoeck and Ruprecht, 1988.

Groh, John. *Nineteenth Century German Protestantism.* Washington, D.C.: University Press of America, 1982.

Grossman, Atina. "Home and Displacement in a City of Bordercrossers: Jews in Berlin 1945–1948." In *Unlikely History: The Changing German-Jewish Symbiosis, 1945–2000,* ed. Leslie Morris and Jack Zipes, 63–99. New York: Palgrave, 2002.

Gutteridge, Richard. *Open Thy Mouth for the Dumb! The German Evangelical Church and the Jews, 1879–1950.* Oxford: Basil Blackwell, 1976.

Halfman, Wilhelm. "Wie sollen wir predigen?" In *Die Stunde der Kirche,* ed. Kurt Jürgensen, 261–63. Neumünster: Karl Wachholtz Verlag, 1976.

Hancock, Ralph C. *Calvin and the Foundations of Modern Politics.* Ithaca, N.Y.: Cornell University Press, 1989.

Harder, Günther. "Christen vor dem Problem der Judenfrage: Evangelisch-jüdisches Gegenüber seit 1945." In *Christen und Juden: Ihr gegenüber vom Apostelkonzil bis heute,* edited by Wolf-Dieter Marsch and Karl Thieme. Mainz: Matthias-Grünewald-Verlag, 1961.

Harling, Otto von, Jr. "Kirche und Israel," *Kirchliches Jahrbuch für die Evangelische Kirche in Deutschland* (1953): 285–335.

Haufler-Musiol, Karin. "125 Jahre Zentralverein: Ein historischer Überblick." In *Auf dem Wege zum christlich-jüdischen Gespräch: 125 Jahre Evangelisch-lutherischer Zentralverein für Zeugnis und Diesnt unter Juden und Christen,* edited by Arnulf H. Baumann. Münster: Lit verlag, 1998.

Hauschild, Wolf-Dieter. "Vom 'Lutherrat' zur VELKD." In *. . . und über Barmen hinaus: Studien zur Kirchlichen Zeitgeschichte, Arbeiten zur kirchlichen Zeitgeschichte,* Series B, vol. 23, edited by Joachim Mehlhausen. Göttingen: Vandenhoeck and Ruprecht, 1995.

———. "Die Relevanz von 'Barmen 1934' für die Konstituierung der Evangelsichen Kirche in Deutschland 1945–1948." In *Die lutherischen Kirchen und die Bekenntnissynode von Barmen,* edited by Wolf-Dieter Hauschild, George Kretschmar, and Carsten Nicolaisen. Göttingen: Vandenhoeck and Ruprecht, 1984.

Hauschild, Wolf-Dieter, Georg Kretschmar, and Carsten Nicolaisen, eds. *Die lutherischen Kirchen und die Bekenntnissynode von Barmen: Referate des Internationalen Symposiums auf der Reisensburg 1984.* Göttingen: Vandenhoeck and Ruprecht, 1984.

Hedenquist, Göte. *The Church and the Jewish People.* London: Edinburgh Press, 1954.

Heimerl, Daniela. "Evangelische Kirche und SPD in den fünfziger Jahren." *Kirchliche Zeitgeschichte* 3, no. 1 (1990): 187–200.

Heineman, Elizabeth. "The Hour of the Woman: Memories of Germany's 'Crisis Years' and West German National Identity." *American Historical Review* 101 (April 1996): 354–95.

Hein-Janke, Ewald. *Protestantismus und Faschismus nach der Katastrophe (1945–1949).* Stuttgart: Alektor Verlag, 1982.

Helmreich, Ernst. "The Freeing of the South German Bishops." *Central European History* 21 (1969): 159–69.

———. *The German Churches under Hitler: Background, Struggle, and Epilogue.* Detroit: Wayne State University Press, 1979.

————. "The Nature and Structure of the Confessing Church in Germany under Hitler." *Journal of Church and State* 12 (1970): 405–20.

Henke, Klaus-Dietmar. *Politische Säuberung unter französischer Besatzung: Die Entnazifizierung in Württemberg-Hohenzollern.* Stuttgart: Deutsche Verlags-Anstalt: 1981.

Herberg, Will. "The Social Philosophy of Karl Barth." In Karl Barth, *Community, State, and Church: Three Essays.* Garden City, N.Y.: Doubleday, 1960.

Herbert, Karl. *Kirche zwischen Aufbruch und Tradition: Entscheidungsjahre nach 1945.* Stuttgart: Radius-Verlag, 1989.

Herf, Jeffrey. *Divided Memory: The Nazi Past in the Two Germanys.* Cambridge, Mass.: Harvard University Press, 1997.

Herman, Stewart W. *It's Your Souls We Want.* New York: Harper and Brothers, 1943.

————. *The Rebirth of the German Church.* Introduction by Martin Niemöller. London: SCM Press, 1946.

Hermle, Siegfried. *Evangelische Kirche und Judentum—Stationen nach 1945.* Göttingen: Vandenhoeck and Ruprecht, 1990.

————. "'Wo ist dein Bruder Israel?' Die Impulse Adolf Freudenbergs zur Neubestimmung des christlich-jüdischen Verhältnisses nach 1945." *Kirche und Israel: Neukirchener theologische Zeitschrift* 4 (1989): 42–59.

Hertz, Karl H., ed. *Two Kingdoms and One World.* Minneapolis: Augsburg Publishing House, 1976.

Heschel, Susannah. "Nazifying Christian Theology: Walter Grundmann and the Institute for the Study and Eradication of Jewish Influence on German Church Life." *Church History* 63, no. 4 (1994): 587–605.

Heydenreich, Renate Maria. "Erklärungen aus der Evangelischen Kirche Deutschlands und der Ökumene zur Judenfrage 1932–1961." In Dietrich Goldschmidt und Hans-Joachim Kraus, eds. *Der Ungekündigte Bund: Neue Begegnung von Juden und christlicher Gemeinde.* Stuttgart: Kreuz Verlag, 1962.

Homrighausen, Elmer G. "Evangelism and the Jewish People." *International Review of Missions* 39 (July 1950): 320.

Hoover, A. J. "God and German Unification: Protestant Patriotic Preaching during the Franco-Prussian War, 1870–71." *Fides et Historia* 18, no. 2 (1986): 20–31.

————. "God and Germany in the Great Wars: The View of the Protestant Pastors." *Canadian Review of Studies in Nationalism* 14, no. 1 (1987): 65–81.

Höpfl, Harro, ed. *Luther and Calvin on Secular Authority.* Cambridge Texts in the History of Political Thought. Cambridge: Cambridge University Press, 1991.

Huber, Wolfgang, ed. *Protestanten in der Demokratie: Positionen und Profile im Nachkriegsdeutschland.* Munich: Kaiser, 1990.

Hübner, Friedrich. "Hans Asmussen und Hermann Sasse in Barmen auf der Bekenntnissynode 1934." In *Barmen und das Luthertum,* edited by Reinhart Rittner. Hannover: Lutherisches Verlagshaus, 1984.

Hunt, Chester L. "Neo-orthodoxy and Totalitarianism: The German and the Soviet Cases." *Journal of Religious Studies* 16, nos. 1–2 (1990): 182–98.

Iwand, Hans. "Die Bekennende Kirche gehört in die Opposition." *Stimme der Gemeinde* (June 1950): 11.

————. "Ende der EKiD? In *EKiD oder nicht?* Eine Aufsatzreihe, zusammengestellt vom Ev. Vortragsdienst in der Mark." Dortmund-Hombruch, n.d.

————. *Frieden mit dem Osten.* Edited by Gerard C. den Hertog. Munich, Kaiser, 1988.

————. "Lutherische Kirche? Warum ich als lutherischer Theologe grundsätzlich Gegner der Vereinigten Evangelisch-lutherischen Kirche Deutschlands bin." *Evangelische Theologie* (1946–47): 385–88.

Jacobs, Manfred. "Konsequenzen aus dem Kirchenkampf: Kirchengeschichtliche und theologische Aspekte." *Lutherische Monatshefte* 8 (1969): 561–67.

Jaspers, Karl. *The Question of German Guilt.* Translated by E. B. Ashton. New York: Capricorn Books, 1961.

Jenkins, Julian. *Christian Pacifism Confronts German Nationalism: The Ecumenical Movement and the Cause of Peace in Germany.* Lewiston/Queenston: Edwin Mellon Press, 2002.

————. "A Forgotten Challenge to German Nationalism: The World Alliance for International Friendship through the Churches." *Australian Journal of Politics and History* 37 (1991): 286–301.

————. "War Theology, 1914 and Germany's *Sonderweg:* Luther's Heirs and Patriotism." *Journal of Religious History* 15, no. 3 (June 1989): 292–310.

Jones, Jill. "Eradicating Nazism from the British Zone of Germany: Early Policy and Practice." *German History* 8, no. 2 (1990): 145–62.

Jones, L. Gregory. *Embodying Forgiveness: A Theological Analysis.* Grand Rapids, Mich.: Eerdmans, 1995.

Judaica: Beiträge zum Verständnis des jüdischen Schicksals in Vergangenheit und Gegenwart.

Jüngel, Eberhard. *Christ, Justice and Peace: Toward a Theology of the State in a Dialogue with the Barmen Declaration.* Edinburgh: T. and T. Clark, 1992.

Jürgensen, Kurt. "Die Schulderklärung der Evangelischen Kirche in Deutschland und ihre Aufnahme in Schleswig-Holstein." In *Kirche und Nationalsozialismus: Beiträge zur Geschichte des Kirchenkampfes in den evangelischen Landeskirchen Schleswig-Holsteins,* edited by Klauspeter Reumann. Karl Wachholtz Verlag, 1988.

————. *Die Stunde der Kirche: Die Ev.-Luth. Landeskirche Schleswig-Holsteins in den ersten Jahren nach dem Zweiten Weltkrieg.* Neumünster: Karl Wachholtz Verlag, 1976.

Kaiser, Jochen-Christoph, and Martin Greschat, eds. *Der Holocaust und die Protestanten: Analysen einer Verstrickung.* Frankfurt am Main: Athenäum, 1988.

Kershaw, Ian. *The "Hitler Myth": Image and Reality in the Third Reich.* Oxford: Oxford University Press, 1987.

Kirchliches Jahrbuch für die Evangelische Kirche in Deutschland. Gütersloh: Bertelsmann Verlag, 1945–55.

Klan, J. S. "Luther's Resistance Teaching and the German Church Struggle under Hitler." *Journal of Religious History* 14, no. 14 (December 1987): 432–43.

Klappert, Bertold. "Barmen V and the Totalitarian State: The Justice and Limits of Governmental Power." In *The Barmen Confession: Papers from the Seattle Assembly,* edited by Hubert G. Locke. Toronto Studies in Theology, vol. 26. Lewiston/Queenston: Edwin Mellen Press, 1986.

————. *Bekennende Kirche in ökumenischer Verantwortung: Die gesellschaftliche und ökumenische Bedeutung des Darmstädter Wortes.* Munich: Kasier, 1988.

Koch, Diether. "Das Erbe der Bekennenden Kirche und die Friedensinitiativen Gustav Heinemanns." *Kirchliche Zeitgeschichte* 4, no. 1 (1991): 188–202.

Koch, Hans-Gerhard. *Staat und Kirche in der DDR: Zur Entwicklung ihrer Beziehungen 1945–1974.* Stuttgart: Quell Verlag, 1975.

Kocka, Jürgen. "Asymmetrical Historical Comparison: The Case of the German Sonderweg." *History and Theory* 38 (February 1999): 40–50.

Koebner, Thomas, Gert Sautermeister, and Sigrid Schneider, eds. *Deutschland nach Hitler: Zukunftspläne im Exil und aus der Besatzungszeit 1939–1949.* Opladen: Westdeutscher Verlag, 1987.

———. "Vergangenheitsverweigerung und Lebenslügen in der Diskussion 1945–1949." In *Deutschland nach Hitler: Zukunftspläne im Exil und aus der Besatzungszeit 1939–1949.* Edited by Thomas Koebner, Gert Sautermeister, and Sigrid Schneider. Opladen: Westdeutscher Verlag, 1987.

Königseder, Angelika, and Juliane Wetzel. *Waiting for Hope: Jewish Displaced Persons in Post–World War II Germany.* Translated by John A. Broadwin. Evanston, Ill.: Northwestern University Press, 2001.

Konukiewitz, Enno. *Hans Asmussen: Ein lutherischer Theologe im Kirchenkampf.* Gütersloh: Gütersloher Verlagshaus Mohn, 1984.

———. "Die Rezeption der Stuttgarter Schulderklärung in Oldenburg." *Jahrbuch der Gesellschaft für Niedersächsische Kirchengeschichte* 84 (1986): 207–43.

Koshar, Rudy. *From Monuments to Traces: Artifacts of German Memory, 1870–1990.* Berkeley: University of California Press, 2000.

Kretschmar, Georg. "Die Auseinandersetzung der Bekennenden Kirche mit den Deutschen Christen." In *Kirche und Nationalismus: Zur Geschichte des Kirchenkampfes,* edited by Paul Rieger and Johannes Strauss, 117–21. Munich: Claudius, 1969.

Künneth, Walter. "Das Judenproblem und die Kirche." In *Die Nation vor Gott: Zur Botschaft der Kirche im Dritten Reich,* ed. Walter Künneth and Helmut Schreiner. Berlin: Wichern, 1934.

———. *Die Öffentliche Verantwortung des Christen.* Berlin: Lutherisches Verlagshaus, 1952.

———. "Zum politischen Weg unseres Volkes: Eine theologische Antwort an den Bruderrat der EKD." *Evangelisch-Lutherische Kirchenzeitung* 2/3 (15 November 1947): 13–16.

Kupisch, Karl. "Dahlem 1934." *Evangelische Theologie* 11 (1959): 487–505.

———. *Die deutschen Landeskirchen im 19. und 20. Jahrhundert.* Göttingen: Vandenhoeck and Ruprecht, 1966.

———. "The Luther Renaissance." *Journal of Contemporary History* 2, no. 4 (October 1967): 39–49.

Lamberti, Marjorie. "Lutheran Orthodoxy and the Beginning of Conservative Party Organization in Prussia." *Church History* 37, no. 4 (December 1968): 439–53.

Large, David Clay, ed. *Contending with Hitler: Varieties of German Resistance in the Third Reich.* Cambridge: Cambridge University Press, 1991.

Latourette, Kenneth Scott. *Christianity in a Revolutionary Age: A History of Christianity in the Nineteenth and Twentieth Centuries.* Vol. 4: *The Twentieth Century in Europe: The Roman Catholic, Protestant, and Eastern Churches.* New York: Harper and Brothers, 1961.

Lehmann, Wolfgang. *Hans Asmussen: Ein Leben für die Kirche.* Göttingen: Vandenhoeck and Ruprecht, 1988.

Lepp, Claudia, and Kurt Nowak. *Evangelische Kirche im geteilten Deutschland (1945–1989/90).* Göttingen: Vandenhoeck and Ruprecht, 2001.

Lessing, Eckhard. *Zwischen Bekenntnis und Volkskirche: Der theologische Weg der Evangelischen Kirche der altpreußischen Union (1922–1953) unter besonderer Berücksichtigung ihrer Synoden, ihrer Gruppen und der theologischen Begründungen.* Bielefeld: Luther-Verlag, 1992.

Lilje, Hanns. "Kritik an Barmen." *Junge Kirche* 2, no. 17 (8 September 1934): 692–99.

———. *The Valley of the Shadow.* Translated by Olive Wyon. Philadelphia: Fortress Press, 1966.

Lindsay, Mark. *Covenanted Solidarity: The Theological Basis of Karl Barth's Opposition to Nazi Antisemitism and the Holocaust.* New York: Peter Lang, 2001.

Littell, Franklin Hamlin. *The Crucifixion of the Jews: The Failure of Christians to Understand the Jewish Experience.* 3rd ed. Macon, Ga.: Mercer University Press, 1996.

————. *The German Phoenix: Men and Movements in the Church in Germany.* Studies in Shoah, vol. 2. Garden City, N.Y.: Doubleday, 1960.

Littell, Franklin H., and Hubert G. Locke, eds. *The German Church Struggle and the Holocaust.* Detroit: Wayne State University Press, 1974.

Locke, Hubert G., ed. *The Barmen Confession: Papers from the Seattle Assembly.* Toronto Studies in Theology, vol. 26. Lewiston/Queenston: Edwin Mellen Press, 1986.

————, ed. *The Church Confronts the Nazis: Barmen Then and Now.* Toronto Studies in Theology, vol. 16. Lewiston/Queenston: Edwin Mellen Press, 1984.

Locke, Hubert G., and Marcia Sachs Littell, eds. *Remembrance and Recollection: Essays on the Centennial Year of Martin Niemöller and Reinhold Niebuhr, and the Fiftieth Year of the Wannsee Conference.* Lanham, Md.: University Press of America, 1996.

Lotz, Martin. *Evangelische Kirche 1945–1952: Die Deutschlandfrage: Tendenzen und Positionen.* Stuttgart: Radius-Verlag, 1992.

Lübbe, Hermann. "Der Nationalsozialismus im Deutschen Nachkriegsbewußtsein," *Historische Zeitschrift* 236 (1983): 579–99.

Lück, Wolfgang. *Das Ende der Nachkriegszeit: Eine Untersuchung zur Funktion des Begriffs der Säkularisierung in der "Kirchentheorie" Westdeutschlands 1945–1965.* Bern: Herbert Lang, 1976.

Lüdtke, Alf. "'Coming to Terms with the Past': Illusions of Remembering, Ways of Forgetting Nazism in West Germany." *Journal of Modern History* 65 (September 1993): 542–72.

Ludwig, Hartmut. "Der Beitrag Hans Joachim Iwands zur Diskussion um das rechte Verständnis der Barmer Theologischen Erklärung." In *Die lutherischen Kirchen und die Bekenntnissynode von Barmen,* edited by Wolf-Dieter Hauschild, George Kretschmar, and Carsten Nicolaisen. Göttingen: Vandenhoeck and Ruprecht, 1984.

————. "Die Entstehung des Darmstädter Wortes." *Junge Kirche* supplement to 8/9 (1977): 1–15.

————. "Ernst Wolf und die Bekennende Kirche." *Junge Kirche* 12 (December 1971): 622–27.

————. "Karl Barth's Dienst der Versöhnung: Zur Geschichte des Stuttgarter Schuldbekenntnisses." In *Zur Geschichte des Kirchenkampfes: Gesammelte Aufsätze II,* edited by Heinz Brunotte and Ernst Wolf. Göttingen: Vandenhoeck and Ruprecht, 1971.

Macfarland, Charles S. *The New Church and the New Germany: A Study of Church and State.* New York: Macmillan, 1934.

Mann, Thomas. *Germany and the Germans.* Washington, D.C.: Library of Congress, 1945.

Marcuse, Harold. *Legacies of Dachau: The Uses and Abuses of a Concentration Camp, 1933–2001.* Cambridge: Cambridge University Press, 2001.

Marshall, Barbara. "German Attitudes to British Military Government 1945–47." *Journal of Contemporary History* 15 (1980): 655–84.

Matheson, Peter, ed. *The Third Reich and the Christian Churches: A Documentary Account of Christian Resistance and Complicity During the Nazi Era.* Edinburgh: T. and T. Clark, 1981.

Mayer, Arno. "Memory and History: On the Poverty of Remembering and Forgetting the Judeocide." *Radical History Review* 56 (1993): 5–23.

McGrath, Alister E. *Reformation Thought: An Introduction.* Oxford: Blackwell, 1993.

Meier, Kurt. *Die Deutschen Christen: Das Bild einer Bewegung im Kirchenkampf des Dritten Reiches.* Göttingen: Vandenhoeck and Ruprecht, 1964.

———. *Der evangelische Kirchenkampf.* 3 vols. Göttingen: Vandenhoeck and Ruprecht, 1976–84.

———. *Kirche und Judentum: Die Haltung der evangelischen Kirche zur Judenpolitik des Dritten Reiches.* Göttingen: Vandenhoeck and Ruprecht, 1968.

———. *Kreuz und Hakenkreuz: Die evangelische Kirche im Dritten Reich.* Munich: Deutscher Taschenbuch Verlag, 1992.

———. "Volkskirchlicher Neuaufbau in der sowjetischen Besatzungszone." In *Die Zeit nach 1945 als Thema kirchlicher Zeitgeschichte,* edited by Victor Conzemius, Martin Greschat, and Hermann Kocher. Göttingen: Vandenhoeck and Ruprecht, 1988.

Meinicke, Wolfgang. "Die Entnazifizierung in der sowjetischen Besatzungszone 1945 bis 1948," *Zeitschrift für Geschichtswissenschaft* 32, no. 11 (1984): 968–79.

Meiser, Hans. *Kirche, Kampf und Christusglaube: Anfechtungen und Antworten eines Lutheraners.* Edited by Fritz and Gertrude Meiser. Munich: Claudius-Verlag, 1982.

———. "Vor der Verwirklichung der Vereinigten Evang.-Luth. Kirche Deutschlands." *Evangelisch-Lutherische Kirchenzeitung* 2, no. 14 (31 July 1948): 127.

Melis, Damian van. "Denazification in Mecklenburg-Vorpommern." *German History* 13, no. 3 (1995): 355–70.

Melzer, Karl-Heinrich. *Der Geistliche Vertrauensrat: Geistliche Leitung für die Deutsche Evangelische Kirche im Zweiten Weltkrieg?* Göttingen: Vandenhoeck and Ruprecht, 1991.

Michael, Robert. "Theological Myth, German Antisemitism and the Holocaust: The Case of Martin Niemöller." *Holocaust and Genocide Studies* 2, no. 1 (1987): 105–22.

Michelson, Arthur U. *Out of the Darkness into the Light: Life Story of Arthur U. Michelson.* Los Angeles: Jewish Hope Publishing House, 1955.

Mitscherlich, Alexander, and Margarete Mitscherlich. *The Inability to Mourn: Principles of Collective Behavior.* Translated by Beverley Placzek. New York: Grove Press, 1975.

Moeller, Robert G. *War Stories: The Search for a Usable Past in the Federal Republic of Germany.* Berkeley: University of California Press, 2001.

———. "War Stories: The Search for a Usable Past in the Federal Republic of Germany." *American Historical Review* 101, no. 4 (October 1996): 1008–49.

Moses, A. D. "The Forty-Fivers: A Generation Between Fascism and Democracy," *German Politics and Society* 17, no. 1 (Spring 1999): 94–126.

Moses, John A. "The British and German Churches and Perception of War, 1908–1914." *War and Society* 5, no. 1 (May 1987): 23–44.

Motschmann, Klaus. "Evangelische Kirche und Nation nach 1945: Staionen des Abfalls vom Vaterland." In *Handbuch zur Deutschen Nation,* vol. 2, *Nationale Verantwortung und liberale Gesellschaft,* edited by Bernard Willms. Tübingen: Hohenrain-Verlag, 1987.

Naimark, Norman. *The Russians in Germany: A History of the Soviet Zone of Occupation, 1945–1949.* Cambridge, Mass.: Harvard University Press, 1995.

Neumann, Peter. *Die Jungreformatorische Bewegung.* Göttingen: Vandenhoeck and Ruprecht, 1971.

Nicolaisen, Carsten. "Der lutherische Beitrag zur Entstehung der Barmer Theologischen Erklärung." In *Die lutherischen Kirchen und die Bekenntnissynode von Barmen,* edited by Wolf-Dieter Hauschild, George Kretschmar, and Carsten Nicolaisen. Göttingen: Vandenhoeck and Ruprecht, 1984.

Niedhart, Gottfried, and Dieter Riesenberger, eds. *Lernen aus dem Krieg? Deutsche Nachkriegszeiten 1918/1945.* München: C. H. Beck, 1992.

Niehammer, Lutz. *Die Mitläuferfabrik: Die Entnazifizierung am Beispiel Bayerns.* Berlin: Dietz, 1982.

Niemöller, Gerhard, ed. *Die erste Bekenntnissynode der Deutschen Evangelischen Kirche zu Barmen.* Vol. 1: *Geschichte, Kritik und Bedeutung der Synode und ihrer Theologischen Erklärung.* Göttingen: Vandenhoeck and Ruprecht, 1959.

Niemöller, Martin. *Die deutsche Schuld, Not und Hoffnung.* Zollikon-Zürich: Evanglischer Verlag, 1946.

———. *Ein Lesebuch.* Edited by Hans Joachim Oeffler et al. Köln: Pahl-Rugenstein, 1987.

———. *From U-Boat to Pulpit.* London: W. Hodge, 1936.

———. *Here I Stand!* Translated by Jane Lymburn. Chicago: Willett, Clark and Company, 1937.

———. *Martin Niemöller: Reden 1945–1954.* Darmstadt: Stimme-Verlag, 1958.

———. *Of Guilt and Hope.* Translated by Renee Spodheim. New York: Philosophical Library, 1947.

———. "Von einer neuen Aufspaltung der evangelischen Christenheit in Deutschland?" In *EKiD oder nicht?* Eine Aufsatzreihe, zusammengestellt vom Ev. Vortragsdienst in der Mark. Dortmund-Hombruch, n.d.

Niemöller, Wilhelm. *Die Bekennenden Kirche sagt Hitler die Wahrheit: Die Geschichte der Denkschrift der Vorläufigen Leitung von Mai 1936.* Bielefeld: Bechhauf, 1954.

———. *Handbuch des Kirchenkampfes.* Bielefeld: Bechauf, 1956.

———. *Kampf und Zeugnis der Bekennende Kirche.* Bielefeld: Ludwig Bechauf, 1948.

———. *Neuanfang 1945: Zur Biographie Martin Niemöllers nach seinen Tagebuchaufzeichnungen aus dem Jahre 1945.* Frankfurt am Main: Stimme-Verlag, 1967.

———. "The Niemöller Archives." In *The German Church Struggle and the Holocaust,* edited by Franklin H. Littell and Hubert G. Locke. Detroit: Wayne State University, 1974.

———. *Die vierte Bekenntnissynode der Deutschen Evangelischen Kirche zu Bad Oeynhausen: Texte—Dokumente—Berichte.* Göttingen: Vandenhoeck and Ruprecht, 1960.

———. *Die zweite Bekenntnissynode der Deutschen Evangelischen Kirche zu Dahlem: Text—Dokumente—Berichte.* Göttingen: Vandenhoeck and Ruprecht, 1958.

Niewyk, Donald L. "Solving the 'Jewish Problem': Continuity and Change in German Antisemitism, 1871–1945." *Leo Baeck Institute Yearbook* 35 (1990): 335–70.

Niven, Bill. *Facing the Nazi Past: United Germany and the Legacy of the Third Reich.* London: Routledge, 2002.

Noormann, Harry. *Protestantismus und politisches Mandat 1945–1949.* 2 vols. Gütersloh: Gütersloher Verlagshaus Mohn, 1985.

Norden, Günther van. *Der deutsche Protestantismus im Jahr der nationalsozialistischen Machtergreifung.* Gütersloh: Gütersloher Verlagshaus Mohn, 1979.

Nowak, Kurt. "Christentum in politischer Verantwortung. Zum Protestantismus in der Sowjetischen Besatzungszone (1945–1949)." In *Christentum und politische Verantwortung,* edited by Jochen-Christoph Kaiser and Anselm Doering-Manteuffel. Stuttgart: Verlag W. Kohlhammer, 1990.

———. *Evangelische Kirche und Weimarer Republik: Zum politischen Weg des deutschen Protestantismus zwischen 1918 und 1932.* Weimar: Hermann Böhlaus Nachfolger, 1988.

———. *Geschichte des Christentums in Deutschland: Religion, Politik und Gesellschaft vom Ende der Aufklärung bis zur Mitte des 20. Jahrhunderts.* München: Verlag C. H. Beck, 1995.

————. "Wie es zu Barmen kam." In *Barmen und das Luthertum,* edited by Reinhart Rittner. Hannover: Lutherisches Verlagshaus, 1984.

Onnasch, Martin. "Die Situation der Kirchen in der sowjetischen Besatzungszone 1945–1949." *Kirchliche Zeitgeschichte* 2, no. 1 (May 1989): 210–21.

Palm, Dirk. *"Wir sind doch Brüder!": Der evangelische Kirchentag und die deutsche Frage, 1949–1961.* Göttingen: Vandenhoeck and Ruprecht, 2002.

Peck, Abraham J., ed. *Jews and Christians after the Holocaust.* Philadelphia: Fortress Press, 1982.

Peitsch, Helmut. "Autobiographical Writing as *Vergangenheitsbewältigung* (Mastering the Past)." *German History* 7, no. 1 (1989): 47–70.

Peterson, E. N. *The American Occupation of Germany.* Detroit: Wayne State University Press, 1977.

Phayer, Michael. *The Catholic Church and the Holocaust, 1930–1965.* Bloomington: Indiana University Press, 2000.

————. "The Postwar German Catholic Debate over Holocaust Guilt." *Kirchliche Zeitgeschichte* 8, no. 1 (1995): 426–39.

Pierard, Richard. "Why Did Protestants Welcome Hitler?" *Fides et Historia* 10, no. 2 (1978): 8–29.

Pressel, Wilhelm. *Die Kriegspredigt 1914–1918 in der evangelischen Kirche Deutschlands.* Göttingen: Vandenhoeck and Ruprecht, 1967.

Proctor, Robert N. *Racial Hygiene: Medicine under the Nazis.* Cambridge, Mass.: Harvard University Press, 1988.

Prolingheuer, Hans. *Kleine politische Kirchengeschichte: Fünfzig Jahre Evangelischer Kirchenkampf von 1919 bis 1969.* Köln: Pahl-Rugenstein Verlag, 1985.

————. *Wir sind in die Irre gegangen: Die Schuld der Kirche unterm Hakenkreuz, nach dem Bekenntnis des "Darmstädter Wortes" von 1947.* Köln: Pahl-Rugenstein Verlag, 1987.

Rabinbach, Anson. *In the Shadow of Catastrophe: German Intellectuals between Apocalypse and Enlightenment.* Berkeley: University of California Press, 1997.

Raiser, Konrad. "Schuld und Versöhnung: Erinnerung an eine bleibende Aufgabe der deutschen Kirchen." *Kirchliche Zeitgeschichte* 4, no. 2 (1991): 512–22.

Raisig, Christoph Matthias. *Wege der Erneuerung: Christen und Juden: Der rheinische Synodalbeschluss von 1980.* Potsdam: Verlag für Berlin-Brandenburg, 2002.

Rausch, Wolf Werner, and Christian Walther. *Evangelische Kirche in Deutschland und die Wiederaufrüstungsdiskussion in der Bundesrepublik 1950–1955.* Gutersloh: Gütersloher Verlagshaus Mohn, 1978.

Rehmann, Ruth. *The Man in the Pulpit: Questions for a Father.* Translated by Christoph Lohmann and Pamela Lohmann. Lincoln: University of Nebraska Press, 1997.

Rendtorff, Rolf. *Hat denn Gott sein Volk verstoßen? Die evangelische Kirche und das Judentum seit 1945: Ein Kommentar.* Munich: Kaiser, 1989.

Rengstorf, Karl Heinrich. "Begegnung statt Bekehrung: Welchen Sinn kann das jüdisch-christliche Gespräch für Christen haben?" In *Juden, Christen, Deutsche,* edited by Hans Jürgen Schultz. Stuttgart: Kreuz-Verlag, 1961.

————. *Das Institutum Judaicum Delitzschianum 1886–1961.* Munster: Achendorff, 1963.

————. "The Jewish Problem and the Church's Understanding of Its Own Mission." In *The Church and the Jewish People,* edited by Göte Hedenquist. London: Edinburgh House Press, 1954.

————. *Die eine Kirche aus Juden und Heiden.* Stuttgart: Quell-Verlag, 1951.

————. "The Spiritual Basis for Jewish Evangelism." *International Review of Missions* 40 (April 1951): 149–55.

Repgen, Konrad. "Die Erfahrung des Dritten Reiches und das Selbstverständnis der deutschen Katholiken nach 1945." In *Die Zeit nach 1945 als Thema kirchlicher Zeitgeschichte.* Edited by Victor Conzemius et al. Göttingen: Vandenhoeck and Ruprecht, 1988, 127–80.

Richmond, James. "God and the Natural Orders: Is There Permanent Validity in Karl Barth's Warning to Natural Theology?" In *Being and Truth: Essays in Honor of John Macquarrie,* edited by A. Kee and E. Long. London: SCM Press, 1986.

Rittner, Reinhart, ed. *Barmen und das Luthertum.* Hannover: Lutherisches Verlagshaus, 1984.

Robertson, Edwin Hanton. "Remembrances of the Work of the Religious Affairs Branch 1947–1949." *Kirchliche Zeitgeschichte* 2, no. 1 (1989): 59–63.

Röhm, Eberhard, and Jörg Thierfelder. *Juden, Christen, Deutsche 1933–45.* 3 vols. Stuttgart: Calwer, 1990–95.

Rosenbaum, Stanley R. "Dietrich Bonhoeffer: A Jewish View." *Journal of Ecumenical Studies* 18 (Spring 1981).

Rürup, Reinhard. "Kontinuität und Diskontinuität der 'Judenfrage' im 19. Jahrhundert. Zur Entstehung des modernen Antisemitismus." In *Sozialgeschichte Heute: Festschriften für Hans Rosenberg zum 70. Geburtstag.* Edited by Hans-Ulrich Wehler. Göttingen: Vandenhoeck and Ruprecht, 1974.

———, ed. *Berlin 1945: A Documentation.* Berlin: Willmuth Arenhovel, 1995.

Saat und Hoffnung: Vierteljahrsschrift für das Gespräch zwischen Christentum und Judentum.

Sasse, Hermann. "Die Einigung der Kirchen und das lutherische Bekenntnis." *Luthertum* (1935): 257–78.

———. *Here We Stand: Nature and Character of the Lutheran Faith.* Translated by Theodore G. Tappert. Adelaide, Australia: Lutheran Publishing House, 1966.

———. *The Lonely Way: Selected Essays and Letters.* Vol. 1: *1927–1939.* Translated by Matthew C. Harrison, with Robert G. Bugbee, Lowell C. Green, Gerald S. Krispin, Maurice E. Schild, and John R. Stephenson. Saint Louis: Concordia Publishing House, 2002.

Scharf, Kurt. *Für ein politisches Gewissen der Kirche: Aus Reden und Schriften 1932–1972.* Edited by Wolfgang Erk. Stuttgart: J. F. Steinkopf Verlag, 1972.

Scharffenorth, Ernst-Albert. "Helmut Thielicke: Ein lutherischer Theologe in der Nachkriegszeit." In *Protestanten in der Demokratie: Positionen und Profile im Nachkriegsdeutschland,* edited by Wolfgang Huber. Munich: Kaiser Verlag, 1990.

Scheerer, Reinhard. *Evangelische Kirche und Politik 1945 bis 1949: Zur theologisch-politischen Ausgangslage in den ersten Jahren nach der Niederlage des "Dritten Reiches."* Köln: Pahl-Rugenstein Verlag, 1981.

Schild, Maurice E. "Sasse and Bonhoeffer: Churchmen on the Brink." *Lutheran Theological Journal* 29, no. 1 (May 1995): 3–10.

Schissler, Hanna, ed., *The Miracle Years: A Cultural History of West Germany, 1949–1968.* Princeton, N.J.: Princeton University Press, 2001.

Schleunes, Karl A. *The Twisted Road to Auschwitz: Nazi Policy toward German Jews 1933–1939.* Urbana and Chicago: University of Illinois Press, 1970.

Schmaus, Michael. "Das Verhältnis der Christen und Juden," *Judaica* V (1949): 182–91.

Schmidt, Dietmar. *Martin Niemöller: Eine Biographie.* Hamburg: Rowohlt, 1959.

Schmidt, Jürgen. *Martin Niemöller im Kirchenkampf.* Hamburg: Leibniz-Verlag, 1971.

Schmidt, Kurt Dietrich, ed. *Die Bekenntnisse und grundsätzlichen Äusserungen zur Kirchenfrage des Jahres 1934.* Göttingen: Vandenhoeck and Ruprecht, 1935.

Schneider, Thomas Martin. *Reichsbischof Ludwig Müller: Eine Untersuchung zu Leben, Werk und Persönlichkeit.* Göttingen: Vandenhoeck and Ruprecht, 1993.

Scholder, Klaus. *The Churches and the Third Reich.* Vol. 1: *Preliminary History and the Time of Illusions 1918–1934.* Translated by John Bowden. Philadelphia: Fortress Press, 1988.

————. *The Churches and the Third Reich.* Vol. 2: *The Year of Disillusionment: 1934 Barmen and Rome.* Translated by John Bowden. Philadelphia: Fortress Press, 1988.

————. "Political Resistance or Self-Assertion as a Problem for Church Governments." In *A Requiem for Hitler and Other New Perspectives on the German Church Struggle.* London: SCM Press, 1989.

————. *A Requiem for Hitler and Other New Perspectives on the German Church Struggle.* London: SCM Press, 1989.

Schwan, Gesine. *Politik und Schuld: Die zerstörerische Macht des Schweigens.* Frankfurt am Main: Fischer Taschenbuch, 1997.

Shanahan, William O. *German Protestants Face the Social Question.* Vol. 1: *The Conservative Phase 1815–1871.* Notre Dame, Ind.: University of Notre Dame Press, 1954.

Siegele-Wenschkewitz, Leonore. *Neutestamentliche Wissenschaft vor der Judenfrage: Gerhard Kittels theologische Arbeit im Wandel deutscher Geschichte.* Munich: Kaiser, 1980.

————. "New Testament Scholarship and the Nazi-State: Christian Responsibility and Guilt in the Holocaust." In *Remembering for the Future,* vol. 3, ed. Yehuda Bauer et al., 2717–27. New York: Pergamon Press, 1989.

Siegele-Wenschkewitz, Leonore, and Carsten Nicolaisen, eds. *Theologische Fakultäten im Nationalsozialismus.* Göttingen: Vandenhoeck and Ruprecht, 1993.

Smid, Marikje. *Deutscher Protestantismus und Judentum 1932/1933.* Munich: Kaiser, 1990.

Smith-von Osten, Annemarie. *Von Treysa 1945 bis Eisenach 1948: Zur Geschichte der Grundordnung der Evangelischen Kirchen in Deutschland.* Göttingen: Vandenhoeck and Ruprecht, 1980.

Solberg, Richard. *God and Caesar in East Germany: The Conflicts of Church and State in East Germany since 1945.* New York: Macmillan, 1961.

Spotts, Frederic. *The Churches and Politics in Germany.* Middletown, Conn.: Wesleyan University Press, 1973.

Steck, Karl Gerhard. "Vom politischen Gottesdienst der Kirche." *Die Wandlung* 2, no. 8 (November 1947): 686–706.

Steinmetz, David C. "Luther and the Two Kingdoms." In *Luther in Context.* Bloomington: Indiana University Press, 1986.

Stern, Frank. "Breaking the 'Cordon Sanitaire' of Memory: The Jewish Encounter with German Society." In *Thinking about the Holocaust: After Half a Century,* ed. Alvin H. Rosenfeld, 213–32. Bloomington: Indiana University Press, 1997.

————. "Evangelische Kirche zwischen Antisemitismus und Philosemitismus." *Geschichte und Gesellschaft* 18 (1992): 22–50.

————. *The Whitewashing of the Yellow Badge: Antisemitism and Philosemitism in Postwar Germany.* Translated by William Templer. Oxford: Pergamon Press, 1992.

Stoll, Christian. "Die Lage der Lutherischen Kirche innerhalb des deutschen Gesamtprotestantismus." In *EKiD oder nicht?* Eine Aufsatzreihe, zusammengestellt vom Ev. Vortragsdienst in der Mark. Dortmund-Hombruch, n.d.

————. *Die Theologische Erklärung von Barmen im Urteil des lutherischen Bekenntnisses.* Bavaria: Verlag der Evang.-Luth. Kirche in Bayern, 1946.

Stupperich, Robert. *Otto Dibelius: Ein evangelischer Bischof im Umbruch der Zeiten.* Göttingen: Vandenhoeck and Ruprecht, 1989.

Tal, Uriel. *Christians and Jews in Germany. Religion, Politics, and Ideology in the Second Reich, 1870–1914.* Translated by Noah Jonathan Jacobs. Ithaca, N.Y.: Cornell University Press, 1975.

———. "On Modern Lutheranism and the Jews." *Leo Baeck Yearbook* 30 (1985): 203–14.

Tappert, Theodore G., trans. and ed. *The Book of Concord: The Confessions of the Evangelical Lutheran Church.* Philadelpia: Muhlenberg, 1959.

Tent, James. *Mission on the Rhine: Reeducation and Denazification in American-Occupied Germany.* Chicago: University of Chicago Press, 1982.

Thadden, Rudolf von. "Dietrich Bonhoeffer und der deutsche Nachkriegsprotestantismus." In *Kirchen in der Nachkriegszeit: Vier zeitgeschichtliche Beiträge,* edited by Armin Boyens, Martin Greschat, Rudolph von Thadden, and Paolo Pombeni. Göttingen: Vandenhoeck and Ruprecht, 1979.

Thielicke, Helmut. *Notes from a Wayfarer: The Autobiography of Helmut Thielicke.* Translated by David R. Law. New York: Paragon House, 1995.

———. "Religion in Germany." *Annals of the American Academy of Politics and Social Science* (November 1948): 144–54.

———. *Theological Ethics.* Edited by William H. Lazareth. 2 vols. Philadelphia: Fortress Press, 1966–68.

Thierfelder, Jörg. "Die Kirchenpolitik der vier Besatzungsmächte und die evangelische Kirche nach der Kapitualtion 1945." *Geschichte und Gesellschaft* 18 (1992): 5–21.

———. *Das Kirchliche Einigungswerk des württembergischen Landesbischofs Theophil Wurm.* Göttingen: Vandenhoeck and Ruprecht, 1975.

———. "Theophil Wurm und der Weg nach Treysa." *Blätter für württembergische Kirchengeschichte* 85 (1985): 149–74.

———. *Zusammenbruch und Neubeginn: Die evangelische Kirche nach 1945 am Beispiel Württembergs.* Stuttgart: Quell, 1995.

Thomas, Theodore N. *Women against Hitler: Christian Resistance in the Third Reich.* Westport, Conn.: Praeger, 1995.

Thompson, W. D. J. Cargill. "Luther and the Right of Resistance to the Emperor." In *Studies in the Reformation: Luther to Hooker,* edited by G. W. Dugmore. London: Athlone Press, 1980.

———. *The Political Thought of Martin Luther.* Edited by Philip Broadhead. Sussex: Harvest Press, 1984.

———. "The 'Two Kingdoms' and the 'Two Regiments': Some Problems of Luther's Zwei-Reiche-Lehre." In *Studies in the Reformation: Luther to Hooker,* edited by G. W. Dugmore. London: Athlone Press, 1980.

Tiefel, Hans. "The German Lutheran Church and the Rise of National Socialism." *Church History* 41 (1972): 326–37.

Tilgner, Wolfgang. "Volk, Nation und Vaterland im protestantischen Denken zwischen Kaiserreich und Nationalsozialismus (ca. 1870–1933)." In *Volk-Nation-Vaterland: Der deutsche Protestantismus und der Nationalismus.* Gütersloh: Gütersloher Verlagshaus, 1970.

———. *Volksnomostheologie und Schöpfungsglaube.* Arbeiten zur Geschichte des Kirchenkampfes, vol. 16. Göttingen: Vandenhoeck and Ruprecht, 1966.

Tillmanns, Adrian. "Die Erklärung von Stuttgart und ihre Interpretationen: Versuch einer psychoanalytischen Kritik." *Kirchliche Zeitgeschichte* 7, no. 1 (1994): 59–82.

Troeltsch, Ernst. *The Social Teaching of the Christian Churches.* Translated by Olive Wyon. 2 vols. London: George Allen and Unwin, 1956.

Turner, Ian, ed. *Reconstruction in Postwar Germany: British Occupation Policy and the Western Zones 1945–1955.* New York: Berg, 1989.

Tyra, Ralf. "Treysa 1945: Neue Forschungsergebnisse zur ersten deutschen Kirchenversammlung nach dem Krieg." *Kirchliche Zeitgeschichte* 2, no. 1 (1989): 239–67.

United States Dept. of State. *Occupation of Germany: Policy and Progress 1945–1946.* European Series 23, publication 2783. Washington, D.C., August 1947.

Unterwegs. Berlin, monthly, 1947–49.

Vogel, Johanna. *Kirche und Wiederbewaffnung: Die Haltung der Evangelischen Kirche in Deutschland in den Auseinandersetzungen um die Wiederbewaffnung der Bundesrepublik 1949–1956.* Göttingen: Vandenhoeck and Ruprecht, 1978.

Vollnhals, Clemens. *Evangelische Kirche und Entnazifizierung 1945–1949. Die Last der NS-Vergangenheit.* Munich: R. Oldenbourg Verlag, 1989.

———. "Die Evangelische Kirche zwischen Traditionswahrung und Neuorientierung." In *Von Stalingrad zur Währungsreform: zur Sozialgeschichte des Umbruchs in Deutschland,* edited by Martin Broszat, Klaus-Dietmar Henke, and Hans Woller. Munich: R. Oldenbourg, 1988.

———, ed. *Die evangelische Kirche nach dem Zusammenbruch: Berichte ausländischer Beobachter aus dem Jahre 1945.* Göttingen: Vandenhoeck and Ruprecht, 1988.

Wall, Donald D. "The Confessing Church and the Second World War." *Journal of Church and State* 23 (Winter 1981): 15–34.

Ward, W. R. "Guilt and Innocence: The German Churches in the Twentieth Century." *Journal of Modern History* 68 (June 1996): 398–426.

———. *Theology, Sociology and Politics. The German Protestant Social Conscience 1890–1933.* Berne: Peter Lang, 1979.

Weber, Max. *The Protestant Ethic and the Spirit of Capitalism.* Translated by Talcott Parsons. London: Harper Collins, 1991.

Webster, Ronald. "American Relief and Jews in Germany, 1945–60. Diverging Perspectives." *Leo Baeck Yearbook* 38 (1993): 293–321.

———. "Opposing 'Victors' Justice': German Protestant Churchmen and Convicted War Criminals in Western Europe after 1945." *Holocaust and Genocide Studies* 15, no. 1 (Spring 2001): 47–69.

Welsch, Helga A. *Revolutionärer Wandel auf Befehl? Entnazifizerungs-und Personalpolitik in Thüringen und Sachsen (1945–1948).* Munich: R. Oldenbourg, 1989.

Wilkens, Erwin. "Zum 'Darmstädter Wort' vom 8 August 1947." In *Zukunft aus dem Wort,* edited by Günther Metzger. Stuttgart: Calwer Verlag, 1978.

Wilkinson, James D. "Remembering World War II: The Perspective of the Losers." *American Scholar* (Summer 1985): 329–43.

Willis, F. Roy. *The French in Germany 1945–1949.* Stanford, Calif.: Stanford University Press, 1962.

Willis, Robert E. "Bonhoeffer and Barth on Jewish Suffering: Reflections on the Relationship between Theology and Moral Sensibility." *Journal of Ecumenical Studies* 24, no. 4 (Fall 1987): 598–615.

Wischnath, Johannes Michael. *Kirche in Aktion: Das Evangelische Hilfswerk 1945–1957 und sein Verhältnis zu Kirche und Innerer Mission.* Göttingen: Vandenhoeck and Ruprecht, 1986.

Wittenberg, Martin. "Hermann Sasse und 'Barmen.'" In *Die Lutherischen Kirchen und die Bekenntnissynode von Barmen,* edited by Wolf Dieter Hauschild, Georg Kretschmar, and Carstens Nicolaisen. Göttingen: Vandenhoeck and Ruprecht, 1984.

Wolf, Ernst. *Barmen: Kirche zwischen Versuchung und Gnade.* Munich: Kaiser, 1970.

———. "Political and Moral Motives behind the Resistance." In *The German Resistance to Hitler,* translated by Peter and Betty Ross. London: B. T. Batsford, 1970.

Wright, J. R. C. *"Above Parties": The Political Attitudes of the German Protestant Church Leadership 1918–1933.* London: Oxford University Press, 1974.

Zabel, James A. *Nazism and the Pastors: A Study of the Ideas of Three Deutsche Christen Groups.* Missoula, Mont.: Scholars Press, 1976.

Zahrnt, Heinz. *The Question of God: Protestant Theology in the Twentieth Century.* Translated by R. A. Wilson. New York: Harcourt, Brace and World, 1969.

Zerner, Ruth. "Dietrich Bonhoeffer and the Jews: Thoughts and Actions, 1933–1945." *Jewish Social Studies* 37 (Summer and Fall, 1975): 235–50.

———. "German Protestant Responses to the Nazi Persecution of the Jew." In *Perspectives on the Holocaust,* edited by Randolph L. Braham. Boston: Kluwer-Nijhoff Publishing, 1983.

Zipfel, Friedrich. *Kirchenkampf in Deutschland 1933–1945: Religionsverfolgung und Selbstbehauptung der Kirchen in der nationalsozialistischen Zeit.* Berlin: Walter de Gruyter, 1965.

INDEX

Page numbers in italics indicate illustrations.

MATTHEW D. HOCKENOS is Assistant Professor of
modern European history at Skidmore College in upstate
New York. His research interests include German church
history, religion and ethics, and Christian-Jewish relations
after the Holocaust.